Communication, Society and Politics

Editors

W. Lance Bennett, *University of Washington*
Robert M. Entman, *The George Washington University*

Editoral Advisory Board

Scott Althaus, *University of Illiniois, Urbana-Champaign*
Larry M. Bartels, *Vanderbilt University*
Jay G. Blumler, *Emeritus, University of Leeds*
Michael X. Delli Carpini, *University of Pennsylvania*
Doris Graber, *University of Illinois. Chicago*
Regina Lawrence, *University of Texas at Austin*
Paolo Mancini, *University of Perugia*
Pippa Norris, *Harvard University*
Barbara Pfetsch, *Free University of Berlin*
Philip Schlesinger, *University of Stirling*
Gadi Wolfsfeld, *The Hebrew University of Jerusalem*
John Zaller, *University of California, Los Angeles*

Politics and relations among individuals in societies across the world are being transformed by new technologies for targeting individuals and sophisticated methods for shaping personalized messages. The new technologies challenge boundaries of many kinds – between news, information, entertainment, and advertising; between media, with the arrival of the World Wide Web; and even between nations. Communication, Society and Politics probes the political and social impacts of these new communication systems in national, comparative, and global perspectives.

Other Books in the Series
C. Edwin Baker, *Media Concentration and Democracy: Why Ownership Matters*
C. Edwin Baker, *Media, Markets, and Democracy*
W. Lance Bennett and Robert M. Entman, eds., *Mediated Politics: Communication in the Future of Democracy*
Bruce Bimber, *Information and American Democracy: Technology in the Evolution of Political Power*
Murray Edelman, *The Politics of Misinformation*

(*continued after the index*)

Digital Media and Political Engagement Worldwide

A Comparative Study

This volume focuses on the impact of digital media use for political engagement across varied geographic and political contexts. It identifies context-dependent and transcendent political consequences of digital media use. As the first decade of theorizing in this field has been based on studies from the United States and the United Kingdom, this volume places those results into comparative relief with other regions of the world. The book moves debates in this field of study forward by identifying system-level attributes that shape digital political engagement across a wide variety of contexts. The volume brings together research and scholars from North America, Europe, Latin America, the Middle East, and Asia. The evidence analyzed across the cases considered in the book suggests that engagement with digital environments influences users' political orientations and that contextual features play a significant role in shaping digital politics.

Eva Anduiza is an associate professor in the Department of Political Science of the Autonomous University of Barcelona, where she is also principal investigator of the research group Democracy, Elections and Citizenship. She holds a PhD in political and social sciences from the European University Institute in Florence. She has published in *European Journal of Political Research*; *International Journal of Regional and Urban Research*; *Information, Communication and Society*; and *Journal of Information Technologies and Politics*.

Michael J. Jensen is a postdoctoral Fellow at the Institute of Government and Public Policy at the Autonomous University of Barcelona. He holds a PhD in political science from the University of California, Irvine. He has been visiting Fellow at Royal Holloway College of London and a visiting professor at the Open University of Catalonia. He has published in *Information, Communication and Society* and *Information Society*.

Laia Jorba holds a PhD in political science from the Autonomous University of Barcelona. She has been a visiting researcher at the New School of Social Research in New York and a postdoctoral researcher with the project Internet and Political Participation in Spain at the Autonomous University of Barcelona. She has published in *Migrations, Société, Revista Migrações, Revista Internacional de Sociología, Revista Española de Ciencia Política,* and *Gestión y Análisis de Políticas Públicas.*

Digital Media and Political Engagement Worldwide

A Comparative Study

Edited by

EVA ANDUIZA
Autonomous University of Barcelona

MICHAEL J. JENSEN
Autonomous University of Barcelona

LAIA JORBA
Autonomous University of Barcelona

CAMBRIDGE
UNIVERSITY PRESS

CAMBRIDGE UNIVERSITY PRESS
Cambridge, New York, Melbourne, Madrid, Cape Town,
Singapore, São Paulo, Delhi, Mexico City

Cambridge University Press
32 Avenue of the Americas, New York, NY 10013-2473, USA

www.cambridge.org
Information on this title: www.cambridge.org/9781107668492

First published 2012

Printed in the United States of America

A catalog record for this publication is available from the British Library.

Library of Congress Cataloging in Publication data

Digital media and political engagement worldwide : a comparative study /
[edited by] Eva Anduiza, Michael James Jensen, Laia Jorba.
    p.   cm. – (Communication, society, and politics)
Includes bibliographical references and index.
ISBN 978-1-107-02142-6 (hardback) – ISBN 978-1-107-66849-2 (paperback)
1. Political participation – Technological innovations – Cross-cultural studies.
2. Communication in politics – Technological innovations – Cross-cultural studies.
3. Internet – Political aspects – Cross-cultural studies.   I. Anduiza Perea, Eva.
II. Jensen, Michael James.   III. Jorba, Laia.
JF799.D56   2012
303.48′33–dc23   2011044841

ISBN 978-1-107-02142-6 Hardback
ISBN 978-1-107-66849-2 Paperback

Contents

List of Tables and Figures

Tables

Figures

Contributors

Eva Anduiza, Autonomous University of Barcelona

Bruce Bimber, University of California, Santa Barbara

Marta Cantijoch, Manchester University

Andrew Chadwick, Royal Holloway, University of London

Clelia Colombo, Institute of Government and Public Policy, Autonomous University of Barcelona

Carol Galais, Autonomous University of Barcelona

Aina Gallego, Stanford University

Allison Hamilton, University of Iowa

Philip N. Howard, University of Washington

Muzammil M. Hussain, University of Washington

Michael J. Jensen, Autonomous University of Barcelona

Laia Jorba, Autonomous University of Barcelona

Martin Kroh, Humboldt University

Hannes Neiss, Humboldt University

Min Tang, Purdue University

Caroline J. Tolbert, University of Iowa

Cristian Vaccari, University of Bologna

Yanina Welp, Zentrum für Demokratie Aarau

Jonathan Wheatley, Zentrum für Demokratie Aarau

Acknowledgments

This book is the result of many exchanges among its contributors, to whom the editors are very grateful. The volume emerged from a seminar held in Barcelona in May 2008 titled "Citizen Politics: Are the New Media Reshaping Political Engagement?" We are particularly indebted to the participants in this event, during which part of the material in the volume was presented in embryonic form. This seminar and this volume would not have been possible without the financial support of the Spanish Ministry of Science and Innovation (research grants SEJ2007–80062, CSO2009–05975-E, and CSO2010–09901-E), the Catalan Agency for Research Grants Management (AGAUR), and the Center for Social Research (CIS). Additionally, special thanks are due to Bruce Bimber from the University of California, Santa Barbara, for his kind support, intellectual insight, and guidance from 2008 through the end of the editorial process. We are also very grateful to Diana Owen and Michael Xenos for their detailed comments on the whole volume, which have improved it significantly. Finally, we are greatly appreciative of the thoughtful comments and feedback from the members of our research group, Democracy, Elections and Citizenship at the Autonomous University of Barcelona.

Bellaterra, August 3, 2011
Eva Anduiza, Michael J. Jensen, and Laia Jorba

Introduction

Michael J. Jensen, Laia Jorba, and Eva Anduiza

Research from the United States and United Kingdom over the past fifteen years shows an increasingly positive relationship between internet use and levels of political engagement. Although the effect might be small at times, more evolutionary than revolutionary, and require certain conditions, it is rarely contested that digital media have an impact on civic and political involvement (Boulianne 2009; Prior 2007; Jensen, Danziger, and Venkatesh 2007; Owen 2006). However, the mechanisms by which internet use makes political engagement more probable remain somewhat elusive. In addition, whether this effect can be observed in other, non Anglo-Saxon political systems is still largely an open question. This question is particularly important given recent events in the Islamic world, where mixed results in citizen-led revolutions have provoked different opinions regarding the consequences of digital media use for democratic politics (Morozov 2011; Zhuo, Wellman, and Yu 2011). To better understand the role of digital media in connecting individuals to the political system, the contributors of this volume examine different aspects of this relationship with a variety of data sources and methodological approaches in a number of diverse contexts.

First, the book analyzes different paths through which digital media are affecting political involvement among citizens. We argue that these paths are both direct and indirect. Digital media have opened new modes of engagement that previously did not exist and that can be used by citizens to express their political views and convey their interests. This book considers a wide variety of different political contexts and political activities available online, and it considers the impact of these activities both on political systems and, most important for our concerns, on citizens. Thus, this volume analyzes online involvement as a direct consequence of digital media use on the way citizens relate to their political environments and the indirect effects that result from internet use via changes in resources, attitudes, and traditional patterns of behavior.

Second, the book studies who is digitally involved in politics. The book explores whether online engagement is associated with an array of different resources and whether those engaged online have different political orientations and constitute differentiated publics. This question moves beyond the reinforcement-versus-mobilization debate that has come to define the field to a great extent. Although this has been largely a useful frame for research questions on digital media, we can progress forward in this debate by considering interactions between different online and offline structural environments that provide mobilizing opportunities. We therefore direct attention to who uses technology and how, taking into consideration differences in the groups of people who are mobilized and are mobilizing online, as well as the types of activities that people perform in the different arenas. Hence, the question is less about whether people become mobilized through internet use and more about who participates online and how people are participating in the different online and offline spaces.

Third, the book analyzes the role of contextual factors in conditioning the relationship between digital media and political engagement. We know from decades of comparative work on political involvement that political participation depends greatly on institutional arrangements, political circumstances, and levels of socioeconomic development. Digital politics should not be different as digital media do not sit apart from political structures and practices. Rather, they innervate and, in part, materially constitute the political structures, institutions, and channels along which participation and mobilization occur (Kallinikos 2004), thereby enabling certain participatory modes and the formation of new political structures (Kriesi 2008; Castells 2009). Comparative work outside of the United States and United Kingdom is scarce. As a result, research in this field is limited in that it has mainly considered a restricted range of institutional arrangements, media systems, and levels of internet diffusion and use. Different contextual aspects, including the characteristics of the political system and its environment, may affect the choice of modes for digital politics engagement, the relevance of digital involvement for specific segments of the population, and the way in which attitudes and resources condition digital politics.

In this introduction we first elaborate a few conceptual clarifications, discuss the literature behind the main research questions of this volume, and finally present the selection of cases and the plan of the book.

Digital Media and the Dimensions of Political Engagement

Before discussing the implications of digital media for political engagement, some conceptual clarification is in order. This discussion intends not to close any conceptual debates but to clarify the meaning of the terms used throughout the book.

Digital media refers to a broad range of digitally networked devices. Digital media are distinguished by the contrast with analog modes of communication.

TABLE I.I. *Dimensions of Political Engagement*

	Offline	Online
Political participation	Representative (e.g., voting, contacting, party activity)	Vertical, unidirectional (e.g., online petition, donation, contact)
	Extrarepresentative (e.g., protest, consumerism)	Horizontal, interactive (e.g., blogging, posting political comments, joining political groups in social networks)
Political information consumption	Exposure to newspapers, television, or radio news offline	Exposure to online sources of information
Political attitudes	Interest in politics, political efficacy, ideological orientations, and so on	

The digitization of information facilitates its compression, manipulation, and transmission (Poster 2001). These characteristics endow users with equal capacities as transmitters and receivers of information (Castells 2009, 22–23). This sufficiency allows for communications to be horizontal and dispersed, thus enabling the formation of flexible and scalable organizational structures (Kallinikos, Aaltonen, and Marton 2010), which are key requisites for functioning networks. The speed of digital communication reduces not only transmission time but also geographic distance (Adams 2009). Digital media therefore include a variety of fixed and mobile devices that can access the internet, where, via a network of networks, digitized information is transmitted instantaneously with global reach (Terranova 2004, 41). The global reach of networks enables each node to engage in "mass-self broadcasting" (Castells 2009, 58), thus representing a qualitative change in the structure of information transmission and circulation in comparison to the broadcast model.

Several chapters in this book take the concept of digital media use as a main independent variable for explaining political engagement. This includes a number of different operationalizations, depending on the specific interests of the chapter and data availability. Indicators used include frequency of internet use; experience in internet use; level of internet skills; and use of specific digital media devices, including mobile devices.

The dependent variables throughout the chapters reference different aspects of political engagement. Without aiming to be exhaustive, we can distinguish at least three dimensions of political involvement: participation, information consumption, and attitudes. Each of the chapters in this book deals with one or several of these dimensions of political engagement. For analytical purposes, the behavioral dimensions of political engagement are classified with respect to the form through which they take shape, either offline or online. Table I.1 presents the three dimensions of engagement with some examples.

As the concept of engagement is already large and encompassing, our definition of political participation is restricted. Here, political participation refers to actions taken by citizens to influence political outcomes (see Teorell, Torcal, and Montero 2007). Traditional studies of political participation emphasized particularly those modes that were related to the institutions of representative democracy, such as voting, joining a party, or contacting a politician (see, e.g., Verba and Nie 1972). Over time, authors have started to pay attention to extrarepresentational forms, such as forms of political protest (e.g., sit-ins, demonstrations, strikes; see Barnes et al. 1979) as well as political consumerism (e.g., boycotts and "buycotts" motivated by political reasons; Micheletti 2003) and the micropolitical processes that influence who has access to and standing in political arenas (Beck 1997; Marsh, O'Toole, and Jones 2007).

Most of these modes of participation can be performed online, as we can contact, petition, donate, or buy through digital media. However, digital media have enabled the creation of new modes of political participation that did not exist before: people could use the web to diffuse their own political views through blogs or comments, upload videos with political content to YouTube, or join political groups in social networks.

The second dimension of political engagement is political information consumption. Given transmission costs, traditional, centrally broadcast media place a significant emphasis on filtering compared to the relatively low entry barriers online, which enable access to a wider range of information sources (both mainstream and alternative; Shirky 2010). It is true that most people who consume online political information do so through mainstream media outlets (Hindman 2009). Online news consumption is, however, different, as readers can directly link to videos and primary sources. Likewise, people can customize their news and exert greater control over information environments online than they can with television or even newspapers (Sunstein 2001; Prior 2007). When official channels of information are suspect or media reporting is highly restricted, online channels are sometimes the only sources of reliable information and, as a result, play a decisive role in civic dynamics.

Although the dimensions presented so far are related to political behavior, the last dimension of political engagement is attitudinal: people may have varying degrees of interest in politics, feelings of political competence, and perceptions regarding the responsiveness of the political regime and authorities. This dimension cannot be crosscut by the offline-online dimension, as attitudes are relatively stable psychological orientations of citizens, not behaviors enacted via different media streams. There is an extensive literature on what a political attitude is and the main categories of political attitudes (Almond and Verba 1963; Martín and van Deth 2007). What is clear is that they are a fundamental component of political engagement with a significant impact on behavior. Thus, they are also considered in several of the chapters of this volume.

The Consequences of Digital Media for Political Engagement

Research on media effects has paid considerable attention to the consequences of media consumption on citizens. Existing research in the United States and the United Kingdom provides two clear departure points in our analysis, thus reflecting behavioral and attitudinal effects associated with digital politics. These relate to the emergence of online involvement and the effect of digital media use on general political engagement. The research presented in this volume is therefore more act and agent centered than media centered.

The Rise of Online Engagement

The most direct consequence of the extension of digital media use for political involvement is the expansion of the repertoire of modes and channels of political participation, communication, and information. The digital interfaces provided by e-mail, blogging platforms, and online social networking sites simplify and facilitate creation and diffusion of political messages as well as political recruitment. Although each of these acts has a history that predates the internet, the structural affordances created by digitally networked media distinguish digital politics in two ways. First, as we noted earlier, digital media enable the formation of ad hoc, flexible networks of political organization and communication outside of traditional civil society networks and media centers. This reduces the impediment of institutional gatekeeping mechanisms. Second, the digital platform is more conducive to a greater range of expression, which can attract different segments of the population and engage them in varied ways. The specific forms of digital politics that emerge at any given time depend greatly on motivations from within concrete political systems.

The relevance of these new opportunities for political engagement is larger in a context of increasing political disaffection that particularly affects representative modes of participation (e.g., voting, party membership) as more political decisions are made outside electorally accountable offices. Hay (2007) notes that although levels of representative or institutionalized participation have been declining significantly, there appears to be some shift in participatory repertoires in the direction of noninstitutionalized or extrarepresentative modes of participation. These noninstitutional modes of politics are highly individualistic and ephemeral (Marien, Hooghe, and Quintelier 2010); less elite driven (Inglehart 1999); derive from lifestyle choices (Beck 1997); and reflect political rather than social capital (Bang and Esmark 2009). Digital networks are highly structurally congruent with these modes of political participation (Bennett 2003; Farthing 2010).

On the one hand, digital media facilitate the development of horizontal political networks. Although the revolution in digital media has provided communication infrastructure that facilitates ad hoc political mobilization (Bimber 2003), "in addition to the 'pull' of opportunities provided by the new media-centered forms of political communication, the 'push' of the declining power of the vote provides an incentive for collective actors to resort to

unconventional forms of participation" (Kriesi 2008, 160). When political
authorities and institutions are perceived as unresponsive, nonhierarchical
channels, which abound online, may seem more attractive for participation
(Little 2008; Bang 2005).

On the other hand, digital media not only allow for grassroots processes but
also open, and increasingly require, political institutions to integrate digital
media into governance practices and service provision (Anttiroiko 2010). In
addition, some politicians and those in government maintain official blogs
and Twitter accounts, and use other social media channels to directly reach
the public, thereby bypassing media outlets (see Chapter 2). This can provide
additional avenues for people to interact with political authorities and agencies
in less formalized contexts.

Digital Media Use as a Predictor of Motivations, Attitudes, and Learning

Digital media use, whether for general or for political purposes, can affect the
resources and motivations necessary for political engagement. The extent to
which people use or are familiar with digital media and their level of internet
skills may be among the most important predictors of online political participation, with more explanatory power than motivations such as political interest
(Anduiza, Gallego, and Cantijoch 2010; Hoff 2006; van Dijk 2005). Beyond
the antecedent condition of physical access, these internet skills reflect cognitive resources, which are fundamental for becoming politically involved online.
They may also reflect greater opportunities for receiving mobilization stimuli,
for contacting political organizations and diffusing political information, and
for escaping governmental control and censorship.

Digital networked communications technologies reduce the costs of acquiring political information, which is a positive motivation for offline political
participation (Tolbert and McNeal 2003; Brundidge and Rice 2009). In addition, digital environments can be a source of accidental or by-product learning
about politics, which can motivate higher levels of political engagement and
participation (Norris 2001, 226; Lupia and Philpot 2005). Digital media use
may also have profound consequences on our conception of the political world
and our own abilities to deal with its complexity (Crozier 2010; Kallinikos
2004). The creativity permitted by digital media structures may motivate some
to participate and other individuals to become more interested in politics. For
these reasons digital media are expected to influence political attitudes and
offline political participation.

Who Is Engaged through Digital Media?

A third aspect inextricably linked to the previous two is the question of who
is engaged through digital media. Scholars have analyzed the extent to which
sociodemographic characteristics; resources including education, income, and
internet skills; and attitudes including ideological self-placement, interest in politics, and political efficacy affect online political engagement. Who participates
online is important for two reasons. First, differences between populations

participating online and offline can give rise to new configurations of political influence. If certain segments of the population participate to a greater extent online and do so effectively, we may find significant differences in the issues raised and in the political forms that emerge online and offline as well as the policies adopted. Second, to the extent that online participation is stratified along the same dimensions as offline participation, this may reinforce previous political inequalities.

The comparison with offline participation is a crucial question in the literature. Scholars have debated at length whether online participation is simply a new mode of engagement used by those already active in politics or whether, conversely, digital media can attract new participants. Debates on this question have shifted somewhat. Earlier work tended to show that those participating online were already politically active offline (Jensen 2006; Best and Krueger 2005; Bimber 2003; Norris 2001; Hill and Hughes 1998).

In general, the evidence for a mobilization effect is based on younger cohorts, a population otherwise more disaffected and disengaged from electoral politics (Jensen, Danziger, and Venkatesh 2007; Owen 2006; Muhlberger 2004). Younger cohorts tend to be more technology savvy, embracing digital media use in multiple domains of life including politics. However, not all online environments provide the same incentives for participation, as web 1.0 environments have more structured architectures of engagement than web 2.0, which characterizes users as co-producers rather than audience members. These varied forms of interactivity may prove more satisfying modes of political activity for certain population segments.

Whether online participation has a mobilizing or a reinforcing effect may not be easily answerable in a general sense for at least three reasons. First, as internet access and use become increasingly common in a political system and the technology becomes more domesticated and integrated into political organizations, workplaces, and homes, the role that it plays may change. Second, internet environments are not uniform. We noted that online engagement is heterogeneous and subject to a changing internet and that there exists some parallel online arenas that might function independently one from another. Therefore, the question is not only who participates but also how they participate – and that changes over time. Third, the larger context of the political system provides differential motivations for participatory forms, as political systems vary in distribution of access to channels of political influence and the role of the internet in structuring the flows of political communications. Hence, in systems in which formalized channels connecting members of a political system with political authorities are closed, or regarded as not reliable, there is often a shift to informal channels (Little 2008).

These three issues suggest that although the reinforcement-mobilization question was a useful orienting framework to deal with changes in and impacts on politics some time ago, that question is showing itself to be somewhat contingent, depending on categories of online participation and on political environments.

The Role of Context in Digital Politics

Individual-level analyses of digital politics, though fundamental, are insufficient: "The disclosure of context-embedded processes through which technology develops or becomes involved in local affairs is indeed essential to the social study of technology" (Kallinikos 2004, 144). Across political systems, different contextual features give rise to differential arrays of opportunity structures, which digital media in turn play a role in constituting. The elucidation of relationships between macrosocial features of political systems and the political use and effects of digital media are far less explored but nevertheless essential for the development of the study of digital politics. To the extent that digital communications expand the number of independent channels for political expression, there are more avenues through which political systems can process inputs. However, a number of contextual elements can shape the range of communications that systems can process and the range of connections possible.

We identify three sets of contextual variables expected to influence the relationship between digital media and political engagement: the digital divide, the media system, and the institutional setting. The relevance of these factors can be inferred from each of the different case studies and comparisons included in this book for the types of digital engagement, the profiles of digitally involved citizens, and the indirect effects of digital media use on political engagement.

First, the digital divide creates differential opportunities for citizens to interact with other individuals, groups, and authorities and political structures (Warschauer 2003; Norris 2001). Internet access varies considerably, with the highest concentration of users in North America and Northern Europe (Internet World Statistics 2009). Given the costs of computer equipment and maintaining an internet connection, in poorer countries with low levels of access, those who are online often represent wealthier, higher educated, and sometimes politically favored segments of the population.

The digital divide is not solely a matter of access; it also refers to the distribution of abilities to use the technology effectively in daily life. Research shows that as strident as the digital divides in access are, the divides in skills, use, domestication (Venkatesh 2008), and motivation (Warschauer 2003, 122) are even greater and less eradicable (van Dijk 2006; Norris 2001). The extent to which digital inclusion exists and the opportunities for internet use vary between countries. This stratification along lines of access, use, and competence therefore affects who becomes involved online.

Second, media systems can also play a significant role in structuring the relative importance and function of digitally mediated participation in a political system. Although media consumption often has a hybrid form in which the transmission and consumption of broadcast media and digital media streams intersect, the media system can shape the motives for digital politics. Beyond that, the integration of media structures into the political process differs greatly across countries (Blumler and Gurevitch 1995). Some media systems are highly regulated by governments and primarily serve a propaganda function, whereas others depend for their legitimacy on independence from the government.

In addition, media systems differ in terms of whether they have a public service charter or are primarily market driven (Currant et al. 2009). Not only is government independence a statutory matter but also media markets may be more or less concentrated and have histories with different levels of partisanship.

In different media systems, digital media can play complementary and countervailing roles. Digital media play a complementary role when they not only serve as another platform for the transmission of media content but also create new ways in which news events are transmitted and experienced. For example, the advent of live blogging, video content live and on demand, and the simultaneous consumption of media streams creates what Chadwick (2007; see also Chapter 2) calls a hybrid media environment. Complementary roles are anticipated more commonly in an open media system. A countervailing posture for digital media is more common when traditional media channels are either closed because of governmental regulation or indirect political pressures from either society or political actors (Smith 2010) or are thought to be a source of misinformation (Castells 2009).

Third, institutions can play a determinative, facilitative, or constraining role in the conduct of digital politics in a political system. Laws regarding political speech are a key dimension. It is clear that in nondemocratic systems, which lack protections for political speech, governments may surveil or censor online speech and prosecute the expression of online opinions that run contrary to official doctrines. This can have significant consequences for the development of civil society as an independent political force. However, even in democratic societies in which freedom of speech is guaranteed by law, government institutions can constrain its practice and exercise. Institutions regulating internet neutrality may legislate on whether service providers can prioritize or prohibit certain forms of internet traffic.

Even institutions not directly tied to the regulation of digital media can affect the role of digital politics in a particular system. Political parties, electoral laws, and even campaign finance provisions can also play a significant role in shaping the opportunities for online politics in different countries (Anstead and Chadwick 2009). Beyond formal institutions, practices of institutional openness and responsiveness can influence the role of parties and other political actors in interactive and broadcast media communication strategies (Witte, Rautenberg, and Auer 2010).

These contextual variables, though not the only system-level variables that influence mobilization, information acquisition, and attitudinal change, condition the role of digital media in a political system and their influence on political engagement. These contextual elements not only function independently but also have interrelated effects; however, it is important to understand variations in individual elements in combination with other aspects of the system from which they derive their particular qualities (Easton 1990, 268). Therefore, the analysis of these contextual variables must be situated in particular cases. For this reason, the chapters in this book proceed in a case-centered rather than a variable-centered manner.

The Choice of Cases and the Plan of the Book

Because the research questions dealt with in this book are closely related, and often each chapter includes several such questions simultaneously, the empirical section of the book is structured according to the choice of cases, starting with the familiar U.S. and U.K. cases and then moving toward increasing levels of heterogeneity by including cases for which empirical material was available. This has involved the analysis of eight individual-level survey data sets, together with data consisting of qualitative and contextual evidence.

The first part of the book opens the volume with research from the United Kingdom and the United States. Because these countries have high levels of economic development, internet diffusion, and long-term democratic consolidation, they provide a unique reference point of cases with highly innovative digital political practices. The second part of the book analyzes Western European countries. This allows us to investigate the extent to which conclusions generated from the U.S. and U.K. cases are generalizeable to other countries with similar levels of political and economic development and the extent to which contextual factors contribute to the understanding of individual-level digital politics. Western European democracies contain great deal of variance in levels of internet diffusion as well as variability in their political and media systems. The third part of the book includes cases outside of the United States and Europe with various levels of economic development (and thus of economic equality and technological development) and different political regimes (corresponding to different levels of protection for fundamental civil and political rights that define both media and institutional contexts). The analysis of these cases allows us to assess the liberalizing role of digital media through their impact on the political engagement of the citizenry and to explore the alternative and diverse political uses of the internet in contrast to the modes most common in representative democracies. We thus move to a most-different-systems research design maximizing variation in the political contexts considered.

Tables I.2 and I.3 present some basic indicators of socioeconomic characteristics, political openness, and internet diffusion for the fifteen countries included in the different case studies of the book. These include population size, degree of urbanization, wealth, equality, human development, literacy, political rights, political institutions, and internet diffusion. These data document the large degree of institutional, socioeconomic, and technological variation that can be found among the cases included in the volume.

Before addressing the empirical analysis, the book begins with a theoretical chapter by Jorba and Bimber that explores key issues regarding citizenship and political engagement across political contexts. Through an extensive exploration of the most recent literature on digital media and political involvement worldwide, the authors acknowledge the convergence of some common interests in the research literature of different countries. This takes them beyond the traditional division in the literature between democratic and nondemocratic regimes, with the former focusing on rates of participation and the latter on surveillance and censorship. The issues they identify go far beyond the

TABLE 1.2. *Basic Demographic and Social Indicators*

	Population[a]	Urban Share Population (%)[b]	GDP ($)[c]	Gini Index[d]	HDI[e]	Adult Literacy (%)[f]
United States	313,232,004	82.3	47184.5	40.8	0.902	99.0
Europe						
Germany	81,471,636	73.8	40508.9	28.3	0.885	99.0
Italy	61,016,804	68.4	33916.8	36.0	0.854	98.9
Spain	46,754,784	77.4	30541.6	34.7	0.863	97.9
United Kingdom	62,698,362	90.1	36099.7	36.0	0.849	99.0
Latin America						
Argentina	41,769,726	92.4	9123.7	50.0	0.775	97.6
Brazil	203,429,773	86.5	10710.1	55.0	0.699	90.0
Dominican Republic	9,956,648	70.5	5195.4	50.0	0.663	89.1
Peru	29,248,943	71.6	5291.0	49.6	0.723	89.6
Uruguay	3,308,535	92.5	11996.0	46.2	0.765	97.9
Africa						
Egypt	82,079,636	42.8	2698.6	32.1	0.620	66.4
Asia						
Saudi Arabia	26,131,703	82.1	15835.9		0.752	85.0
China	1,336,718,015	44.9	4392.6	41.5	0.663	93.3
Indonesia	245,613,043	53.7	2945.5	39.4	0.600	92.0
Pakistan	187,342,721	37.0	1006.9	31.2	0.490	54.2

[a] Population for 2011; U.S. Census Bureau, International Data Base (http://www.census.gov/ipc/www/idb/).

[b] Data for 2010, based on national definitions of what constitutes a city or metropolitan area. UN Development Programme data (http://hdr.undp.org/en/).

[c] Data for 2010. Gross domestic product per capita (current prices, U.S.): market value of all final goods and services in the borders of a country in a year. World Development Indicators, World Bank (http://data.worldbank.org/).

[d] Data for 2009. The Gini coefficient is a statistical dispersion measure of the inequality of income. The index ranges from 0 (absolute equality) to 100 (absolute inequality). World Development Indicators, World Bank (http://data.worldbank.org/).

[e] Data for 2010. HDI = Human Development Index: high (HDI ≥ 0.8); medium (0.5 ≤ HDI < 0.8), low (HDI < 0.5). The HDI is composed from data on life expectancy, education, and per capita gross domestic product. UN Development Programme data (http://hdr.undp.org/en/).

[f] Estimates from censuses or surveys conducted between 1999 and 2007. Adult literacy (15 years-above): ability to understand, both read and write, a short simple statement (http://www.uis.unesco.org).

central research questions of this book, but they situate them in a wider research agenda regarding the relation between citizenship practices and digital media, and they advance some implications for different political contexts.

In Chapter 2, Chadwick analyzes trends in online participation in the United States and United Kingdom regarding the effects on both individuals and

Michael J. Jensen, Laia Jorba, and Eva Anduiza

TABLE 1.3. *Political Openness and the Digital Divide*

	Country Freedom[a]	Press Freedom[b]	System of Government	Centralization of Government	Internet Users (%)[c]	Internet Subscribers (%)[d]
United States	Free	Free	Presidential republic	Decentralized	79.0	26
Europe						
Germany	Free	Free	Parliamentary republic	Decentralized	81.9	24.3
Italy	Free	Partially free	Parliamentary republic	Decentralized	53.7	34.4
Spain	Free	Free	Parliamentary monarchy	Decentralized	66.5	22
United Kingdom	Free	Free	Parliamentary monarchy	Centralized	85.0	32.7
Latin America						
Argentina	Free	Partially free	Presidential republic	Decentralized	36.0	9.4
Brazil	Free	Partially free	Presidential republic	Decentralized	40.6	8.3
Dominican Rep.	Free	Partially free	Presidential republic	Centralized	39.5	4.3
Peru	Free	Partially free	Presidential republic	Centralized	34.3	3.7
Uruguay	Free	Free	Presidential republic	Centralized	43.4	8.6
Africa			Presidential republic			
Egypt	Not free	Partially free	Presidential republic	Centralized	26.7	3.4
Asia						
Saudi Arabia	Not free	Not free	Absolute monarchy	Centralized	51.0	7.3
China	Not free	Not free	Single-party system	Decentralized	34.3	11.3
Indonesia	Free	Partially free	Presidential republic	Centralized	9.1	0.8
Pakistan	Partially free	Not free	Parliamentary republic	Centralized	16.8	2.1

[a] Data for 2011. Composed index measuring political rights and civil liberties, ranges from 1 (highest degree) to 7 (least amount of freedom): free (1.0–2.5), partially free (3.0–5.0), not free (5.5–7.0) The ratings are determined by a checklist of twenty-five questions, ten of which address political rights (electoral process, political pluralism and participation, functioning of government) and fifteen of which address civil liberties (freedom of expression and belief, associational and organizational rights, rule of law, personal autonomy, and individual rights; http://www.freedomhouse.org).

[b] Data for 2010. Index ranging from 0 (best) to 100 (worst) on the basis of twenty-three questions divided into three subcategories: legal environment, political environment, and economic environment: free media (0–30), partially free media (31–60), not free media (61–100; http://www.freedomhouse.org).

[c] Data for 2010. Internet users' percentage is an estimated index of those using the internet from any device (e.g., mobile phones) in the previous twelve months. http://www.itu.int/ITU-D/icteye/Indicators/Indicators.aspx#.

[d] Data for 2009. Percentage of people with fixed internet access, including dial-up, broadband, cable modem, and leased-line internet subscribers. Only active subscribers who have used the system in a reasonable period of time are included. http://www.itu.int/ITU-D/icteye/Indicators/Indicators.aspx#.

emergent political structures. He observes recent changes in the online environment leading to new directions for research and new conceptualization and understanding of the complex relationships among digital media, information, and political engagement. Drawing on recent literature and examples from the United Kingdom and the United States, the author highlights three key forces of web 2.0: granularity, informational exuberance, and by-product political learning. These concepts call for a new research agenda that demands closer attention to the emergent properties of online politics.

Hamilton and Tolbert focus Chapter 3 on two central issues: first, the estimation of the effect of online involvement on political interest and voter turnout, controlling for prior levels of political involvement; second, analysis of which segments of the population are mobilized online. The authors use a unique six-wave 2008 election panel survey (Cooperative Campaign Analysis Panel) that includes a sample of twenty thousand registered U.S. voters during the 2008 U.S. presidential primaries and general election.

Jensen and Anduiza present a systematic comparison of the political participation of internet users in the United States and Spain. In Chapter 4, they analyze the differences among web 1.0, web 2.0, and offline participation in the two countries. The authors test resource and attitudinal models of participation across cases and online environments. They find that contextual elements matter as much for online modes of participation as they do for offline modes of participation.

Chapter 5, by Colombo, Galais, and Gallego, starts the second part of the book, which extends the analysis to Western Europe. They address the relationship between internet use and two fundamental political attitudes: political interest and efficacy. To this end, they use data from the first four waves of the European Social Survey (2002–2009) and provide the first systematic comparative evidence of the impact of internet use across fifteen European countries with relatively high levels of internet use. The chapter further explores the nature of the relationship between internet use and political attitudes through quantitative and qualitative data for the case of Spain.

Cantijoch attempts in Chapter 6 to disentangle the role of digital media use in promoting offline involvement through by-product learning, taking into account different modes of political participation. She frames the reinforcement-versus-mobilization debate by distinguishing representational and extrarepresentational modes of offline participation and by insightfully drawing citizen motivation profiles. She uses a 2007 survey of more than 3,700 citizens representative of the Spanish population in a context of low political mobilization.

In Chapter 7, Vaccari shifts attention to online engagement and the importance of context in his analysis of digital politics in Italy. Like Spain, Italy has low levels of attitudinal engagement and internet use compared to Northern Europe and the United States. The Italian political and media systems also present a unique situation as Silvio Berlusconi has not only led the country for 17 years but he, along with his family, also controls a significant portion of the traditional media outlets. Using a survey conducted during the 2008 Italian general election of four thousand respondents representative of the Italian population, the author analyzes who is digitally involved and the extent to which internet use reproduces offline participation in relation to specific features of the Italian context, thus showing how the media system can significantly influence digital political participation.

The last contribution of the second part of the book, Chapter 8 by Kroh and Neiss, assesses the causal direction of the relationship between digital media use and political involvement that is often found in cross-sectional data. By using panel data for the German household panel from 1995 (a time when private internet access was uncommon in Germany) to 2005, they conclude that although internet users do have higher prior levels of engagement, there is still a positive causal relationship between internet use and involvement that increases over time.

Welp and Wheatly begin the third part of the book by examining the different incentives and constraints to digital media use for social movements operating in five Latin American countries: Argentina, Brazil, the Dominican Republic, Peru, and Uruguay. They investigate the extent to which digital media are used in different protest movements. The study is based on interviews with key actors and specialists, as well as secondary sources to contextualize each case. The analysis shows that levels of internet diffusion, sociodemographic characteristics of protesters, organizational features and past campaign experience of movements, and political context are relevant factors that, through complex configurations and interactions, explain differences in digital media use in these social movements.

In Chapter 10, Hussain and Howard study the role of digital media in four countries from the Islamic world: Pakistan, Egypt, Saudi Arabia, and Indonesia. These countries have various degrees of institutional openness in both their media systems and their practices of censorship and surveillance online, as well as differences in their historical patterns of political development. The authors analyze changes in the patterns of political communication in the four countries since the introduction of new digital media, which have affected information acquisition, engagement in social networks, and mobilization of specific segments of the population. Their analysis is based first on a cross-country comparison of available statistical data on public opinion and political communication and then on qualitative individual case studies. Their results show that although it would be naive to say that digital media "opened" closed regimes in the Islamic political world, they certainly have changed the configuration of the public sphere, thus creating opportunity structures for new voices.

Tang, Jorba, and Jensen provide a final case study of China, a country with 384 million internet users (Internet World Stats 2009) where, although communications are highly constrained, digital media provide some venues for citizens to express and communicate, and to look for alternative information. Digital media are far less controllable than traditional media outlets.

The chapter shows how online information seeking affects attitudes regarding political trust and views on democracy. The analysis is based on a cross-sectional survey, the second wave of Asian Barometer carried out in 2008 and representative of the adult population of China. Tang, Jorba, and Jensen show that in a country where internet sites are fairly constrained and access is more limited to urban centers, there is still a significant relationship between internet use and attitudes that are more critical of the current regime. Furthermore, internet use is associated with higher levels of political efficacy, which suggests that internet users may be more likely to act on those critical beliefs than are other segments of the population.

Finally, in the Conclusion we bring together the main findings on the questions with which we started this project: What are the consequences of digital media use for political engagement? Who is involved online and how are they involved? Can the conclusions of the analyses performed in the United States and the United Kingdom be generalized to other political contexts? How do contextual characteristics condition online engagement and its explanations? In summarizing the main findings of the book, we provide general explanations for some of these questions.

I

The Impact of Digital Media on Citizenship from a Global Perspective

Laia Jorba and Bruce Bimber

1.1. Introduction

As new technologies are evolving worldwide, many theoretical challenges have arisen that surpass the frameworks used so far to pose questions about digital media and citizens' lives. There is a great need for broader perspectives to understand what is common and what is different in emerging political practices across nations. That need motivates this chapter, which starts from the observation that a great deal of research on digital media and politics since the late 1990s has centered on one of two sets of issues. In the United States and the United Kingdom, and to some extent in other European countries, a central concern has been whether the use of digital media increases political participation or civic engagement. In research on authoritarian regimes, however, questions of censorship and state control over media have dominated the discussion. Although these two frameworks for analysis have been productive, they are ultimately quite limited in addressing the broad range of changes in the character of citizenship that is underway because of digital media.

The transformations associated with digital media extend well beyond how many people vote or how much content is circumscribed by state control. In many nations, both democratic and nondemocratic, the changes are similar or overlapping or common, whereas in others they differ because of political institutions and culture, or other aspects of political context, and as a result of different stages of internet diffusion. The goal of this chapter is to examine some common theoretical issues in digital media across nations as a framework for understanding citizenship practices in a broader way. We focus on five issues: political attitudes, political practices, sociality of politics, political voice, and transnational allegiance. In each, we account for some commonalities and differences across regimes.

1.2. The Digital Context and Citizenship

The rapid diffusion of digital media for mass use is no longer limited mainly to industrialized countries, where the average rate of access to the internet is about 70 percent (United Nations 2010). In China, about 30 percent of people use the internet (United Nations 2010; Central Intelligence Agency 2011), and about half have mobile phones (International Telecommunication Union 2011). In Egypt, around 20 percent of people use the internet and two-thirds have mobile phones, and in Syria the figures are roughly the same. In Tunisia, about a third of the population uses the internet and more than 90 percent have mobile phones. In sub-Saharan Africa, where infrastructure for the internet is the least developed, a third of the population nonetheless has access to cellular telephony. Worldwide, there exist about 5 billion active mobile phones, for a global population of slightly less than 7 billion at the end of 2010, and globally, almost one in four people has access to the internet through a computer (United Nations 2010). Even though these figures are still far from those of most industrialized countries, and as the visible role of social media in the events of the Arab Spring of 2011 shows, it is not necessary that all citizens in a nation use digital media for those technologies to play a role in political change. In many places, sufficient numbers of people are already online to shape politics.

Social media specifically are increasingly global in scale. At the time of the Egyptian revolution of 2011, Facebook was the third most popular website in that country, behind Google and Yahoo! (Shapiro 2009). Although Facebook dominates social networking in the United States and many other places, a wealth of language-specific and regional sites exist as well. For instance, Orkut is widely used in Brazil; hi5 in Mongolia, Thailand, and parts of Africa; and Sonico in Latin America. By one estimate (comScore 2010), there were 53 million social networking site users in Latin America in 2008, and 30 million in Africa and the Middle East, which was the fastest-growing region of the globe. With 200 million users located in Asia, plus those in Latin America and Africa, roughly half of people using social networking sites live outside Europe and North America. This means that people around the globe are confronting a new potential to connect with like-minded others, to share views or concerns, to act as citizen-journalists by posting imagery or tweeting real-time observations of political events, and to search for information relevant to public affairs.

Certainly, the expansion of digital media is neither complete nor uniformly distributed, and there continue to be important digital divides. In Africa, advances in mobile telephony have been substantial, and growth rates in computer-based internet access are much higher than in industrialized nations, which are reaching a saturation level for current generations of users. But lack of adequate infrastructure and administrative capabilities in most of Africa means that technologies will not continue to diffuse toward industrialized levels anytime soon. And of course digital divides exist within countries, as well as across them, as early adopters are typically different from those further along the diffusion curve. Because much of the internet was in English in its early years, language exclusions were important. Today, the profusion of languages online enables wider use. Mandarin Cantonese is nearly equal to English in presence online, followed by Spanish, Japanese, and French (Internet World Stats 2010).

The boundaries created by language use online increasingly reflect offline diversity and barriers to common communication, although a growing body of translation tools is emerging. It remains the case that language differences belie the notion of anything like a single global public sphere. Nonetheless, the expanding use of the internet in so many places and in so many languages suggests that opportunities are increasing for substantial numbers of people in many types of political regimes and circumstances to have some kind of political experience online.

As the technologies themselves spread out in geographic and political contexts, signs of a shift toward a new generation of research are evident as well. This new generation of work is rightly moving beyond the emphasis on the politics and practices of the United States and United Kingdom that dominated the first decade or more of research about digital media. As Klotz (2004, 189) wrote some years ago, "Since the internet is a global communication infrastructure, no work on the internet should be complete without a consideration of the situation outside the United States."

The diffusion of digital media has indeed reached a point at which it is possible to conduct comparative work. It is increasingly feasible to look for patterns across democracies and nondemocracies that would have been impossible to examine ten or even five years ago. Data are scarce and not very systematic for some countries and regions, but comparative work is emerging, thus making possible intraregional (Howard 2008; Ho, Kluver, and Yang 2003; Hoff, Horrocks, and Tops 2000) and interregional (Deibert et al. 2008; Gunther, Montero, and Puhle 2007; Jenkins and Thorburn 2003; Norris 2001; Eickelman and Anderson 1999) comparisons. As more data become available, broader and more refined comparative work is possible.

Little is known about the extent to which effects that have been shown in the United States or the United Kingdom will be present as well in other democracies – for instance, whether digital media use is associated with increased political participation. Further, it is not obvious how relevant these experiences are to issues in nonliberal regimes. It is clear that one should expect to find considerable variation in the digital media context across nations. Media effects are highly contingent in both democratic and nondemocratic states (Gunther and Mughan 2000; Kalathil and Boas 2003; Lee 2009). With variation in the extent of modernization, in the structure of civil society and political opportunity, in culture, and in the policies of regimes toward digital media itself, one should expect to find a rich array of outcomes as comparative scholarship expands (Norris 2002). But it is also true that some of the affordances of technology are common to nearly all places and contexts: technology tends to expand people's choices about whom to communicate with and how, as well as about what information they attend to. Use of digital media also has common implications for temporality, as it accelerates the speed of many kinds of communication and flows of information. How these and other aspects of digital media play out differently across contexts, and the most salient questions to ask about digital media and politics, will all vary between countries.

Until recently, many of the dominant questions in the Anglo-American literature on the internet have involved political participation rates and campaign effects, as well as other topics such as selective exposure and opinion polarization. At the same time, the small body of research on digital media in semidemocratic and authoritarian states has focused almost exclusively on how regimes have attempted to censor and control use of digital media. These research problems have therefore largely spoken past one another. The simplest observation about this state of affairs is that the United States is not an adequate model for studying political uses of digital media on a global scale, just as there is more of interest in the digital politics of authoritarian states than censorship, as the revolutions in Tunisia, Egypt, and Libya show. Some common issues may be emerging across nations, even though the ways that technology is incorporated into public life in those nations differ greatly.

In this chapter, we pursue the possibility of some common thematic issues in digital media across nations. Our approach is to focus on the citizen and to consider the common issues or themes relevant to citizenship that are emerging in the literature on democracies and that might also bear on citizenship in nondemocracies. We then ask the same question from the perspective of nondemocracies: What issues are emerging in research on citizenship in authoritarian or quasi-authoritarian states that are common across regimes and that also bear on citizenship in democracies? To do this, we start from the idea of citizenship rather than political participation, public opinion, campaigns, or other concerns largely specific to democracies. Five issues result from this inquiry: attitudes, political practice, sociality of politics, political voice, and transnational allegiance. In what follows, we discuss these and offer some theoretical reasons why they may be important in general.

1.3. From Studying Democratic Participation or Censorship to Studying Citizenship

The study of digital media and political participation is more than a decade old, and it has been largely based on research in the United States and the United Kingdom. After years of debate, there is an emerging consensus in the literature that positive though small associations exist between digital media use and certain kinds of civic engagement and political participation. For example, evidence supports the existence of a very modest association between voter participation rates and use of the internet in the United States (Bimber 2003; Mossberger, Tolbert, and McNeal 2008; Prior 2007). Evidence also suggests associations between digital media use and a range of other participation-related outcomes. These include, among others, discussion and political talk, civic engagement, knowledge, interest, donations, attendance at political events, participation in calls for action by interest groups, and communication with government (Bimber 1999, 2003; Pasek, More, and Romer 2009; Bimber, Stohl, and Flanagin 2009; Jennings and Zeitner 2003; Mossberger et al. 2008; Xenos and Moy 2007). However, effects vary across type of participation and across country, as well as across elections and events, which suggests a good deal of contingency.

Where the U.S. literature reflects a strong concern with the decline in voter participation rates that occurred in the United States between the 1960s and the early 1990s, a key emphasis in the European literature has been on democratic quality, distrust, and political skepticism. One concern in the European context is the increasingly candidate-centric nature of campaigns against a backdrop of declining party membership in many places. Whether digital media will provide a tool for parties to better target messages or otherwise provide some bulwark against organizational decline, or whether digital media will increase the independence of candidates from party organizations, or both, is a central problem reflected in some of the literature (Gibson and Römmele 2001; Zittel 2009).

Although case studies of election campaigns in many European countries are available, in general the campaign literature has been dominated by U.S. and British studies (Bimber and Davis 2003; Coleman 2001; Gibson, Nixon, and Ward 2003; Gibson and Ward 2000; Jackson and Lilleker 2009; Foot and Schneider 2006), whereas the European literature has mainly focused on political practices among elites (Mazzoleni 1999; Kalnes 2009; Kluver et al. 2007). In this vein, a lot of literature has been devoted to the use of digital technologies by trade unions (Ward and Lusoli 2003), as well as by political parties in relation to their members (Gibson et al. 2003; Carlson and Djupsun 2001; Farmer and Fender 2005; Newell 2001; Löfgren 2000; Schweitzer 2005), in relation to competition among parties (Semetko and Krasnoboka 2003; Shynkaruk 2005; Resnick 1998), and with respect to internal effects on party organization and structure (Löfgren 2003; Gibson, Lusoli, and Ward 2005; Pedersen and Saglie 2005; Chadwick 2007).

Another concern in the European context has been the democratization of government through the study of e-government possibilities, either from a top-down perspective (Hoff et al. 2000; Chen et al. 2008; Macintosh 2003; Macintosh, Coleman, and Lalljee 2005; Chadwick and May 2003; Chadwick 2003) or from a bottom-up empowerment perspective (Tsagarousianou, Tambini, and Bryan 1998; Coleman 2005; Chadwick 2006). But only recently a line of development has emerged about the effects of the internet on citizens and different forms of participation (Cantijoch, this volume; Anduiza, Gallego, and Cantijoch 2010; Vissers et al. 2009; Quintelier and Vissers 2008).

Outside the context of liberal democratic politics, a key concern in research on digital media has been matters of censorship and control, as well as whether digital media will play a role in democratization (Ho et al. 2003; Lyon 2003; Penfold 2003; Harwit and Clark 2001; Abbott 2001; Yang 2003; Guillén and Suárez 2005; Rodan 1998; Kok Wah and Teik 2002; Soon and Kluver 2007; Franda 2001; Deibert et al. 2008; Hughes and Wacker 2003). Since Sola Pool (1990) too optimistically predicted the positive role that technology would play in developing countries in advancing liberalization and democratization, many voices have challenged or supported that thesis, but most have paid attention to the multidimensional interconnections among culture, economic development, and the various trade-offs that reveal digital media to be deeply embedded socially. Several authors have argued that the development of civil societies and the adoption of digital media are coevolutionary. In China, across North Africa and the Middle East, and in authoritarian regimes in other places, emergent civil society organizations and nascent public spheres have adopted digital media and have advanced and expanded through technology as well (Ho et al. 2003; Howard 2011; Kalathil and Boas 2003; McGlinchey 2009; Tai 2006; Yang 2009). In this sense, technology affords opportunities for political voice and for political organizing and development, but it hardly compels action. Its use can erode the power of states slowly, as may be happening in China, or it can play a role in precipitating abrupt changes in places where pressure for transition has been building and where other conditions are right, as in the case of Arab Spring. This coevolutionary character of technology means that the question should be not whether technology is democratizing but how affordances of technology affect processes of political and social development, whatever those may be.

Much research has also been devoted to exploring the state of digital diffusion and reasons for impediments to infrastructural expansion in developing countries (Franda 2001; Rao and Klopfenstein 2002; Kagami, Tsuji, and Giovannetti 2004; Hughes and Wacker 2003; Mercer 2005; Banda, Tettey, and Mudhai 2009). Beyond this basic problem, once a threshold level of digital media use is reached in those countries and data become available, new questions about matters such as campaigns and parties, and political organizing in general, arise (Karan, Gimeno, and Tandoc 2009; Lee 2009), as do questions about possibilities for e-government practices (Xing et al. 2008; Zhang et al. 2008; Ouyang 2005) and political attitudes.

Despite substantial gaps and different foci of the literatures on the United States and United Kingdom, other democracies, and nonliberal regimes, there are several emerging themes that cut across contexts, and all bear in some way on the meaning and practice of citizenship and its coevolution with digital media. In identifying such common themes and theoretical problems, which is our goal in this chapter, the question is not whether different people's use of digital media has a single set of outcomes regardless of context, as that would be nonsensical. It has been amply demonstrated that media effects are contingent on many factors. The factors influencing participation and engagement also vary: citizen resources and motivation, socioeconomic development, the character of civil society, and many other factors affect the character of participation (Norris 2002). It is doubtful, therefore, that digital media use would exhibit the same outcomes across nations. So instead, we ask how the affordances of global technology interact with various national and regional contexts to produce a range of influences on citizenship, some of which may be similar to one another. We start by considering three issues mainly developed in the behavioral literature in the U.S. and U.K. contexts but that appear to be of increasing importance in other contexts as well, ranging from other democracies to authoritarian states: attitudes, political practices, and the sociality of politics. Then we consider two issues not rooted in democratic regimes: political voice and allegiance of transnational citizenship.

1.3.1. *Digital Media and Political Attitudes*

If anything has been shown in a decade of research on digital media in the United States, it is that the effects on political participation and civic engagement are connected to people's attitudes, interest, and motivation rather than simply to reduced transaction costs or easier access to information. Use of digital media clearly affects certain political attitudes and interacts with those attitudes to affect participation.

The complex of attitudes related to political interest, political knowledge, and political sophistication is central to this story. A significant problem in the literature over the past decade has been whether internet use predicts various forms of engagement and participation when political interest is controlled – which creates an enormous endogeneity problem for researchers (Boulianne 2009). This is relatively well settled: interest does drive use of digital media, so results are misleading without controlling for interest, but digital media use has a small influence on participation when interest is controlled (Boulianne 2009; see also Chapter 3).

The U.S. literature is moving beyond this problem to examine the interdependence of digital media use and interest in public affairs. Two studies set the boundaries for this work. Xenos and Moy (2007) show that internet use and political interest interact in predicting civic and political participation and that the interaction term is greater than the internet term alone. It is not simply that people who use the internet are engaged more when controlling for interest; those who are already politically interested become more politically engaged as a result of their internet use. Prior's (2007) results are consistent but add a new dimension relative to entertainment preference. Those who have stronger preferences for being entertained exploit the high degree of choice offered by digital media to indulge those preferences at the expense of attention to public affairs. Such empirical work moves beyond questions of participation rates to show that digital media are significant because of how they affect the way people express and act on beliefs and tastes, especially with respect to their preferences across the many kinds of communicative actions possible through digital media. One key to the effects of digital media on politics may be intensification of the salience of interest and motivation for participation patterns.

In addition to interest and motivation, a second set of attitudes appears to be connected to the use of digital media, and this set involves efficacy and trust. For instance, Kenski and Stroud (2006) find that with controls for political interest, demographics, and a variety of uses of traditional media, internet access predicts both internal and external political efficacy, and among those with internet access, use of the internet to access campaign information predicts internal efficacy. In a similar line, Tedesco (2007) shows how more interactive uses of the internet increase political efficacy as well as interest and involvement.

A number of studies have shown a positive association between digital media use and trust (Kraut et al. 2002; Katz and Rice 2002; Pasek et al. 2009). For example, Shah, Kwak, and Holbert (2001) model relationships between informational, recreational, and other types of internet use and interpersonal trust, life contentment, and civic engagement, as well as generation. They show that whether internet use generates trust and social capital is a function of motives and purposes for the use of technology. This work further suggests that digital media can be conceptualized as affecting the expression of beliefs rather than simply making certain kinds of political action easier or less costly in game-theoretic terms.

Similar results are emerging in other countries, indicating the importance of attitudes such as interest and efficacy in understanding digital media. Kroh and Neiss (in Chapter 8) examine political interest in the German context by using fixed-effects panel models on data over thirteen years. Their results are consistent with U.S. results: self-selection by more interested citizens for use of digital media for politics explains a good deal, but not all, of the relationship between technology use and various participation measures. After controlling for those effects, a small but robust effect in the direction from internet use to participation remains. More politically interested citizens are more likely to use digital media, and they benefit from its use with even more participation. Internet use appears to intensify the salience of interest for political participation. In Spain, Cantijoch (in Chapter 6) shows a relationship between internet use and some dimensions of political participation when interest is controlled, although she does not explore interaction effects. Also Cantijoch, Jorba, and San Martín (2009) demonstrate a positive correlation between internet use and internal political efficacy in Spain.

In nonliberal states, attitudinal issues are also central to understanding digital media, but they take on different forms from those in liberal states. The most important attitudes involve support for regimes and the question of whether digital media use contributes to a sense of citizenship rights, liberties, and duties. It is not yet known whether people with more critical views of regimes or with stronger conceptions of citizenship rights would be most likely to use digital media in political ways and to deepen their attitudes as a result. But some aspects of the problem are coming into focus. A pattern in studies across nations is that the public attitudes evinced online are essentially mixed with respect to regime support and nascent citizenship concepts. Yang (2009) documents the formation of an emerging consciousness of rights and an initial notion of citizenship in China. He bases his conclusions on an increasing number of appeals to the legal system and lawsuits claiming protection of individual rights, as well as cases of local environmental advocacy and organizing around other issues that do not threaten the legitimacy of the state and so are tolerated by Beijing. Tang, Jorba, and Jensen (in Chapter 11) also center their analysis on China and show that internet use has no significant effect on people's evaluation of the regime but is negatively related to citizens' trust in politics and positively related to democratic orientation.

Several studies show that citizen attitudes expressed in chat rooms, blogs, and other venues contain a good deal more contestation and criticism than is possible publicly through state-controlled media (Sun 2002; Graham and Khosravi 2002; Kok Wah and Teik 2002; Eickelman and Anderson 1999). For example, in his review of nine Arabic-language websites, Rinnawi (2009) found an emergent public sphere in which previously little existed because of state-controlled media. Following the April 6 Youth Movement in Egypt, Facebook pages took on explicitly political orientations and were used throughout 2009 and 2010 to organize small-scale protests, both about domestic issues and about the Israeli-Palestinian conflict. Egyptians experimented widely with YouTube to post images of police brutality and repression in the years before the revolution of 2011. More generally across the Islamic world, the public gained opportunities for expressing political views and learning about those of others (Howard 2011). It is no surprise that by early 2011, when people revolted against the regimes in Tunisia and Egypt, they would employ digital media in their efforts to express resistance to the state.

It is interesting to note that attitudes in emergent public spheres are not uniformly prodemocratic. In research conducted before the Arab Spring, Rinnawi (2009) found a range of political attitudes online in Arab states, including a considerable degree of ethno-nationalism combined with fairly little explicit critique of religious authorities. Notably, he found a greater degree of support for al-Qaeda's September 11, 2001, attacks in online forums than was present in traditional Arab state-controlled media. Digital media not only are a breeding ground for antiregime views but also support the expression and development of a range of attitudes and pluralism in a broad sense. Findings from content analysis in China are similar. Cases exist showing nationalistic attitudes supportive of the regime and of expanding pluralism, which results not only from internet use but also from other developments in civil society (Hughes 2000; Taubman 1998; Yang 2003; Tai 2006).

Limited survey data are emerging to support the thesis that attitude change associated with internet use is a function of the extent to which regimes censor discussion online. McGlinchey (2009) compared Central Asian autocracies using survey data. In his results, the comparison between Uzbekistan, where the state aggressively filters the web, and Kyrgyzstan, where no state filtering occurs, is intriguing. In censored Uzbekistan, internet use is unrelated to trust in the national government or international organizations. In uncensored Kyrgyzstan, internet users show less trust in the national government and more trust in international organizations. In this regard it is worth observing that the Mubarak regime did not censor the internet in Egypt as it had print media. But on the contrary, as pointed out earlier, distrust in institutions is associated with internet use in China, a country with one of the most sophisticated online censorship systems in the world (MacKinnon 2006).

Of course, it would be premature to announce the arrival of democratic public spheres in most authoritarian regimes, because of the effectiveness of regimes in controlling the internet where they choose to, especially in China, and in Saudi Arabia.

Empirical work on authoritarian regimes at this early stage is clearly far behind that on democratic states in the individual-level analysis of attitudes and public opinion, and it will not likely ever reach a comparable level of development. However, it is increasingly clear that, just as in democracies, digital media use in nondemocracies is shaping the formation and expression of attitudes and influencing worldviews and that conceptualizing technologies in this way is much more profitable than viewing them simply as tools of easier participation.

1.3.2. Changing Political Practices

A second major theoretical issue in the participation literature involves changing practices of being political. Some of what people do politically online does not fit traditional theoretical and empirical categories, and some is tightly connected to activities such as protest and participation in electoral politics. From expressive acts such as friending a politician to collective actions such as organizing protests via Twitter, it is clear that citizens are being political online and are using digital media to shape their offline actions. These affordances of digital media for politics are emerging when broader changes in political practices of citizenship have been underway for some time. A good deal has been written on modernization, changing values, and changing conceptions of participation that implicate media, especially broadcast and mass media in early modernization, and digital media in demonstrations, political consumerism, and environmentalism. Norris (2002, 208) shows increasing citizen involvement in petitions, demonstrations, and boycotts between 1970s and the mid-1990s, and she writes, "The internet has altered this dynamic by electronically promoting the diffusion of protest ideas and tactics quickly and efficiently across national borders." These trends involve greater emphasis on civic engagement than political participation (Dalton 2008; Zukin et al. 2006); an interest in personal forms of political expression and political identity creation, especially among younger people (Bennett 2008); and a turn away from elite-driven and institution-centric forms of participation toward other forms of political action, such as protest or consumerism (Stolle, Hooghe, and Micheletti 2005; Inglehart 1997).

A small but growing body of comparative literature has suggested that digital media have citizenship implications associated with changing practices and attitudes. Norris (2001) argued fairly early in the global diffusion of digital media for the emergence of a cyberculture involving postmaterialism: progressive social values, individualism, environmentalism, and cosmopolitanism. She argues that digital media will generally exert positive forces on societies, primarily benefiting the political periphery: "minor and fringe parties, loose coalitions of protest organizations, and alternative social movements" (Norris 2001, 23; see also Norris 2011).

Empirical work specifically on digital media and changing political practice
is rare but suggestive. Dalton (2008) finds that online participation is positively
associated with newer norms of engaged citizenship, which involve greater
independence and a broader conception of what constitutes politics, such as
being concerned with the welfare of others; he finds no association between
use of internet forums and more traditional duty-based citizenship norms.
Consistent with Dalton, Cantijoch (in Chapter 6) and Cantijoch, Jorba, and
San Martín (2009) show the existence of several distinct dimensions of political
participation in Spain corresponding to conventional participation, protest,
and political consumerism. Both studies show that internet use is predictive of
protest and consumerism but not conventional participation.[1]

This emerging work suggests that across democratic contexts, it may be
more useful to ask how use of digital media changes the styles and expands the
portfolios of political practice than to continue to search for turnout effects or
other participation-rate issues. A similar question can be posed in the case of
authoritarian regimes, where the central issue is not so much the expansion
or modification of participation repertoires but the emergence of repertoires
of engagement with civil society and participation in nascent public spheres.
The question of where and when political experiences happen for people, and
where and when people engage with public affairs or avoid them, is entirely
appropriate to ask in nondemocracies.

In China, an incipient civil society exists, and its emergence coincided
roughly with the development of the internet in the 1990s. Yang (2003) argues
that expanding internet use and expanding civil society practices are coevolutionary in the sense that each is dependent on the other. He finds considerable
evidence of internet use associated with emergent community groups and unreg-
istered social groups of various kinds, environmental groups, a new tradition
of online literature, and practices of expressing personal stories and views on
public issues. Use of the internet in Chinese civil society actually outpaced
commercial and state use as of the early 2000s. Yang also shows evidence
from content analysis of public discussion that at least some Chinese citizens
think of the internet explicitly as a tool of political discussion and expression.
Of course, the incipient civil society in China is the product of a number of
factors – generational change, economic development leading to diversified
economic and social interests, globalization, and somewhat diminished state
control of traditional media.

Particularly of interest are questions about how digital media affect the
making public of private concerns and identities and how they affect the extent
of public discussion and contestation of issues. In China, the government is
tolerating a good deal of online discussion and advocacy around issues that
are not threatening to the legitimacy of the state or its positions on major
issues such as Tibet. The resulting space for people to engage publicly with

---

[1] The multiplying forms of political practice make traditional typologies of participation problematic (Cantijoch and Gibson 2011).

issues has resulted in small-scale activism of all kinds there (Tai 2006; Yang 2009). However, censorship by the state remains powerful and surprisingly effective (Lagerkvist 2010). Norris (2001) argued a decade ago that technology would exert the greatest influence in this regard on consolidating democracies by strengthening civil society in countries such as Taiwan, Brazil, and South Africa. The Arab Spring is a counterexample, although it is too soon to draw conclusions about this hypothesis.

In both democracies and nondemocracies, and in those that are transitioning, digital media appear to affect how people act politically and when and where they are political. In the former, digital media promote diversification of repertoires, whereas in the latter they may represent the most accessible venue for political participation. What seems true in both cases, though for different reasons, is that digital media are more relevant for unconventional forms of political participation than for conventional ones.

1.3.3. Sociality of Politics

A third issue in research on digital media concerns the social basis of politics and how that basis may be growing more salient. There is a consensus in the literature that the social media and related tools presently called web 2.0 offer some qualitatively different social and political opportunities from prior technologies, and that those opportunities involve social experience and networks (Kalnes 2009; Jackson and Lilleker 2009; Benkler 2006; Chadwick 2009a). Observers give various reasons for this, but most concur that there are at least two facets to the phenomenon. The first is the high degree of horizontal communication among citizens and groups of citizens rather than between elites and citizens. For instance, the vast majority of Facebook's 500 million participants use the medium to communicate with other individuals, not with corporations or states. In this sense, they are qualitatively different from the audiences or readerships of mass media. Moreover, the structure of this communication is organized greatly around social networks among citizens rather than by subscriberships or the regional and demographic factors that underlie broadcast and cable audiences. The second, and closely related, facet is that the experience of media is shaped so much by citizens themselves, who make key decisions about when to speak and about what documents, images, sounds, and symbols will be communicated. This is evident in wikis, where authoritative content is produced collaboratively by citizens, and in video- and photo-sharing sites, as well as other social media, where people produce personalized content in the social context.

What do these features of social media mean when people use them for politics? The answer is still unclear, but it is likely to be important across nations. The behavioral literature has begun to focus on potential differences in citizen-level effects from web 2.0 tools, although a thorough empirical exploration of the theoretical differences between generations of digital media is likely a long way off. For instance, in a somewhat skeptical analysis, Schlozman, Verba, and Brady (2010) show that in the United States, traditional internet use does not alter the basic socioeconomic basis of participation, but they also find that civic engagement involving blogs and social networking sites shows some potential for altering these patterns in the long run. They indicate that the traditional pattern of relatively unengaged younger citizens and more engaged older ones is less pronounced online and that digital media offer some promise of less socioeconomically stratified participation as young people age.

Others are coming to similar conclusions. Using Spanish and American samples, Jensen and Anduiza (in Chapter 4) find differences between web 2.0 online environments and web 1.0 environments with respect to how political interest and knowledge predict participation. Pasek and colleagues (2009) demonstrate a relationship between social media use and civic engagement. Interestingly, they also show that the relationships between use of social networking sites and civic engagement, political knowledge, and trust vary between the major sites in the American market, Facebook and MySpace. They find Facebook use to be associated with more civic engagement in the form of participation in clubs and greater political knowledge, whereas MySpace use is unrelated to civic engagement and negatively associated with political knowledge and trust. Their work suggests that "social networking sites" is not necessarily a meaningful construct, but it reinforces the emerging view that the personal-scale media of the web 2.0 revolution have potentially new implications in advanced democracies.

Certainly, reasons exist to think that differences between web 1.0 and web 2.0 may transcend a lot of boundaries and contexts, including nondemocratic systems. The availability of horizontal and social forms of communication through digital media could be especially important in countries with fewer alternative means of social communication, provided that sufficient civil society infrastructure exists. In authoritarian regimes, the horizontal and social character of digital media may have even larger implications, because political communication flowing through social networks is more difficult to control than traditional websites are. Friedman (2005) addresses the potential of horizontal dissemination through the internet of information and political practices by studying cases in Mexico, Argentina, and Brazil. She argues that the horizontal construction of networks does not inevitably lead to greater democratization but can allow for the inclusion of marginal groups and voices in the realm of politics. Tai (2006) also explains the changing nature of Chinese civil society as facilitated by new technologies. He argues that civil society has evolved from a corporatist and vertical structure to a more horizontal and autonomous one. Beyond that, horizontal politics also allows for the reformulation of identities and the formation of plural communities (Graham and Khosravi 2002), as we will see here. Finally, horizontal politics in nondemocratic states challenges the hierarchical interpretation of facts and events. Li, Xuan, and Kluver (2003) analyze the Qiangguo website, sponsored by the *People's Daily* newspaper, the voice of the Chinese Communist Party. The authors conclude that, despite constant cleansing and censoring by employees, online discussion there does include challenges to official versions of controversial events. They also suggest that Chinese people outside of the country contribute to the online debate. In this sense they conclude that "the Internet has seriously undermined the ability of the Chinese government to define the political agenda, and in many ways has internationalized the news flow into China in unanticipated ways" (Li et al. 2003, 156).[2]

These facets of social media technologies raise some interesting challenges. As several authors have pointed out (e.g., Bennett and Iyengar 2008; Jackson and Lilleker 2009), much of the study of political communication in democracies and its relationship to public opinion and participation is contained in a paradigm organized around persuasive messages and comparatively centralized communication, even if these also include two-step flows. It is elites who frame messages, news media and public officials who set agendas, editors and business offices who act as gatekeepers, and candidates for office who prime issues. To the extent that political communication shifts toward horizontal messages with citizen-created media experiences, with flows shaped by social networks, it shifts outside some of the key theoretical models that have been employed to study media and politics.

Something similar can be said about professional practitioners of campaign politics, whose skills and organizational strategies are heavily rooted in mass media. A number of scholars have found that in democracies, campaign organizations and parties are unsure what to make of social media. It is customary in many nations for such organizations to offer social media as part of their campaigns but to fail to incorporate it into their strategies in any kind of serious way. This has been shown in the United States, the United Kingdom, and Norway (Jackson and Lilleker 2009; Kalnes 2009; Foot and Schneider 2006). In many ways, political professionals' use of social media appears much like their use of the web a decade ago; their actions appear less as well-planned strategic efforts than as ill-defined attempts to join a bandwagon for fear of missing an opportunity that is still obscure to them in concrete strategic and tactical terms (Bimber and Davis 2003). Yet while professionals struggle to exploit social media purposefully, for many citizens, social media are already seamlessly woven into daily life.

1.4. From Studying Surveillance and Control to Citizenship: Problems from outside the Democratic Context

The three issues of attitudes, practice, and sociality have arisen so far mainly in the case of research on a limited number of democracies, but as we suggest, they raise pertinent issues in a variety of settings. In this sense they constitute

---

[2] There is some debate in the literature about China regarding the comparative influence of internet use at the level of civil society (Yang 2003, 2009; Tai 2006) as opposed to changing norms and decisions in the regime (Lagerkvist 2008, 2010; Jiang 2010). Lagerkvist (2010) argues that the state's capacity to censor online media and to use it for propaganda remain powerful and that change in China as a result of digital media must be understood not only from the bottom up but also from the perspective of technocrats and policy makers attempting to walk a fine line between use of the internet to advance the state's goals and tolerance of its use by emergent civil society.

part of the larger set of common citizenship concerns relevant to digital media in comparative context. We turn to inquiring about what issues might be added to that set from the study of digital media in nondemocratic regimes. For the most part, this question has not been developed in the literature on political communication, because research on digital media in authoritarian regimes is dominated by concerns with surveillance, control, and democratization, which are less directly salient in liberal democracies. However, when we reframe issues in authoritarian regimes around the concept of citizenship, we find two interesting problems that resonate with advanced democracies or involve them directly: political voice and allegiance and transnational citizenship.

1.4.1. *The Possibility of Voice*

Voice is a basic element of citizenship of all kinds. Raising our voices as citizens, in Hirschman's (1970) terms, entails making our claims heard and attended to by governments in order to express the dissatisfaction that can lead to political and social changes. Voice is relevant in different ways in different conditions. In pluralistic and complex democracies, problems of voice often reflect uneven access to the public sphere, cases in which the voice of minorities can be ignored or damaged, or simply cases in which the cost of voice is high in crowded arenas of attention and communicative contestation. However, the opportunity to exercise voice and its interaction with digital media are posing different challenges in liberal and nonliberal regimes.

In nonliberal countries, technology enters a somewhat sterile environment for citizenship because public spheres are nonexistent or insufficiently vibrant for an engaged and open public discussion. Internet spaces can be one of the few, if not the only, domains for the expression of dissent, thanks to a measure of anonymity afforded by the internet compared with offline politics, as well as the fast spread of alternative news and means for evading state control. In this sense the potential impact of the internet on voice in such countries may be much more substantial than in Western ones that have long had many public and open spheres for the expression of opinions (Ferdinand 2000a; Zheng and Wu 2005; Howard 2010). In fact, as Hill and Sen (2000) observe, once nations have achieved a qualitative leap toward liberalization, the distinctive role of digital media tends to fade. Moreover, as noted by Abbott (2001), when undemocratic regimes do open, competition for voice on the internet, accessibility to foreign voices, and greater marketing of those spaces make it less likely that the internet will play a distinctive role in further democratization.

The dilemma faced by many regimes is, then, shaping the rate of openness and expansion of digital media, as they are so much more difficult to control than traditional media. The motivations of certain regimes to promote the extension of digital media can be related to administrative efficiency and economic competitiveness, but once the decision has been made to open the door to a popularly available internet, the political and social consequences are multidimensional and in many cases uncontrollable (Egorov, Guriev, and Sonin 2009; Zheng and Wu 2005; Ho et al. 2003; Ferdinand 2000b). For instance,

D'Costa (2003) analyzes new technological elites in Asia who emphasize meritocracy to the detriment of traditional and oligarchic elites who face a gradual erosion of their traditional powers. Even when digital enterprises or businesses employing the internet align with governments, there can be side effects involving increased transparency that work toward openness or democratization of governments (Egorov et al. 2009). This has been also the main argument and justification of companies like Google, Yahoo!, and Skype, which, to operate in China, have had to accept restrictions set by the government and to deliver some personal data about internet users to Chinese authorities (MacKinnon 2006).

From another perspective, Tekwani (2003) points to the fact that governments that confront insurgent actors or challenges to their authority simply cannot stifle all digital practices and voices; from his point of view governments finally need to accept the trade-off entailed in using digital media and even provide information as a route to legitimacy. In this sense, digital media use can start a war over information that goes well beyond the fight to silence dissident voices. Different regimes have made different choices: China censors some political topics but not others, Saudi Arabia may surpass China in the extent of its efforts to control digital media, and Egypt opted against applying the same level of censorship of new stories as it had imposed on printed news media.

The symbiosis between voice and internet use occurs in specific historical moments when incipient but sufficient civil society is able to adopt the technology (Yang 2003, 2009); when other channels for free expression in civil society are limited; and when a minimum technological structure exists among citizens, beyond enterprises and public institutions.

The audience for political voice is important and varies: it can be international in scope, it can involve groups in societies, or it can be states themselves. A first level, especially when citizens' voice will not be heard internally, is speaking to the international sphere, with the hope of gaining global alliance or sympathy that might create external pressure on the domestic political agenda (Li et al. 2003). A paradigmatic case of success was the Chiapas conflict (Froehling 1997; Cleaver 1998; Castles 2002; Tarrow 2005). This started in 1994 with the occupation by the Zapatista movement of seven towns in the Mexican state of Chiapas, to advance indigenous people's rights. Despite Mexican state domination of traditional media, within a short time the pro-Zapatista movement rallied an international community of supporters, from nongovernmental organizations (NGOs) to political parties, through an intense internet information campaign. As Froehling (1997, 302), puts it, "The pro-Zapatista Internet mobilization efforts were successful information rhizomes because they produced flows that foreshortened the options available to the Mexican government and boosted Zapatista efforts." The internet provided a sphere of international voice about the conflict that accompanied many offline political actions: aid caravans, peace camps, international observers' campaigns, and mobilizations in front of many worldwide Mexican embassies. It is interesting that the

Mexican government also tried to provide information through ad hoc websites. However, these had no real impact, as they could not take advantage of anything like the nonhierarchical organizations' network structure to develop and forward communication. What matters here is that international visibility and voice largely denied to the Zapatistas by traditional Mexican media but made possible by the internet changed the conflict in Chiapas; it contributed to the government's avoidance of a direct military confrontation and its participation in rounds of negotiations with the guerrillas. Other indigenous movements have also found space on the internet to defend their rights (Kearney 1995).

But success is not automatic; nothing guarantees that voices heard will be acted on (Tarrow 2005), and it remains unclear how significant constraints really are and under what circumstances efforts to overcome them are likely to succeed. The Tibet case is a well-known example in which many NGOs' advocacy claims in the defense of Tibet's rights, along with considerable publicity, failed to persuade the Chinese government to take steps to solve the conflict except through repression (Ferdinand 2000b; Zheng and Wu 2005; Bray 2000). Tibet advocacy groups hoped that the internet would make a difference in the national and international political debate on Tibet. The historical contest between the People's Republic of China government in Beijing and the Dalai Lama's government in exile in northern India has indeed gone online. Digital communication has been a complementary route to other traditional media campaigns. But online communication has changed neither the nature of the arguments nor the strategy of the contest. And although the Tibetan cause has gained more international support and audience online, facilitating some campaigns including boycotts (Bray 2000), it has not changed China's policies. Bray (2000) points to the hope of activists that, despite the lack of adequate sympathy to the Tibetan cause, some new support is emerging around human rights arguments.

This last point brings us to the possibilities of voice addressed to internal audiences. The internal civil society itself is an important audience for voice, which may shape relations among groups of citizens with plural interests and values, or among differing speech communities (Eickelman and Anderson 1999), or among groups and parties otherwise in opposition to one another (Semetko and Krasnoboka 2003; Kok Wah and Teik 2002). The chief concerns in such cases are diversity and plurality of voices, and the possibility of questioning traditions and official political and cultural interpretations. This kind of voice is essential to building new identities (Ho et al. 2003) and to challenging the monopoly of governments (Guillén and Suárez 2005). The questions, then, are how the use of digital media affects the dynamics of internal voice; what the composition of online voices and its audiences are; and whether these can be translated to civil community self-recognition and, in the ultimate step, be an engine of major changes toward tolerance and democratization.

The third audience for voice is the responsible authorities and political elites of the country. As Zheng and Wu (2005) write, it is rational in civil society, even in a rights-limited regime, to choose a strategy of voice over one of direct confrontation. They argue that direct confrontation against the Chinese regime is very unlikely to succeed, whereas lateral claims that are a challenge but not a threat allow for some space for a positive reaction, as happened in the case of the severe acute respiratory syndrome (SARS), or the death of Sun Zhigang, a graduate student from Zhongshan University, at the hands of police. In the first case, Chinese negligence in publicizing the spread of SARS in November 2003 in Guangdong Province opened the door for internal dissidents to give a real account of what was happening, despite the silence imposed by Chinese authorities. Internal voices and international pressure led the Chinese government to take measures to contain the epidemic, and many officials were removed from office. In the second case, a man held in a Guangzhou custody and repatriation center was beaten to death, thus causing a cascade of discussion on the internet about similar cases. This fed a campaign to make those centers unconstitutional; they were abolished in August 2003. Liu Xiaobo, the Chinese dissident and winner of the 2010 Nobel Peace Prize, has called the internet "God's present to China," writing, "The government can control the press and television, but it cannot control the internet.... It has allowed a new generation of intellectuals to emerge and created folk heroes such as the military doctor Jian Yanyong," who called attention to SARS (Liu 2009).

The Chinese government takes an official position welcoming citizen voice so long as it helps make government appear responsive and does not entail fundamental challenges to state power. For example, state media covered the case of a municipal real estate official who was fired for corruption after having drawn the attention of people online, where photos were posted of his lavish lifestyle. According to one observer in China, this was an effort by the government to channel rising civic awareness into outlets compatible with the maintenance of the state (Chun 2009). In this interpretation, the official position of the Chinese state is that internet-oriented political participation constitutes appropriate and orderly input into decisions of the government, especially at the local level, to make it more efficient. To the extent that this turns out to be true in general, then the internet has become an important channel for both the government and ordinary Chinese people to hear and to be heard, something that creates a dialectic between the regime and the civil society that could lead to a progressive drift toward liberalization rather than a revolution or breakdown of the regime (Howard 2010; McGlinchey 2009; Yang 2009; Eickelman and Anderson 1999).

Voice is an issue in liberal democracies as well, though in a somewhat different way. There, the question is not so much the capacity to speak but the possibility of being heard. These states typically exhibit modern economies that are highly saturated with media and civil society organizations, and so on; the challenge for voice is not the liberty to express oneself or the vehicles with which to do so, but competing in a marketplace of voices. Voice possibilities in liberal countries are channeled through many different roads and media, including digital media. Although diversity is one of the positive effects of the

extension and inclusion of digital media, not all voices have equal opportunity
to be heard. In practice, the ability to influence is more concentrated in a
limited number of elites than is commonly thought, and despite the long tail
of many smaller voices online, those rich voices at the head of the distribution
are very influential (Hindman 2009). The problem of the representativeness of
these voices and the pressure they exercise on policy makers is not a minor
one, especially when the overload of information and inputs from citizens can
reduce their ability to manage all the information available and give them even
and balanced treatment (Ferdinand 2000a).

A second issue for voice in these countries is polarization. Having a competitive market of voice means plurality, but that plurality can succumb to
fragmentation or polarization, as famously outlined by Sunstein (2006). Most
scholars of selective exposure argue, in effect, that Sunstein's case is not wrong
but overstated (Iyengar and Hahn 2009; Garrett 2009; Mutz and Martin
2001; Wojcieszak and Mutz 2009). Evidence is clear for the polarization of
views online, although considerable numbers of people are exposed to challenging voices. Two of the most interesting problems are where online political voice is expressed and where conditions exist for diverse voices to meet.
Wojcieszak and Mutz (2009) show that political talk occurs quite frequently
in many nonpolitical forums online, which is to say that political communication among citizens is suffused throughout their online lives rather than being
bounded by explicitly political environments. They also find that exposure to
political difference is typically more common outside political forums than in
them.

Although the foci in liberal and nonliberal countries differ quite a lot with
respect to voice, parallels do exist regarding who speaks out and who is heard,
often as a question of building and expressing identities online, an issue that
goes beyond the division between liberal and nonliberal countries.

1.4.2. Allegiance, Identities, and Transnational Citizenship

An emerging issue that is still taking shape involves transformations in the
concept of citizenship as a result of the permeability and porosity of borders,
as well as global migration flows. Transnational movements are not new, but
in recent years they have taken on features that challenge the more territorial
conception of citizenship. Castles (2002, 1157) outlines the issues well: "At the
dawn of the twenty-first century, globalization is undermining all the modes of
controlling difference premised on territoriality. Increasing mobility; growth of
temporary, cyclical and recurring migrations; cheap and easy travel; constant
communication through new information technologies: all question the idea of
the person who belongs to just one nation-state or at most migrates from one
state to just one other (whether temporarily or permanently)." The processes
that Castles lists create new spaces for configuring multiple identities linked
not to just one specific country but to more than one. In addition to multiple national identities, these identities may be tied to diverse communities and

ethnic groups, and they may have special attributes tied uniquely to the experience of sharing migration experiences.

Greater mobility and communication allow for migration processes to include return and circular movements rather than permanent integration into host societies, and this is possible because of both physical mobility and new possibilities for communication. The resulting relational processes (Tarrow 2005) or circular migration (Castles 2002) may mean that some people do not settle in any one location in which they can build identity and citizenship. Such migration can foster a sense of belonging to a diaspora and to being unbounded by borders and countries with respect to citizenship (DiMaggio et al. 2001). What does the practice of transnational citizenship actually entail? It can manifest in a wide range of ways, from financial remittances to cooperation in the electoral campaigns in the country of origin and mobilization for the defense of certain rights. The majority of transnational practices are not strictly political (Morales and Jorba 2009), but many important ones can be or can affect politics through the configuration of new identities and the expansion of online communities.

From normative perspectives on citizenship, a trade-off can exist between transnational engagement and integration in the host society. Although it is logical that transnational activities and communication promote the continuing attention to the country of origin and may promote isolation in a host society, it is also true that transnational engagement can have positive spillover effects, empowering individuals and translating skills and abilities from one sphere to the other (Portes, Guarnizo, and Landolt 1999; Morales and Jorba 2009, 2010; Tarrow 2005).

Norris and Inglehart (2009) defend the convergence-of-values hypothesis, arguing for a growing orientation toward a more liberal and individualistic culture across nations. In this sense, online communities and new technologies are facilitating the emergence of a new global citizen, aided by physical movement and multiple allegiances. Moreover, increasing technological power may allow the overcoming of language barriers (Ho et al. 2003; Tekwani 2003), which facilitates access to English websites and communities. However, the result can be ambiguity and fluidity of identities and subjectivities (Rinnawi 2009; Sun 2002), such that it is difficult to clearly identify loyalties. This means that the temptation to adopt a simplistic model of cosmopolitanism versus ethnicism as a way of understanding citizenship should be avoided (Castles 2002).

Digital media are implicated throughout this process, from facilitating easy electronic remittances to facilitating common identities through sharing stories and symbols for people living in different countries (Kunreuther 2006, 330; Sun 2002). For example, Rinnawi (2009) explores the possibility opened by the internet to reinterpret what it means to be Arab and to challenge the official political and religious traditions that had previously reduced individuals to identification only with their particular nations and ethnicities. This has helped overcome ethnicity and build a sense of pan-Arabism. Specifically, a shared language and some common political, social, and cultural concerns in the Arab world help create commonalities in the online sphere, thus facilitating an interchange between individuals in the Arab world and through Arabs living outside it. The internet helps open up the exchange of ideas and a more nuanced diversity of views, projects, and expressions of both pan-Arabism and concern for national identity. At the same time, it may enhance the desire for democratization and openness throughout the entire Arab world, beyond the claim of the right for equal access to the Arab public sphere and the sharing of ideas.

This is a case of constructing what is sometimes called the common-imaginary features of shared culture, values and imagination. This process is not always challenging or based on resistance, as it can be built from nostalgia for a country (Sun 2002). But even when online communities and transnational identities oppose the official image promoted by the country of origin, that voice is usually not uniform but pluralistic, contradictory, and conflicting. For example, Graham and Khosravi (2002) describe the pluralism and dynamic response that occur in the Iranian diaspora communities and the subsequent construction of a more pronounced individuality. Basing their study on the Iranian migrant communities in Stockholm and Los Angeles during the period 1994 to 2001, the authors conclude that cyberspace has contributed to promote "discussion in a wide range of political phenomena including political mobilization and censorship, intergenerational communication, identity formation, sexuality, sense of belonging, and forms and location of symbolic capital" (Graham and Khosravi 2002, 219). This makes visible a degree of social and cultural heterogeneity, as well as contradictory and conflicted views among Iranians, thus fostering a sense of distinction and individuality as well as a greater reflection on one's self-identity. One can hope that this kind of communication spanning different contexts will promote tolerance and the recognition of individual rights in a way that affects societies of origin (Castles 2002).

Finally, Lim (2003) points out that the internet can be used to promote violence and exacerbate radical nationalism (Kalathil and Boas 2003; Anderson 1997). The possibility that the survival and growth of violent groups and the formation and maintenance of insurgent groups through fund-raising practices are greatly facilitated by the internet and digital media cannot be disregarded (Tekwani 2003). "Diasporas are increasingly functioning as nonstate actors in international conflict, and governments dealing with terrorist groups and insurgents within their borders are finding out that power balances are shifting away from their favor" (Tekwani 2003, 189–190).

Although it is true that citizenship is still strongly associated with the borders of nation-states, these trends toward various enactments of transnational citizenship are expanding and are of growing importance – directly for transnational citizens themselves and indirectly for others influenced by their increasing presence on national and international stages.

1.5. Conclusion

In several ways, common citizenship issues associated with digital media manifest in varying national contexts. For instance, where nonliberal countries are concerned, a major normative issue has been having sufficient contestation of ideas and challenges to regimes. Where liberal countries are concerned, a major issue has been too much cynicism and mistrust of institutions, as well as extreme contestation of attitudes that is deliberately harmful. Both cases can be understood in terms of critical voice, which suggests an underlying autonomy of the citizen, built in opposition or even in relation to a particular political system, the performance of its institutions, or toward some specific sets of values. The development of this individuality fits much better with new technologies that allow for richer and more diverse forms of communication and participation than it does with mass media.

These five issues – attitudes, practices, voice, sociality, and transnationalism – do not exhaust the list of connections between digital media and citizenship, but they do establish that the connections may be both broad and deep. Together they suggest that some qualitative changes in the character of citizenship are intertwined with the diffusion of digital media and with people's explorations of ways to incorporate these media into their private and public lives. A crucial theme across many of these issues is the coevolution of digital media and politics. Rarely, if ever, is it right to say that digital media cause anything, in the sense that people's use of technology is the cause of a particular social or political outcome. That kind of statement is sometimes a convenient shorthand that falls more or less far from being correct but never hits the mark. It is also true that the people who build and sell new technologies rarely have social or political goals that are important to their innovations, although exceptions exist. But it is true that digital media have crucial characteristics and affordances that for the most part are invariant across cultures, such as speed of communication and a decentralized structure. Digital media are very different from analog broadcast media, and this is as true in Catalonia as it is in California.

By themselves, technologies do not do anything, nor do the opportunities and agency they afford compel people to act, and so their implications are felt as people take them up and incorporate them into their practices. In this sense, digital media do not create civil society or introduce new practices of citizenship. But where these are incipient or contested, use of technology can support, reinforce, or amplify trends. As some people's use of technology supports social or political innovation, subsequent cycles of adoption and practice can emerge that fuel the market for further technological innovation and diffusion. This is the coevolution of citizenship and media.

This, of course, means that there is nothing inevitable about the process, nor is it necessarily linear or predictable. Modest or even tiny differences across settings in attitudes, practices, sociality, voice, or allegiance may be amplified differently by the availability of digital media, which means that trajectories of citizenship differ across place. The portrait we have drawn of these issues in this chapter has been citizen-centric, at the cost of paying little attention to differences in cultures, institutions, and political economy, which are among the most important influences on how digital media and citizenship develop together. These do not provide small differences in initial conditions but large and continuing differences in context. As a result, we do not expect citizenship to move in the same direction across nations, but we expect these five dimensions to be key to the interconnections of citizenship and digital media in diverse societies.

2

Recent Shifts in the Relationship between the Internet and Democratic Engagement in Britain and the United States

Granularity, Informational Exuberance, and Political Learning

Andrew Chadwick

2.1. Introduction

The internet is evolving into one the most significant enablers of political inno-vation since the emergence of mass democracy. Over the past decade, few areas of social and political life have escaped its influence. Because of the potentially huge scope of the internet (see Chadwick and Howard 2009b; Chadwick 2006), this chapter has two interrelated objectives. First, following a brief explication of concepts, it discusses significant recent shifts in what we know, or should seek to know, about the internet's role in promoting political knowledge and political engagement, with reference to some important strands of literature from the United States and Britain. Second, it generates some hypotheses about the likely effects of recent changes in the online environment, through discus-sion of British and U.S. examples of what is widely called web.2.0. The broad argument is that continuing to frame research in this area in terms of traditional understandings of engagement, participation, and deliberative democracy risks missing the significance of three key forces in the contemporary political context of these two countries: granularity, informational exuberance, and by-product political learning.

2.2. Web 2.0, Granularity, and Informational Exuberance

Though widely used, the concept of web 2.0 has eluded precise definition. Originally the creation of Silicon Valley technologists, web 2.0 has long since escaped the business community and is an idea that loosely organizes a variety of concerns across a range of scholarly disciplines. O'Reilly is widely regarded to have been the first to popularize the term in 2003. His technology-focused approach defined web 2.0 in terms of seven key principles: "the web as plat-form," "harnessing collective intelligence," "data is the next 'Intel inside,'" "the end of the software release cycle," "lightweight programming models," "software above the level of a single device," and "rich user experiences"

(O'Reilly 2007, 18, 22, 27, 30, 31, 33, 34). Chadwick and Howard (2009a) begin from these technological principles but explicate their relevance for politics and suggest the following formulation: "the internet as a platform for political discourse; the collective intelligence emergent from political web use; the importance of data over particular software and hardware applications; perpetual experimentalism in the public domain; the creation of small scale forms of political engagement through consumerism; the propagation of political content over multiple applications; and rich user experiences on political websites" (Chadwick and Howard 2009a, 4).

Granularity is a metaphorical concept that has long been used in computer science, but it has recently spread into other fields, such as management, information systems, and law. Benkler extends the computer science approach by observing that most successful examples of online collaboration involve breaking up large projects into smaller modules. In Benkler's (2006, 100–101) terms, granularity is understood as the "size of the modules, in terms of the time and effort that an individual must invest in producing them." He goes on to argue that success is more likely when the majority of modules are "relatively fine-grained," (Benkler 2006, 101) although there are instances of projects with coarse-grained contributions, as in the collaborative production of Linux, the open-source computer operating system.

Building on Benkler's approach, in this chapter *granularity* refers to the extent to which the creation of informational public goods may be disaggregated into tasks of varying magnitude, where magnitude is understood as a function of resources, such as time, knowledge, experience, cognitive processing, and so on, which people are able to mobilize in the pursuit of individual and collective goals. Sociotechnical environments that have different degrees of granularity designed in – to allow citizens to innovate and perform citizenship in diverse ways – are more likely to be successful and to produce greater aggregated effects, where success and effects can be defined in any number of ways beneficial to democracy. One-size-fits-all environments in which classically deliberative encounters are the expectation require citizens to complete tasks that are of a much greater magnitude than those expected in nondeliberative environments.

By *informational exuberance* I mean to capture the increasing willingness of nonelites to contribute to the collective production, reworking, and sharing of media content, with the conscious or unconscious aim of creating public goods for formal and informal political organization, coordination, and aggregation. These may include, for example, firsthand reports of events, personal narratives, conversations, commentary, opinion, archives, spatial and temporal information, and lifestyle and consumption behavior, all of which may be expressed in textual and/or audiovisual forms. In the United States and Britain, much of citizens' public informational exuberance as it relates to politics takes place online or is conducted through mechanisms that involve rapid and subtle switching between online and offline realms. Because of the granularity that characterizes the most popular online environments for politics in the two countries, most informational exuberance is nondeliberative, if deliberation is understood in the classical Athenian or Habermasian senses. By this, I mean that the small-scale forms of political engagement that have proliferated online over the past half-decade are far removed from the demanding models of the deliberative and discursive democracy that provided the yardsticks for so many interpretations of the internet – both positive and negative – during the early years of scholarship in the field. And I believe that these new forms may be all the more powerful for that.

Granularity and informational exuberance present challenges to deeply embedded assumptions about the relationship of media, information, and politics, but they arguably form the social roots of a new phase in the evolution of political participation, collective action, and democratic innovation.

2.3. Information, Learning, and Engagement

Social scientists have long sought to understand how information shapes political participation. Early empirical studies of U.S. public opinion from the 1940s and 1950s often found that individuals rarely lived up to the ideal of the informed citizen. Although citizens usually reported some basic awareness of political events, most devoted more energy and attention to nonpolitical information, particularly entertainment. However, some scholars argued that individuals were able to derive sufficient information from the press, radio, and television through "by-product learning." This concept, first elaborated by Downs (1957), assumes that, if given the choice, most citizens will avoid consuming political information and will instead seek out entertainment. In the context of a media environment in which choice is limited, citizens are often exposed to political information by accident: their daily diet of sports, music, movies, and celebrity gossip is interspersed with television and radio news bulletins that are hard to avoid. Downs concluded that a basic level of political knowledge – certainly sufficient to enable informed participation in elections – was a healthy by-product of a mixed information ecology. By-product learning was said to soften informational inequalities between social groups; ensure broad popular awareness of key political events; and most crucially, spur us to act on that knowledge come Election Day.

Since Downs's study, the proliferation of multichannel television and the internet have radically increased the quantity of information available to the majority of citizens in advanced Western democracies, and the original conditions under which by-product learning was first proposed have vanished. But what of the aggregate effects of those developments? The argument for by-product learning was hatched in an era of relative media scarcity, but for some scholars it has started to look less secure in the rather different context of a virtually limitless choice of media content. In an early study of the internet's contribution to democracy, Sunstein (2001) argued that individuals were predisposed to filter and sort information about the social world in ways that accord with their preexisting preferences. When the technological tools to do this are highly refined and widely available, as they now are online, Sunstein argued that citizens created information echo chambers: meticulously personalized spheres of communication that reflect, but do not challenge, their predilections and prejudices.

Prior (2005, 2007) has demonstrated empirically that, in the United States, individuals with a preference for entertainment have far greater opportunities for avoiding news than they did during the so-called golden age of broadcast television from the 1950s to the early 1980s. Before the diffusion of cable and satellite television and the internet, Prior argues, individuals watched a lot of television, but this was not a bad thing. Learning about politics via this medium was easier than learning through print media because television relied on images and the spoken word. For those predisposed to watching entertainment programming, by-product learning about politics while watching television played an important role in encouraging them to vote. During the mid-1960s (terrestrial broadcast television's heyday in the United States) each household had access to an average of just 6.8 stations. Similarly, in late 1970s Britain there were only three stations per household. Today, 85 percent of American and 90 percent of British households face a bewildering, yet empowering choice of cable and satellite stations, and substantially more than two-thirds of those populations can access vast swaths of online content at home (Internet World Stats 2008; United Kingdom Office of Communications 2010). In 2010, 88 percent of the population of the United Kingdom owned a mobile phone, 40 percent watched television online, and 23 percent reported using their mobile devices to access the internet and watch television programs (U.K. Office of Communications 2010).

The high-choice media environment in the United States and Britain enables those with a preference for politics to satisfy their cravings in ways that were unimaginable only a couple of decades ago. But for Sunstein and Prior, in this environment it is much less likely that those uninterested in politics will be accidentally exposed to political content. As Prior (2007, 134) puts it, "Even though political information is abundant and more readily available than ever before, political knowledge has decreased for a substantial portion of the electorate: entertainment fans with access to new media. Ironically, the share of politically uninformed people has risen since we entered the so-called 'information age.'"

More recently, these and several related assumptions have been placed at the center of Bennett and Iyengar's (2008) argument that we are entering a new era of "minimal effects," as media fragmentation becomes more deeply embedded and aligned with broader social changes associated with postindustrialism, such as the decline of solidaristic social and political institutions. Paradoxically, therefore, abundant information is said to create incentive structures that increase political apathy and polarization at the same time as they further stratify civic and political engagement. But is this always the case? Recent shifts in the literature on the internet and engagement, discussed next, suggest that things might not be this straightforward.

2.4. Some Recent Shifts in the U.S. and British Literature

In the radically fragmented media environments of the contemporary Anglo-American democracies, researching the diverse ways in which individuals interact with media, and precisely how those interactions may or may not shape political behavior, has become a huge challenge.

2.4.1. Analytical and Methodological Uncertainty

An initial contextual point here is that, despite the growth of the literature base over the past decade, the study of the internet and engagement has been characterized by a general sense of analytical and methodological uncertainty. Although this could be said of many areas of the social sciences, it is a sign that political communication is a field in transition following a major exogenous shock.

Most early behavioral studies of the effects of internet use on civic and political participation emerged from the United States and tended to find that the internet's overall influence was minimal. The medium was more likely to provide further opportunities for political engagement for those who were already politically engaged (Bimber 2001; Hill and Hughes 1998; Scheufele and Nisbet 2002). In the late 1990s and early 2000s, only a small minority of citizens used the internet for political information. Early British studies tended to reinforce these findings. For example, anywhere between 4 percent and 10 percent of survey respondents, depending on the survey, used the medium for information during the 2004 European Parliament and 2005 general election campaigns (Lusoli and Ward 2005; Norris and Curtice 2007). Meanwhile, some U.S. empirical studies of online behavior substantiated the argument for the end of by-product learning by observing, for example, how people actually consume online news. Tewksbury's (2003) analysis of website logs found that readers of online news tended to avoid content about public affairs and instead preferred that about sports and entertainment.

A recent meta-analysis of thirty-eight mainstream empirical studies of the internet and engagement in the United States unearths a total of 166 separate effects (Boulianne 2009). It reveals that most studies have attempted to use as dependent variables some fairly standard measures of civic and political participation derived from pre-internet political science in the American pluralist tradition (e.g., Verba, Schlozman, and Brady 1995). Political participation is usually operationalized as traditional behaviors that are obviously focused on political institutions and shaping policy, such as voting, donating money, attending meetings, letter writing, discussing issues, and so on, although it may also include less formal behavior such as protesting in marches and demonstrations, volunteering in the local community, and signing petitions. The standard independent variables have usually included internet use or nonuse, number of hours spent online, different technology uses (e.g., e-mail, web browsing, instant messaging), or online and offline media consumption habits. The consumption of news has, for understandable reasons in liberal democratic contexts, been perceived as a particularly important independent variable for political engagement. Most of the U.S. studies have used multivariate statistical analysis and have controlled for variables that shape participation, such as education and income. A surprisingly high proportion of empirical work has used web surveys to gather data, and many studies have focused on subsamples of internet users derived from random-digit-dialing telephone surveys. The majority of studies model internet use as affecting participation, but some studies reverse this, by assessing how prior levels of engagement affect internet use. Some include only online activity in their measures of political participation (e.g., Kobayashi, Ikeda, and Miyata 2006). Some combine online and offline behavior into composite scales but do not distinguish between effects on online and offline action (e.g., Weber, Loumakis, and Bergman 2003; Wellman et al. 2001). The majority test internet use effects only on offline action. These uncertainties raise questions that arguably deserve greater attention, especially given the recent shifts in the nature of the online environment.

2.4.2. *The Abundance and Complexity of Information*

Although she does not explore it in detail, a key finding of Boulianne's (2009) meta-analysis is a consensus that the internet has a small but positive effect on participation and that the effect is becoming stronger over time. What might underlie this development? Contrary to the thesis on the end of by-product learning of Sunstein and Prior, or the argument of a new era of minimal effects of Bennett and Iyengar, some have theorized that the characteristics of political information online – its quantity, richness, timeliness, and accessibility – create a media environment more beneficial for the acquisition of the knowledge and skills required for politics. In an ongoing series of team-authored studies, Shah, Kwak, and Holbert (2001) and colleagues integrate several large U.S. data sets to examine whether informational uses of the internet encourage civic and political engagement when compared with traditional media, especially newspapers. Their early results revealed that the internet played only a minor role in this regard, although a significant finding from a 2001 study was that using the internet to exchange political information generates higher levels of political trust than uses of traditional print and broadcast news media (Shah, McLeod, and Yoon 2001).

The latest U.S. studies, however, are beginning to get under the skin of the internet's functions in everyday communication about politics and how these functions may lead to civic and political engagement. They reveal the emergence of a more complex political communication environment, with the internet rivaling, and in some U.S. work, exceeding, television and newspaper consumption as a spur to engagement (Shah et al. 2005). A range of mediation and interaction effects among traditional media use, direct campaign messages, interpersonal communication, and online interactivity have been observed (Shah et al. 2007). As Shah and colleagues (2007, 696) put it, "Online news use and interactive political messaging – uses of the web as a resource *and* a forum – both strongly influence civic and political participation." And these findings have been reinforced by a recent book by Mossberger, Tolbert, and McNeal (2008, 47–66), who discover that across three American national election campaigns (2000, 2002, and 2004), those who read political news online were more likely to have higher levels of political knowledge and political interest and were more likely to engage in discussions about politics.

This shift toward a more complex understanding of the internet and engagement is starting to inform the British literature. For example, Norris and Curtice's (2007) analysis of internet use during the 2005 British general election finds evidence of a classic two-step flow of communication. The two-step flow model, first proposed by Lazarsfeld, Berelson, and Gaudet (1944) and much discussed since, argues that specialized forms of political communication, such as manifestos, speeches, and website content, are unlikely to reach a mass audience but are highly likely to reach informed activists. Those activists, called opinion leaders, engage in interpersonal discussion with those in their immediate surroundings, thus indirectly informing the less engaged. Norris and Curtice (2007) demonstrate that those who go online to acquire political information are statistically more likely to talk to others about the election (both online and offline) than those who do not go online. As they conclude, "it appears that the reach of the internet during the 2005 election campaign was rather greater than appears to be the case from simply looking at how many people used the Internet for themselves to find out about the election" (Norris and Curtice 2007, 11).

The discovery of more complex, often interpersonal flows of political information and more diverse internet usage patterns by citizens in Britain and the United States should come as less of a surprise if we consider how the supply of opportunities for online political activity has increased since the internet's early period of diffusion in the mid-1990s. As web technologies have evolved and expanded over the past decade, so, too, have the political repertoires available to citizens. Early work in this area was based on the assumption of an online realm in which basic websites formed the core experience of those wishing to pursue politics online. Few could have foreseen the recent rapid innovations in networked online software services. Not only do American and British citizens now have many more opportunities to participate in mediated politics, but also the means by which they are able to do so are far more granular and interpersonal than they once were.

2.4.3. Revisionist Perspectives on Deliberation
A recent shift in the U.S. literature on political deliberation also has implications for the internet and engagement. Deliberation has provided an important organizing perspective and normative model for scholarship on the internet and politics (for an overview, see Chadwick 2006). Yet just as the literature on the internet and engagement has recently shifted toward an emphasis on granularity and complexity, so, too, has the broader literature on deliberative

democracy. These revisionist approaches ought to inform studies of democratic innovation online.

There has long been a divide between normative and empirical approaches to deliberation (Thompson 2008). Mutz (2008, 522) has gone as far as to suggest that "frustration remains on both sides due to our inability to accept one another's assumptions and even to understand one another's terms." Studies of the internet, especially those studies in the United States, have replicated this divide because they have often been fueled by highly unrealistic expectations of citizen behavior, not just in normative terms but also empirically. At stake here is the extent to which the ethical justifications for the promotion of deliberative democracy may be operationalized as testable hypotheses and applied to deliberation in real-world settings by social scientists, where the real world firmly includes the online environment. Mutz argues that studies of deliberation should move away from all-or-nothing approaches, such as the assumption that deliberation creates legitimate consensus. Instead, she advocates a new orientation based on Merton's (1957) well-known idea of theories of the "middle range" (Mutz 2008, 522). Taking Mutz's view on board means moving away from deliberation as the supreme independent variable and universally positive outcome, and toward exploring mechanisms that "partially comprise deliberation" (Mutz 2008, 531). Rather than seeking to construct increasingly elaborate normative edifices that can then be applied to deliberative encounters, we ought to generate more circumscribed hypotheses about the conditions under which specific desiderata from deliberative theory may or may not be achieved. We ought also to consider whether deliberative modes of decision making are in fact always suitable for the production of particular outcomes desirable for democratic politics, such as citizens' political interest, sense of political efficacy, and so on.

Part of the problem here is that the majority of the studies of online democracy begin from the assumption that "true" deliberation is, in itself, always and everywhere, intrinsically valuable; they then tend to conclude that an online environment is or is not deliberative (e.g., Hindman 2009). In terms of Mutz's critique, such studies have developed criteria that may be used to assess online communication for its deliberativeness without questioning either whether a setting that meets those criteria actually produces the desired outcomes or, more important for my argument, whether nondeliberative contexts are capable of producing the democratic goods that deliberative contexts are supposed to create, but so often fail to do so.

2.5. Web 1.0 to Web 2.0: Three Arguments on the Transition

At least three important arguments flow from these recent shifts in the U.S. and U.K. literatures on the internet, engagement, and deliberation.

The first is that citizens' digital network repertoires (Chadwick 2007) have expanded considerably and studies of online engagement in the United States and Britain are steadily catching up. Work that conceptualizes the internet as a simple conduit for the vertical transmission of messages from source to receiver appears limited. Even the two-step flow model is a limited tool for making sense of these trends. The internet is a multifaceted medium, and it partly functions as a series of network mechanisms for the organization of horizontal, interpersonal, communication among citizens. The useful knowledge that flows through these networks stimulates involvement in political campaigns and other civically beneficial activities, and this knowledge is increasingly, though not exclusively, derived from online, not traditional, sources (Shah et al. 2007). There is also evidence that these kinds of effects are more strongly created by, and experienced among, those who are less involved in traditional political activity, such as women and young people (Pasek et al. 2009; Gibson, Lusoli, and Ward 2005).

With so many recent quantitative and qualitative shifts in online behavior, as greater numbers of people have become involved not only in the consumption but also in the production of digital content, we need to disaggregate what we mean by "the internet" and operationalize the diverse range of activities that occur in the online environment when compared with much simpler, one-to-many media such as television. Although there are, at the time of writing, no published studies that explore this question (but see Bode 2010), as I have argued previously (Chadwick 2009a), it is a reasonable hypothesis that hugely popular user-generated content sites such as YouTube and social networking environments such as Facebook encourage more by-product learning about politics than do static web pages. Although the internet's enormous potential for political information retrieval does not imply that individuals will always use it for those ends, and it is clear that attitudinal variables such as partisanship will act as important mediators, there is a danger that we neglect opportunities for by-product learning in the online environment. A recent review of the literature on online news posits, among other things, that many use the internet in the same way that they use other media, and general browsing is just as important as echo-chamber-style filtering (Tewskbury and Rittenberg 2009). Other studies have found that it is practically impossible for citizens to avoid dissonant views in the online environment (Garrett 2005); that ideological segregation online is typically lower than in face-to-face social interactions (Gentzkow and Shapiro 2010); and that citizens typically engage in much political discussion in online arenas that are formally nonpolitical, such as those related to hobbies and lifestyles (Wojcieszak and Mutz 2009). Indeed, there is evidence that even during the period of the early web, before blogging, social networking sites, and user-generated content expanded, individuals sought out dissonant views (Brundidge and Rice 2009; Stromer-Galley 2003) and they did experience by-product learning effects (Tewksbury, Weaver, and Maddex 2001). In other words, media fragmentation may not always lead to minimal effects; it may simply be that the sources and modalities of these effects are different in the new media environment (Holbert, Garrett, and Gleason 2010).

The second point to be made about these recent shifts is that it is less analytically useful to conceptualize engagement and participation along the lines first established during the early wave of empirical research. Many of the current assumptions about how to measure engagement date from the wave of studies from the Anglo-American world of the late 1980s and early 1990s (see, e.g., Verba et al. 1995; Parry, Moyser, and Day 1992). But given that solely online political expression is a growing part of citizens' political behavior, is it sufficient to model the effects of simple internet-use variables (e.g., time spent online) on solely offline behaviors (e.g., voting, attending town hall meetings)? Foot and Schneider (2006) convincingly argue that political websites should be understood as distinctive zones of political action: "surfaces on which campaigns' production practices are inscribed over time and evolving structures that simultaneously manifest and enable political action." I have argued elsewhere that "repertoire switches" spatially (between online and offline realms) and temporally (within and between campaigns) characterize political mobilization (Chadwick 2007, 283). How citizens use and contribute to informational exuberance, together with the rapid expansion of a diverse range of meaningful online opportunities for political action, present challenges to the assumptions of the first wave of literature on the internet and engagement.

The third point is that revisionist critiques of the deliberation literature (Mutz 2008; Fung 2007) are highly pertinent for understanding recent shifts in the nature of the internet's role in democratic innovation. Although these critiques do not use the term, these approaches assume granularity. There is no natural, immutable link between a set of normative principles and institutional design across all policy problems and contexts. Equally, there ought to be no assumption that democratic goods are always more likely to emerge from classically deliberative encounters. As Fung (2007, 445–456) puts it, "A democrat for whom deliberation and public reason are cardinal values need not prescribe citizen deliberation, or even deliberation, for every problem.... Democratic theorists should widen their sources of inspiration and constraint to include the disciplined consideration of the consequences of the fullest range of institutional alternatives for collective decision making and action."

In the remainder of the chapter, by way of illustration, I sketch out a range of intriguing themes that emerge from recent developments in the United States and Britain. These ought to be on the research agendas of all scholars interested in the internet and engagement.

2.6. Granularity in Web 2.0 Politics

The internet's role in daily life has changed a great deal over the past five years.[1] Contemporary web applications are dominated by a distinctive usability ethos that was often absent from the earlier phases of web development. Early critical accounts of internet-mediated politics often bemoaned the growth of a digital divide between do-it-yourself websites and the glitzy, professionalized sites of the wealthy and powerful. Although it would be a mistake to

---

[1] This section and the following section expand on Chadwick 2009b, 26–33.

ignore the sophisticated backend technologies that enable web 2.0 sites to function, the usability doctrines of figures such as Nielsen (1999) and Maeda (2008) have had a major influence on the look and feel of the contemporary web. Accessibility and ease of use are the core principles of extremely simple messaging platforms such as "tumblelogs" (see http:///www.tumblr.com) and Twitter (http://www.twitter.com). The U.K. MySociety projects are based on the principle that small is beautiful, and they enable citizens to do one simple thing, easily and elegantly (http://www.mysociety.org). TheyWorkForYou (http://www.theyworkforyou.com), for example, provides an intuitive searchable interface to Hansard, the record of all British parliamentary proceedings. Debates are listed in an easy-to-follow format, but more important, they allow citizens to comment on specific parliamentarians' speeches. Once submitted, citizens' comments appear alongside the original speeches, and citizens are able to comment on the comments of others. The site also provides opportunities to learn about the views and behavior of members of Parliament, including their voting record, speeches, committee membership, and entries in the register of members' interests. In granular sociotechnical environments such as this, complexity emerges from the aggregation of many simple contributions.

High-, medium-, and low-threshold tools for democratic innovation exist side by side in a panoply of online environments, such as threaded discussion forums, group and individual blogs, wikis, audio messaging, video messaging, social networking profile pages, friend lists, shared calendars, shared address books, shared document databases, shared spreadsheets, and shared tag clouds. This list could be extended. Many web services rely on large numbers of individuals behaving with regularity in low-threshold ways. A threshold is here understood to be a function of an individual's calculation about the expected utility of participating in a given activity, on the basis of the likelihood of participation by others (Granovetter 1973; Miller and Page 2004; Olson 1965). The key point about low-threshold political behavior online is that much of the technological architecture of web 2.0 applications designs in low- and high-threshold activities and many variants in between. An example is the division of labor typified by many news aggregators and blogs such as Digg (http://www.digg.com), BBC News Online (http://www.bbc.co.uk), and AOL News (http://news.aol.com). This user-generated content circulates around reactive, storytelling models and a division of labor. Citizens write stories, and the sites open a sample of these to comments and ratings. Some tell the stories, others make brief comments, and others rate both the story and the comments with a simple click. Highly rated stories rise to the top of the list. Many of these stories begin life as stories about other stories – remixed versions of the content of others. A good policy example comes in the form of Frank, a user-generated element on the U.K. government's drug-awareness site for young people (http://www.talktofrank.com). The page allows users to write and upload their own stories, thus providing an interesting combination of an information site with a public health agenda that relies on user content to help fulfill its role. The popularity of this approach is explained by the fact that it is a granular, not an all-or-nothing, model.

Quantitatively and qualitatively different forms of contribution are facilitated by the technological architecture. Many citizens seem to find mixing together sources of digital content originally created by others to be a compelling and worthwhile experience. Although it would be an exaggeration to say that the political economy of political content creation has been transformed, it has shifted in significant ways.

Just as these environments lower thresholds for citizens, they also lower them for political elites. A major disadvantage of deliberative models is their high-stakes, one-size-fits-all approach. Many risk factors present themselves in this environment (Chadwick 2011a), but three are particularly salient. First, forum participation rates will be low, which will attract negative media coverage and, over time, deter citizens from entering a forum for fear of standing out. Second, the forum descends into irrelevance, or flame wars, and becomes heavily censored or an embarrassment. Third, the forum's sponsors fear losing control of their agenda and so design in severe restrictions, overmoderate it, or disown it.

Granular environments, in which different repertoires of engagement sit side by side, from postings to comments, ratings, wiki editing, and so on, do not eliminate these risks but do reduce them. Consider, for example, the U.K. Foreign Office's group blog (United Kingdom Foreign Office 2008). This features entries by the U.K. foreign minister, junior ministers, career civil servants, and occasionally guest writers. David Miliband, the British foreign secretary from 2007 to 2010, began blogging while a minister at the Department of the Environment. Miliband's blog concentrated on policy and ministerial work and featured a commenting facility. The entries were moderated and rarely received large numbers of comments, although they were read by many (Hansard Society 2007). But the advantage of the blog format is that comments and interaction are not pivotal to the experience: many blogs have no comments, but this is generally accepted as part of the blogging ecology and does not deter their authors. The general sense of an ongoing flow of material in a conversational style also avoids the perception of a high-stakes, tightly managed environment. The amount of time and staff resources required to run a group blog are also less than those required to run a deliberative forum. Skeptics point to the fact that some politicians' blogs are ghostwritten, but many are not. For example, the Hansard Society's (2007) researchers found that Miliband wrote his own entries.

The hypothesis that increasing granularity reduces the risk of failure also relates to the presentation of politicians' and officials' online personae. Politicians' blogs and YouTube videos tend to avoid jargon and formal stump-speech and press release genres. Microblogging services such as Twitter, the ultimate in low-threshold action because it permits individual messages only 140 characters long, take this informality to extremes. Yet many politicians have adopted microblogging with relish. As with blogging, there is much skepticism regarding politicians' use of Twitter. Barack Obama was criticized for supposedly suspending his Twitter feed once elected in November 2008. However, the account was not in fact suspended and was used to publicize the White House's Open for Questions initiative of March 2009, for which, according to the White House site, "92,937 people submitted 103,981 questions and cast 3,602,695 votes" (U.S. White House 2009). Twitter has also provoked controversy on the grounds of its superficiality and transience, but it has evolved into a distributed back-channel medium at political meetings, as those present use it to converse with one another and with broader networks of followers. Twitter is also playing a major role in contributing to the hybridization of new and old media, by reconfiguring intraelite communication among journalists and politicians, and by occasionally integrating nonelite members of the public into news-making assemblages during important political events that are simultaneously mediated via other channels, most notably television (Chadwick 2011b).

The granularity of web 2.0 also offers more powerful means of increasing trust among online participants than the older models of political discourse based on open web pages, discussion forums, and Usenet. Trust is one of the most valuable and most elusive forces in online politics. Anonymity and pseudonymity may encourage freedom of expression, but they also constantly undermine sustained collaboration in problem solving. Government-run online consultations in Britain have been criticized for their insensitivity to how the sociotechnical environment encourages or undermines trust (Wright 2006). Web 2.0 environments do not wholly solve these problems, but in recent years some interesting models have emerged for sustainable co-production, reflecting a blend of self-governance and regulation (see Benkler 2006). Wikipedia relies on a mix of spontaneous self-correction by the army of volunteer Wikipedians and an expanding conception of hierarchy (entries are frequently locked down; prominent warnings are increasingly displayed at the top of contentious or incomplete entries). Politicians have started to experiment with such mechanisms. During the 2010 British general election campaign, the Conservative Party (now in government) ran two major wiki-style crowd-sourcing initiatives, the first on the Labour government's final budget and the other on Labour's manifesto. The budget consultation was particularly intriguing. Opposition parties in the United Kingdom are always at a disadvantage in the immediate aftermath of a new budget, where the information asymmetry is most acute as a result of the government's ability to draw on civil service expertise for its approach. Minutes after the government's document was published, the Conservatives uploaded it to an interactive website that enabled Conservative supporters to highlight and comment critically on the budget's key priorities. The site received approximately a thousand comments, and those went on to shape the party's response in the mainstream media.

2.7. Informational Exuberance and Political Learning in Web 2.0 Politics

It would be naive to suggest that co-production environments such as Wikipedia and Digg create the high levels of trust that are typical of face-to-face encounters such as deliberative polling. But they do encourage voice and loyalty while

discouraging exit (Hirschman 1970). In this sense, the small-scale interactions
in these environments offer potentially valuable lessons for online deliberative
consultations, where ease of exit has long been perceived as a barrier to citizen and government participation. Some of the online mechanisms of web 2.0
encourage greater trust through a variety of means that tap into citizens' informational exuberance: use of real names, continuous presence, clear archives,
inclusion of photos, address details, and so on. These provide for a richer representation of a citizen's real-life identity. Interactions among citizens in these
environments are a long way from the freewheeling libertarian ethos of Usenet
in the 1980s and 1990s – much admired by the early e-democracy movement
in the United States – but they do reduce the risk of politically embarrassing
comments, and they offer balance by providing political elites with a greater
sense of control over the terms of engagement.

Social networking sites provide areas in which individuals express many
different facets of their identities and in which diverse lifestyles and values play
out. The affordances of social network environments encourage us to build
our lives online. As discussed already, it has been argued that the internet is
a purposive medium and is therefore less likely to have by-product learning
effects than other media, such as television, where serendipitous encounters
with political information occur in the context of entertainment. But although
this may have been true of earlier phases of the internet, the emergence of
social networking applications has altered the context. Political life in Facebook
occurs amid the everyday-life characteristics of the environment, in much the
same way as third places function in community building, social capital, and
civic engagement away from the home and the workplace (Oldenburg 1997).
Politics here aligns itself with broader repertoires of self-expression and lifestyle
values. Politics in Facebook goes to where people are, not where we would
like them to be. In 2007, when Facebook opened up its code as a means of
encouraging programmers to create extra features, this unleashed a wave of
new applications. The majority of these applications are concerned with the
expression of lifestyle choices and consumerism, but political applications, of
which there were more than 1,200 by early 2009, include Causes, which in
April 2009 averaged 22.3 million monthly active users mobilized around a
vast array of topics, such as the environment, human rights, health care, trade,
poverty, and organizations including political parties, advocacy groups, and
trade unions (Facebook 2009a, 2009b).

Many Facebook profile pages are a mishmash of content and genres; music,
film, and fashion sit alongside political campaigns, donation drives, and slo-
gans. There is a substantial amount of political engagement around the technological affordances of Facebook itself, chiefly organized around civil libertarian
mobilizations against the company's somewhat cavalier attitude to users' privacy. This is, therefore, a fragile and uncertain arena for politics, one that may
erode at some future point as rival services meet demand for different principles for their sociotechnical environments. Although we must await empirical
work in this area, it is a reasonable hypothesis that online social networking

sites encourage greater by-product learning about politics than the simple web-sites of the past and, perhaps, the multichannel television environment. And we should not lose sight of the fact that Facebook is, again, a low-threshold communication environment, with features such as status updates, a wall, and groups, which allow users to comment on others' profiles and to hold ongoing conversations in semipublic spaces.

The quality of citizens' informational exuberance is, of course, the subject of debate. Some commentary on web 2.0 has focused on the rise of highly individualized forms of online expression and how these contribute to a broader social narcissism (Keen 2007). Some of the journalistic accounts of blogs and YouTube, for example, have criticized what are perceived as self-obsessed, egotistical communication genres. Some lament the rise of audiovisual content online, complaining that it signals the end of an innocent ideal of text-based communication free of the constraints of physical markers such as ethnicity, appearance, accent, and social class. As O'Loughlin (2001) shows, many of the early advocates of e-democracy celebrated the egalitarian quality of textual computer-mediated communication.

The emergence of visual communication genres online presents challenges to understandings of e-democracy. But is the news all bad? Over the past decade or so, some have sought to broaden the concerns of social and political theory to encompass the role of affective dimensions in the regulation of social life. Young (2000, 53–57) has written of political deliberation's "internal" exclusionary dynamics, which subtly devalue informal and emotional discourse. More recently, Papacharissi (2009, 236–239), drawing on Inglehart and Welzel (2005), has argued for a "civically motivated narcissism," based on the view that "self-expression values are connected to the desire to control one's environment, a stronger desire for autonomy, and the need to question authority" and the claim that "self-expression values are not uncivic." Citizen-produced audio and video deviate from the ideal of textual deliberative discourse, but in genres such as YouTube we can hypothesize that they democratize political expression by creating a new grassroots outlet for the affective in politics. We can see how certain policy sectors are more attuned to this style of discourse than others. The site of the British National Health Service review, started in summer 2007, features the "Have Your Say" section, complete with a news and announcements blog that allows for public commentary. The site also incorporated Lord Darzi's personal blog, online surveys for National Health Service stakeholders and members of the public, and an accompanying YouTube stream (U.K. National Health Service 2008).

Although there remains much empirical work to be done in this area, we can also hypothesize that citizens are more at ease uploading a quickly recorded video delivered in an informal, conversational style than being asked to do so formally and deliberately in a staged setting. Thus, although the egalitarian effects of text-based computer-mediated communication will in some respects diminish, it is not at all clear that audiovisual online culture will have entirely negative effects on citizen engagement. An excellent example here is

Barack Obama's unedited, thirty-seven-minute "More Perfect Union" speech delivered in Philadelphia in March 2008. By Election Day of November 2009, more than 6 million people had viewed the speech on YouTube. But more significant, many citizens chose to upload short films narrating their own personal reactions to it.

A final point about informational exuberance concerns legitimacy and the importance of numbers. Faced with low participation rates, many online democracy initiatives have fallen back on the argument that numbers do not matter and that it is the quality of political deliberation that counts. The best-known formal deliberative schemes have never grown beyond communities of a few hundred and have therefore faced legitimacy problems. Indeed, the reliance by interest organizations on low-threshold form e-mails and web templates that enable many thousands of citizens to send comments to policy makers has been criticized for its cheap-talk effects as the ease of communication may undermine its impact (Shulman 2006).

But should we be so quick to devalue large numbers of citizen actions, even if those actions carry little cost for the individuals who act? Web 2.0 environments enshrine participation by thousands in scalable ways. The most powerful web 2.0 applications – and this is most obvious for online social network sites – derive their value from the predictable network effects associated with large numbers of participants. Most interactions on these sites are low threshold but may involve huge numbers of people. Consider Netmums (http://www.netmum.com), the popular British parenting and health advice community, with 275,000 users (Mayo and Steinberg 2007), or TheStudentRoom (http://www.thestudentroom.co.uk), with its forums containing upward of 19 million messages and (as of October 2009) a nine-thousand-page user-generated wiki covering a wide variety of topics related to higher education.

Political networks in Facebook and Twitter, because they are not tied to a deliberative model, have been able to grow comparatively quickly, and the more people participate, the more value there is in the network. The first signs of this dynamic emerged during the 2004 U.S. presidential primaries, when it became obvious that citizens, often many citizens, were willing to add simple, one-line comments to blog posts. Yet these efforts were utterly eclipsed by Obama's 2008 campaign. According to Obama's new media director, Joe Rospars, the campaign raised $500 million from 6.5 million online donations, encouraged four hundred thousand blog posts, regularly e-mailed a database of 13 million Americans, established its own social network (MyBarackObama.com) of 2 million supporters, and managed to garner the support of a further 5 million members of commercial social networking sites (Rospars 2009). The Pew Internet and American Life Project's tracking survey on the internet and the U.S. election, conducted before the height of the campaign in April and May 2008, reported that 40 percent of Americans accessed political news and information online and that 46 percent "used the internet, email, or phone texting to get news about the campaigns, share their views, and mobilize others." Some 10 percent of all Americans used social networking sites for political activity – a total of 40 percent of all those who maintain social networking profiles (Smith and Rainie 2008).

Although it has been criticized for its lack of deliberative mechanisms, if judged in terms of the number of participants, the British prime minister's E-Petitions website, which ran from 2007 to 2010 (when the new Conservative government abandoned it), was one of the most successful e-democracy projects of all time. In its first year, more than twenty-nine thousand petitions were submitted. Accepted petitions attracted 5.8 million signatures from 3.9 million unique e-mail addresses (U.K. Prime Minister's Office 2008). E-petitions of all kinds have quickly become part of the online repertoire of citizen groups in Britain and the United States, as well as elsewhere, and they have viral characteristics. For example, a 2008 search on Facebook revealed a number of groups formed around specific U.K. e-petitions (Facebook Downing Street E-Petitions 2008).

2.8. Conclusion

This chapter has sought to establish the importance of the hypothesis that innovation in democratic practice is more likely to result when the principles of granularity, informational exuberance, and by-product political learning are embedded in a political communication environment. Nowhere can this hypothesis be more compellingly investigated than in the dynamic complexity of the chaotic transition in which we find ourselves. As ever, the pace of change in the real world of internet-enabled citizen behavior continues to outstrip the pace of change in the academy. Scholars have much to learn from these changes, as do those who seek to bridge the normative-empirical divide in social sciences.

Emphasizing the importance of these principles for democratic innovation does not involve the assumption that citizens lack the motivation to think about and discuss politics. Not only is this assumption empirically disputed (Delli Carpini, Cook, and Jacobs 2004) but it is also unnecessary. Most citizens fall into categories along a continuum from motivated to apathetic, and it is highly unlikely that they will remain in one category in perpetuity. Most of us occupy positions between these two extremes, depending on our contexts.

Equally, although they owe much to the web 2.0 wave, these principles are not exclusively dependent on the specific online services that are currently in vogue. The network effects of YouTube, Facebook, and Twitter are extremely powerful, but these services are likely to evolve or be replaced by others in the future. But it seems safe to assume that the success of these three particular examples means that their foundational rationales will survive in one variant or another. In other words, the internet will continue to provide sources of democratic innovation – and the need for scholarly interrogation – for many years to come. It is not as if things were not interesting enough already. They are about to get even more so.

3

Political Engagement and the Internet in the 2008 U.S. Presidential Elections

A Panel Survey

Allison Hamilton and Caroline J. Tolbert

3.1. Introduction

In the run-up to the 2008 U.S. presidential election, the media buzz about online mobilization was palpable. Expectations were set high. Following in the footsteps of Howard Dean in the 2004 presidential election, President Barack Obama raised $600 million, much of it from small online donations by individuals (Luo 2008). Without question, the internet is an integral part of politics in the twenty-first century, as America quickly has become a nation of digital citizens (Mossberger, Tolbert, and McNeal 2008) residing in a digital public sphere (Howard 2005). During the 2008 presidential election, 55 percent of the U.S. adult population used the internet for some type of political activity, ranging from looking up information on candidates to reading political blogs, watching YouTube videos, and using candidates' websites (Smith 2009). There is a growing body of research demonstrating that internet use can increase political participation and is associated with higher levels of voting and participation in election campaigns (Bimber 2003; Tolbert and McNeal 2003; Krueger 2002, 2006; Mossberger et al. 2008). But is online politics engaging new participants, or is it only expanding activity among those who are already interested and active, as many scholars have found (Norris 1999b; Margolis and Resnick 2000; Prior 2005)? If the latter is the case, online politics may be increasing the gap between the informed and the uninformed.

Most previous research has relied on cross-sectional survey data that do not allow us to measure how change in use of the internet for politics is associated with change in civic engagement and traditional political participation, such as voting over the course of a single campaign season. One recent study provides a meta-analysis of the current work on the internet's effect on engagement (Boulianne 2009). Results show that the internet's effect is nonnegative. However, the meta-analysis itself draws on studies using cross-sectional survey data. Using a unique six-wave panel survey from the 2008 U.S. presidential elections that includes a national sample of twenty thousand registered voters from before the presidential primaries through the general election, we measure who changed their level of online political engagement and how it affected political interest, as well as traditional (offline) political behavior and voter turnout. Does change in digital media use for politics covary positively with change in general interest in politics, when other factors are held constant? We explore who is mobilized through engagement on the internet and whether this expands interest in politics in general and political participation offline as well.

Can exposure to online political information "accidentally" mobilize voters (Graber 1988; Howard 2005; Howard and Jones 2004; Bimber 2003), even those with only modest levels of interest in politics? Using Pew Research Center surveys, some new research suggests that even those with modest levels of interest may be mobilized by online political information (Mossberger, Tolbert, and Bowen 2007). In this chapter we measure accidental mobilization by whether people seek out political information or are exposed to political information online. Political news headlines may appear as online ads when an individual closes a Yahoo, Hotmail, or Google e-mail account, and these may catch the eye of someone who otherwise lacks interest (or does not have a conscious self-perception as politically interested). The literature on accidental learning argues that political behavior cannot be disentangled from the web environments in which it occurs (Howard 2005; Bimber 2003). For instance, most websites, including Google, contain cookies that track the computer usage of anyone who does a search. This tracking information enables political advertising to appear on an individual's computer screen that marketing analysis deems will interest that individual consumer.

Using thick description rather than quantitative data, Howard (2005) exposes this evolution of political marketing online and the confluence of two powerful institutions in American politics: the networked computer and political campaigns. He uncovers the power of hypermedia, implanted campaigns (cookies), political redlining, and how these affect what people see when they log in to their e-mail accounts or search using Google: what he calls your political "data shadow" (Howard 2005, 189). His research exposes the community of young high-tech consultants as they seek to win elections, and at the same time empower a better informed electorate. This increasingly high-tech, ever-evolving digital public sphere is the causal mechanism that allows for accidental political mobilization. Howard's book shows us the motivations of the people behind the digital campaigns and how they seek to engage and inform the public about politics. But do online media campaigns work?

Unlike previous research, we test this accidental mobilization hypothesis, and technology use and political behavior more generally, using a nationally representative panel survey. Panel surveys allow for measurement of dynamic change, as the same individuals are interviewed repeatedly over the nine months surrounding the 2008 presidential election. The advantages of using a panel study to investigate changes over the course of an election outweigh concerns about repeated interviews increasing respondents' interest. This allows us to control for the selection bias or endogeneity problems that have plagued previous media use studies; for instance, the fact that individuals who are online for politics select to do so and thus are more likely to participate in all forms of politics because they are predisposed to be interested in politics.

This chapter tests the impact of changing levels of online politics, such as information seeking and communication, on changing levels of political interest and in turn on offline participation, such as voting. First, we examine previous research about the internet and participation to identify ways technology may engage new participants. We then use the 2008 panel election survey of the U.S. population to test our hypotheses. The survey analysis demonstrates that internet use for political information can engage some new participants in politics, thereby increasing civic engagement and offline political participation.

3.2. Digital Democracy and Political Participation

Political participation, as measured by voting, has been in decline or at best stable in the United States for the past three decades (Putnam 2000; Wattenberg 1996; McDonald and Popkin 2001; Dalton 2008).[1] Although the 2004 and 2008 elections saw increased participation, especially among the young, it is still unclear whether those elections were anomalies or the start of a new trend of increasing participation. Many scholars bemoan low voter participation rates in the United States, where in recent presidential elections slightly more than half of the eligible population has voted. Putnam (2000, 35) argues that "voting is by a substantial margin the most common form of political activity, and it embodies the most fundamental democratic principle of equality. Not to vote is to withdraw from the political community." Explanations for decline are varied, including lower trust and confidence in government (Donovan and Bowler 2004; Keele 2005), changes in the party system, a larger block of peripheral voters who lack an enduring attachment to either of the two major political parties (Wattenberg 1996; Patterson 2002), and a decline in the social capital that motivates political participation (Putnam 2000; Levi and Stoker 2000; Nye, Zelikow, and King 1997). Political knowledge and interest have also plummeted over the past four decades: "Political knowledge and interest in public affairs are critical preconditions for more active forms of involvement. If you don't know the rules of the game and the players and don't care about the outcome, you're unlikely to try playing yourself" (Putnam 2000, 35).

Some argue that the internet has the potential to reverse these trends, making information gathering, discussion, and political mobilization easier and participation more accessible (Rheingold 1993; Barber 1997; Norris 2001; Krueger 2002; Bimber 2003; Chadwick 2006; Chadwick and Howard 2009b). Past research has revealed beneficial effects of internet use (especially for election

---

[1] McDonald and Popkin (2001) show that if turnout is measured by the voting eligible population (VEP) excluding noncitizens and those ineligible to vote, rather than the voter age population (VAP), turnout has been relatively stable since the 1960s.

news) on offline participation, including voter turnout (Bimber 2003; Tolbert and McNeal 2003), campaign contributions (Bimber 2001, 2003; Kenskiand Stroud 2006), attendance at campaign meetings or volunteering for a campaign (Kenski and Stroud 2006), and involvement in community activities (Shah et al. 2005). Research shows that political uses of e-mail, chat rooms and/or blogs, and online news all increase the probability of voting and offline political participation more generally (Mossberger et al. 2008), even when controlling for factors that cause individuals to use online news in the first place.

Does this mean, however, that new participants are being brought into the political sphere? Or are those already more likely to participate in politics the ones who gain the most from the convenience, information, and interactivity of online politics? Verba, Schlozman, and Brady (1995) argue that political participation requires motivation, capacity, and mobilization, and that there is some evidence that the internet may influence all three of these. For example, research using cross-sectional survey data and two-stage models to control for selection bias showed that use of online news is associated with higher levels of political interest (motivation), political knowledge (capacity), and offline discussion of politics (mobilization), and that these effects are significant even when controlling for the use of other media, such as newspaper and television. The impact on political knowledge was most pronounced among the young, though significant for all ages (Dalton 2008; Mossberger et al. 2008; for a literature review, see Mossberger and Tolbert 2010). Online campaigns naturally provide mobilization (Bimber 2003).

One way to determine whether digital politics draws in new participants is to explore whether online participants are demographically different from those who are active offline. As a group, younger individuals are more likely to be online using political information. Political interest and participation traditionally increase with age (Wolfinger and Rosenstone 1980), but young people are consistently more likely to participate online in a range of political activities (Bimber 2003; Muhlberger 2003; Gibson, Lusoli, and Ward 2005; Best and Krueger 2005; Mossberger et al. 2008). Krueger (2002, 2006) argues that the internet has the ability to engage some individuals who otherwise would not be involved in politics and that this pattern is most evident among younger individuals.

In other ways, online politics may not produce fundamental change. Education is an important determinant for involvement in politics online, just as it is strongly associated with voting and other forms of offline participation (Bimber 2003; Muhlberger 2003; Best and Krueger 2005). Inequality in information technology access and skill, or information literacy, also excludes some individuals from online engagement (Norris 2001; Mossberger, Tolbert, and Stansbury 2003). Although citizens with lower socioeconomic status may be increasingly online, they may not consume political information.

Political participation online requires access to broadband internet access; Putnam (2000) warned more than a decade ago that the digital divide may

limit the potential of digital political participation. The 2009 Current Population Survey of 129,000 Americans from the U.S. Census Bureau indicates that
63.5 percent of households have high-speed or broadband internet access. The
National Telecommunications and Information Administration estimates that
in 2009, 32 percent of Americans did not use the internet anywhere, 35 percent did not use the internet at home, and 40 percent lacked broadband access
at home. Latinos were the least likely to have broadband at home (40 percent of Latino households), followed by African American households, and
both groups significantly lagged behind white non-Hispanics. If home access
and high-speed access are necessary for digital citizenship, Mossberger et al.
(2008) argue, then 60 percent of Americans would qualify as digital citizens.
Thus, four in ten Americans are still offline or have limited technology access.
Nationally, 40 percent of Americans were either offline entirely or less connected in 2009 than in previous years.

When those with no high-speed broadband or home access were asked the
main reason they did not have access, 26 percent cited cost ("too expensive"),
and 18 percent noted a lack of technology skills or access ("no computer").
These disparities remain despite the rapid diffusion of the internet, and they
are based on age, education, income, race, and ethnicity (National Telecommunications and Information Administration 2010). According to the Organisation for Economic Co-operation and Development (OECD), the United States
ranked fifteenth in broadband subscribers per hundred inhabitants, and tenth
in advertised fastest connection speeds. Twenty OECD nations had lower average monthly subscription rates than the United States (OECD 2009). Limited
access and a lack of broadband in the United States, compared to many European nations, mean exclusion from the growing world of campaign information
online; this places a ceiling on the potential of accidental political mobilization
online.

Despite inequality in access, an important question for this research is
whether technology use can involve those who are only moderately interested in
politics and who may otherwise often remain on the sidelines (Boulianne 2009;
Mossberger et al. 2007). Early studies (Norris 1999b; Margolis and Resnick
2000) contend that there is little evidence that the internet will expand the
engaged public through its information capacity, let alone increase the actively
engaged public. Others predict that the internet may lead to declining participation and greater disparities overall (Putnam 2000). Prior (2005) argues that
politically interested individuals are becoming more active because of the effects
of greater information available on the internet and cable television, whereas
those who are less interested are becoming decreasingly informed and less
active, given that they have more options to avoid political news and information. In the past, exposure to political information through network news led to
passive learning and some accidental mobilization among citizens with modest
levels of political interest (Graber 1988). Prior (2005) argues that such accidental mobilization is less likely today in a world of online media. In contrast,

Tewksbury, Weaver, and Maddex (2001) conclude that there is potential for accidental mobilization on the internet.

3.3. Accidental Online Political Mobilization

One way the internet may lead to new forms of indirect or accidental political mobilization is by reducing the costs of finding political information, political expression, and political communication. The internet lowers information costs through its twenty-four-hour availability, searchable databases and search engines, e-mail mobilization, and customized alerts, as well as through the wide variety of information sources on the web. The interactivity of the web allows for political expression through blogs, social networks such as Facebook and Twitter, YouTube videos, and other sites. Easy entrance and exit also characterize internet participation. The internet may also facilitate broader mobilization through the low marginal costs of sending information or appeals through e-mail and discussion boards, and through hyperlinked websites and blogs (Mossberger et al. 2007). For this reason, those who are moderately interested in politics, or are perhaps interested only in a particular issue, may be persuaded to occasionally participate online.

Mossberger et al. (2007) find some evidence that, among those only modestly interested in politics, the internet may mobilize new participants by increasing passive exposure to politics through campaign ads, online news, discussion boards, and forwarded e-mails. The authors argue that even accidental exposure to political information results in some learning and mobilization (Graber 1988). Portals such as Google and Yahoo routinely display news headlines on home pages, targeted online political advertising (Howard 2005), and online microcampaigning (Hillygus and Shields 2008). Scholars have found that political advertising can lead to learning, political knowledge, and interest (Kahn and Kenney 1999). Exposure to campaign advertising, even to negative ads, results in citizens who are more interested in politics and who know more about the candidates (Freedman, Franz, and Goldstein 2004). Although previous research on political ads was conducted primarily in relation to television, the finding may apply to the internet as well. The headlines alone may have a priming effect, and repetition of information is important for accidental mobilization (Graber 1988; Tewksbury et al. 2001). Some research indicates that frequency of internet use increases accidental exposure to political information, and that such exposure is associated with more knowledge of current affairs (Tewksbury et al. 2001).

The accidental mobilization thesis is bolstered by theories of participatory democracy (Pateman 1970; Barber 1984). These theorists contend that if democratic institutions offer people greater opportunities to participate in decisions, those institutions may have an educative effect on them (Smith and Tolbert 2004). With more opportunities to act politically online, citizens may learn to participate more and come to believe that their participation has meaning.

DelliCarpini and Keeter (1997) argue that political knowledge leads to increases in voter participation, and Niemi and Junn (1998, 9) find that knowledge is a "prerequisite to successful political engagement." Plutzer (2002) shows that once the young are engaged in politics, they continue to be active politically throughout their lives (see also Dalton 2008). The interactivity, ease, convenience, and even excitement of politics online may educate individuals to be democratic citizens, even those who were previously unengaged.

The 2008 presidential election showed the potential of the internet for fund-raising and electoral outcomes and mobilization across broad geographic areas. In 2008, record-setting fund-raising was the result of the largest group of individuals turning out to make campaign donations than in any previous election. Historically, political contributions (to either candidates or political parties) were a relatively rare activity among the general public. From 1952 to 2000, fewer than 10 percent of Americans contributed per election during this period (Keller 2010). This number increased in the 2004 election to 13 percent, and in 2008, the number of individuals who donated doubled from 2000 to a record 17 percent of Americans (Pew Research Center for People and the Press 2008). As the use of the internet grows for electoral campaigns and for issue activism, it is important to reexamine who is being mobilized online and whether current technologies have the capacity to broaden participation. The following hypotheses structure our analysis and test whether accidental political mobilization occurred in the 2008 presidential elections.

3.4. Hypotheses

In this chapter we investigate whether changing use of digital media for political purposes during a single election season increased levels of political interest and participation in politics. We test whether changing online engagement and political interest increased the likelihood of participating in the primary and/or caucus process and voting in the general election. We present the following hypotheses, consistent with the arguments on accidental mobilization:

> H1: Change in online political engagement increases levels of political interest.
>
> H2: Change in online political engagement increases voter turnout in the primaries and/or caucuses.
>
> H3: Change in online political engagement increases voter turnout in the general election.

Furthermore, we consider whether this accidental online mobilization translates into other traditional forms of participating. An index was created of four common offline participation activities to consider whether newly mobilized citizens carried over their interest and participation to traditional forms of participation.

H4: Change in online political engagement increases offline participation in the month before the general election.

3.5. Data and Methods

We expand on previous research using cross-sectional American National Election Study (ANES) and Current Population Surveys (CPS) to study online political engagement (Bimber 2003; Krueger 2002; Tolbert and McNeal 2003; Mossberger et al. 2008) by drawing on national panel survey conducted before and after the 2008 elections. Our data come from the 2008 Cooperative Campaign Analysis Project (CCAP) conducted by Polimetrix (Jackman and Vavreck 2009).[2] The survey sampled twenty thousand respondents in six panel waves (December 2007, and January, March, September, October, and postelection November 2008) with a common battery of questions comparable to the ANES or General Social Survey (GSS), but with sample sizes many times larger than those omnibus surveys.[3] The same individuals answered questions throughout the nine-month presidential campaign, which allowed us to track changes in their use of online political information and participation levels over time. The unique panel data, in which the same individuals are interviewed over multiple waves, allow us to precisely measure how change in online political engagement from the baseline wave (in December 2007) shaped levels of political interest, as well as offline political participation, in later waves.

To investigate our hypotheses, we create an index of four common online political behaviors (for detailed information on the coding of all variables in the analysis, see the Appendix). Respondents were asked, "In the last week, how many days have you used the internet to visit news websites, visit political blogs, post comments on a news website or political blog, or exchange political e-mails with friends and family?" The online politics questions were asked in three of the six waves of the survey; thus, we have three time periods throughout the 2008 election cycle to track change over the year. This gives us three indices of online political engagement measured in December 2007 (baseline),

---

[2] The Cooperative Campaign Analysis Project (CCAP; Jackman and Vavreck 2009) is a collaborative effort to produce a six-wave panel study conducted on the internet. This sample is constructed using a technique called sample matching (Vavreck and Rivers 2008). The researchers create a list of all U.S. citizens from the U.S. census to generate a set of demographic, political, and behavioral characteristics that should be mirrored in the survey sample. Then, using a matching algorithm, the researchers select respondents who most closely resemble the census data from a pool of opt-in participants. The sample is stratified to ensure large samples within states (see Jackman and Vavreck 2010 for a description of the sample). More information regarding sample matching is available at http://web.mit.edu/polisci/portl/cces/material/sample_matching.pdf. The models are estimated using survey weights. Using this same technique, the 2006 Cooperative Congressional Election Survey (CCES) produced more precise estimates than more conventional probability designs such as random-digit-dialing phone surveys (Vavreck and Rivers 2008).

[3] With all panel data, attrition is a concern. Each wave has approximately thirty thousand respondents. Almost one thousand respondents failed to complete one or more waves and thus are not included in our analysis.

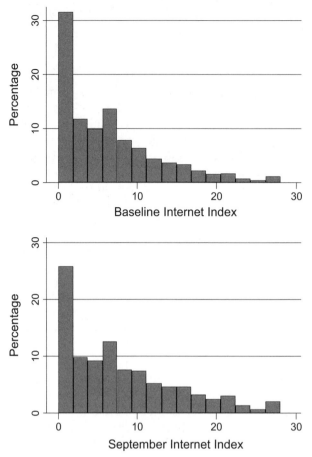

FIGURE 3.1. Online political engagement in December 2007 (baseline) and September 2008. *Source:* 2008 CCAP, panel data.

March 2008, and September 2008 that run on a twenty-nine-point measure (seven days a week multiplied by four online activities).

The primary predictor variable we use is change in online political engagement. Figure 3.1 provides a graphical depiction of the distribution of individuals' online engagement in December 2007, before the presidential nomination process, compared to September 2008, two months before the general election. It is immediately apparent that in both time periods, more than 25 percent of respondents claim to have participated in no online political activities. The percentage reporting no online engagement drops from more than 30 percent in the December 2007 wave to slightly more than 25 percent in the September wave, which indicates increased mobilization over the course of the campaign. In the September wave, on the eve of the general election, more individuals

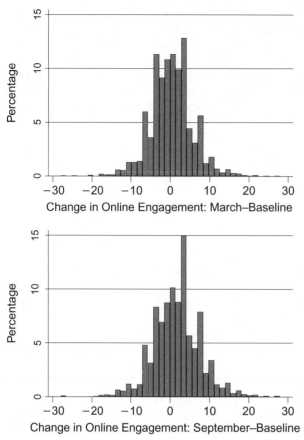

FIGURE 3.2. Change in online political engagement. *Source:* 2008 CCAP, panel data.

reported high online engagement. Using these multiple waves with measures of online political engagement, we create two variables measuring change.

The change in online political engagement is measured by taking the later measure (March or September) of the variable and subtracting from it the earlier measure (baseline December). We create one change variable, which is the change in online political engagement from before the presidential election began (baseline December 2007) to after most states held their presidential primaries (March 2008; see Figure 3.2). To create this variable, we subtracted the respondents' twenty-nine-point online political engagement index measure from the baseline from their March measure. This gives us a change variable that ranges from −28 to 28. We create a second change measure over a nine-month period from the baseline (December 2007) to before the November general election (September 2008), also presented in Figure 3.2. This change variable is constructed the same way as the December-to-March variable.

This variable measuring change in online political engagement is the key explanatory variable in our study.

Figure 3.2 graphs the percentage of Americans in the sample who changed their online engagement over the three-month period (baseline to March) and the nine-month period (baseline to September), with individuals who did not change their use of online political information omitted (approximately 35 percent of the sample). Both graphs follow a relatively normal distribution. Note that those individuals frequently engaging in politics online before the presidential campaign and those still frequently online during the election have a low change score (near 0). Similarly, individuals who were not using the internet for political engagement before the campaign and did not become engaged online also have a 0 score. But individuals who increased use over the course of the presidential campaign have positive values, whereas individuals who decreased their online engagement over the course of the election have a negative score. Comparing the two graphs in Figure 3.2, by September more individuals had increased their online political engagement.

Unlike previous studies of technology and politics that largely rely on static cross-sectional survey data, these dynamic panel data allow us to measure those who are newly engaged in politics online. The panel data provide a way to control for selection bias, or endogeneity, by measuring change in online media use. A primary hypothesis is that those who increase their online political engagement become more interested in the election. Political interest, in turn, is understood as a primary antecendent to political participation.

The first outcome variable measures individuals' level of political interest. Respondents were asked, "How interested are you in politics?" This variable was recoded so that "very interested" was the highest category, coded as 3; "somewhat interested," coded as 2; and "not interested," coded as 1. The ordinal political interest variable was asked across the six waves in our study, and for the analysis, we measure interest in the presidential election at the baseline (December 2007), March 2008, September 2008, and October 2008 waves, to correspond with our measures of online political engagement. With these repeated measures, the models predict who changed their interest in politics over the nine-month presidential campaign and the one month before the 2008 general election using lagged terms. We measure long-term change in political interest with a lagged term, using individuals' political interest score in the baseline wave (December 2007) to predict their level of interest in September 2008, nine months later. We also measure short-term change in political interest by using individuals' political interest score in September 2008 to predict their level of interest in October 2008, over one month. The models measure who changed their political interest during the election.

Once individuals are engaged in the election and interested, we hypothesize that they are more likely to participate offline in traditional ways. These hypotheses involve panel models of offline participation and turnout in both the primaries and the general election. We test whether change in online engagement (the newly mobilized) and greater political interest before the election (time period 1) increases the likelihood of offline participation (time period 2).

We consider three measures of offline participation. The first is whether respondents voted in their state's presidential primary or caucus, for which there is typically much lower turnout than general elections. Respondents in the March wave were asked whether they turned out to vote in their state's primary or caucus. Respondents in states that had not held their primary or caucus were dropped from this analysis. Of the four possible answers (1 = "I made it to the polls," 2 = "voted early," 3/4 = "did not vote") responses 1 and 2 were combined to create a "yes voted" (coded 1), and 3 and 4 were combined and coded as 0 "did not vote."

The third hypothesis is that individuals engaged online were more likely to vote in the general election. In the postelection wave (November) respondents were asked, "Which candidate did you vote for?" Any response with a candidate named was coded 1 ("did vote"). Anyone reporting a nonvote was coded as 0 ("did not vote").

The final hypothesis is that individuals engaged online were more likely to participate offline. An index of four common offline participation actions asked in the October wave, on the eve of the general election, was created as the outcome variable. Respondents were asked, "Thinking about the presidential candidates and their campaigns, did any of the following things happen to you yesterday?" The offline political activities indexed are "donated money to a candidate," "wore a button for a candidate," "discussed a candidate with someone," and "went to hear a candidate speak." Respondents were coded anywhere between 0 and 4, depending on the number of traditional political activities they engaged in. We use the measure for change in online engagement that is closest to when the traditional activity was measured. For primary turnout, we use the change from baseline to March; for turnout in the general election and offline participation measured in October, we use the change from baseline to September. Political interest is measured at one wave prior for all models.

When considering online engagement and offline participation, we control for any attempts by political parties and campaigns to mobilize voters. Does online political engagement matter, above and beyond traditional forms of party mobilization? For the offline participation and general election voting measures, we include an index of common attempts by campaigns to mobilize the public. The questions that we used to create this mobilization variable come from the October 2008 wave. These questions were also part of the item list that followed "Thinking about the presidential candidates and their campaigns, did any of the following things happen to you yesterday?" The mobilization responses were "saw a campaign ad on TV," "received a piece of mail," "received a pamphlet on my door," "received a visit from a campaign worker," "heard a radio ad for a candidate," "saw a yard sign for a candidate," "got a phone call from a campaign," and "heard about a candidate at religious services." We also include controls for other forms of gaining political information. This includes two variables measuring frequency of television watching and reading the newspaper. Other control variables include the typical demographics (for the full list and coding, see the Appendix).

3.6. Findings

3.6.1. Who Changed Their Use of Online Political Information during the Campaign?

Table 3.1 presents ordinary-least-squares regression results predicting engagement in politics online, to gain an understanding of our key explanatory variable. Model 1 provides results for the December 2007 baseline measure, which runs from 0 to 28. Consistent with previous research (Krueger 2002; Tolbert and McNeal 2003; Bimber 2003; Mossberg et al. 2008), individuals who are already interested in politics are more likely to be active politically online. This suggests that a selection bias exists when measuring digital media use, as those who are already interested in politics are most likely to seek out information on the web. Younger individuals, as well as those with higher education and wealth, are more likely to be online politically, and men are more likely to be online than women. In addition, individuals who regularly read the newspaper or watch television news are more likely to use online political information, which suggests some substitution effects.

Models 2 and 3 explain changes in online political engagement over the 2008 presidential campaign, from the baseline to March 2008 (Model 2) and from the baseline to September 2008 (Model 3). Although political interest continues to be a statistically significant predictor of change in online engagement, the size of the regression coefficients is reduced tenfold. Demographic predictors of change in online political engagement are different than predicting who is online politically. Over the nine-month presidential campaign, women and nonwhites were more likely to be among the newly mobilized than were men and whites. Individuals who are less likely to read a daily newspaper were more likely to become engaged in politics online. Thus, it appears that online engagement may be more than simply a substitute for traditional forms of information gathering. Although young individuals were significantly more likely to be online to begin with, older individuals were more likely to increase their online engagement (or go online at all) as the election progressed. Older individuals appear more likely to be newly mobilized. These findings are consistent with our accidental mobilization hypothesis, as those individuals least likely to be engaged in politics online are the most likely to increase their engagement with the web over the course of the campaign. These results give us confidence that our primary explanatory variable is working as expected.

3.6.2. Does Change in Online Political Engagement Predict Change in Levels of Political Interest?

Table 3.2 provides a simple cross-tabulation of the percentage change in online political engagement from the baseline wave in December 2007 to September 2008 by levels of political interest in September. Among individuals who did not change or who decreased their online engagement over this time, 46 percent reported that they were very interested in politics two months before the general election. Among individuals who increased their level of online

TABLE 3.1. *Explaining Change in Online Political Engagement in the 2008 Presidential Elections*

	Baseline (Dec. 07) Model 1 b (s.e.)	Change From Dec. 07 (baseline) to Mar. 08 Model 2 b (s.e.)	Change From Dec. 07 (baseline) to Sept. 08 Model 3 b (s.e.)
Political interest	3.777**	0.361**	1.00**
(Dec. 07, baseline)	(0.203)	(0.098)	(0.128)
White	0.323	−0.237	−0.272+
	(0.229)	(0.201)	(0.14)
Male	1.412**	−0.112	−0.507**
	(0.22)	(0.13)	(0.163)
Education	0.391**	0.062	0.146**
	(0.049)	(0.038)	(0.050)
Income	0.063*	−0.011	0.068*
	(0.029)	(0.02)	(0.027)
Age	−0.030**	0.011**	0.01*
	−0.030**	(0.004)	(0.004)
Democrat	−0.376*	0.064	0.353*
	(0.161)	(0.122)	(0.147)
Republican	−0.422*	−0.103	−0.181
	(0.184)	(0.169)	(0.176)
Read newspaper	0.068**	0.001	−0.024*
	(0.020)	(0.014)	(0.011)
Watch television news	0.204**	−0.005	−0.074+
	(0.068)	(0.06)	(0.039)
Constant	−5.0**	−1.09**	−2.163**
	(0.434)	(0.339)	(0.409)
R	0.219	0.005	0.025
F	276.07	4.95	10.78
N	8,244	7,917	7,893

Note: Unstandardized regression coefficients with standard errors in parentheses. Models estimated using survey weights.

Model 1: Dependent variable is an index of four online engagement measures that range from 0 to 28.

Model 2: Dependent variable is the March index minus the baseline index for a range of −28 to 28.

Model 3: Dependent variable is the September index minus the baseline index for a range of −28 to 28.

** Significant at 99%. * Significant at 95%. + Significant at 90%.

Source: 2008 CCAP, Panel data.

TABLE 3.2. *Change in Political Online Engagement (baseline to September) by Levels of Political Interest in September 2008, Frequencies and Percents*

	Political Interest in September 2008			
	Not Interested	Somewhat Interested	Very Interested	Total
No change, or decreased	986	2,400	2,864	6,250
	15.8%	38.4%	45.8%	100%
Increased	277	1,781	3,619	5,677
	4.9%	31.4%	63.8%	100%
Total	1263	4,181	6,483	11,927
	10.6%	35.1%	54.4%	100%
	Pearson $\chi^2 = 551.3$; Pr = 0.0001			

Source: 2008 CCAP, Panel data.

political engagement over the eight-month campaign season, 64 percent were highly interested in politics by September 2008, a difference of almost twenty percentage points. Table 3.2 suggests that individuals with the greatest change and/or increase in use of political information online over the eight-month campaign season were significantly more likely to be interested in politics at the end of the election (the chi-square test shows that this relationship is statistically significant). For a more robust test of this causal relationship, we present a multivariate analysis.

Table 3.3 presents the multivariate findings for our first hypothesis, which posits that online engagement affects political interest. Both models in Table 3.3 are estimated using ordered logistic regression, as the dependent variable, change in interest in politics, is measured on a five-point scale. Individuals who changed and/or increased their online engagement over the campaign season were more likely to increase their interest in politics both over the long term (December 2007 to September 2008), shown in Model 1, and over the short term (September to October 2008), shown in Model 2. The results hold even after controlling for a battery of factors associated with higher interest in politics, including use of traditional media such as television and newspapers.

Model 1 of Table 3.3 measures change in individuals' interest in politics from the baseline to September (using a lagged term for political interest) as a function of the change in online political engagement from the baseline to March. Model 2 of Table 3.3 measures change in individuals' political interest in the month before the general election (September to October 2008) as a function of the change in online engagement over the nine-month campaign (baseline to September). In both models the lagged term for political interest is statistically significant: individuals more interested in politics in the previous time period are more likely to be interested in politics in the later time period. Despite this strong predictive effect, use of political information online has an independent effect on increasing levels of political interest over the long and

TABLE 3.3. *Explaining Change in Political Interest in the 2008 Presidential Elections*

	Change in Interest (Dec. 2007–Sept. 2008) Model 1 b (s.e.)	Change in Interest (Sept.–Oct. 2008) Model 2 b (s.e.)
Change in online political engagement (Dec. 2007–March 2008)	0.021* (0.011)	–
Change in online political engagement (Dec. 2007–Sept. 2008)	–	0.039** (0.009)
Political interest (December 2007)	3.083** (0.074)	–
Political interest (September 2008)		3.147** (0.09)
White	0.115 (0.104)	0.001 (0.135)
Male	0.391** (0.07)	0.325** (0.067)
Education	0.085** (0.027)	0.108** (0.022)
Income	0.063** (0.012)	0.037* (0.015)
Age	0.002 (0.003)	−0.001 (0.003)
Democrat	−0.002 (0.105)	0.218* (0.095)
Republican	−0.027 (0.01)	0.139 (0.122)
Read newspaper	0.026** (0.006)	0.028** (0.006)
Watch television news	0.066** (0.024)	0.077* (0.036)
Cut 1	5.33 (0.271)	5.1 (0.252)
Cut 2	9.09 (0.269)	8.92 (0.297)
Pseudo R^2	0.394	0.398
Wald χ^2	3,438.13	2,553.69
Log pseudolikelihood	−4,313.77	−3,700.49
N	7,906	7,147

Note: Unstandardized ordered logistic regression coefficients, with standard errors in parentheses. Models estimated using survey weights.

Dependent variable from the question "How interested are you in politics?" with responses including "very much" (3), "somewhat" (2), and "not that much" (1). The dependent variable measures change in interest on a −2 to 2 scale.

** Significant at 99%. * Significant at 95%. + Significant at 90%.

Source: 2008 CCAP, Panel data.

TABLE 3.4. *Likelihood of Changing Levels of Political Interest from Moderate to High from September to October 2008 (from Model 2 of Table 3.3)*

	Likelihood of High Interest (%)	Change from Mean
Change online politics index set to minimum (set at −28)	38	−25
Change online politics index set to 25th percentile (set at −1)	62	−1
Change online politics index set to mean (set at 0)	63	
Change online politics index set to 75th percentile (set at 4)	66	+3
Change online politics index set to maximum (set at 28)	83	+20

Note: Predicted probabilities created using Clarify software. All other variables were set at their mean or modal categories.
Source: 2008 CCAP, panel data.

short terms. Those who are newly engaged online (measured by the change in online engagement) are more likely to increase their level of interest in politics from low or moderate to high during the presidential campaign. The models also show a significant effect for traditional information sources. Both reading a newspaper and watching the news are significant, positive predictors of higher levels of interest. These findings hold controlling for a battery of demographic factors, and they are robust to different model specifications beyond those shown here (available from the authors on request). Increasing online engagement increases political interest, and this finding is consistent with the accidental mobilization hypothesis.

To understand the substantive effect of changing online engagement on interest in politics, we estimate predictive probabilities of being interested in October 2008 from Model 2 of Table 3.3, holding all other factors in the model constant at their mean or modal values. Thus, these probabilities are for a hypothetical woman who reported no strong partisan attachment and moderate interest in politics just one month before. Table 3.4 provides the predicted probability of changing one's level of interest from moderate to high as the measure for change in online engagement varies from the minimum to the maximum values. The mean of online change was zero, and at this measure, this hypothetical person has an approximately 63 percent chance of being very interested in politics by the October wave. Moving the change in use of online political information from the twenty-fifth to the seventy-fifth percentiles (−1 to 4) results in a three-percentage-point increase in the probability of becoming very interested in the last month of the election. The same change in use of online political information results in an even greater probability of moving an individual from not being interested in politics to a moderate level of interest. Varying use of online political engagement from minimum to the maximum values results in an almost a fifty-percentage-point change in the probability of being very interested in the election in the last month.

3.6.3. Does Change in Online Political Engagement Predict Offline Political Participation?

Table 3.5 presents three models to test Hypotheses 2–4, which argue that online engagement should increase turnout and offline political participation. A logistic regression model is reported in Model 1 for predicting turnout in the presidential primaries or caucuses as a function of change in online political engagement from the baseline to the March wave and relevant controls. Political interest is a significant predictor of increased turnout in the presidential primaries; however, our change in online engagement measure from baseline to March is not. Thus, Hypothesis 2, which expected higher online engagement to increase primary turnout is not supported.

Model 2 of Table 3.5 presents the results for our third hypothesis, which states that individuals who increased their online engagement would be more likely to vote in the general election. This model is also a logistic regression. Unlike in the primary turnout model, change in online engagement (from December 2007 to September 2008) is a positive, significant predictor of whether an individual voted in the November elections. Thus, our hypothesis that online engagement would increase the likelihood of voting is confirmed. This suggests that those who are newly engaged in politics on the web are more likely to vote in the general election.

Model 3 of Table 3.5 provides an ordered logistic regression predicting offline political participation in October 2008 using a five-point measure to investigate our fourth hypothesis. Again, change in online political engagement from December 2007 to September 2008 results in an increased probability of being engaged politically offline.

Although two of our three hypotheses are confirmed in Table 3.5, what do these results substantively mean? Table 3.6 presents predicted probabilities of traditional political participation from Model 3 of Table 3.5. At the mean change (equal to 0) in online engagement over the course of the campaign, a hypothetical woman who does not affiliate with either the Democratic or Republican parties has a 66 percent chance of participating offline the previous day in at least one of our four offline participation measures. With all other variables in the model set at their mean or modal values, the likelihood of participating offline increases as change in online engagement rises. With all other variables held constant, our hypothetical respondent, with a change in online engagement of plus-two standard deviations from the mean (11), has nearly an eight-percentage-point increased chance of participating in at least one traditional political activity the previous day over those with mean (0) change. Although substantively one could argue that this is modest, it must be remembered that we are measuring offline participation at the end of a long campaign

TABLE 3.5. *The Effect of Change in Online Political Engagement on Offline Political Participation in the 2008 Presidential Elections*

	Turnout in Presidential Primaries (Mar. 08) Model 1 b (s.e.)	Turnout in General Election (Nov. 08) Model 2 b (s.e.)	Offline Participation (Oct. 08) Model 3 b (s.e.)
Change in online political engagement (baseline to closest wave)	0.004 (0.006)	0.041** (0.015)	0.036** (0.005)
Political interest (at closest wave)	0.581** (0.086)	0.908** (0.118)	1.063** (0.061)
Party and/or candidate mobilization	–	0.337** (0.090)	0.638** (0.021)
White	−0.296[+] (0.157)	−0.479[+] (0.266)	−0.014 (0.078)
Male	−0.001 (0.058)	0.054 (0.203)	−0.033 (0.052)
Education	0.092** (0.023)	0.046 (0.083)	0.083** (0.024)
Income	0.047** (0.010)	0.139** (0.024)	0.030** (0.010)
Age	0.006[+] (0.003)	0.011 (0.007)	−0.012** (0.002)
Democrat	0.520** (0.132)	0.896** (0.290)	0.297** (0.070)
Republican	0.322** (0.106)	0.609** (0.234)	0.035 (0.066)
Read newspaper	0.018[+] (0.009)	0.056** (0.021)	0.011[+] (0.006)
Watch television news	0.004 (0.026)	0.022 (0.081)	0.006 (0.023)
Constant	−2.206** (0.227)	−2.015** (0.528)	
Cut 1	–	–	3.618 (0.219)
Cut 2	–	–	6.517 (0.232)
Cut 3	–	–	8.509 (0.214)
Cut 4	–	–	10.928 (0.360)

	Turnout in Presidential Primaries (Mar. 08) Model 1 b (s.e.)	Turnout in General Election (Nov. 08) Model 2 b (s.e.)	Offline Participation (Oct. 08) Model 3 b (s.e.)
Pseudo R^2	0.063	0.225	0.161
Wald χ^2	174.09	240.39	2,523.78
Log pseudolikelihood	−5,009.22	−1,294.21	−6,278.1
N	7,917	6,879	7,037

Note: Unstandardized logistic regression coefficients, with standard errors in parentheses (Models 1–2). Unstandardized ordered logit coefficients, with standard errors clustered by state of residency in parentheses (Model 3).
Model 1: Dependent variable is response to whether respondent voted in the state's primary or caucus.
Model 2: Dependent variable measures turnout in the general election.
Model 3: Dependent variable is an index of four offline participation behaviors
** Significant at 99%. * Significant at 95%. $^+$ Significant at 90%.
Source: 2008 CCAP, panel data.

season as well as the probability of participating yesterday, which has a lower probability than if we were modeling political participation over the previous week or the course of the entire political campaign. Individuals experiencing the maximum change in online political engagement, or accidental mobilization, are almost certain to have participated in at least one traditional political

TABLE 3.6. *Predicted Probability of Participating in Politics Offline in October 2008 (from Model 3 of Table 3.5)*

	Predicted Likelihood of Offline Participation	Diff. from Mean Online Engagement
Change in online politics index (set at −28)	44.2%	−21.9%
Change in online politics index −2 SD (set at −11)	57.8%	−8.3%
Change in online politics index mean (set at 0)	66.1%	
Change in online politics index +2 SD (set at 11)	73.6%	7.5%
Change in online politics index maximum (set at 28)	81.4%	15.3%

Note: Predicted probabilities created using Clarify software. All other variables were set at their mean or modal categories. Probabilities shown are likelihood of predicted value of 1–4 on the 5-point index combined.
Source: 2008 CCAP, panel data.

activity the previous day (0.81 probability) and a 0.15 increased probability of being active offline, in comparison with those with the mean use of politics on the web.

3.7. Conclusion

Building on previous research that has relied primarily on cross-sectional survey data to study use of online political information and offline participation, this research uses a large-sample panel survey in which the same individuals are measured repeatedly over the course of a presidential election. A key question was whether changing levels of engagement in politics online were associated with higher levels of political interest, as well as voting and offline participation more generally. This is one of the first studies to use panel survey data to study online media use and political participation. Results are for the most part consistent with our expectations, and they illustrate that online engagement translates into increased political interest and other forms of traditional political participation. Contrary to what some researchers expect, these findings shed a more positive light on the changing nature of political campaigns. The results suggest that the shift to online information gathering and participation does influence offline participation and may increase interest in politics, even for those who are uninterested in politics. Online participation and information gathering can also increase the likelihood of voting. The research suggests that the internet can lead to accidental political mobilization; political campaigns on the web can accidentally mobilize the public and lead to more interest in politics and participation in politics in traditional ways, such as voting.

From this research, there remains the question of whether the young were actually the ones most influenced by digital media. Plutzer's (2002) insights regarding habitual voting are important here, because he finds that the mobilization of younger voters has permanent rather than ephemeral effects, as it initiates them into a habitual pattern of higher turnout that can endure in later elections. The young are clearly more likely to use political information online. However, our analysis suggests that older individuals were the most likely to change or increase their use of online political websites over the course of the 2008 campaign (Table 3.1). Were the tech-savvy younger individuals able to selectively screen information online, whereas older individuals who are less proficient came into contact with more targeted information? Future research should consider whether it was truly the young online or older individuals who benefited the most from extensive digital campaigns used in the 2008 U.S. presidential elections.

3.8. Appendix

Age. (profile51). Age was coded by subtracting the respondent's year of birth from 2008. Although this is not an exact measure of the respondents' ages, as the data were collected over an entire year, it is a consistent measure from which to distinguish the effects of being older or younger.[4]

Baseline online engagement index (December 2007 wave). A scale ranging from 0 to 28 was created by using four 0–7 days-a-week variables. The first variable is bcap820, the second was bcap821, the third was bcap822, and the fourth was bcap823. The question wording for each of these variables follows. Each started with: "In the last week, how many days have you used the internet to ... "

  bcap820 Visit news websites
  bcap821 Visit political blogs
  bcap822 Post comments on a news website or political blog
  bcap823 Exchange political e-mails with friends and family?

Change in online engagement, baseline to March. To create this change variable, we subtracted the respondents' online engagement index measure (0–28 points) from the baseline from their March measure. This gives us a change variable that ranges from −28 to 28.

Change in online engagement, baseline to September collapsed (from Table 3.2). The above online engagement index was collapsed so that −28 to 0 were "no change or decrease," and respondents with an increase from 1 to 28 were coded as 1, "increased engagement."

Change in online engagement, baseline to September. To create this change variable, we subtracted respondents' online engagement index measure (0–28 points) from the baseline from their September measure. This again gives us a change variable that ranges from −28 to 28.

Education (profile57). Respondents were asked the last level of schooling they had completed. There were six categories, ranging from less than high school to postgraduate education.

Frequency of television watching. Queries regarding five types of television watching were asked during the December 2007 wave. Each of the five is a binary variable, with "no" recoded from 2 to 0. The five questions combined all began, "And what kinds of things have you watched on television in the last seven days ... " The results were summed into a combined measure.

  Bcap2_3 "prime time shows"
  Bcap2_4 "news programs"
  Bcap2_5 "late night shows"
  Bcap2_6 "daytime talk shows"
  Bcap2_7 "political talk shows"

---

[4] Variable used in the chapter analysis: coding, construction of variables, and survey question wording (alphabetically ordered).

Income (profile59). Respondents were asked their family income. There were fourteen categories, from less than $10,000 to more than $150,000.

Male (profile54). The value of female was recoded from 2 to 0 to provide a binary variable for gender.

March 2008 online engagement index. This index was created in the same way as the base online engagement index. The same four variables were asked of respondents again in March 2008, and then recoded and indexed as with the other online engagement indices.

Newspaper readership. The newspaper readership question was asked in the March and September waves. Because this is simply used as a control variable for other forms of media intake, the two were simply added together to give us a general idea of how often respondents were reading newspapers. The variables were coded 0–7 days a week readership:

> Mcap815, Scap815 "How many days in the past week have you read a daily newspaper?"

November 2008 general election voter. A variable for voters who turned out in the general election was created by recoding PCAP600 (vote choice). Respondents who reported voting for Obama, McCain, or "other candidate" were coded as 1. Respondents who reported, "I didn't make it to the polls," were coded as 0.

October 2008 offline participation index. An index of four offline participation variables was created. The four variables used are listed here, where 1 indicates doing the behavior and 0 indicates all others. The binary variables were then indexed, and those missing were dropped from the analysis. The question was as follows:

"Thinking about the presidential candidates and their campaigns, did any of the following things happen to you yesterday?"

> Ocap400_3 "donated money to a candidate"
> Ocap400_5 "wore a button for a candidate"
> Ocap400_6 "discussed a candidate with someone"
> Ocap400_10 "went to hear a candidate speak"

October 2008 party/candidate mobilization index. An index of eight offline mobilization variables was created. The eight variables used are listed here (all variables had a "no" response recoded from 2 to 0 to create binary variables that were then indexed; those missing were dropped from the analysis). The question stem for all variables is as follows:

"Thinking about the presidential candidates and their campaigns, did any of the following things happen to you yesterday?"

> Ocap400_1 "saw a campaign ad on tv"
> Ocap400_2 "received a piece of campaign mail"

Ocap400_4 "received a pamphlet on my door"
Ocap400_7 "received a visit from a campaign worker"
Ocap400_8 "heard a radio ad for a candidate"
Ocap400_9 "saw a yard sign for a candidate"
Ocap400_11 "got a phone call from a campaign"
Ocap400_13 "heard about candidate at religious service"

Partisanship, baseline wave (bcap8). Recoded from a seven-point ideology scale. Strong Democrats and Democrats coded as 1 (all others as 0) for Democrat, and strong Republicans and Republicans coded as 1 (all others as 0) for Republican.

Political interest, December 2008 (baseline; bcap813). "How interested are you in politics?" This variable was recoded so that very interested was the highest category (3). "Not sure" and "don't know" were recoded as missing.

Political interest, March 2008 (mcap813). Coded the same way as the baseline interest variable.

Political interest, September 2008 (scap813). Coded the same way as the baseline interest variable.

Primary and/or caucus turnout in March 2008 wave (mcap7t_aux). Respondents were asked whether they turned out to their state's primary or caucus. Of the four possible answers (1 = "I made it to the polls," 2 = "voted early," 3/4 = "did not vote"), answers 1 and 2 were combined to create a "yes voted" (coded 1) and 3 and 4 were combined to "did not vote" (coded 0).

September 2008 online engagement index.Created the same way as the base online engagement index. The same four variables were asked of respondents again in September 2008. These four were recoded and indexed the same way as the other online engagement indices.

White (profile55). Originally a seven-point nominal variable, white was left coded as 1, and 2 through 7 were recoded as zero, thus providing a white and nonwhite variable.

4

Online Political Participation in the United States and Spain

Michael J. Jensen and Eva Anduiza

4.1. Introduction

The diffusion and integration of digital media in social and political life are said to be creating new forms of political organization and new opportunities for political participation (Castells 2009). This chapter is a comparative study of how and why people get involved in different offline and online participatory environments in the United States and Spain. Researchers have differentiated forms of participation in digital milieus according to their architectures, which enable more or less participation (Jackson and Lilleker 2009; Chadwick 2009a; Chapter 2). Digital environments contain varied structures for communicative interaction. Although web 1.0 involves a fixed content transmitted from a sender to a receiver, web 2.0 is distinguished by the role the receiver plays in the co-production of content. That is, web 1.0 is characterized by closed architecture (Lessig 2006), whereas web 2.0 is widely regarded as having a participatory architecture (O'Reilly 2007). In addition, researchers have developed theories connecting participation with resources such as experience, time, money, and civic skills (Verba, Schlozman, and Brady 1995). Modes of participation have been further distinguished by the attitudinal factors that motivate certain forms of participation but not others (Dalton 2008; Marsh, O'Toole, and Jones 2007). From a comparative perspective, research indicates the existence of differences in the categories of individuals and of attitudes motivating different forms of participation across systems (Dalton 2008). This chapter seeks to contribute to this line of research by examining the role the political context plays in shaping the forms of participation and the resources and attitudinal motivations behind them. We expect macro-level differences between the United States and Spain in political communication structures to have an impact on micro-level participatory practices in the two countries.

Understanding political involvement is important today, as declining levels of formal political participation and of trust in political institutions and political authorities have generated considerable attention in advanced industrialized countries (Dalton 2004; Stoker 2006; Wattenberg 2007). Beyond the salience of socioeconomic stratifications in political participation, researchers are finding that "voter cynicism" is "growing most rapidly amongst sections of the population previously characterized by the highest levels of political engagement, party identification and participation" (Hay 2007, 20). Well-educated and affluent young adults – otherwise expected to be among those most likely to identify with a political party, contribute to political campaigns, and vote – are becoming increasingly disengaged from politics. This cohort of "critical citizens" (Norris 1999a) tends to have lower levels of political efficacy and confidence in political authorities and institutions. Yet these are the same citizens who are among the heaviest users of digital media, and some evidence suggests that younger cohorts may be more attracted to participating online than offline (Bakker and de Vreese 2011; Schlozman et al. 2010; Owen 2006; Jensen, Danziger, and Venkatesh 2007). This may point to the emergence of new stratifications in participation, reflecting differences in the mode and manners of engagement with the political system.

This chapter compares modes of participation considering web 1.0 and 2.0 in relation to offline participation in the United States and Spain. It connects the macro-level political structures with micro-level political behaviors, attitudinal motivations, and resources (Easton 1990). The chapter begins by bringing together the literatures on digital media use and political participation. We then detail the cases, identifying the main features related to the media and political systems expected to condition internet use and political participation. The following two sections address the empirical analysis, first descriptive and then explanatory. Finally, we discuss our results.

4.2. Digital Media Use and Political Participation

Scholars have focused extensive attention on the consequences of digital media diffusion and use on political engagement. We can distinguish four thematic dimensions addressed by the literature.

First, many scholars have noted that the structural affordances of online environments reduce the costs of participation in terms of time and effort. Online, some traditional modes of participation, such as contacting, donating, and signing petitions, entails lower costs in terms of time and effort. Digital environments facilitate communication by reducing the temporal requirements for participation in politics. Communication technologies reduce the time necessary to transmit a message over distance (Adams 2009, 48–50). The structures of e-mail, social networking sites, and Twitter enable users to quickly disseminate information and ideas across a significantly larger audience than would be possible by word of mouth. For this reason, interest groups routinely create mass e-mail campaigns whereby a form letter is disseminated to supporters to forward to the appropriate agency or authority, often overwhelming recipients

(Shulman 2009), and politics is characterized by an abundance of information (Bimber 2003).

For individuals, these campaigns consume a fraction of the time and civic skills necessary to formulate one's own thoughts and attend a meeting or directly contact an official through offline communication channels (Verba, Schlozman, and Brady 1995). Likewise, websites and e-mail lists are often used by political campaigns to solicit donations and, more generally, facilitate processes of political engagementor users. Given that these online communications can often be asynchronous, users can defer online participation until it presents less pressure on time. Hence online participation may be more flexible with respect to time than offline participation, and thus the temporal structures of digital media may facilitate traditional forms of political participation (see Chapters 6 and 8). At the same time, this structural opening may also create a countervailing incentive to indefinitely postpone participation absent the imposition of temporal constraints.

Second, digital media expand the repertoire of modes of political participation, thereby creating new channels for political communication and organization between citizens as well as between citizens and political authorities. The digital interfaces provided by e-mail, blogging platforms, and online social networking sites simplify and facilitate the creation and diffusion of political messages, commenting on political messages, and recruitment to political causes. These modes of political participation did not exist before the creation of digital media, particularly the internet. Hence, digital media provide a range of opportunity structures for political communication and participation.

The study of online politics is forcing scholars to rethink what constitutes political participation. Historically, studies of political participation had a bias toward electoral politics (Verba, Nie, and Kim 1978; Milbrath and Goel 1977). At one point, protest was largely regarded in psychological rather than political terms as the expression of maladjusted youth (Mitscherlich and Francis 1970). However, political participation gradually expanded to include protest (Barnes et al. 1979) and ad hoc forms of participation (Inglehart 1999; Norris 2002). More recently, political consumerism has come into general usage as a new mode (Stolle and Hooghe 2004). Although these "new" forms of participation have always coexisted with more institutionalized electoral and campaign participation, they have been increasing in political importance as more political decisions and policy making have been occurring outside electorally accountable offices (Hay 2007) and as people are increasingly distant from political parties.

Although the revolution in digital media has provided communication infrastructure that facilitates ad hoc political mobilization (Bimber 2003), "in addition to the 'pull' of opportunities provided by the new media-centered forms of political communication, the 'push' of the declining power of the vote provides an incentive for collective actors to resort to unconventional forms of participation" (Kriesi 2008, 160).

The structural affordances of digital media are particularly, though not exclusively, conducive to the enactment of ad hoc, informal, and noninstitionalized forms of participation (Castells 2006; Collin 2008; Farthing 2010). Digital media can thus broaden the array of participatory opportunities for individuals (Bimber, Stohl, and Flanigan 2009) and support new, nonhierarchical political forms (Marsh et al. 2007), particularly through web 2.0 applications. In contrast to offline electoral politics, online politics tends to have a more diverse repertoire. With communication as the primary currency of online politics, participation can be more ad hoc, individualistic, and granular (see Chapter 2). Digital environments provide a platform that enables a diversity of interactions and activity (Bimber et al. 2009) from highly institutionalized participation to highly entrepreneurial and creative intersections of politics and popular culture. E-mails, blog posts, online petitions, and videos are the tools for participation in network society as "the battle of images and frames, at the source of the battle for minds and souls, takes place in multimedia communication networks" (Castells 2009, 302). When political authorities and institutions are perceived as unresponsive, this may channel participation toward the informal and nonhierarchical channels that abound online (Little 2008; Bang 2005).

Third, many scholars have examined the relationship between the digital divide and participation. This relationship takes on two dimensions that go beyond antecedent access to the internet. The first is one's competence in using digital media as a cognitive category (van Deursen and van Dijk 2010; Anduiza, Gallego, and Cantijoch 2010; Min 2010). Digital media use develops and produces new resources that may facilitate and motivate participation (van Dijk 2005; Hoff 2006). Previous research has found that these skills are the most important predictors of online political participation; they have more explanatory power than motivations such as political interest (Anduiza et al. 2010). The second is the level of internet domestication, or the extent to which technology use has become integrated into a domain activity (Helle-Valle and Slettemeas 2008; Venkatesh 2008). Independent of one's ability to use a given technology, domestication of the technology may vary depending on the extent to which it plays a role in daily life; and this variance can often reflect differences in the opportunity to use a technology in a given context. Though analytically distinct, the domestication or taming of a technology often implies the achievement of a level of skill in its use. Therefore, in practice, the skills divide and the domestication divide are typically measured as a behavioral category reflecting the range of one's habitual uses of a given technology.

Fourth, studies have shown that there is a statistical relationship between internet use and political participation (Boulianne 2009), although the mechanism by which internet use makes political participation more probable and the contextual limitations of this effect remain somewhat elusive. Politics today is very media and information centered (Castells 2009). On the one hand, the increasing rendition of political life as digital objects represents a quantitative change in the volume of information transmitted between political actors (Bimber 2003), as well as a qualitative shift in political practice, as the strategic communication of information "has become an integral part of the contemporary political calculus in all aspects of the political system" (Crozier 2008, 3). On the other hand, the indexing of the internet by search engines makes information more readily available to individuals. Digitally networked communications technologies reduce the costs of acquiring political information, which serves as a positive motivation for offline political participation (Tolbert and McNeal 2003; Norris 2001; Brundidge and Rice 2009). Although there is debate over the extent to which prior political interest plays a role in motivating online information seeking (see Prior 2007; Chapters 6 and 8), political information is structurally easier to access and disseminate. In addition, we can also expect that, at least to some extent, a combination of lower information costs and by-product learning provokes political interests and raises one's internal political efficacy – both well-known predictors of political participation (see Chapter 5).

To the extent that digital media facilitate access to various centers of decision making, their uneven distribution may result in unequal influence. The question that has been intensely debated is whether the internet can be said to mobilize political participation of those who would not otherwise participate or reinforce political inequalities by adding new participatory modes to the citizens who are already active. Debates regarding this question have shifted somewhat. Earlier work tended to show that those participating online were also already politically active offline. Bimber (2003) found no relationship between online information seeking and voting or other forms of offline political expression. Likewise, Best and Krueger (2005), along with Jensen (2006), Norris (2001), and Hill and Hughes (1998), argue that those participating online are also politically active offline, have similarly high levels of political interest, and tend to have higher levels of income and education – all robust predictors of offline participation. However, these findings may be changing over time, as the internet is becoming increasingly domesticated by users and integrated into politics by political actors.

In general, the evidence for a mobilization effect is based on younger cohorts, who tend to be more disaffected and disengaged from electoral politics (Schlozman et al. 2010; Jensen et al. 2007; Owen 2006; Muhlberger 2004). This generation also tends to be more technology savvy, embracing digital media use in multiple domains of life, including politics. Hence, even if political interest remains a salient predictor of participation for younger cohorts, those cohorts are finding an outlet to express their politics across digital domains to a greater extent than across offline domains. Not all online environments provide the same incentives for participation, as web 1.0 environments have more constrained architectures of engagement than web 2.0 environments, which characterize users as co-producers rather than audience members.

In addition, there are a number of online conduits that evidence shows can mobilize participation. Although users have more control over their online experiences than they have in other media environments (Prior 2007; Sunstein 2001), we have noted that the internet facilitates political information access, which can motivate political participation. In addition to by-product learning, formalized campaigning makes extensive use of targeted political advertisements (Howard 2006). Finally, viral campaigning can often catch the attention of people otherwise disengaged from politics.

Conversely, although online politics may open new doors to participation for some, it also creates new barriers to participation. Just as political participation is notably stratified along socioeconomic status (Verba et al. 1995; Dalton 2008), so, too, is internet access (Warschauer 2003). Given that the attitudinal and ability dimensions are even more stratified along the same dimensions as the access divide (van Dijk 2005; Norris 2001), online channels may not facilitate greater access and influence in politics for those on the low end of socioeconomic measures.

Whether online participation has a mobilizing or reinforcing effect may not be answerable in a global sense for three reasons. First, as internet access diffuses throughout an area, and as the technology becomes more domesticated and integrated into political organizations, workplaces, and homes, its role may change. Second, internet environments are not uniform. We already noted that online participation and digital participatory environments are both heterogeneous and subject to a changing internet. Therefore, we must consider who participates and how they participate. Third, the larger context of the political system provides differential motivations for participatory forms, as political systems vary in distributions of access to channels of political influence and the role of the internet in structuring the flows of political communications. Hence, in systems in which formalized channels connecting members of a political system with political authorities are more often perceived as closed, we expect communications to be directed in more informal manners.

Finally, political participation depends greatly on the political structures, institutional arrangements, and cultural practices and beliefs existing in a political system at a given time. Kitschelt (1986, 58) describes the political opportunity structure as the "specific configurations of resources, institutional arrangements and historical precedents for social mobilization." Although particular opportunity structures may vary from issue to issue, the integration of digital media into political institutions and processes has created new opportunity structures (Castells 2009). "The media-centered public sphere," Kriesi (2008, 154) observes, has produced a "transformation of both parties and political communication with important implications for mobilization of the vote. It also opens new opportunities for the mobilization of the public beyond the vote." Digital media such as the internet do not sit apart from or rest on top of political structures, cultures, and institutions. Rather, they innervate and, in part, materially constitute these political structures and institutions, organizing human activity in situated domains of deployment – not by defining a singular course of action but by "inviting specific courses of action" (Kallinikos 2002, 289; 2004). Hence, participation is a function of different individual-level

resources and motivations mediated by analog and digital political communication structures, institutions, and historical patterns of participation.

We therefore analyze the impact of differences between the United States
and Spain on different modes of online and offline participation. This chapter
addresses who participates and how they participate in the two countries. We
pose two specific research questions.

First, to what extent do political participation and its explanations vary
across countries? As the two countries vary significantly in their contextual
features (political, cultural, and technological), we expect differences in the
levels of political participation across differently mediated structures (offline,
web 1.0, and web 2.0) at the aggregate level and in the relative weight in the
United States and Spain of individual explanatory factors in terms of both
resources and motivations.

Second, to what extent do different resources, demographic categories, and
attitudes play a different role in offline and online participation? Although the
structure of these technologies contains the same functionalities and closure
regarding their use across countries, different institutional and political contexts are expected to play a role. That is, we expect different motivations to
prevail across the digital architectures of web 1.0 and web 2.0 and that these
will also be affected by the larger political and nonpolitical environment in
each country. In this respect we do not expect online participation to be any
less dependent on context than offline participation (see Chapter 1). But we
expect certain resources (e.g., internet skills) to be more important for online
participation, particularly web 2.0. We also expect that political attitudes will
be less important motivations of online than offline politics (Anduiza et al.
2010) and that age will be differentially associated with participation (positive
for offline modes, negative for online modes).

4.3. The Cases

Online political behavior is ripe for comparative research. On the one hand,
the global architecture and (relatively) global reach of the internet result in an
intersection between the global "space of flows" and the local spaces of places
(Castells 1989, 126). That is, although the network society contains a "cen-
tripetal and homogenizing pull of the global mass," it also provides resources
for the expression of regional cultural and political practices (Terranova 2004,
49). Hence, even though the architecture of the internet remains common across
contexts, the motivations for use – that is, the attitudinal, socioeconomic factors, and the institutional environments that give rise to different forms of
participation – may vary considerably on the basis of contextual features.

To investigate these expectations on the relationship between digital media,
political contexts, and political participation, we have chosen to compare two
countries, the United States and Spain.

The data used are from two surveys conducted roughly one year apart
but based on the same questionnaire. The Spanish survey was collected using
face-to-face interviews at respondents' homes in fall 2007, before the 2008

general election campaign began.[1] These data therefore represent the Spanish citizenry at a low point of mobilization, indicative of ordinary patterns of internet use and political participation. The survey contains a total of 3,716 respondents representative of the Spanish population, with an oversampling of adults between the ages of eighteen and forty to maximize the pool of internet users. The margin of error is +/– 1.61 percent with a 95 percent confidence interval. As a result of the oversample of eighteen- to forty-year-olds, the results for the Spanish sample are presented on the basis of weighted data. The weighted data indicate that 50.7 percent of respondents in our survey are internet users, which is close to the International Telecommunication Union (ITU) estimate for 2007 (52 percent).

The U.S. survey used a nationally representative, random-probability telephone sample of six hundred respondents.[2] This sample size is sufficient to produce a margin of error of +/– 4 percent with a 95 percent confidence interval. The data collection was conducted in November 2008 over the course of two weeks following the national election. This captures the U.S. political system in the wake of a particularly mobilized moment when the internet is said to have played a significant role. The geographic distribution of respondents included 37.1 percent from the southern United States, 21.7 percent from the Mountain and Pacific time zones, 21.8 percent from the Midwest, and 19.3 percent from the Mid-Atlantic and New England regions. The sample was 52.5 percent female and 47.5 percent male, and 79.7 percent white, 8.7 percent black, 2.3 percent Hispanic, and 1.3 percent Native American. The sample contains 74.5 percent internet users, which is very similar to the ITU estimate from the year earlier (72.5 percent).

Both surveys asked a variety of questions regarding internet use (for any purpose), political attitudes, knowledge about the political system, and online and offline political participation. The U.S. and Spanish surveys were not entirely identical, but they included several overlapping modules with exact translations or similarly worded questions that are the basis for our analysis here. These modules were translated from Spanish to English using double translation, with a process similar to that used for the U.S. census (Harkness, Pennell, and Schoua-Glusberg 2004) and the European Social Survey. The survey was

---

[1] The Spanish survey was carried out by the Polnet project on Political Participation in Spain, financed by the Spanish Ministry of Science and Innovation (Grant No. SEC2007–60082). The data are available at http://www.cis.es. We are grateful to the Centro de Investigaciones Sociológicas for carrying out the Spanish survey.

[2] The U.S. survey was conducted by the People Organizations and Information Technology Project at the Center for Research on Information Technology and Organizations, University of California, Irvine. The use of different survey collection methods is not unusual (Fowler 2002). In 1996, the American National Election Survey used a similar approach with a split sample of data collection using both face-to-face surveys along with random-digit dialing to contact survey respondents. Although the response rate was greater for face-to-face surveys, the results of item measures were not statistically significant (Ellis and Krosnick 1999). Some of the difference in response rates is mitigated by the fact that telephone surveys enable interviewers to contact households that they may not otherwise be able to reach for a face-to-face interview, at least in the U.S. context (Dilman 1978).

translated into English from Spanish by both the Spanish and U.S. teams. In cases when an item on the Spanish survey was based on a question from surveys such as the World Values Survey, for which an English translation is already available, that wording was selected. In other cases, discrepancies between survey translations were resolved in favor of the translation fitting most closely the U.S. linguistic context. In some instances questions were reworked or responses were enumerated differently across the surveys. These are noted in the relevant places.

Although a comparison of only two cases does not allow us to make broad generalizations about the explanatory power of contextual variables, it provides a useful base to explore the role of differences in a political system and its environment for several reasons.

First, the United States and Spain have very different histories of political development. In the United States, the adult population was enfranchised over time and the boundaries of the political system have expanded, but the structure of the democratic regime has remained basically the same over its entire political history. By contrast, Spain is a third-wave democracy, which occurred after a long period of dictatorship. A significant percentage of the adult population came of age before democratization and remembers life under dictatorship. The transition process has had significant consequences for the political culture. Spain is well known to have lower levels of political institutional support, and Spaniards tend to have lower levels of political efficacy than their American counterparts. Gunther, Montero, and Botella (2004, 14) attribute this to the aftermath of Spain's transition to democracy, which they argue has resulted in a great disconnect between Spanish citizens and political authorities: "The depolarization and mass demobilization that were essential components of the 'politics of consensus'... may have contributed decisively to the establishment of a stable, consolidated democracy... but they also contributed to weak institutionalization in certain secondary organizations and low levels of interest and involvement in politics."

Research shows that there are profound generational differences in repertoires of participation in Spain. Across nearly all forms of political activity, and particularly unconventional forms of participation, generations born before 1942 were less participatory in 1980 than younger cohorts, and that trend remains evident over the subsequent twenty years (Morales 2005). These differences in political attitudes that summarize the political culture of both countries are presented in Table 4.1.[3]

Second, institutionally, the U.S. presidential system and Spain's parliamentary system create differential incentives for online politics in each country

---

[3] Note that the political interest variable in the American case is measured as interest in the 2008 presidential election. Although we expect political interest to be lower in Spain than the United States, given the characteristics of Spanish political culture, this difference is amplified in the figures reported here, given interest generated by the election, which is often different from general levels of political interest at less mobilized times during the electoral cycle.

TABLE 4.1. *Political Attitudes in the United States and Spain*

	United States		Spain	
	Mean (s.d.)	N	Mean (s.d.)	N
External efficacy[a]	0.428 (.252)	586	.283 (.242)	3,515
Internal efficacy[b]	0.520 (.206)	592	.404 (.244)	3,457
Political interest[c]	0.807 (.269)	597	.335 (.301)	3,702
Political knowledge[d]	0.604 (.207)	599	.481 (.339)	3,666

Note: All variables are measured between 0 and 1; see the Appendix for question wording.
[a] Additive index of two items.
[b] Additive index of two items.
[c] In the U.S. survey political interest refers to interest in the campaign.
[d] Additive index of three items in Spain and four items in the United States.

along two dimensions. The U.S. system of electoral primaries requires candidates to create their own campaign organizations centered on individual candidates rather than on weak parties. In contrast to the U.S. single-member plurality districts, Spain has a proportional representation electoral system that uses closed party lists. This centers campaigning not on individual candidates but on the parties, which make the electoral elites. Although U.S. electoral campaigns are based on ad hoc organizations, Spanish campaigns are conducted by party organizations that have more inertial infrastructures, designed to endure beyond an election cycle. The dependence of U.S. candidates on individual supporters is more conducive to the integration of the internet into their campaign organizations (Anstead and Chadwick 2009).

These cases are also differentiated in terms of the electoral systems. Single-member districts facilitate a close connection between representatives and constituents, as a representative is a direct target for accountability and support. This may favor a culture of direct contacting with political authorities in the U.S. system, which should also appear in the online arena.

Comparatively, the Spanish political system discourages direct contact: the president is indirectly selected by the parliament, and the electoral system is based on multimember districts that, though not large, make it difficult for Spaniards to identify their district representatives. Large parties are reluctant to give up control over campaigning or the policy agenda. There are more parties in Spain than in the United States, but Spanish politics is still dominated at the national level by two main parties, which leaves few opportunities for nonsupporters of those parties to find institutional avenues for political expression. Because governments in Spain emerge from the parliament, representation centers on the strength of parties rather than on preferences for individual candidates. For this reason, in Spain political representation is constructed around parties, whereas in the U.S. system, there is a closer tie between the electorate and individual politicians.

Third, according to our data, Spain has significantly lower levels of internet access and use (50.7 percent) than the United States (74.5 percent).[4] In comparison to Spain, postindustrial development is more evenly distributed in the United States, particularly in the knowledge economy (Giner, Tolosa, and Fuster 2004; Tabellini 2005). The inequalities across Spain in integration into the digitally networked knowledge economy are more strident than the differences in economic production across regions, and Spain considerably lags behind Northern Europe and the United States in terms of its overall integration in the network society. However, education conditions internet access to a greater extent in the United States than in Spain, and whereas in the United States age is positively related to use, in Spain this relationship is negative. This points to a cohort effect regarding technology adoption and use in Spain, with internet use more concentrated across younger cohorts.

Among internet users there are secondary digital divides, which refer to the ability to use the internet effectively and the level of its domestication (van Dijk 2005; Venkatesh 2008). *Secondary* here does not indicate marginal or less significant, as previous research has shown that this divide is more stratified and enduring than the access divide (Norris 2001; van Dijk 2005). It denotes a nested relationship to the prior access divide. We measure this variable in terms of a scale of online nonpolitical activities including using e-mail, shopping online, banking or paying bills online, maintaining a blog or website, making a phone call online, and surfing the web without a concrete objective.[5] Table 4.2 presents the figures from our Spanish and U.S. surveys regarding levels of internet access and average levels for each of these six uses.

Once online, Americans report that on average they use the internet for a greater diversity of items than their Spanish counterparts. However, there are two notable exceptions: online calling and, more significant, maintaining a website or blog. Because online calling is often a free or lower cost form of communication than traditional international telephone calls, there are several potential explanations for this higher level of online calling in Spain, including higher levels of interaction with other EU countries, which is facilitated by international exchange programs that contribute to the development of international social networks, or the higher costs of traditional international calls.

---

[4] More recent data show that this gap has narrowed to 62.2 percent in Spain compared with 78.2 percent in the United States (Internet World Statistics, http://www.internetworldstats.com, accessed July 9, 2011).

[5] This measure is preferable to subjective self-assessments of internet use for two reasons. First, it presents an objective measure of capacities that is more readily interpretable and reliable than categories of self-assessment that may be subject to different interpretations by individual respondents. Second, this measure also shows the extent to which the internet is domesticated for our respondents. A behavioral measure is preferable because we are interested not in innate abilities but in the degree to which the internet is integrated into their lives.

TABLE 4.2. *Uses of the Internet in the United States and Spain*

	United States		Spain	
	% Users (% over total sample)	N	% Users (% over total sample)	N
Percentage of internet users over population	74.5		50.7	
Effect of education on internet use[a]	1.51***		0.78***	
Effect of age on internet access[a]	0.02**		−0.06***	
E-mail	95.1 (70.7)	424	84.8 (42.7)	1,588
Surf to pass the time	79.4 (59.2)	355	66.2 (33.3)	1,238
Buy online	81.0 (60.3)	362	37.0 (18.7)	696
Online banking and paying bills	62.9 (46.8)	281	40.7 (20.6)	764
Online phone call	13.0 (9.7)	57	14.9 (7.5)	277
Maintain blog and/or website	10.3 (7.7)	46	21.5 (10.8)	403
Mean number of items out of 6	3.45 (s.d. 1.10)		2.66 (s.d. 1.42)	

[a] Binary logistic regression coefficients for internet use predicted by age and education.
** $p < .01$. *** $p < .001$.

The digital divides with respect to internet skill levels and the domestication of online activities are distinguished here in terms of their measurement, as the diversity of online activity constitutes evidence of both. However, even though domestication does not conceptually require a hierarchical relationship between one type of technology use and another, internet skills imply that there are higher and lower levels of ability, differentiated by the range and frequency of use. Hence, to measure the scalability of these items as an indication of internet skills, we created an item-response scale using a Rasch model to verify that the items are evidence of a latent variable. In contrast to standard reliability scales, we do not expect uniform response patterns across the items, as each item is assumed to have a different level of difficulty. Items of higher difficulty such as maintaining a blog or website are assumed to indicate higher levels of internet skills than sending an e-mail. The higher a respondent's level of internet skills, the more likely the respondent is to have completed more difficult tasks online. Rasch scaling has been used extensively to identify latent variables, as it measures the proximity of the items to a Guttman scale (Rizopoulos 2006). The item-response curves for Spain and the United States are plotted in Figures 4.1a and 4.1b, respectively.

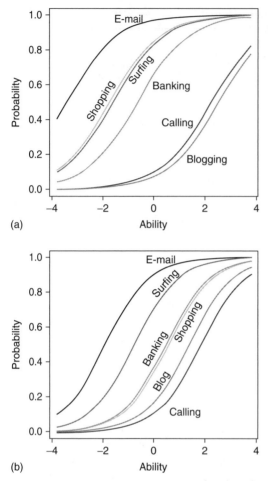

(a)

(b)

FIGURE 4.1. (a) Item-response curves for digital media use (United States). (b) Item-response curves for digital media use (Spain).

These results confirm that the scale is monotonically increasing and, in general, converging as internet skills and domestication increase. Iterated simulations show that in both cases, the results are not spurious.[6] The results from the U.S. case show that maintaining a website or blog and making a phone call online converge less rapidly with the other items than in the Spanish sample. This may be a result of the significantly higher rates of blogging and website maintenance, combined with slightly higher rates of online calling, in Spain than in the United States. This suggests that the remaining four items are

[6] To test the strength of the scale, the observed data were compared with fifty randomly generated samples of data using a bootstrapping operation (Rizopoulas 2006). In neither case was there a statistically significant association between the observed data and randomly generated data.

widely used among Americans online, whereas maintaining a blog or website and making an online phone call are comparably less common. Differences in the rate of convergence may reflect contextual differences, as previous research has shown that the overall integration of technology into one's life depends to a significant extent on social influences in personal networks and on messages transmitted through the media (Venkatesh 2008).

These system-level factors can affect the trajectories of online participation in Spain and the United States. They involve technological differences in the distribution of internet access, different institutional incentives, and different patterns of political culture.

There are several implications that can be derived from the comparison between the United States and Spain. First, considering the characteristics of the political culture and the institutional setting of both countries, we expect lower levels of participation directed at formal institutions and authorities in Spain than in the United States, both offline and online. Similarly, given differences in political culture and where each country is at in their electoral calendars, we expect that levels of political interest and political efficacy (internal and external) will account for a larger percentage of political contacting in Spain than in the United States and these effects will be more notable offline than online, as online contacting entails fewer costs. We also expect that given differences in political socialization across the cases, after controlling for internet access and skills, older cohorts in Spain will participate less online, especially in web 2.0. We expect that, given the political consensus that formed after the transition to democracy and the political socialization that occurred under Francisco Franco, members of this generation are less politically engaged outside of formal structures and elite-initiated modes.

Second, considering the levels of internet diffusion, skills, and domestication, we expect that all forms of online participation will be more frequent and less subject to stratification by internet skills and domestication in the United States than in Spain, where the range and intensity of online activities are, on average, more constrained in daily life. We also expect that younger cohorts are more likely to participate online in Spain, whereas in the United States we expect age differences to be less pronounced because of differences in access and cohort identification with internet use.

4.4. Participation in Spain and the United States

Table 4.3 presents the levels of web 1.0, web 2.0, and offline political participation in Spain and the United States among internet users.[7] The results show relatively similar levels of petition signing and campaign donations across countries. Even though the figures are for internet users, both signing a petition and donating are still more common offline than online in both countries.

---

[7] We have restricted our analyses in this section to internet users, to control for internet access and to be able to compare frequency and explanations of online modes with offline modes.

TABLE 4.3. *Political Participation in Spain and the United States (over internet users)*

	United States		Spain	
	%	N	%	N
Offline participation				
Sign petition	27.3	164	21.7	806
Contact official	26.4	158	7.4	275
Donation	24.8	149	25.3	942
Any of these	50.3	301	39.7	1,454
Web 1.0				
Sign petition online	18.6	83	14.4	269
Contact official online	25.5	114	4.6	86
Donate online	9.8	44	8.4	158
Any of these	37.4	167	27.1	503
Web 2.0				
Comment on online forum, web, or blog	10.5	47	20.2	378

The main difference lies in the levels of direct contacting, which are much higher in the United States than Spain, both offline and online. In the United States 26 percent of internet users have contacted a political official online versus only 4.6 percent in Spain. These figures are very similar for offline contact, with 26 percent of U.S. and 7.4 percent of Spanish internet users having contacted a political official in the previous year. Although the differences in the levels of direct contacting are expected, more remarkable is the similarity in the levels of participation both offline and online, despite differences in the mobilization frame of the countries. Citizen-initiated contacting is not a common form of campaign politics, but there are only slight differences between the cases with respect to petition signing and political donations.

The result is different for web 2.0. Although Spanish internet users show a smaller portion of participation through web 1.0 mechanisms (27 percent in Spain versus more than 37 percent in the United States), the proportion of internet users who have posted a comment is twice as high in Spain as in the United States. E-mail from personal networks of course plays a particularly important role in U.S. political communications, as 70.7 percent (results not shown in Table 4.3) of U.S. internet users have received an e-mail with political content from friends and family. By contrast, only 35.8 percent of Spanish internet users report receiving an e-mail with political content from any source (results not shown in Table 4.3). Certainly, Americans connect with one another in horizontal networks, although this tends to be through closed channels such as e-mail, whereas in Spain there is more of a preference to avoid politics in personal e-mail networks in favor of blog-centered communications. Hence, the differences between the participatory architectures favored by Spaniards

TABLE 4.4. *Explanatory Models of Political Participation*

	Offline		Web 1.0		Web 2.0	
	U.S. b (s.e.)	Spain b (s.e.)	U.S. b (s.e.)	Spain b (s.e.)	U.S. b (s.e.)	Spain b (s.e.)
Intercept	−3.90*** (0.03)	−2.13*** (0.33)	−3.62*** (0.87)	−4.12*** (−0.02)	−4.93*** (1.19)	−3.41*** (0.43)
Age	0.03** (0.01)	0.02** (0.01)	0.01 (0.01)	−0.02** (0.01)	−0.01 (0.01)	−0.03*** (0.01)
Resources						
Education	1.90*** (0.48)	0.81*** (0.24)	0.78 (0.48)	0.65* (0.30)	−0.09 (0.61)	0.25 (0.33)
Digital divide	0.77 (0.55)	0.69* (0.27)	1.86** (0.58)	2.96*** (0.33)	2.47*** (0.75)	3.07*** (0.36)
Attitudes						
Interest in politics	1.42** (0.48)	1.49*** (0.25)	2.43*** (0.58)	2.00*** (0.29)	3.22*** (0.89)	1.90*** (0.31)
Internal efficacy	0.42 (0.62)	−0.15 (0.31)	−0.76 (0.63)	0.49 (0.37)	−0.31 (0.81)	0.09 (0.39)
External efficacy	−0.37 (0.45)	0.41 (0.26)	−0.16 (0.46)	0.00 (0.30)	0.34 (0.57)	0.24 (0.31)
Akaike information criterion	493.88	1,629.70	480.68	1,298.90	343.55	1,158.10
N	387	1,368	387	1,373	388	1,381

and their U.S. counterparts revolve around American preferences for personal connection and Spanish aversion to vertical communications with political authorities. Contextual differences favoring certain types of political communications therefore seem to affect online modes of political communication as much as offline modes.

Turning to the individual explanatory factors of participation, Table 4.4 presents the estimation of a binary logistic regression model including resources and attitudes as explanatory factors for the three participation modes in each country. The Appendix includes a detailed explanation of the question wording and coding details for each variable. The dependent variable is coded as 1 if the respondent has participated in any of the items for each measure reported in Table 4.3 (offline, online web 1.0, and online web 2.0). All explanatory variables apart from age are normalized, with values ranging between 0 and 1 so the coefficients can be roughly compared. The results for key independent variables are converted into predicted probabilities in Figure 4.2.

The results show a great deal of similarity across the cases, particularly in the offline models. Thus, the overall explanatory model of political participation based on resources and motivations appears quite general. Offline participation is positively affected by age, education, and interest in politics, but not by

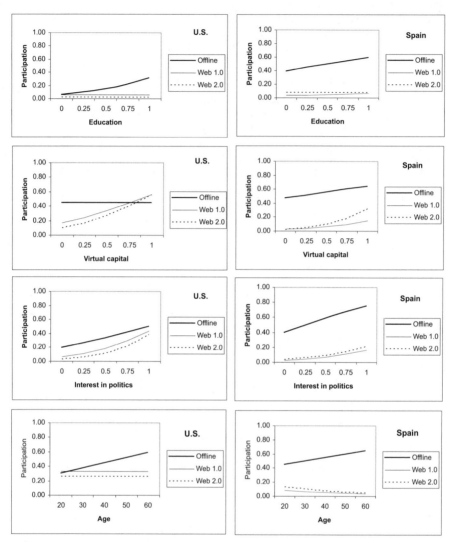

FIGURE 4.2. Predicted probabilities for the three modes of participation by age, education, digital media domestication, and interest in politics in the United States and Spain.

income.[8] In addition, we find similar results in both countries regarding the importance of internet domestication and skills. With regard to the resource account of participation, in contrast to offline participation for which formal education is a resource, in an online environment, internet skills are more

---

[8] Note that this may have been different if we considered the whole sample and not only internet users, who have higher income levels.

important, which suggests that different modes of participation require different resources. One's facility with the medium substitutes the cognitive resources in offline politics for which education is a proxy.

In general, the secondary digital divide plays a stronger role in accounting for participation in Spain. In Spain, this variable is even associated with offline participation. Although the domestication of nonpolitical activities spills over into online political participation in both the U.S. and the Spanish cases, in Spain the relationship is substantially stronger. Whereas in the United States participation appears to emerge from one's ideational engagement with politics, in Spain, online participation – and to a certain extent, offline participation – appears to emerge more directly from one's ability to use the internet and its domestication. This is not to say that internet use necessarily transforms individuals into politically active agents. However, it does point to differences between the cases regarding the diffusion and use of the internet: in Spain, where the digital divide is more evident, those who are engaged online represent not only an informational elite but also a politically active minority. This may be further confirmed by the earlier noted link between income and online participation in Spain, which is absent in the United States. However, this does not mean that internet skills are irrelevant in the United States. Remarkably, among U.S. internet users with high levels of internet skills, political participation is more likely to happen online as the crossing curves in Figure 4.2 show.

Also in both countries, and for all modes of participation, political interest is a strong positive predictor of participation. However, quite unexpectedly, neither internal nor external efficacy is related to political participation in any of the models for any country. This suggests that at least for internet users, political alienation has no effect on nonelectoral forms of political participation, and this result holds independent of the medium of participation and the country considered.

We find the greatest differences between the countries in the web 1.0 and 2.0 models. Although age is inversely related to internet access in Spain, once online, we could expect the traditional positive effect of age (see Muhlberger 2004; Jensen et al. 2007). This is observed in the United States, where the coefficient for age is positive but insignificant for the web 1.0 and 2.0 participation modes. However, in Spain the data show that age is inversely related to online political models in the United States. This may be evidence supporting the expected generational effect by which older age cohorts do not identify with new forms of political participation, but it also may be evidence that younger cohorts, for whatever reason, are more inclined to participate via the digital opportunity structures that exist online rather than traditional offline channels.

4.5. Conclusion

This chapter indicates that the political, cultural, and technological environments of a country are implicated in both the patterns of online and offline political behavior and the resources and attitudinal characteristics that give rise to participation. As with offline participation, the distribution of resources and prevalence of opportunity structures within a political system render some modes of participation more attractive and feasible than others.

The answers to our research questions posed earlier in the chapter assist in elaborating these conclusions. The first question examined differences in the extent to which citizens participate through different modes and in the factors that explain these participation modes. Comparatively, Americans use the internet more often to communicate with political authorities, whereas Spaniards use the internet more often to communicate with other members of the political system and are particularly unlikely to contact authorities. Cross-country differences were greater in online modes than in offline modes of participation: online is not, therefore, any less affected by differences in political structures than offline participation. In addition, the degree to which people have access to the internet and have incorporated it into their daily lives is an external structure that varies across countries and serves as a constraint on online participation. Hence, although internet diffusion and domestication are not necessarily in themselves a political structure, they are certainly politically relevant in their effects.

The second research question queried the extent to which different modes of participation are conditioned by sociodemographic factors and political attitudes. Although our results find general support for the traditional models based on resources and attitudes, showing that education, income, and age are important predictors of participation, particularly offline, this model is less applicable online. In an online environment, the cognitive resources and social status afforded to those more educated are replaced by people's ability to use the internet and the extent to which the internet is integrated into daily life. Hence, those who are better connected technologically are also more politically connected in the sense that they participate more.

The cases are distinguished, however, in terms of the "categorical groupings" that are structurally connected to channels of political influence and decision making (Easton 1990, 71). In the United States, those who have integrated digital media more into their nonpolitical lives and who participate online are not necessarily from the ranks of higher income brackets or higher levels of education, which is consistent with previous research indicating that there is greater political equality in unconventional modes of participation than there is in electoral participation (Marien, Hooghe, and Quintelier 2010). In Spain, however, those who participate online also come from higher socioeconomic categories, which mirrors offline participants to a greater extent. This may be indicative of a greater degree of normalization in online forms of participation in the United States than in Spain.

In addition, age plays an important role in understanding participation and its effect varies across cases and modes of participation. We find that there is greater equality across age groups participating online than offline in the United States. However, in Spain, in direct contrast to offline participation, younger cohorts are more likely to participate online. This may in part reflect generational differences in Spain revolving around technology diffusion, integration, and domestication. Given that internet access is more evenly distributed among age groups in the United States but in Spain is concentrated in the younger generation, this can have a normative effect: even if someone has access, that individual is still less likely to integrate the technology into daily life and politics because he or she does not identify as strongly with the technology (Warschauer 2003). Hence, both historical patterns of participation and cultural orientations toward technology can affect whether someone participates online.

The second research question asked about the relationship between political attitudes and differences in online modes of participation in Spain and the United States. We addressed this question at both a system level and an individual level. At an aggregate level, levels of external and internal efficacy are much lower in Spain than in the United States, and there is considerably more web 2.0 participation in Spain than in the United States. By contrast, the American cultural preference for directly contacting elites is evident in equal measure online and offline. Those findings appear consistent with what we know about the political cultures in both the United States and Spain. However, at an individual level, we found no relationship between levels of political efficacy (internal or external) and the probabilities of participation for any mode of participation in either country. Just as the inference from the aggregate- or system-level data to individual-level conclusions commits the ecological fallacy, one cannot extrapolate directly from individual-level data to a system level. Hence, if there is a relationship between efficacy and participation, it is likely mediated by other factors and structures. Nevertheless, there are clear indications that the communication architecture of different environments between web 1.0 and web 2.0 carries significance for Spain and the United States.

Whether the internet or other digital media mobilize or reinforce political inequalities cannot be assessed at an aggregate level. Rather, our comparison of Spain and the United States shows that how the internet is used for participation reflects prevailing motivations embedded in a political system, as we find mobilization for certain modes of online participation but not for others. Online mechanisms for participation are more or less available depending on the configurations of access, abilities, and other individual-level resources, as well as the cultural and institutional parameters of a political system that differentially integrates communication technologies to serve varied interests. These contextual factors mediate whether the political opportunity structures of particular digital communication channels open pathways for participation that mitigate or exacerbate political inequalities. Finally, we expect the interactions among political institutions; social, economic, and political structures; and participation to vary over time as political authorities and citizens find new ways to incorporate the technology into their political strategies.

4.6. Appendix

External efficacy. Respondents were asked to indicate on a five-point scale the degree to which they agreed with the following statements: "Public officials don't care about what people like me think" and "Politicians always put their own political interests first."[9]

In the U.S. survey, the question wording was "People use the internet to share their opinions publicly, while others do not. Please tell me how often you used the Internet in the following ways in the months leading up to the election to post a comment on a political blog or online discussion forum – everyday or almost every day, several times a week, several times a month, rarely, or never?" In the Spanish survey, this item was coded as a binary (yes or no). To ensure comparability in the analyses, we recoded the U.S. responses into a binary item.

Interest in the campaign and interest in politics. In the U.S. survey, interest in the campaign and politics was measured in terms of interest in the election, given that the period of measurement was immediately after the election. The question was worded as follows: "How closely did you follow news about the 2008 presidential election? Very closely, somewhat closely, not too closely, or not at all closely." In the Spanish survey, this question was worded as follows: "How interested would you say you are in politics? Very interested, quite interested, hardly interested, not at all interested."

Internal efficacy. On a five-point scale, respondents were asked to indicate the degree to which they agreed with the following statements: "Politics and government are so complicated that a person like me really cannot understand what's going on" and "I am better informed about politics and government than most people."

Internet skills. This item is composed of six internet uses. In the U.S. survey, respondents were asked, "Please tell me if you used the internet to do any of the following things in the past 12 months: send or read e-mail; go online for no particular reason, just for fun or to pass the time; buy a product or a service; pay a bill online; make a phone call online; create or work on your own online journal or blog." The items in the Spanish survey were similarly worded: "In the last 12 months, for which of the following activities have you used the internet: receive or send e-mail; navigate the internet without a concrete objective; buy a product or service; conduct a bank transaction; make a phone call online; maintain your own blog or web page." In both surveys the responses were coded as a binary (yes or no) response.

Offline participation. The offline participation measure is composed of three items. Respondents were asked whether they had signed a petition, contacted a political official or candidate, or contributed to a campaign in the previous year. The responses were measured as a binary (yes or no) on both the U.S. and Spanish surveys.

---

[9] Variable used in the chapter analysis: coding, construction of variables, and survey question wording (alphabetically ordered).

Web 1.0 participation. The web 1.0 participation measure is the online equivalent of the offline measures, including contacting officials online, signing a petition online, and donating to a political candidate or campaign online. The wording in the U.S. survey was "Please tell me how often you used the internet in the following ways in the months leading up to the election – every day or almost every day, several times a week, several times a month, rarely, or never: E-mail a candidate or elected official, sign a petition online, donate money to a candidate online." To ensure comparability in responses and between differences in the question wordings across the individual items and the binary response option in the Spanish survey, all items were recoded such that 0 = never and 1 corresponded to any frequency with which the respondent had reported engaging in each action.

Web 2.0. Web 2.0 was a single item consisting of commenting on blogs or in online political forums.

5

Internet Use and Political Attitudes in Europe

Clelia Colombo, Carol Galais, and Aina Gallego

5.1. Introduction

Political attitudes are relevant for a variety of reasons. Interested and critical citizens can actively monitor their government's activities and thus foster accountability. People who think that they are able to influence government are more likely to participate in politics, vote in elections, and follow political news. Thus, the level of political interest or efficacy of a population is critical to the proper working of democratic countries. However, political attitudes vary widely cross-nationally and are undergoing profound changes in advanced industrial democracies (Dalton 2002, 2008; Pharr and Putnam 2000; Norris 1999b).

In this chapter we use different approaches to investigate the extent to which digital media contribute to shape some relevant political attitudes. First, we look at the impact of internet use on political attitudes from a large cross-national perspective. This is a novel contribution to the literature on digital politics. Because most of the core works in this field deal only with the United States or a limited range of other case studies, we lack a reliable comparative picture of the relationship between internet use and political attitudes. To do this, we use the European Social Survey and examine the link between internet use and political attitudes in fifteen European countries. Then, we consider in depth a particular case, Spain, analyzing both quantitative evidence (survey data from fall 2007) and qualitative data (from focus groups carried out in fall 2008).

5.2. Political Attitudes and Digital Media

The internet is deeply embedded in the everyday life of a large part of the population of Western European societies and has transformed many aspects of social and economic relationships. The initial works on the effect of the internet on political behavior expected this medium to produce large impacts. Authors were quite clearly divided between those who anticipated that the changes would result in the atomization of society (Davis 1999; Margolis and Resnick 2000; Sunstein 2001; Putnam 2002) and those who expected an increase in civic attitudes and participation as a result of lower communication and participation costs, and greater amounts of political information available online (Negroponte 1995; Bonchek 1997; Wellman 1997). After the first empirical studies were conducted, proponents of the normalization hypothesis argued that the use of the internet had modest, if any, impact on civic engagement and attitudes such as political efficacy, political knowledge, and political interest (Drew and Weaver 2006; Uslaner 2004; Bimber 2003; Jennings and Zeitner 2003; Scheufele and Nisbet 2002).

In the last past few years, the normalization hypothesis itself has been challenged. The internet seems to foster involvement in certain unconventional modes of engagement such as participation in social movements, civic associations, local communities, protest activities, and political consumerism (see Chapter 6; Kavanaugh et al. 2008; Norris 2005). Boulianne (2009) has argued that the impact of the internet on political participation is positive, and more recent studies have argued that it is greater (Borge and Cardenal 2011; De Zúñiga, Copeland, and Bimber 2011). This suggests that effects are visible only after people have integrated the internet into their daily lives and that some characteristics of current developments such as the web 2.0 may have political consequences.

The causal mechanisms that link internet use to political participation are less clear. There are two kinds of paths that might explain this impact on political behavior (see Introduction; Bimber 2003). First, the internet has direct effects on participation because it lowers its costs. For example, it is cheaper and quicker to send an e-mail to a politician than to send a letter. Second, there are indirect mechanisms because internet use may produce changes in political attitudes, which in turn affect behavior. In this later stream of work, some studies have found that internet use is positively related to attitudes such as internal political efficacy (Eveland and Scheufele 2000; Kaye and Johnson 2002; Scheufele and Nisbet 2002; Lee 2006), political information efficacy (Tedesco 2007), interest in electoral campaigns (Tolbert and McNeal 2003), and general political interest (Johnson and Kaye 2000; Kaye and Johnson 2002; Di Gennaro and Dutton 2006; Kenski and Stroud 2006).

There are a variety of theoretical arguments that predict a positive influence of internet use on political attitudes relevant to political engagement. First, internet users are potentially exposed to more political stimuli because of the abundance of online political information, that can be actively searched for. Moreover, political information can be encountered accidentally as many websites intertwine some political information with other contents, and many internet users receive unsolicited political e-mails (see Chapter 6). The result can be increased by product learning (see Chapters 2 and 3). If political information is unintentionally encountered in the online, those users belong to an inadvertent audience that does not include nonusers. Users are exposed to additional political stimuli and are encouraged to develop political interest and the feeling that it is possible and quite easy to contribute to this amount of information (Weber, Loumakis, and Bergman 2003). In addition, the internet allows citizens to obtain political information directly from primary sources, avoiding intermediaries such as journalists or press agencies and bypassing traditional media gatekeepers (Römmele 2003). This characteristic may positively affect citizens' feelings of political competence.

Second, the characteristics of interactivity and horizontality, which are particularly important in web 2.0 environments, might foster feelings of political efficacy and enhance engaged citizenship. We know from previous research that horizontal relations at school or at work – that is, nonhierarchical relationships with a high degree of autonomy and involvement in decisions, – can positively affect internal political efficacy (Milbrath and Goel 1977; Mason 1982; Greenberg 1986; Peterson 1992; Sobel 1993; Greenberg, Grunberg, and Daniel 1996; Torney-Purta 2004; Jian and Jeffres 2008). Furthermore, according to some points of view, the horizontality of the internet may enhance users' discursive skills and attitudes. Habermas's (1996) theory of communicative action requires openness, discursive equality, fair play, and freedom for the success of social discourse. The ability to reflect on, express, and understand political arguments (i.e., their effects on internal political efficacy) might be positively affected by some uses of the internet, as Habermas's theory of discourse has been used as a guide to develop information systems and online tools to support public discourse (Heng and de Moor 2003).

Interactivity, understood as "a contextualizing facility that mediates between environments and content and users and enables the generation of further content" (Richards 2006, 532), has dramatically increased in recent years as well. With web 2.0 people produce and share their own data, work with a constant actualization of information and contents, and collaborate and cooperate in the construction of information and participation through the internet. This includes blogging, wikis, social bookmarking, and use of other sites created by user-produced content (e.g., Flickr, YouTube) and networking applications such as Facebook or Twitter. These new tools make possible the collective participation of internet users in the production of web content (Breindl and Francq 2008; see also Chapter 2). A new leading role for citizens in the political sphere online would contribute to enhancing internal efficacy. This is not to claim that every internet user posts political content online, but rather that many users feel that they can intervene easily and have different tools available if they wish to do so.

Interactivity can also be applied to the possibility of a more direct relationship between citizens and their representatives. Digital media can make contacting public officials and institutions easier. Many politicians maintain their blogs, answer their e-mail, and seek to create a virtual relationship with some citizens. This might help citizens to better understand the political process and the political actions of their representatives.

Another characteristic of the internet is anonymity, which can have different effects on attitudes, such as a negative impact on interpersonal trust. However, anonymity may help shy people overcome fears of expressing their opinions, avoid feelings of inferiority, and dilute implicit hierarchies in communicative interactions. So, the anonymity of the internet may reduce public embarrassment and improve internal political efficacy levels (Cornfield 2003).

Finally, the internet has the specific function of connecting people. The virtual community is an alternative to geographically located communities, and it has the same value and usefulness (Rheingold 1993) thanks to improved wireless portability, globalized connectivity, and high bandwidth. Internet users have an advantage with regard to their social capital, because they tend to have wider social circles than nonusers (Uslaner 2004) and a richer social life, even offline (Neustadtl and Robinson 2002). Internet use helps build social connections because virtual social networks and e-mail facilitate meeting new people and keeping in touch with friends and relatives. We know from previous research that big networks – and their politicization and degree of homogeneity – foster positive attitudes toward political participation (Leighley 1990). In addition, belonging to virtual networks has a positive impact on interpersonal trust (Kobayashi, Ikeda, and Miyata 2006), which is positively related with interest in collective issues. Indeed, it has been found that the more a person uses the internet, the more he or she feels able to change networks, thus increasing self-efficacy (Furutani, Kobayashi, and Ura 2007). Certainly, there are many opportunities for joining online communities and being aware of or exposed to the political opinions of those communities' members. But even internet users who do not belong to a specific virtual network may feel that they share some technological skills, relationship patterns, and a set of particular interests, different from those of non-internet users. As long as they develop a sense of belonging to the internet community and some group consciousness, they will improve their levels of trust, their engagement as citizens, their internal political efficacy, and their interest in politics (Gurin and Epps 1975; Gurin, Hatchett, and Jackson 1989; Tate 1994; Anderson 2005).

There are, however, counterarguments to the proposed paths that connect internet use with political efficacy and political interest. Interactivity can discourage people, as it is not probable that public officials answer their contact efforts (Johnson and Kaye 2003). Users may become more isolated, using the internet mainly for leisure purposes and avoiding people with different profiles and motivations, thus becoming invulnerable to the internet's effects of political socialization (Kavanaugh and Patterson 2001; Putnam 2002). Moreover, anonymity may entail distrust, and political information available on the online might be chaotic, inaccurate, imprecise, and difficult to handle, which may lead to political disinterest or only attract those already interested (Graber 1996; Norris 2001; Prior 2007).

Political interest and internal political efficacy, understood as the belief that citizens can understand and influence politics,[1] are often considered the minimal attitudinal component of political engagement (Almond and Verba 1963;

---

[1] This is different from the feeling of external political efficacy, which entails the belief that government is responsive to the citizen's demands.

Verba, Schlozman, and Brady 1995). Thus, we limit our analyses to these two dependent variables and test the effect of internet use on them following a research design that goes from more general evidence to more detailed data. First, we look at this relation cross-nationally. Given that the effect of the internet on engagement is greater when the adoption rates of the technology are high (Boulianne 2009), we focus on the first fifteen countries integrated into the European Union (EU15), which have had relatively high adoption rates for a longer time than other European countries. Then we move to the Spanish case for a closer look at both quantitative and qualitative evidence.

5.3. Internet Use and Political Attitudes in Europe

The four first waves of the European Social Survey (ESS) have been merged in a database, covering a span of seven years, from 2002 to 2009, resulting in a sample of almost one hundred thousand people.[2] The only indicator of internet use included in the European Social Survey is frequency. It is well known that not every person is equally likely to use the internet: internet use is related to socioeconomic resources and age, which are also related to political attitudes. Thus, these factors have to be controlled for in the multivariate analysis. The set of control variables include gender, age (measured in years), and education (measured in years of full-time education completed). Furthermore, it could be argued that there is a problem of reverse causality if people who are very interested in politics to start with use the internet more frequently, precisely because it allows them to search for political information quickly and efficiently. To account for this possibility, we add two controls that capture the propensity to search for political information: exposure to news and current affairs on an average weekday, broadcasted either on TV television or on the radio, and reading newspapers.[3]

Table 5.1 displays the unstandardized coefficients of the multivariate analysis of two explanatory models of political interest, one including traditional socioeconomic variables and the other adding exposure to news and frequency of newspaper reading. The coding details for all variables are reported in the Appendix.

---

[2] The data can be downloaded from http://www.europeansocialsurvey.org. We took into account the nesting of the data by country (fifteen groups) and year or wave (four groups) using clustered standard errors to account for the fact that observations are more likely to be similar in the sixty resulting groups. Appropriate weights have been applied to correct for the different sizes of the populations across countries.

[3] We have to acknowledge, though, that there is a risk of endogeneity (political attitudes causing internet use and not the other way around), which because of the nature of the data, we cannot exclude. This question is dealt with particularly by Hamilton and Tolbert and Kroh and Neiss in this volume, and we base our interpretation of the analysis in this Chapter on their conclusion that digital media use has an effect on involvement, even when adequately taking into account the possibility of reverse causality.

TABLE 5.1. *Political Interest and Internet Use in the EU15*

	Interest in Politics, b (S.E.)	
Internet use	0.06***	0.05***
	(0.00)	(0.00)
Male	0.23***	0.16***
	(0.01)	(0.01)
Education	0.18***	0.13***
	(0.01)	(0.01)
Age	0.01***	0.01***
	(0.00)	(0.00)
Exposure to news on television and radio		0.11***
		(0.01)
Newspaper reading		0.20***
		(0.02)
Constant	0.09	0.12**
	(0.04)	(0.04)
R^2	0.182	0.223
Obs.	92,954	65,046

Note: Clustered standard errors in parentheses.
* $p < 0.05$. ** $p < 0.01$. *** $p < 0.001$.

Interest in politics increases as the frequency of internet use increases. Controlling for media exposure does not reduce the effect a great deal. Thus, in the EU15 during the period 2002–2009, and all else being equal, internet use is positively related to citizens' degree of political interest, as anticipated by our theory.

This analysis captures the effects of internet use on political interest for all of the EU15 countries. This relationship may vary across countries, or the results could be due to a single case in which the effect is particularly strong. We thus performed the same analyses on a country-by-country basis. Figure 5.1 displays the regression coefficients of the effect of internet use on interest in politics in each of the EU15 countries between 2002 and 2009, controlling by the variables showed in the second model. As can be observed in Figure 5.1, the coefficients are similar across countries, and the majority are significant and positive. It is worth mentioning that the coefficients for Greece, Portugal, and Italy are not significant, as shown by the large confidence intervals, so it cannot be confirmed that internet use affects political attitudes in these cases. Nevertheless, the remaining observations support our hypothesis, as twelve of the coefficients are significant, positive, and similar in magnitude: the greater the use of the internet, the greater is the interest in public affairs in the EU15.

We ran the same models with citizens' internal political efficacy as dependent variables. As can be observed in Table 5.2, internet use significantly increases internal political efficacy after controlling for socioeconomic variables and exposure to news on traditional media. Figure 5.2 displays the coefficients of

TABLE 5.2. *Internal Political Efficacy and Internet Use in the EU15*

	Internal Political Efficacy, b (S.E.)	
Internet use	0.07***	0.06***
	(0.01)	(0.01)
Male	0.78***	0.72***
	(0.02)	(0.02)
Education	0.34***	0.26***
	(0.02)	(0.01)
Age	0.01***	0.01***
	(0.00)	(0.00)
Exposure to news		
Television and radio		0.07***
		(0.01)
Newspaper reading		0.27***
		(0.02)
Constant	1.76***	1.88***
	(0.09)	(0.09)
R^2	0.155	0.151
Obs.	91,106	64,085

Note: Clustered standard errors in parentheses.
* $p < 0.05$. ** $p < 0.01$. *** $p < 0.001$.

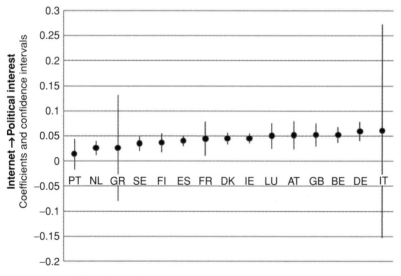

FIGURE 5.1. Effect of internet use on interest in politics by country. Control variables: education, gender, age, exposure to news on television and radio, newspaper reading. PT (Portugal), NL (Netherlands), GR (Greece), SE (Sweden), FI (Finland), ES (Spain), FR (France), DK (Denmark), IE (Ireland), LU (Luxemburg), AT (Austria), GB (Great Britain), BE (Belgium), DE (Germany), IT (Italy).

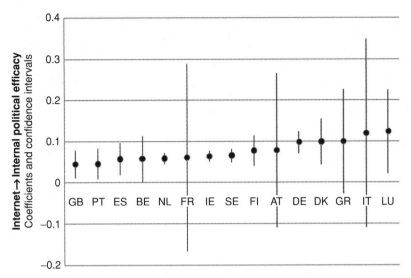

FIGURE 5.2. Effect of internet use on internal political efficacy by country. Control variables: education, gender, age, exposure to news on television and radio, newspaper reading. PT (Portugal), NL (Netherlands), GR (Greece), SE (Sweden), FI (Finland), ES (Spain), FR (France), DK (Denmark), IE (Ireland), LU (Luxemburg), AT (Austria), GB (Great Britain), BE (Belgium), DE (Germany), IT (Italy).

the effect of internet by country, showing greater differences across countries than in the case of interest in politics. This points to possible interactions of the effects of internet use with other contextual conditions. There are some nonsignificant coefficients: the internet does not seem to play a significant role in the development of internal political efficacy among the citizens of Belgium, France, Austria, Greece, and Italy.

5.4. Internet Use, Interest in Politics, and Internal Political Efficacy in Spain

Spain is a perfect case for testing the hypothesis that internet use affects political attitudes. Since Spain's transition to democracy in the late 1970s, Spanish citizens have shown persistent traits in their attitudinal profile: low public commitment, lack of political interest, low rates of political efficacy, (both internal and external), and other symptoms of political disaffection (Gunther, Montero, and Botella 2004; Martín 2005; Bonet, Martín, and Montero 2006). According to rational-culturalist theories, the behavior of political elites produces disaffection, whereas modernization theories point to economic and institutional development as explanatory factors for understanding this phenomenon. The arrival and spread of the internet may be a new factor affecting political attitudes and engagement. Spain belongs to the group of developed democracies that have still not reached the highest rates of internet adoption. Within its population are people who have quickly embraced the technology, people who do not want to use it, and people who cannot access it. In 2007 about half the population had access to the internet, according to the Spanish National Statistics Institute (see also the Introduction), which provides sufficient variation to test for internet effects on the user population. Furthermore, low levels of interest and efficacy render the detection of positive changes in political attitudes easier than in countries where these variables are already high.

To produce more robust conclusions about the relationship between internet use and political engagement for the Spanish case, we rely on both quantitative and qualitative evidence. We first use survey data from a face-to-face survey conducted in Spain in November 2007 ($N = 3,739$).[4] The dependent variables included in the quantitative analysis of the Spanish case were political interest and internal political efficacy. Internet use is measured according to experience and proficiency: years of internet use and internet abilities. We introduce the same controls as in the comparative analysis, as well as political activism. Details on the coding can be found in the Appendix.

The qualitative analysis complements survey evidence. We use the information provided by two focus groups that were conducted in the city of Zaragoza in fall 2008. Participants in both groups were people between twenty and forty years old who had secondary education but had not completed university education and who had similar educational and socioeconomic statuses. Political activists, such as members of political parties or civic organizations, were purposely excluded from both groups. One group was composed of frequent internet users (e.g., people who use the internet almost every day), whereas the members of the other group used the internet only rarely or never (less than once a week). The groups were asked about their opinions and feelings toward politicians, democracy, and politics in general. The discussions lasted for about one hour and were fully transcribed. The analysis of the textual information was initially inductive and aimed to identify common themes and categories. The common issues were organized so that a comparative analysis of the discourses on internet users and nonusers could be made.

5.4.1. *Interest in Politics*

More than 70 percent of Spaniards in our sample acknowledge that they are interested in politics a "little" or "not at all," whereas fewer than 7 percent are "very" interested. Table 5.3 and Figure 5.3 display the results of linear regression models that predict interest in politics with internet use and include appropriate controls.

Years of internet use do not seem to affect interest in politics. Internet abilities do, but the effect is not significant when controlling for political activity. This could be interpreted in two different ways. First, it is possible that some

---

[4] The survey was carried out by the Centro de Investigaciones Sociológicas (CIS study 2736) for the project Internet and Political Participation in Spain, funded by the Spanish Ministry of Science and Innovation (SEJ2007–60082). Data can be downloaded from http://www.cis.es.

TABLE 5.3. *Interest in Politics and Internet Use in Spain*

	Interest in Politics, *b* (S.E.)		
Years of internet use	0.00	0.00	0.00
	(0.00)	(0.00)	(0.00)
Index of internet abilities	0.01***	0.01***	0.01
	(0.00)	(0.00)	(0.00)
Male	0.07***	0.06***	0.07***
	(0.01)	(0.01)	(0.01)
Age	0.00***	0.00***	0.00***
	(0.00)	(0.00)	(0.00)
Education	0.20***	0.17***	0.13***
	(0.02)	(0.02)	(0.02)
Income (imputed values)	0.03***	0.02***	0.02***
	(0.00)	(0.00)	(0.00)
Exposure to news		−0.05***	−0.04***
Television and radio		(0.00)	(0.00)
Newspaper reading		−0.02***	−0.02***
		(0.00)	(0.00)
Index of political activity			0.05***
			(0.00)
Constant	−0.09**	0.14***	0.10**
	(0.03)	(0.04)	(0.04)
R^2	0.181	0.220	0.281
Obs.	3,695	3,685	3,545

* $p < 0.05$. ** $p < 0.01$. *** $p < 0.001$.

political activists have come to use the internet, motivated by its importance as a space for political activity. In that case, we would be facing a problem of reverse causality, and the positive link between internet abilities and political interest in the previous models would be misleading. A second possibility is

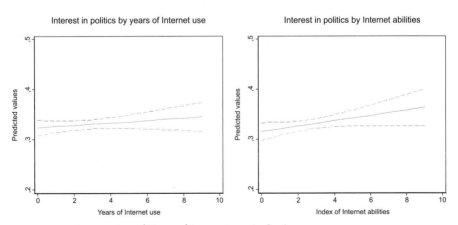

FIGURE 5.3. Interest in politics and internet use in Spain.

that those who have become more interested in politics because of their use of the internet have also become more active and engaged in politics. In that case, more political activity would be a consequence of increased internet use, which would be in favor of our theory. Without adequate longitudinal panel data available, we turn to our qualitative evidence.

The study of the focus groups points to the existence of relevant differences between the political attitudes of internet users and nonusers. Nonusers feel distant from representative politics and repeatedly insist on the issue of their feeling of alienation. They indicate a wide range of reasons for their pronounced disinterest. First, politics is perceived as irrelevant to their lives, even as nonstimulating and unpleasant. The background of their discourse is that it makes no sense to be interested in politics because it is an obscure and malicious sphere. According to one member of the nonusers group:

MAN: When politicians reach power, they all get corrupted in a way or in another. In the end, they all do the same thing [;] that is, they don't listen to those who have voted for them and they just share out the money and discuss among themselves. . . . When people are young, and they start thinking, and they are a little bit aware of the things that are happening, they would say: "I like this party or this person." But after a while, they don't even feel like listening to them on TV.

A second reason for the lack of interest reported by nonusers is that there is no clear difference among available political options. Repeatedly, they point out that all political parties are similar, and that politics is a sphere dominated by hypocrisy and by apparently intense but pointless debates. The real differences in the standpoints of the political parties, as visible in the daily political debate, are minimal. For the group of non non-internet users, fights among political parties resemble a theater performance, but parties do not represent and communicate substantively different policy positions:

WOMAN: They [the politicians] don't look for a solution, they only fight.
MAN: But when they agree on a solution it seems as if they had been life-long friends.
w: Yes, that's what I'm telling you, after the fight they go for a drink and to have dinner together.
m: I frequently think that they just perform a circus such as the ancient Romans who did that thing with the circus. When Caesar wanted to he organized lion fights. Politicians do exactly the same thing.

On the contrary, the group of internet users did not display those deep feelings of disinterest and disappointment. As with most Spaniards, they were not highly interested in politics, but they justified their lack of strong ties to politics with pragmatic and instrumental reasons: being interested in politics would not make much sense for them because people's opinion does not have a strong influence in the political world. However, group members reported that

TABLE 5.4. *Internal Political Efficacy and Internet Use in Spain*

	Internal Political Efficacy, b (S.E.)		
Years of internet use	0.01**	0.01**	0.01**
	(0.00)	(0.00)	(0.00)
Index of internet abilities	0.01***	0.01***	0.01*
	(0.00)	(0.00)	(0.00)
Male	0.08***	0.07***	0.08***
	(0.01)	(0.01)	(0.01)
Age	0.00***	0.00**	0.00**
	(0.00)	(0.00)	(0.00)
Education	0.23***	0.20***	0.18***
	(0.02)	(0.02)	(0.03)
Income (imputed values)	0.02***	0.02***	0.02***
	(0.01)	(0.01)	(0.01)
Exposure to news		−0.03***	−0.02***
Television and radio		(0.01)	(0.01)
Newspaper reading		−0.02***	−0.01**
		(0.00)	(0.00)
Index of political activity			0.03***
			(0.00)
Constant	0.10***	0.25***	0.22***
	(0.03)	(0.04)	(0.04)
R²	0.194	0.206	0.224
Obs.	3,596	3,586	3,451

* $p < 0.05$. ** $p < 0.01$. *** $p < 0.001$.

they had some general interest in public affairs. The reasons for their lack of engagement in politics were rather of a rational nature:

M: Most people are disappointed with politics.
M: Yes. I'm very young but I don't know a single case in which the opinion of the people really made a difference.

However, the members of this group are able to perceive some differences between the left and the right of the political spectrum. The ability to select between clear options makes the acts of voting and following political debates more meaningful.

5.4.2. Internal Political Efficacy
Table 5.4 displays the results of the regression models that predict internal political efficacy using the same explanatory variables as for interest in politics. According to these results, internet users feel more able to influence politics than nonusers, even after taking into account that users tend to have a higher socioeconomic status and are more politically active. Moving from the minimum to maximum levels of experience and abilities with internet use would

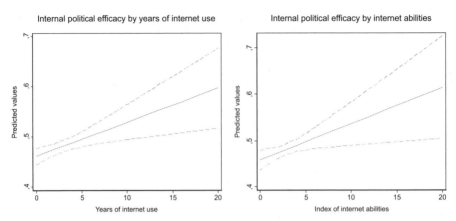

FIGURE 5.4. Internal political efficacy and internet use in Spain.

produce approximately a 10 percent increase in individuals' internal political efficacy. Figure 5.4 plots the predicted levels of internal political efficacy when moving from the maximum to the minimum of the two internet variables, setting all other variables to their means.

In line with the results of the quantitative analysis, the two focus groups show that internet users and nonusers differ markedly in their reported internal political efficacy. Nonusers feel very strongly that they are unable to have an influence on the political system. They report that they cannot understand properly what happens in the political world, which is characterized by its lack of transparency and its complexity. They feel easily overwhelmed by discussions on public issues, and thus avoid discussing or even thinking about political topics. As some explain:

w: I don't know much about politics. I'm not interested about this topic because when I hear them [the politicians] on television and so on, I don't understand much. . . .
m: And then they [the politicians] do what they want with you because when you get to discuss with them, they fool you. In the end you tell them that they are right but just because of boredom and tiredness, you let it go. . . .
m: I think that we don't even get to realize, not even realize, what they are telling us and what they want to tell us.

Nonusers insist on the idea that any difficulty in understanding what happens in the political world and what can be done to influence it is only partially because of their lack of interest. Politicians are also responsible for their apathetic attitudes because they frequently do not clearly communicate their ideas. Furthermore, politicians are unclear in their communication with the public on purpose, to keep people unaware of some relevant political issues.

m: With this issue of the economic crisis it is as if they spoke in Morse and if you can't speak Morse, you won't get anything of what they are saying.

When they want to be great they say "look at what we have done, and look at that" they speak extremely clear. It's as if you go to see the doctor and he speaks in a technical language. You don't get anything until he says: "Look, what you have is related to your heart." I think that with politicians it is the same. If they don't want people to understand the issue so that there aren't any protests, then they speak in Morse. And you say "Well, what have they said? I didn't get what they said, whether at the very end they will fix things or they won't."

Internet users have, on the contrary, higher levels of internal political efficacy. In some circumstances they can imagine themselves taking action with the aim of influencing the government, and they do not distrust their own ability to understand what is going on in the political world. The idea of internal political efficacy was not as frequently discussed in the conversation of internet users as in the group of nonusers, but it appears that users do have confidence in their abilities to understand the political world and eventually to try to influence it.

w: We [Spaniards] don't even take part in demonstration properly....
m: And why would we join a general strike?.... Yes, we can stop the country, but after that it's us who lose the most because we get fired.

5.5. Conclusion

In this chapter we have analyzed whether internet use has an impact on political attitudes such as interest in politics and internal political efficacy. Although the available data do not allow us to directly examine the causal mechanisms (something future research should do), we have suggested five arguments by which internet use could increase this attitudinal dimension of political involvement and thus enhance interest in politics and internal political efficacy: greater exposure to political stimuli, horizontality, interactivity, anonymity, and the feeling of belonging to an online community.

In general terms the analyses confirm our expectations. Both European and Spanish data reveal a small but significant, positive impact of internet use on these two political attitudes related to political engagement. The fact that internet use variables were consistently related to political attitudes in the expected direction in almost all countries and that the effect was significant in most of the EU15 countries gives robustness to our results. The results also suggest that the effect is stronger in the case of internal political efficacy than for interest in politics. Thus, if internet adoption can influence political involvement, it may do so largely through feelings of internal political efficacy. If the internet plays a role in citizens' self-perception of their ability to understand, act, or form opinions about political issues, this may contribute to perceptions of internal political efficacy.

These effects are, however, not homogeneous across countries, which suggests that there are interaction effects with contextual factors – cultural, institutional, and socioeconomic. Future research should thus also consider the specific way context conditions the extent to which internet use can reinforce attitudes of political engagement.

5.6. Appendix

5.6.1. *Variable Coding for the EU15 Analysis*
Age is measured in years.[5]

Education is measured in years of full-time education completed.

Exposure to news and current affairs on an average weekday broadcast either on television or radio and reading newspapers are measured on an eight-point scale ranging from 0 (no time at all) to 7 (more than three hours).

Frequency of internet use is measured on an eight-point scale from 0 (no access at home or work) to 7 (daily use).

Interest in politics is measured on a four-point scale coded from 0 to 3 (0 = not at all, 1 = hardly interested, 2 = quite interested, 3 = very interested).

Internal efficacy is an additive scale of two internal efficacy indicators. The first item pertains to how often the individual feels that politics are too complicated to understand what is going on. The possible answers were coded on a five point scale (never = 4, seldom = 3, occasionally = 2, regularly = 1, frequently = 0). The second item pertains to how difficult the individual thinks it is to make his or her mind up about political issues. The answers were coded from 0 to 4, where 0 = very difficult and 4 = very easy. The addition of both variables results in a nine-point scale of internal political efficacy (Cronbach's alpha = 0.627).

Male is a dummy variable.

5.6.2. *Variable Coding for the Spanish Analysis*
Age was measured in years.

Education was coded in four categories from less than no primary education (0) to primary education completed (0.33), secondary completed (0.67), and university degree (1).

Exposure to news on TV television or radio and *frequency of press consumption* were measured on a five-point scale (4 = every day, 3 = 3–4 days a week, 2 = 1–2 days a week, 1 = less frequently, and 0 = never).

Income was measured in ten categories ranging from 300 euros of household total income per month (1) to more than 6,000 euros (10). Missing cases are imputed.

---

[5] All variables in the Appendix are in alphabetical order.

Internal political efficacy was measured on a five-point Likert scale in response to the sentence "Generally politics is so complicated that people as me cannot understand what it is going on." Responses were recoded to range from 0 to 1 (0 = strongly agree, 0.25 = agree, 0.5 = neither agree nor disagree, 0.75 = disagree, 1 = strongly disagree).

Internet abilities is an additive scale of a battery of nine different online activities, such as using e-mail, shopping, searching for information, telephoning, or maintaining a blog or website. People who are not users are coded as having no abilities (0), and for users, positive answers to each activity are aggregated in an index (ranking ranging from 0 to 9). This index is similar to the one proposed by Krueger (2002), which showed considerable construct reliability. The index's Cronbach's alpha is 0.616. We assume that these variables are not measuring online political activities or online political participation. The correlation with other online political activities is significant, but the coefficients are very low (less than 0.1), which indicates that they are not alike.

Male is a dummy variable.

Political activism was measured with an additive scale. Respondents were asked whether they had participated in nine political activities (e.g., attending a demonstration, boycotting products, signing petitions) in the previous twelve months. Those who had were coded as 1. The variable political activity is the sum of the participation score in any of these activities. It ranges from 0 to 9 and aims at measuring respondents' degree of political activity.

Political interest was a four-point scale recoded to range from 0 to 1 (not at all, little, quite, and very interested).

Years of internet use was measured as the number of years of regular internet use.

6

Digital Media and Offline Political Participation in Spain

Marta Cantijoch

6.1. Introduction

The literature on the impact of digital media use on political behavior has debated whether the internet has a positive or a negative effect on citizens' political engagement. Among those defending a positive effect, the reinforcement hypothesis argues that digital media offer new opportunities for those who were already participating before securing their access to the internet (Hill and Hughes 1998; Norris 2000; Weber, Loumakis, and Bergman 2003; Curtice and Norris 2004). In contrast, the mobilization hypothesis supports the idea that digital media will contribute to a more participative society by attracting previously less active members of the public (DelliCarpini 2000; Ward, Gibson, and Lusoli 2003; Tolbert and McNeal 2003; Stanley and Weare 2004).

This chapter addresses this question by taking into account the multidimensional character of political participation. Internet use may have an impact on specific forms of political participation and not on others. We analyze political participation, distinguishing between representational and extrarepresentational activities (Teorell, Torcal, and Montero 2007). The representational mode includes formal activities conducted in the frame of institutional rules and procedures typical of representative democracy (e.g., party-oriented activities, voting, contacting an official), whereas extrarepresentational conduct includes informal activities such as protest and newer forms of political consumerism. Although the former have decreased in recent decades across most industrial countries, the latter are increasing.

At the same time, different studies have identified a growing amount of public discontent with the mechanisms and institutions of representative democracy (Dalton and Wattenberg 2000; Pharr and Putnam 2000; Dalton 2002; Norris 1999a). Political dissatisfaction may be the motivation for decreasing levels of representational activities in some sectors of the public. Meanwhile, critical but still involved citizens are not willing to renounce their capacity of intervention in the political sphere, and they tend to resort to contentious participatory activities to voice their demands.

This changing nature of citizen politics has attracted the attention of political scientists, as it can be argued that questioning the institutional mechanisms threatens the democratic system. However, it can also be argued that these transformations foster political engagement of citizens in a way that challenges institutional elites, putting pressure on the system to meet their demands. The growing diffusion of the internet is a phenomenon to be considered as a factor contributing to this transformation.

In this chapter it is argued that the increase in the amount of information available on the internet allows for escape from the mainstream discourses and the agenda setting established by traditional elites. A greater diversity of information is available, and involved citizens will access it voluntarily or through unplanned exposures. This exposure to more diverse discourses would contribute to the impulse of extrarepresentational modes of participation. Furthermore, we expect this phenomenon to affect those individuals who are not experiencing discontent and dissatisfaction but who remain loyal to the formal institutional rules and procedures.

Section 2 of the chapter discusses the literature dealing with the relationship among participatory repertoires, political attitudes, and technology use. In addition, this section also discusses the role of digital media in the production of an information-saturated political environment and the consequences this has for political participation. Section 3 describes the data and the methods used. Section 4 includes the analyses of the consequences of internet use for different modes of participation and attitudinal profiles in Spain. Finally, the concluding section discusses the results.

6.2. Political Participation, Political Attitudes, and Internet Use

6.2.1. The Multidimensionality of Political Participation

Verba and Nie (1972) showed that political participation is multidimensional and that distinct modes of participation are often engaged in by different profiles of participants. These authors distinguished four modes of participation: turnout, campaign activities, communal activities, and parochial participation (Verba and Nie 1972; Verba, Nie, and Kim 1978). Parallel to these developments, several authors conducted the first analyses on political protest and established a typology that has been widely used in the past decades: the distinction between conventional and unconventional political participation (Marsh 1977; Marsh and Kaase 1979). Although the activities analyzed by Verba and colleagues belong to the first group, unconventional participation refers to unorthodox actions such as attending a demonstration or a protest political meeting, boycotting products, and taking part in a strike or in violent activities.

Although in recent years protest actions have become less rare and exceptional (Parry, Moyser, and Day 1992; Verba, Schlozman, and Brady 1995; Dalton 2002; Norris 2002; Torcal, Montero, and Teorell 2006; Rucht 2007), these activities still have particular attributes differentiating them from conventional participation. An interesting approach to this distinction is the one focusing on the channel employed to carry out the action, differentiating between representational and extrarepresentational forms of participation (Teorell et al. 2007). This distinction is based on whether the activity is executed within formal democratic institutions or outside them. Some of the conducts previously named as conventional are activities developed in the framework established by the institutions of the state (e.g., political parties, government institutions). This means that the activities not only address a message to these actors but also follow procedural rules determined and even controlled by them: the clearest examples are voting or campaign and party activities.

Conversely, extrarepresentational actions are activities in which, even though participants can equally be trying to reach an institutional agent as the target of a demand, the action is realized outside the formal institutional framework.[1] Certainly, lawful protest actions must observe legal regulations (e.g., in general, permission needs to be requested to hold a demonstration). But when conducting these activities, the participant keeps control over the ability of initiating the action, shaping its form and determining its issue content. In this sense, Dalton (2002, 60) refers to these as "citizen-initiated activities."

This distinction enables us to highlight important trends in political participation in advanced industrialized democracies. In the past decades, several studies have detected a decline in electoral and representational participation in most industrial countries (Rosenstone and Hansen 1993; Verba et al. 1995; Whiteley and Seyd 1998; Blais 2000; Gray and Caul 2000; Scarrow 2007) concomitantly with a rise in protest and other forms of extrarepresentational participation. Thus, a change in participatory repertoires is taking place (Inglehart 1990; Topf 1995; Tarrow 2000; Dalton 2002; Norris 2002; Inglehart and Catterberg 2003; Stolle and Hooghe 2004; Stolle and Micheletti 2005; Zukin et al. 2006; Rucht 2007).

One of the explanations the literature has provided for this transformation of repertoires is related to the attitudinal changes detected in Western democracies. In the past decades, increasing dissatisfaction toward the institutions of representative democracy has been found (Norris 1999a; Dalton and Wattenberg 2000; Pharr and Putnam 2000; Dalton 2004). Some evidence suggests that this reflects discontent with the ability of governments to meet demands in bureaucratic and hierarchical systems (Dalton 2000).

However, negative evaluations and low trust in public institutions do not always result in apathy and disaffection. In fact, as Montero, Gunther, and Torcal (1997) point out, political disaffection is different from discontent. On the one hand, disaffection entails the development of feelings of powerlessness, confusion with respect to politics, and estrangement from the political system (Torcal and Montero 2006). Thus, disaffected citizens are both less psychologically engaged in politics (low levels of interest in politics or internal political

---

[1] A different distinction would be whether the targets are state or nonstate agents (Norris 2003; Stolle and Micheletti 2005; Torcal et al. 2006).

TABLE 6.1. *Description of Three Attitudinal Profiles and Their Expected Political Behavior According to the Literature*

Profile	Attitudinal Characteristics	Expected Behavior
Disaffected	Low political involvement (low interest in politics and low internal efficacy) Dissatisfaction with the political system (low trust in formal institutions and low external efficacy) Low feelings of either engagement or citizen duty	Inactive Lower proclivity to engage in any mode
Critical	High political involvement (high interest and internal efficacy) Dissatisfaction with the political system (low trust in formal institutions and low external efficacy) Conceptions of citizenship more toward engagement	Active Greater proclivity to engage in extrarepresentational modes
Institutional	High political involvement (high interest and internal efficacy) Low dissatisfaction with the political system (high trust in institutions and external efficacy) Conceptions of citizenship more toward citizen duty	Active Greater proclivity to engage in representational modes

efficacy) and dissatisfied with the political system, thereby evincing low levels of trust in institutions or external efficacy. Accordingly, the expected behavior of this profile of individuals is inactivity, in that they refrain from participatory actions of any kind.

On the other hand, for another segment of the citizenry, a lack of confidence in political institutions and elites can actually foster the search for forms of participation outside their domain. These "critical" citizens remain politically involved, as they do not want to give up their right to do so in spite of (or even because of) their lack of confidence in traditional representative institutions (Norris 2002; Dalton 2004). As opposed to disaffected citizens, they do not lack political efficacy or interest in politics, among other things, because their civic and political involvement remains high (Dalton 2008). However, contrary to other engaged individuals who define their participation in the confines of formal institutions, the critical profile has greater proclivity for extrarepresentational forms of participation to voice their demands (Dalton 2002).

We can thus derive three attitudinal profiles and their expected forms of participation: disaffected, critical citizens, and institutional citizens (or citizens who participate in ways structured by formal institutions). Table 6.1 describes these profiles.

6.2.2. The Impact of the Internet on Political Participation:
Attitudinal Profiles and Political Information

How does digital media use influence political participation? Our argument here is twofold: First, internet use changes the access to political information. Second, the effect of internet use (and of exposure to online political information) depends on the attitudinal profiles.

The internet increases the amount of political information available and reduces information access costs (Bimber 2001). Citizens' access to information and their ability to retransmit it are essential elements to many conceptions of citizenship. On the one hand, the strategic communication of information is used by political actors to frame political events and shape citizen perceptions (Mulder 1999). On the other hand, access to political information facilitates the development of political sophistication as individuals become informed about the political system (Luskin 1990). Moreover, access to political information has consequences for knowledge as a cognitive precursor to participation. As Delli Carpini and Keeter (1997, 155) note, "Less informed segments of the public – in part because of their lack of political knowledge – are less able to discern their political interests, less likely to participate in politics, and, most important, less likely to connect their political interests effectively to their political participation." Therefore, we expect that higher levels of exposure to political information should promote greater levels of political sophistication and perceptions of efficacy, which in turn can motivate political participation.

The reinforcement hypothesis contends that political information seeking is mainly limited to segments of the population that are already politically interested and active (Hill and Hughes 1998; Norris 2001; Bimber 2003). First, it is argued that exposure to information is not passive, and therefore prior motivation to look for political information is needed. Internet use is an individual activity requiring more engagement and attention than, for example, watching television (Nie and Erbring 2002). This means that political contents can more easily be avoided. In fact, the search for political information is not the most common online activity, at least in advanced democracies. Most people use the internet for activities without any explicit political relation, such as social communication, work, and entertainment.[2]

Use of nonpolitical sites, the reinforcement thesis contends, does not promote political engagement (Shah, Kwak, and Holbert 2001). Accordingly, only access to political content on the internet would foster political participation. If the internet enables greater selectivity and control over information

---

[2] In Spain, 95.3 percent of internet users search for general information (e.g., work, study, health, travel), 84.8 percent for sending or receiving e-mails, and 75.7 percent for downloading files (e.g., documents, music, video, software). Only 45.2 percent use the internet to search for political information, and 9.6 percent have consulted the web page of a political party or candidate (Anduiza et al. 2010). For data on nonpolitical uses of the internet in authoritarian regimes, see Chapter 11.

exposure, then internet use should reinforce the political knowledge gap between those already politically engaged and those who are politically disinterested, promoting participation among engaged population segments while leaving the disinterested unaffected (Delli Carpini and Keeter 2002; Bonfadelli 2002; Weber et al. 2003; Prior 2005, 2007).

Second, the reliability of the information available on the internet is often doubtful (Davis 1999; Noveck 2000; Clément 2002). Although the internet's archives of information and search mechanisms may facilitate information acquisition, digital media lack the vetting mechanisms traditionally associated with broadcast media. Thus, even when attention to political contents has been established, users must deal with the costs associated with discerning the reliability of online information, which requires additional cognitive effort to assess content (Eveland and Dunwoody 2000). In addition, the abundance of information online – far from being a democratic virtue – can exacerbate this problem by causing information overload. It can overwhelm the public's ability to discriminate, evaluate, and interpret the information available online (Noveck 2000; Clément 2002; Bimber 2003; Karakaya 2005). On the whole, the reinforcement hypothesis establishes that a radical transformation of current patterns should not be expected.

On the other hand, mobilization theories argue that the new features associated with digital media foster an increase in political participation by engaging previously inactive members of the public (Delli Carpini 2000; Tolbert and McNeal 2003; Ward et al. 2003; Stanley and Weare 2004). Digital media rely more on horizontal interpersonal exchanges rather than on linear and hierarchical modes of information transmission (Yildiz 2002; Ward and Vedel 2006). Besides, they are not just a tool for retrieving information; they also allow the user to become an information provider through contact and discussions with other users (Flanagin and Metzger 2001), thus enabling an exponential spread of information.

E-mails from friends and participation in online social networking sites, chats, and forums can result in unsolicited and unplanned exposures to political information for even nonpolitically interested users. Certain online behaviors, though not explicitly political, can become an involuntary or unplanned learning process (Tewksbury, Weaver, and Maddex 2001), which can motivate political participation (Gibson, Lusoli, and Ward 2005).

But mobilization can occur among the already politically interested and active, as digital media can also transform participatory practices. In digital environments, citizens can access a greater diversity of information sources. Although establishing its validity complicates the information-vetting process, it also weakens the ability of gatekeepers to establish or control the political agenda (Mossberger, Tolbert, and McNeal 2008; Tewksbury and Rittenberg 2009). Instead, "the new media environment with its multiple points of access and more continuous news cycle has increased the opportunities for the less mainstream individuals and groups to influence public discourse" (Williams and Delli Carpini 2004, 1225). When online, users can avoid the mainstream channels of information provision, explore interests not available in traditional media, and establish communications with nonstate actors and other individual citizens (Althaus and Tewksbury 2000; Bimber 2001).

Following the logic of the reinforcement theory, it can be argued that, to prevent cognitive dissonance, citizens will search for information only in accordance with their previous opinions. Then, even when individuals surf the internet to actively look for political information (when able to select and process that information), they will pay attention only to the sources and contents that strengthen their position, thus polarizing their views and reinforcing their previous behavior (Davis 1999; Noveck 2000; Sunstein 2007). This means that a reinforcement effect is expected among individuals not only regarding their proclivity to look for information but also regarding their previous attitudes and opinions about the political system.

Dissatisfied citizens can find in digital media an alternative entry into the conventional political sphere where the institutional discourse prevails. If they perceive a discrepancy between their views and the mainstream discourse – mostly supplied by conventional media – this media dissociation will promote their aim to search for alternative information on the digital environment. In turn, this use of the internet will foster their engagement in extrarepresentational forms of participation (Hwang et al. 2006). Thus, the critical citizens would strengthen their opinions, and their likelihood to be active in extrarepresentational modes of participation would increase.

Those supporting formal institutions would use the new media to pursue previous habits. Access to political information in digital media would constitute an extension of exposure to traditional media by means of searching for online counterparts (Norris 1999a; Karakaya 2005). Therefore, exposure to mainstream discourses prevails and the effects on greater proclivity to take part in representational modes of participation are reinforced as well.

However, the possibility of accessing more diverse information will affect all profiles of previously involved individuals, including the institutional one. These citizens will also be exposed to the new diversity of discourses, including more critical viewpoints, because they are involved in politics. Internet use for gathering information is additive to other media use (Bimber 2003; Shah et al. 2005). Not perceiving a discrepancy with the mainstream discourse does not mean that these individuals will not take advantage of the information available on the internet to gain political knowledge and fulfill what they consider a responsibility: to be informed. This is particularly true for individuals with high levels of cognitive skills, as previous evidence has shown that sophisticated individuals are more attentive to reasoned arguments (Luskin 1990). As a consequence, internet users "have greater overall exposure to political arguments, including those that challenge their candidate preferences and policy positions" (Mossberger et al. 2008, 52).

Then, given the increase in opportunities to avoid gatekeepers, together with the possibility of being involuntarily exposed to political information, even those who are not mistrustful of mainstream institutional discourses will

TABLE 6.2. *Reconceptualization of the Positive Effects of Digital Media According to Previous Attitudinal Profiles*

Attitudinal Profile	Disaffected	Critical	Institutional
Previous participatory proclivity	Lower engagement in any mode	Higher engagement in extrarepresentational participation	Higher engagement in representational participation
New conceptualization of the effects of digital media	Mobilization	Reinforcement	Mobilization

be exposed in the digital environment to more critical views and will be able to incorporate these arguments into their evaluation of the political process and capture at least some nuances regarding their previous opinions. Online access to more diverse information, then, could contribute to the attitudinal change exposed in the previous section, and institutional individuals would be attracted to the extrarepresentational modes of participation. In that case, we could be talking about a mobilizing process toward specific forms of participation.

To sum up, our aim in this chapter is to address the general research question of the impact of digital media on political participation, taking into account that we are dealing with a multidimensional phenomenon. As such, our main hypothesis not only specifies an expectation regarding a positive effect of internet use but also determines a distinction according to different modes of participation. The hypothesis can be stated as follows:

H1: Internet use has a positive effect on the extrarepresentational modes of political participation, but not necessarily on voting or on other representational modes of participation.

If this first hypothesis is validated, and given that the literature on the impacts of digital media has not paid attention to distinguishing different modes of participation, we need to review the conceptualizations of these effects, as shown in Table 6.2. Critical citizens were already prone to take part in extrarepresentational forms of participation (e.g., protest activities). If we find evidence supporting that their use of digital media has a positive impact on this form of participation, we can consider it a reinforcement effect. On the contrary, for institutional individuals whose previous participatory proclivity was toward representational modes of participation, a positive effect on extrarepresentational modes should be categorized as a mobilization process. Finally, disaffected citizens could be mobilized toward the extrarepresentational mode of participation overcoming their expected low levels of involvement.

Finally, we need to disentangle which are the specific facets of digital media that enhance political participation (Bimber 2000; Karakaya 2005). We have focused here on the digital media's ability to supply more diverse information as one of the traits that can foster participation in extrarepresentational activities. Accordingly, our second hypothesis is as follows:

H2: Exposure to political information online has positive effects on the likelihood of engaging in extrarepresentational activities, both through intended information gathering and through unintended exposure.

6.3. Data and Variable Operationalization

To test these hypotheses, we analyze Spanish data. Political participation rates in Spain are among the lowest in Europe (Torcal et al. 2006; Ferrer 2005). Nevertheless, levels of extrarepresentational participation are high and have increased over the past twenty years, especially in activities like taking part in demonstrations or strikes and signing petitions (Morales 2003). If our hypotheses are verified, this trend could be reinforced by the extent of internet use that is taking place in this country. In 2007, 55 percent of the Spanish population eighteen or older had used the internet in the previous three months (Anduiza, Gallego, and Cantijoch 2010). The rate of internet diffusion has grown by 440 percent since 2000; only the new eastern members of the European Union have higher growth rates of internet diffusion (Internet World Stats 2010).

We use data collected from a survey conducted in November 2007. The survey sampled 3,700 respondents representative of the Spanish population, with an oversample of eighteen- to forty-year-olds, among whom there are notably higher levels of internet adoption. The questionnaire includes variables measuring a wide range of political attitudes and behaviors. It also includes several batteries of questions about internet access and use.[3]

Regarding the dependent variables, we used an exploratory factor analysis of nine items a respondent may have engaged in to identify the dimensions of participatory activities. The results of the analysis are presented in Table 6.3.

We obtain three factors corresponding to three dimensions of political participation outlined in the literature (Teorell et al. 2007). The first factor represents political consumerism, as conceptualized by Stolle and Micheletti (2005). The second factor corresponds to political protest activities. These two categories reference extrarepresentational forms of participation. Finally, the third factor groups the two forms of participation most closely tied to interactions with formal political authorities, such as attending a political meeting and contacting political officials. We add a fourth variable to account for turnout in the previous general election. Although this is clearly a form of representational political participation, it is often treated separately (Verba and Nie 1972; Verba et al. 1978; Parry et al. 1992). Four dependent variables have been constructed to account for whether the individual has engaged in each type of

---

[3] The survey was carried out by the Centro de Investigaciones Sociológicas (CIS Study 2736) in the context of the project Internet and Political Participation in Spain, funded by the Spanish Ministry of Science and Innovation (SEJ2007–60082). The survey can be downloaded at http://www.cis.es.

TABLE 6.3. *Factor Analysis of Political Participation Activities*

	Factor		
	1	2	3
Buycott	0.838	0.057	0.049
Boycott	0.805	0.105	0.040
Donation	0.597	0.023	0.228
Strike	0.037	0.736	0.019
Demonstration	0.212	0.691	0.174
Illegal protest	−0.041	0.617	0.098
Petition	0.432	0.454	0.124
Contact politicians	0.164	0.062	0.811
Attend political meeting	0.092	0.216	0.795

Note: Principal components analysis, Varimax rotation; KMO: 0.752.

participation: whether he or she voted and whether he or she engaged in at least one or none of the activities included in each of the three groups of items defined by the factor analysis. As these are dummy variables, we ran binary logistic regressions.

Regarding the main explanatory variables, we first consider the effect of frequency of internet use. We assume that more frequent use of the internet is associated with engaging in a greater number of activities, including those involving access to political information. Then we introduce the distinction between intentional and accidental information exposure. Voluntary exposure to political information is measured through an item on active search. The propensity to be involuntarily exposed to political information is based on an index including uses of the internet to establish contacts and interpersonal exchanges (receiving e-mails, taking part in chats and forums, and keeping a personal web page or blog) and to surf the web without a specific aim.

Regarding attitudinal variables, we distinguish among three kinds of indicators. First, we consider indicators of psychological involvement (following Verba et al. 1995; Martín and van Deth 2007), such as interest in politics and internal political efficacy. Second, we include indicators measuring the degree of satisfaction with the political system (Montero et al. 1997; Zmerli, Newton, and Montero 2007), including external political efficacy and confidence in political institutions (e.g., political parties, local and central government). Third, we consider indicators of different conceptions of citizenship, typically found in the literature (duty based or engaged; Dalton 2008). We also include the standard sociodemographic controls: gender, age, education, and income (see the Appendix for coding details).

6.4. Internet Use and Offline Participation in Spain

Table 6.4 shows the analyses conducted to test the explanatory capacity of being a more frequent internet user on the probability of carrying out each

TABLE 6.4. *Predicting Representational Participation, Extrarepresentational Participation (protest and consumerism), and Turnout*

	Representational Participation		Voting		Protest		Consumerism	
	Coef.	s.e.	Coef.	s.e.	Coef.	s.e.	Coef.	s.e.
Gender (female)	−0.128	0.112	0.126	0.110	0.386**	0.090	0.543**	0.085
Age	−0.006	0.004	0.172**	0.017	−0.014**	0.003	0.005	0.003
Age2	—	—	−0.001**	0.000	—	—	—	—
Education	−0.363	0.283	0.825**	0.306	0.502*	0.230	0.896**	0.213
Income	0.811*	0.375	0.953*	0.378	−0.001	0.302	0.561*	0.284
Interest in politics	1.936**	0.223	0.610**	0.230	1.600**	0.179	1.457**	0.170
Internal efficacy	0.999**	0.283	0.572*	0.274	0.622**	0.223	0.667**	0.208
Trust in institutions	−0.093	0.315	0.744*	0.295	−0.815**	0.249	−0.698**	0.231
External efficacy	0.301	0.246	0.151	0.264	0.488**	0.203	−0.123	0.194
Duty citizenship	1.865**	0.387	2.585**	0.322	0.348	0.281	0.268	0.265
Engaged citizenship	−0.685	0.368	−0.586	0.339	0.579*	0.290	0.762**	0.272
Freq. of internet use	0.196	0.166	0.016	0.163	0.459**	0.129	0.458**	0.121
Constant	−3.999**	0.424	−6.470**	0.514	−2.257**	0.325	−3.415**	0.312
Nagelkerke R²	0.165		0.247		0.181		0.172	
N	2824		2799		2797		2826	

$* p < 0.05$. $** p < 0.01$.

of the four modes of participation considered: representational participation, voting, protest, and consumerism.

The first model in Table 6.4 predicts the representational mode of participation. Our main explanatory variable, frequency of internet use, has a positive but nonsignificant effect. Thus, we cannot conclude that, all other variables held constant, using the internet more frequently increases the likelihood of taking part in representational forms of participation. The analysis also shows that there is a positive and significant relationship between interest in politics and representational participation, after controlling for the other variables included in the model. We observe the same relationship regarding internal political efficacy. On the contrary, none of the two indicators of system perception (confidence in formal institutions and external political efficacy) predict this form of participation. A duty-based conception of citizenship increases the probability of taking part in representational activities, but an engaged conception of good citizenship has no significant effect. The results for voting, in the second model, are pretty much the same.

In the third and fourth models, the same variables are used to predict participation in protest actions and political consumerism. Frequency of internet use increases the probability of taking part in protest actions and in consumption-based activities, and this relationship is significant after controlling for other predictors.

Interest in politics and internal efficacy have both positive and significant impacts on these forms of participation. Confidence in institutions reduces the likelihood of protesting, whereas an engaged conception of citizenship increases both protest and consumerism.

Consequently, and assuming that the relationship is not endogenous, we find support for a mobilization effect from internet use in the Spanish case as far as protest and political consumerism are concerned, but not for voting or representational activities, as our first hypothesis stated.

A second aim of this chapter was to test whether this process could be affecting citizens differently according to their attitudinal profiles. The results show that, for all the individuals in the sample, the more frequently they use the internet, the more likely they are to be active in extrarepresentational forms of participation. Nevertheless, this conclusion does not deny the possibility of the internet fostering extrarepresentational repertoires of action in different degrees for specific groups of citizens according to their attitudinal characteristics. If the effect of internet use is much stronger among critical citizens, who are already expected to be attracted to repertoires not controlled by elites, we could consider this phenomenon a reinforcement process. On the contrary, if institutional individuals are similarly increasing their likelihood of engaging in extrarepresentational activities, it would be a mobilization process toward this type of participation.

To illustrate this idea, Figures 6.1 and 6.2 show the predicted probabilities (calculated from the previous models) of taking part in each of the extrarepresentational forms of participation at different levels of frequency of internet

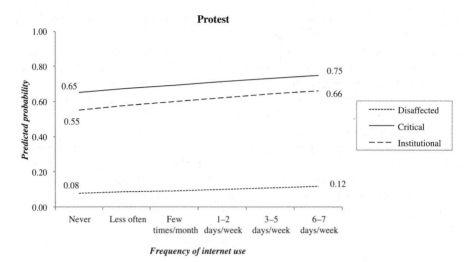

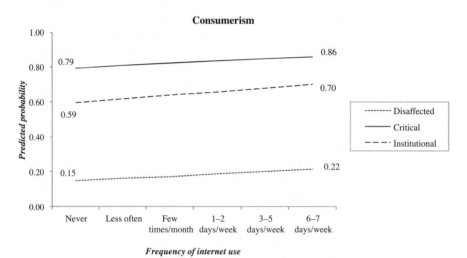

FIGURES 6.1 AND 6.2. Predicted probabilities of taking part in a protest or a consumerism activity as a function of internet use for three attitudinal profiles. *Note:* Probabilities estimated from models in Table 6.4.

use for the three specific profiles of individuals presented earlier (details on the values given for the estimation are provided in the Appendix).

Figures 6.1 and 6.2 show that the predicted probabilities for political consumerism are higher than for protesting, for all profiles. This is probably due to the lower costs associated with these consumerism actions (especially in the case of boycotting products) as compared with protest. The figures also show some differences across the profiles that we anticipated from the literature: in general, critical citizens are the most likely to engage in protest and consumerism activities. The institutional profile is also likely to become active but at lower levels. Disaffected individuals show low levels of likelihood to engage in these type of activities.

The effect of internet use is slight in the case of the disaffected (only 6 percent in consumerism and 4 percent in protest). In contrast, both for the institutionally centered and the critical profiles, the likelihood of participating in protest or consumerism increases about ten points when moving from the lowest level of frequency of internet use (never) toward the highest (six or seven days a week). The predicted probability of participating in protest actions for the most frequent internet users among critical citizens is 75 percent, ten points higher than for nonusers. Although this citizen profile was expected to be more likely to participate in extrarepresentational activities regardless of the level of internet use, the results show that internet use also makes a difference. Thus, there is a process of reinforcement of previous behaviors among critical individuals due to a frequent use of the internet.

Most interesting, this effect is similar for the institutional profile. We observe similar increases in their predicted probability of participating in protest and consumerism when the frequency of internet use rises. Although this profile is less active in this type of participation in general, the changes observed due to an increase in the frequency of internet use are similar or even greater than the ones observed for the critical profile. What is more, the likelihood of protesting for institutional citizens who use the internet on a daily basis (66 percent) is greater than the probability of protesting of critical citizens who never use the internet (65 percent). As a consequence, these analyses show that there is also a mobilization process toward protest and consumerism, which affects individuals who were already more likely to be active in representational modes of participating according to their attitudinal profile.

We have also argued that in an environment richer in diversity of information like the internet, citizens would be more exposed to diversity of opinions. This takes place either by actively searching for information or through by-product learning or accidental exposure to information. By analyzing specific online mechanisms through which the mobilization effect occurs, we are better able to allay concerns that the internet mobilization effects are endogenous. Table 6.5 shows the analyses conducted following the same methodology as in Table 6.4 to predict political protest and consumerism, substituting the variable of frequency of internet use with two indicators accounting for different kinds of online information exposure: the active search for political information and a propensity for unplanned exposure to political information.

The results show interesting effects when incorporating different uses of the internet to the analyses. Our proxy for unplanned political information exposure increases the likelihood of taking part in protest activities. However, the active search for online political information does not increase one's likelihood to protest. In the consumerism model, we obtain positive and significant effects for both variables. Holding all other variables constant, searching for information online voluntarily increases the probability of engaging in

TABLE 6.5. *Predicting Protest and Consumerism*

	Protest		Consumerism	
	Coef.	s.e.	Coef.	s.e.
Gender (female)	0.400**	0.091	0.558**	0.086
Age	−0.013**	0.003	0.008*	0.003
Education	0.600**	0.229	0.927**	0.212
Income	−0.100	0.301	0.557	0.285
Interest in politics	1.566**	0.185	1.368**	0.175
Internal efficacy	0.608**	0.225	0.604**	0.211
Confidence in institutions	−0.853**	0.251	−0.672**	0.233
External efficacy	0.541**	0.205	−0.185	0.197
Duty citizenship	0.307	0.283	0.221	0.268
Engaged citizenship	0.551	0.291	0.783**	0.274
Voluntary search of political inf. online	0.121	0.151	0.488**	0.154
Probability of involuntary exposure to political information online	0.631**	0.176	0.712**	0.171
Constant	−2.262**	0.332	−3.146**	0.321
Nagelkerke R²	0.183		0.187	
N	2771		2800	

* $p < 0.05$. ** $p < 0.01$.

consumption-based activities, and so does having a greater proclivity to be involuntarily exposed. Independent of debates over information compartmentalization and selective exposure, this evidence shows that accidental or unplanned learning, when it does occur, can have significant effects on one's propensity for extrarepresentational participation. Our second hypothesis is thus partially confirmed.

Figures 6.3 and 6.4 show the predicted probabilities calculated from these models for the three attitudinal profiles. On this occasion, we have estimated the probabilities of participating in protests and consumption-based activities at the minimum and maximum levels of exposure to political information (voluntarily or not).

We observe that a mobilization process takes place for the three groups when they actively look for political information on the internet and conduct the greatest amount of online activities involving a propensity to be involuntarily exposed. However, the effects differ depending on the attitudinal profile of individuals. The results show that the change in the predicted probabilities of participating is greater among institution-centered citizens both in protest and in consumerism. Also, as a result of a maximum exposure to political information from digital media, their predicted probability of participating in the two extrarepresentational activities is greater than for critical citizens with minimal exposure. And we can also see that the mobilizing effect is considerable

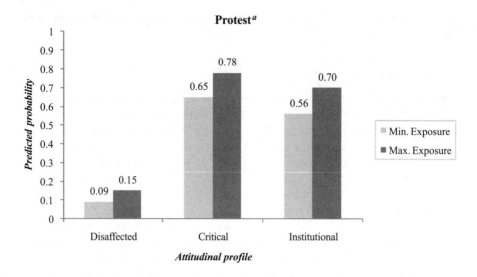

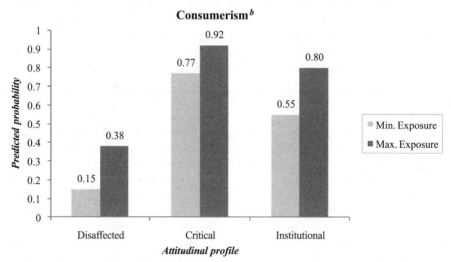

FIGURES 6.3 AND 6.4. Predicted probabilities of taking part in protest and consumerism activities as a function of exposure to political information on the internet. *Note:* Probabilities calculated from models shown in Table 6.5.

[a] Probability of involuntary exposure to political information online at the minimum and maximum levels. All other variables at the levels presented in the Appendix. We opted to leave "voluntary search of information online," which was not significant, at its mean.

[b] Voluntary search for information online and probability of involuntary exposure to political information online at the minimum and maximum levels. All other variables at the levels presented in the Appendix.

for disaffected citizens regarding their likelihood to be active in consumption-based participation.

6.5. Conclusion

The analyses conducted to test the impact of internet use on political participation find support for the mobilization thesis in Spain as far as extrarepresentational participation is concerned. We raised two hypotheses – that internet use would increase the likelihood of extrarepresentational forms of political participation but not representational forms and that online political information, independent of its source, would increase the likelihood of extrarepresentational participation. Using the internet more frequently increases the likelihood of being active in political protest and consumerism. This mobilizing process can be explained by the effects of searching for political information on the internet and engaging in online interpersonal exchanges or surfing the internet with no specific purpose. Our findings also reveal that the internet use effect exists among critical citizens, who are already expected to be attracted to repertoires not controlled by elites or political authorities. We have categorized this relationship as a reinforcement process of the preexisting proclivity to engage in extrarepresentational modes of participation. But we have also found that institution-centered citizens exhibit a similar response. The effects for disaffected citizens were positive but almost imperceptible. Then, our conclusion is that the reinforcement (for critical citizens) and mobilization (for institutional citizens) hypotheses are both verified. They are not exclusive but complementary.

It could be argued that these findings do not necessarily support the existence of a mobilization effect among institutional citizens, as these individuals were already involved in politics. Indeed, the evidence provided by our analyses suggests that we should move away from the simple dichotomous debate between reinforcement and mobilization. Citizens are not simply divided into two categories according to their previous levels of involvement and engagement (active versus inactive). We need to consider a more differentiated approach to analyze the effects of digital media in a way that properly takes into account the complex links that exist between different attitudinal profiles and engagement in distinct modes of participation. Applying this nuanced approach to the Spanish case, we have found that a mobilization process is also taking place among previously engaged individuals. The implications of these findings are relevant because they suggest that digital media might be a key factor contributing to a broader process of transformation of citizen politics toward a more critical style of engagement.

A recent example of this trend can be found in the protest movement that arose in Spain in spring 2011. The 15M movement, also called the Indignados, emerged as a series of (ongoing) protests originated, coordinated, and mobilized mainly through online social networks. Although the movement was initially aimed at rejecting the management and consequences of the economic crisis, the protest rapidly became a movement of denunciation against some of the failures of the conventional political system.

However, our analysis does not allow us to conclude that internet use is fostering the transformation of repertoires more generally, as we observed this relationship in the Spanish context in only a given moment in time (2007). Further research should take a longitudinal perspective to assess change over time and to improve the measures of exposure to specific online contents.

6.6. Appendix

6.6.1. *Variable Coding for Multivariate Analyses (in Alphabetical Order)*

Name	Codification
Age	18–95 years old
Confidence in state institutions	Three variables of confidence in political parties, local government, and central government. Additive index (mean), recoded 0–1
Consumerism participation	Boycotting products Donating money Deliberatively buying products 0 = has not participated in any of the actions in the last 12 months 1 = has participated in at least one of the following actions in the last 12 months
Education	1 = less than primary 2 = primary 3 = secondary 4 = tertiary Recoded 0–1
External political efficacy	A factor analysis was conducted on four items to detect the two dimensions of political efficacy. The external efficacy dimension included the following items: "I think public officials do not care much about what people like me think" and "Politicians are always in search of their personal interest" (1 = Agree strongly; 2 = Agree; 3 = Neither agree nor disagree; 4 = Disagree; 5 = Disagree strongly) Mean, recoded 0–1
Frequency of internet use	0 = never (nonuser) 1 = less often 2 = few times a month 3 = 1–2 days a week 4 = 3–5 days a week 5 = 6–7 days a week

(*continued*)

Name	Codification
Gender	0 = male 1 = female
Good citizenship	A factor analysis was conducted on five items on conceptions of good citizenship. Two dimensions were found, similar to the ones described by Dalton (2008): – Citizen-duty conception: voting in elections, not evading taxes, always abiding by the law and rules – Engaged conception of being a good citizen: thinking more about others than oneself, having one's own opinion For each of the good citizenship conceptions, additive indexes were constructed (mean scores), recoded 0–1.
Income	1 = Less than or equal to €300 2 = €301–600 3 = €601–900 4 = €901–1,200 5 = €1,201–1,800 6 = €1,801–2,400 7 = €2,401–3,000 8 = €3,001–4,500 9 = €4,501–6,000 10 = more than €6,000 Missing values imputed (method: regression) Recoded 0–1
Interest in politics	1 = not at all interested 2 = hardly interested 3 = quite interested 4 = very interested Recoded 0–1
Internal political efficacy	Items related to internal political efficacy in the factor analysis: "Usually politics and government seem so complicated that a person like me cannot really understand what's going on" and "I think that I am worse informed about politics and government than most people." Mean, recoded 0–1
Proclivity to involuntary exposure to political information online	Additive index of number of activities conducted online, including: receiving e-mails, taking part in chats and forums, keeping a personal web page or blog, and surfing the web without specific aims. Recoded 0–1.
Protest	– Taking part in a lawful demonstration – Taking part in a lawful strike – Taking part in an illegal protest – Signing a petition 0 = has not participated in any of the actions in the last 12 months 1 = has participated in at least one of the following actions in the last 12 months

Name	Codification
Representational participation	– Contacting – Attending a political meeting 0 = has not participated in any of the activities in the last 12 months 1 = has participated in at least one of the activities in the last 12 months
Voluntary search of political information online	0 = does not search for political information 1 = searches for political information
Voting	0 = did not vote in the last general election 1 = voted in the last general election

6.6.2. *Description of Profiles Used to Estimate Probabilities*

		Profiles		
Variables		Disaffected	Critical	Institutional
Involvement	Interest in politics	Minimum	Maximum	Maximum
	Internal efficacy	Minimum	Maximum	Maximum
System perception	Confidence in state institutions	Minimum	Minimum	Maximum
	External efficacy	Minimum	Minimum	Maximum
Civic orientations	Duty citizenship	Minimum	Mean	Maximum
	Engaged citizenship	Minimum	Maximum	Mean
Others	Socioeconomic status (control variables)	Means	Means	Means

7

Online Participation in Italy

Contextual Influences and Political Opportunities

Cristian Vaccari

7.1. Introduction

As in other Western democracies, the internet has become an increasingly viable environment for political participation in Italy. At the time of this writing, the latest and most powerful demonstration of the new media's effectiveness in helping people self-organize for political action was the "No Berlusconi Day," a rally held in Rome on December 5, 2009, to request the resignation of center-right Prime Minister Silvio Berlusconi after a wave of scandals. The demonstration – organized entirely online, mostly via blogs and the social networking site Facebook – partnered effectively with various left-wing media, successfully branded itself by using the violet color (which no political party in Italy has ever used, thus giving the initiative a nonpartisan allure), and gathered a remarkable amount of people.[1] Before that, the internet had been successfully used to mobilize citizens by the movement against neoliberal globalization (Mosca 2010) and by Beppe Grillo, a comedian whose blog has become the most read political blog in Italy, and whose supporters, mostly collaborating online through MeetUp.com groups, helped organize various rallies against political malfeasance and corruption. The first and biggest of these occured on September 8, 2007, when fifty thousand people gathered in the main event in Bologna and related rallies were hosted in 225 Italian cities and 30 foreign ones (Vaccari 2009); Grillo's supporters and the movement against globalization subsequently organized citizen lists that ran in various local elections between 2008 and 2010, polling as high as 10 percent in some constituencies (Mosca 2010).

By contrast, institutional political parties and their candidates have been quite reluctant to fully embrace the internet's participatory potential, mostly

---

[1] Typical of Italian politics, there was an enormous gap between estimates by the organizers, who claimed that 1 million people participated, and those by police authorities, who scaled the number down to a less impressive ninety thousand. As is usually the case for Italian political rallies, the real number lies somewhere in between.

due to their bureaucratic nature and reluctance to cede control over message production and distribution, as well as the relatively low levels of internet diffusion in Italy (Bentivegna 2006; Vaccari 2008a, 2008b). Although this aloofness from political insiders has limited the avenues for online participation, it has also provided a window of opportunity for citizens, associations, and social movements, which have not found the online political battlefield occupied by institutional political actors and have thus enjoyed greater freedom to experiment and less-than-fierce competition from more resourceful players.

Beyond that, online political participation in Italy must be understood in light of the peculiar characteristics of the country's political culture and political communication system. First, the political culture in Italy has historically been characterized by a low sense of efficacy, little interest in politics, low propensity to participate in the political arena, and high distrust of politics (see Bardi and Pasquino 1995; Pasquino 2002). This process was accelerated and intensified by the crisis of the polarized pluralism party system (Sartori 1976) that has characterized Italian politics since 1946. In 1993 and 1994, the system rapidly dissolved amid corruption scandals and was replaced by a fragmented bipolar system constituted by a center-right dominated by former media tycoon Silvio Berlusconi and a center-left guided, albeit much less firmly, by the heirs of the former Communist Party. Although the parties of the First Republic (as the dissolved system came to be known) were undergoing a deep crisis due to electoral dealignment and voters' increasing detachment from parties (Bardi 2002), the parties of the Second Republic have not been able to restructure solid attachments and loyalties among voters (Maraffi 2002). The latest available data (Eurobarometer 2009) show that only 19 percent of Italians express confidence in political parties, a percentage that, though equal to the average of the twenty-seven EU member countries, places Italy closer to the new democracies of Eastern and Southern Europe than to the more established Western European polities.

In organizational terms, Italian parties have undergone transformations similar to their European counterparts, with a significant reduction in membership rates; the use of public funding as the main source of financing; and the severing of relationships with economic, social, and cultural collateral organizations that had previously contributed to parties' territorial entrenchment (Bardi, Ignazi, and Massari 2007). Especially the center-left parties have recently attempted to counter these trends in two ways: first, by submitting relevant party decisions (e.g., candidate nominations and the election of the party leader) to popular vote and, second, by trying to recruit and involve not only members but also sympathizers (Bosco and Morlino 2007). These strategies, both of which aim to expand the pool of citizens the parties interact with, might find a valuable ally in online tools, which could expand the participatory repertoire of citizens and offer parties a new channel to reinvigorate their relationships with their supporters.

A second set of factors that needs to be taken into account has to do with the peculiar structure of the Italian media system. One aspect is the central place occupied by broadcast television in Italians' information diet; newspapers, in contrast, have never reached circulation levels in Italy comparable to other Western democracies. Moreover, although the internet has certainly changed the way many people acquire information on public affairs and participate in politics, the diffusion of the new media among the Italian citizenry has been much slower than in most of the European Union. According to Eurostat, in 2009 just 52 percent of Italian households had internet access, significantly lower than the 65 percent European Union average; only 42 percent of the Italian population went online once a week or more often, whereas the comparative figure for the whole European Union was 60 percent. Where 29 percent of European citizens had used the internet to interact with public authorities in the previous three months, only 17 percent of Italians had (Eurostat 2010). As a result, the internet has so far failed to pose a serious threat to the hegemony of broadcast television as a channel of political information. During the general elections of 2008, television was the main source of information for 78.3 percent of Italians, with newspapers a very distant second at 20.8 percent, while only 7.6 percent named the internet as a relevant source (Censis 2008). The limited development of digital media combined with an aloof and distant political culture thus constitutes a ceiling to the diffusion of online participation among Italians.

A third contextual condition that must be taken into account has to do with the competitive environment in Italian political communication. Since a bipolar party system has been in place, Italian television has been uniquely characterized by the dominance of the leader of the center-right coalition, Silvio Berlusconi. Owning three private broadcast television channels and, when in government, being able to effectively steer at least two of the three public channels, surely helped Berlusconi achieve visibility in the most important channel of political communication: his skills in news management, agenda-building, and image making were of equal importance in this endeavor. The end result has been an endemic imbalance between the center-right and the center-left on television, which, as we have seen, accounts for most of Italians' informational diet. Although progressive parties tend to enjoy better reporting and, especially, editorial treatment in newspapers, the press is a much less important source of political information for Italian voters. Berlusconi's dominance on television thus translates into a more generalized competitive advantage in the whole realm of political communication. Combined with the fact that since the 2001 elections the center-left has been in opposition for most of the decade and will most likely be until 2013 (when the next general elections will be held), such a scenario suggests that the Italian progressive coalition could be in a position similar to that of the Democratic Party in the United States, which for most of the past decade has been more innovative online than its Republican counterpart because its out-party status provided strong incentives to innovate in campaigning and communication practices, thus resulting in stronger online infrastructure and a large and engaged base of internet supporters (Karpf 2009). Indeed, survey data on the 2006 Italian election showed that the majority of Italians who claimed to visit political websites identified with either the left or the center-left and had voted for the progressive coalition (Vaccari 2006), and quantitative analysis of party websites demonstrated that center-left parties tended to outperform center-right ones in both the 2006 (Vaccari 2008b) and the 2008 elections (Vaccari 2008a). The successful use of digital media by extrainstitutional political actors, particularly social movements and Beppe Grillo, all catering to broadly defined left-wing constituencies, seems to confirm that there is greater potential and predisposition for online participation among progressive than conservative voters. Indeed, this might be true regardless of the incentives provided to left-wing supporters by their parties' oppositional status and competitive disadvantage in the mass media, as Italian progressive voters historically have been more interested in politics; have felt more politically efficacious; have subscribed to parties, unions, and associations; and have tended to participate in politics more than conservative voters (Pasquino 2002). This political participation divide is particularly relevant in light of the fact that the internet is a predominantly selective medium, which implies that online politics mostly provides people who are already eager to participate with avenues for deeper engagement (Bimber and Davis 2003).

We thus expect mutual reinforcement among three different factors: differentiated political subcultures between left-wing and right-wing voters, dominance of television by the conservative leader, and out-party incentives to invest in new campaign and communication technologies.

One final contextual factor that needs to be taken into account has to do with parliamentary and media representation of political actors that occupy extremes of the ideological spectrum. As a result of the proportional electoral law that was introduced in late 2005 by the Berlusconi government (Pasquino 2007) and changes in both the center-right and center-left coalitional strategies, both the radical left and the radical right have been excluded from the Parliament that was elected in the 2008 general election. This has resulted in political marginalization for most of these groups, which especially on the left disbanded into a coterie of unviable fringe parties and near disappearance from the media – especially from television, which by and large covers only parties that are represented in Parliament. As a consequence, these parties and their supporters might have particularly strong incentives to resort to the internet as the only viable channel to communicate with their voters and supporters.

Most of the contextual factors that I have discussed have not received specific attention in previous studies of online politics in Italy. I next turn to summarizing the main findings and limitations of the existing literature.

7.2. Literature Review

As Bentivegna (2006, 101) notes, most of the literature on internet politics in Italy "has studied and reflected on the nature and development of e-politics starting from the production by political actors rather than its interpretation by citizens." Moreover, when it has addressed citizens' role in internet politics,

Italian research has suffered from the fact that most studies have not featured representative samples, which makes results impossible to generalize to the whole population or even to the subsets of the population (e.g., internet users, students) targeted in each study.

Most studies of online citizen politics in Italy are based on self-selected respondents. Among these, Bentivegna (2006) reports the results of an online survey to which participants responded by clicking on a banner on the website of the left-leaning newspaper *La Repubblica*. Although the data are, as Bentivegna (2006, 103) readily acknowledges, "devoid of any pretense of statistical representativeness," the survey shows some interesting trends among Italian voters. One is "a propensity among internet users to stay away from the official campaign conducted by parties and candidates on their websites" (Bentivegna 2006, 122). Thus, if we are to fully understand the online political behavior of Italian citizens, we need to look beyond internet platforms provided by institutional actors. Bentivegna (2006) also found that Italians tend to have a moderately optimistic view of the role of the internet in campaigns and democracy, as more than three-quarters of respondents agreed that digital media allow citizens to create innovative forms of political participation; however, the outlook is grimmer with respect to relationships with parties and other established subjects, as only four in ten respondents agreed that the internet reduces distances between citizens and political actors. The survey also found that internet use complements television and newspapers as channels of political information rather than replacing them.

Two important studies on Italians' online participation were based on students. Calenda and Mosca (2007) conducted surveys of Italian students with nonprobabilistic sampling and found positive correlations between online and offline forms of political participation for both moderate actions (e.g., online petitions) and more radical ones (such as e.g., net strikes that entail collective action by groups of internet users to overwhelm a website and temporarily render it inaccessibe). On the basis of these and other findings, the authors concluded that "people already engaged in offline social and political networks use the Internet to consolidate their participation" (Calenda and Mosca 2007, 39) and that it was especially organizational involvement, rather than political action decoupled from membership in political groups, that stimulated online participation. Similarly, Calenda and Meijer (2008) studied students younger than thirty-five years in Italy, Spain, and the Netherlands, and they found that both time spent online and offline political participation correlate positively with online participation, but that political habits overall have stronger effects than technological ones. Moreover, different types of online participation are influenced differently by technological and political variables. The authors argued that "the online political world is indeed a natural extension of the offline world" and envisioned the possibility of a virtuous circle by which "online political participation may trigger more offline participation and, conversely, offline political participation may trigger more online participation" (Calenda and Meijer 2008, 893). These studies suggest that online participation might reinforce and reinvigorate traditional engagement and that analysis of internet involvement should account for the nuances of the various types of behavior that it comprises rather than treating it as an undifferentiated phenomenon. The main limitations of these studies lie in their focus on a specific subset of the population, rather than the whole citizenry, and in their use of nonrepresentative samples.

Unfortunately, the only available studies that are based on representative samples of the Italian population deal with online habits that entail information rather than participation. For instance Vaccari (2006) found that during the campaign for the 2006 general elections, 80 percent of Italians never logged onto political websites and only eight 8 percent claimed to do so "often." Among this smaller subset, age, education, student status, interest in politics, frequency of political discussion, mass media exposure, ideological left-wing orientation, and voting for the left-wing coalition were all positively associated with visiting political websites. However, the study only reports bivariate associations, which foreshadow the individual impact of each independent variable.

Aside from the literature on Italian citizens, studies of online political behavior have suffered from lack of comparative analyses, a gap that this book aims to fill. One of the few exceptions that can be found in the literature is Lusoli's (2005) research on the 2004 European Parliament elections, in which citizens from twenty-five member countries were surveyed. Although the study focuses on internet use for electoral information rather than participation, the analysis offers some interesting insights. First, Italy is among the countries whose citizens are least likely to use the internet for campaign-related information, in comparison with other EU countries. Second, "young, male, university educated citizens are more likely to use the Internet for political purposes" (Lusoli 2005, 253), and respondents' occupation was also found to significantly affect this behavior (although less so in Italy than in other countries). Third, a factor analysis found that internet use for political information is associated with activities such as discussing the election with friends and attending rallies and public meetings, which demand more citizen involvement than watching television or being contacted by parties.[2] On the basis of these findings, Lusoli (2005, 262) claimed that "the Internet goes hand-in-hand with citizen-centred campaigns, where the individual takes a more active role in information gathering, in taking part to [sic] political discussion and in attending public electoral events" and that "the Internet is embedded in the dynamics of production and rebroadcasting of the electoral message more than it is related with passive consumption of electoral information and electoral apathy." Thus, even though the internet can lower the costs of political action, its political uses resemble active and engaging endeavors rather than latent participation and relatively passive exposure to politics.

---

[2] In Lusoli's (2005) analysis, among Italians, only attending public meetings coloaded with internet use for political information.

In summary, the literature on Italian online politics is limited by the lack of samples representative of the whole population and suggests that online political habits are closely related to offline attitudes and behaviors, particularly those that demand active involvement. Furthermore, a more nuanced understanding of the factors influencing different types of online participation is needed, as previous studies hint that online information differs from online participation, and that in the latter realm there are important specificities to be appreciated as well. These were the goals of our study, whose methodological choices we illustrate in the following section.

7.3. Research Questions and Methodology

Both the literature surveyed here and the scientific goals of this book encourage us to answer various research questions. First, are differential propensities to offline participation among Italians reproduced online? Second, to what extent does online engagement reinforce and reproduce offline habits, and to what extent does online involvement supplant or supplement offline information and participation? Third, are different types of online political action influenced differently by social and political factors, and if so, how? Finally, do the specific features of the Italian context, particularly citizen disaffection and the unequal balance in offline political communication between the center-right and center-left, have any significant repercussions on political engagement via digital media?

To address these questions, we analyze the results of a random-digit-dialing survey conducted on the voting-age (eighteen years and older) population in four weekly waves in December 2009 (total $N = 4,021$).[3] The data were weighted to accurately represent the distribution among the voting-age population of standard sociodemographic variables and of political preferences, measured by voting choices in the last (2008) general election. In the sample, 53.3 percent claimed to have internet access, a figure consistent with Eurostat's 52 percent estimate. Of those having internet access, two-thirds claimed to log on at least every day (46.3 percent more than once a day, 21.2 percent once a day), which shows that, once the barrier of access is removed, Italians are becoming frequent and intense digital citizens.

Our survey featured eight questions related to different types of political engagement, four of which occur offline and four online. Among offline activities, two questions dealt with informational habits – reading newspaper articles about politics and watching political programs on television – and two with more engaging activities, such as talking about politics with friends and acquaintances and participating in rallies and meetings organized by parties and groups. The questions regarding online activities (asked only of respondents who claimed to have internet access) measured respondents'

[3] I am immensely grateful to IPSOS Public Affairs and in particular Professor Paolo Natale for sharing the data with me.

propensity to visit candidates' or parties' websites; to sign online petitions; to participate in offline political events after receiving an invitation online (thus measuring offline spillover effects of online mobilization); and to express their political viewpoints on forums, blogs, and social networking websites. For all these activities, respondents were asked whether in the last year – which included the campaign for the 2009 European Parliament elections – they had undertaken each of these activities "often," "sometimes," or "almost never or never." These questions allow us to sketch a comprehensive portrait of online political participation in Italy and its relationship with offline engagement.

Our first goal was to understand the extent to which the various types of online participation measured in our survey constitute a unique dimension, and whether and how these activities are related with offline participation and media usage. To achieve this goal, we conducted a factor analysis of the eight variables that have just been described. We undertook this part of the analysis with the LISREL software package (Jöreskog and Sörbom 1996) because, unlike most other statistical software packages, LISREL accounts for the fact that the level of measurement of the variables is ordinal rather than interval. We first ran an exploratory analysis to estimate the number of factors to be extracted on the basis of root mean square error of approximation (RMSEA), and we subsequently ran a confirmatory analysis to identify which variables loaded on the relevant factors and to calculate the respective factor loadings. We also ran a conventional factor analysis with SPSS treating the data as interval level to compare the results of the two methods.

Our second goal was to explain the relationship between internet-based political action and three sets of variables: sociodemographic, political, and frequency of traditional media use and offline political participation. The first set of variables has to do with the social stratification of online activity, which is related to the digital divide and the representativeness of the public that is engaged online vis-à-vis the voting population. The second set of variables allows us to address the issue of motivation for online political action, which has to do with political interest and with two aspects of citizens' ideological self-placement: one is whether they identify with the left or the right, which is relevant in light of the aforementioned communication imbalance favoring the center-right in mass communication; and whether they place themselves at the extremes or the middle of the political spectrum, which addresses the question of whether the internet is more hospitable to intense and radical political viewpoints, which could imply that the demands articulated through the medium are not representative of the general population's. Finally, the third set of variables helps us understand whether online participation is positively related to mass media use, thus suggesting integration and mutual reinforcement between the two, or whether use of some mass media is negatively correlated to internet-based engagement, which could imply substitution effects. Furthermore, assessing the impact of offline participation on internet-based political action helps us understand whether online engagement mirrors inequalities in traditional political participation or has opened new windows of opportunity for citizens who do not ordinarily undertake traditional forms of political action.

To achieve these goals, we ran four hierarchical logistic regression models in which the dependent variables were the four online engagement variables in our surveys, recoded as dichotomous variables for which those who claimed to have undertaken each activity either "often" or "sometimes" were coded as 1, whereas those who answered "almost never or never" were coded as 0.[4] To understand the effects of the three types of variables we identified as relevant, each logistic regression was divided into three steps: in the first, only sociodemographic variables were included; in the second, political variables were added; in the third, the model was completed with variables measuring mass media use and offline political participation.

7.4. The Role of Online Participation in Italians' Habits of Political Information and Engagement

To understand the role and potential of online participation, we need to place it in the context of the broader set of activities by which Italians acquire information on and participate in politics. Table 7.1 shows the frequencies with which respondents claimed to engage in various informational and participative efforts, both online and offline.

The data on mass media use confirm that television maintains a dominant position among Italians' sources of political information, although newspapers are less distant than other surveys have shown, with eight in ten respondents claiming to get some information via the former and seven in ten via the latter. By comparison, visiting political websites of parties or candidates clearly does not rival the mainstream media, as only one-eighth of Italians (but almost one-quarter among citizens with internet access) report at least occasionally visiting them. Similar imbalances between offline and online behavior were found for political discussion: although three in four respondents report talking about political issues with their friends and acquaintances, only 13.7 percent (25.8 percent among internet users) report expressing their political viewpoints on internet discussion forums, blogs, and social networks. The difference between the online and offline realm is more muted with respect to participation in political rallies and events: just 10 percent of respondents report having at least occasionally taken part in an offline event that was publicized online, and only slightly more (14.6 percent) report having participated in events organized by parties, unions, and groups. Thus, there seems to be significant potential among the Italian public to develop the organizational power of online tools to create and populate offline events, as shown by the success

---

[4] See the Appendix for full information on question wording and construction of the variables included in the models.

TABLE 7.1. *Frequency of Various Types of Political Engagement among All Respondents (N = 4,021)*

	Often	Sometimes	Almost Never or Never
Mass media use			
Following political programs on television	44.2	34.8	21.0
Reading about politics on newspapers	36.8	31.4	31.8
Offline political participation			
Talking about politics with friends and acquaintances	38.3	37.4	24.3
Participating in rallies and other political activities organized by parties and political groups	3.7	10.9	85.4
Online political activities			
Using a forum, a blog, or a social networking website to express political viewpoints	6.7	7.0	86.3
Signing an online petition	2.9	9.0	88.1
Visiting the website of a candidate or party	2.3	10.5	87.2
Participating in an offline event after receiving an online invitation	2.2	7.8	90.0

of the online organized political rallies that were mentioned at the opening of this chapter. This point is reinforced by the fact that, unlike all the other activities that we have analyzed so far, among internet users, participation in online organized events actually surpasses participation in traditional political rallies: 18.8 percent versus 17.2 percent. We can thus conclude that, although online participation is still a minority affair among the general population, it involves about one-quarter of the growing segment of internet users, which in turn comprises slightly more than half the adult population. Even though the new media cannot compete with television, newspapers, and everyday political conversations, their presence is rather significant.

To better understand the mutual relationship between online and offline participatory activities, we conducted a factor analysis that accounted for the ordinal-level nature of our data. In the exploratory phase of the analysis, we found that the structure of our data would be best represented by a model with two factors. As is commonly accepted, we set an RMSEA equal to .08 as the cutoff point (see Bollen 1989), so that solutions with lower values on this statistic were excluded. Thus, although the solution with two factors had an RMSEA of .088, the one with three factors had an RMSEA of .072 and so was ruled out. Table 7.2 shows the factor loadings of the eight variables in

TABLE 7.2. *Factor Analysis of Variables Measuring Offline and Online Participation, with Varimax Rotation, Only Internet Users (N = 2,218)*

	Factor 1	Factor 2	Unique Variance
Reading about politics on newspapers	.771	(.142)	.658
Talking about politics with friends and acquaintances	.734	(.211)	.326
Following political programs on television	.672	(.051)	.599
Participating in rallies and other political activities organized by parties and political groups	.678	.404	1.118
Visiting the website of a candidate or party	.482	.433	.693
Signing an online petition	(.305)	.709	.778
Participating in an offline event after receiving an online invitation	(.198)	.762	.794
Using a forum, a blog, or a social networking website to express political viewpoints	(.077)	1.418	1.636
Eigenvalues	2.587	1.292	
Percentage variance explained	32.3	16.1	

Note: Factor loadings of less than .40 are shown in parentheses. Eigenvalues and percentage of variance explained are derived from an SPSS-run analysis treating variables as interval level. All other values are derived from a LISREL-run analysis treating variables as ordinal.

the solution with two factors after varimax rotation. As can be seen from the bottom of the table, the model accounts for almost half the total variance in the data.

The analysis finds support for two distinctive factors, one dominated by reading political articles on newspapers and discussing politics with other people (but with a significant contribution from attending rallies and watching political programs on television), and the other dominated by expressing political viewpoints online (with significant contributions from attending offline events after receiving an online invitation and signing an online petition). The factor structure thus confirms that most Italians tend to be either offline or online citizens, with few crossing the fence between the two worlds. If we take a loading of .60 as a cutoff point to include a variable in a factor, we see that no overlapping is observed between online and offline participation, and visiting candidate or party websites is left out of either factor. However, if we take, as is conventionally done, a less demanding loading of .40 as a threshold for including a variable in a factor, the results for visiting political websites and attending rallies highlight some nuances between online and offline engagement, as both variables load on both factors, with visiting websites exhibiting remarkably similar loadings (and, indeed, a higher loading for the offline than the online factor).

These findings corroborate Lusoli's (2005) claim that acquiring online political information is more related to those offline endeavors that require some commitment, such as attending rallies, than to low-involvement actions, such as watching politics on television. Our data also confirm the conclusions of other studies that have found that the audience of political websites tends to be mostly composed of party members and sympathizers (Norris 2003). However, the fact that we measured different types of online engagement allows us to take a step further and highlight that visiting websites seems to be a shared trait between offline and online participation, as it loads similarly on both factors. This finding is understandable given that visiting a candidate or party website is arguably the least demanding among the online behaviors that we measured but also the one that is most closely related to institutional political actors, who tend to loom large in organizing offline participation.

We can conclude from this evidence that, although offline and online political behaviors by and large constitute two separate and internally homogeneous dimensions, there are more commonalities between them than is normally granted, and there are more internal differences within each of them than the catchall construct of online participation signifies. Thus, in the following section we analyze each type of online political engagement separately in search of similarities and dissimilarities among them.

7.5. Factors Affecting Online Political Participation

In this section we discuss the results of the four regression models that we ran to estimate how different types of online political action are affected by sociodemographic cleavages, political attitudes, and offline political information and participation. We originally ran hierarchical regressions to better appreciate the differential impact of the three sets of independent variables that we considered, but we show only the final step in this chapter because of space constraints. However, we discuss the main findings of the two first steps before illustrating the models that combine all independent variables.

When we included only sociodemographic variables such as gender, age, education, and professional status, we found all forms of internet-based political engagement to be significantly related to gender, with males more likely than females to report partaking in all four activities; age, with younger respondents more likely to engage in all actions but online petition signing; and education, with holders of higher degrees more engaged than citizens with fewer years of instruction. Professional status, by contrast, did not significantly and systematically correlate with online political action, as the only pattern that emerged from the data was students' greater propensity to engage in these activities than retirees, housewives, and unemployed citizens. Thus, consistent with earlier studies (Norris 2001), there still exists a digital divide in online political participation; that is, the propensity to engage in these activities is significantly influenced by sociodemographic variables, and those imbalances result in barriers to equal participation and representation. Although these findings have important implications for the social representativeness of online participation, none of the four models' first steps explained a very large part of the variance in the dependent variable (measured by Nagelkerke R^2), from .053 for visiting websites to .131 for expressing political viewpoints online. Although the digital political divide is still real, it is by no means the whole story.

Given our previous considerations regarding the Italian political context, our ability to predict internet-based political engagement should be significantly enhanced by taking into account political attitudes such as interest in politics and ideological self-placement. These were included in the second step of our regressions, which showed a remarkable increase in the models' explanatory power, with variance explained (Nagelkerke R^2) almost tripling for visiting websites (from .053 to .148), doubling for signing petitions (from .076 to .152), and increasing by one-half and one-quarter, respectively, for participating in online-initiated events (from .118 to .177) and expressing political viewpoints online (from .131 to .164). Thus, political attitudes do make a difference in Italians' online engagement. In the second step, interest in politics had the strongest effect on all types of internet participation, while ideological location toward the left wing of the political spectrum was found to positively and significantly correlate with three of the four types of online engagement, the lone exception being online political discussion. Moreover, in the second step, respondents' propensity to declare ideological extremity was found to correlate significantly with visiting political websites and signing online petitions, whereas the effects on the other two dependent variables were negligible. Because the direction and significance of most of these coefficients did not change in the third and final step of our regression models, we now turn to discussing the impact of these variables in relation to the complete model, which is shown in Table 7.3. The final models estimate between one-quarter and one-fifth of the total variance in the dependent variables, with sizable increases over the previous step, which implies that offline political information and participation are quite relevant predictors of online engagement.

When all independent variables were included, the effects of gender and education were muted (though not canceled), and the influence of professional status remained negligible. Age, however, maintained a significant, negative relationship with three of the four types of online political engagement, which implies that younger citizens are more likely to participate in politics on the web even after accounting for their education levels, interest in politics, and political orientations, as well as offline engagement.

Interest in politics showed a strong and consistent effect on all four types of online involvement, turning out to be the strongest predictor of expressing political viewpoints on the internet, the second strongest predictor of visiting candidate and party websites, and the third strongest predictor of signing online

TABLE 7.3. *Effects of Sociodemographic Characteristics, Political Variables, and Offline Information and Participation on Four Types of Online Political Action, Only Internet Users (N = 1,974)*

	Visiting Website of a Candidate or Party	Signing Online Petition	Participating in an Offline Event after Receiving an Online Invitation	Expressing Political Viewpoints Online
Gender (male)	.076	.035	.103	.239*
	(.124)	(.124)	(.135)	(.121)
Age	−.025***	−.009	−.035***	−.048***
	(.005)	(.005)	(.006)	(.005)
Years of education	.001	.084***	.052**	.009
	(.017)	(.017)	(.019)	(.017)
Professional status				
Self-employed workers	−.024	−.404*	.306	−.293
	(.189)	(.195)	(.216)	(.188)
Public and private employees	−.309	−.378*	−.042	−.410*
	(.165)	(.164)	(.193)	(.162)
Students	.107	−.123	.504*	.027
	(.237)	(.243)	(.255)	(225)
Interest in politics	1.184***	.874*	1.205***	1.214***
	(.315)	(.314)	(.346)	(.295)
Ideological self-placement	.528*	1.404***	1.227***	.233
	(.247)	(.253)	(.280)	(.240)
Political extremism	.118	.451	−.379	.094
	(.235)	(.237)	(.258)	(.225)
Frequency of internet use	.486***	.944***	1.267***	1.209***
	(.144)	(.156)	(.190)	(.154)
Reading about politics on newspapers	.796***	.842***	.702***	−.223
	(.186)	(.187)	(.202)	(.168)
Following political programs on television	.485**	−.364*	−.307	−.024
	(.186)	(.184)	(.199)	(.175)
Talking about politics with friends and acquaintances	.890***	.639**	.150	.553**
	(.213)	(.209)	(.225)	(.197)
Participating in rallies and other political activities	1.442***	.235	1.105***	.645**
	(.212)	(.218)	(.228)	(.217)
Constant	−3.163***	−4.694***	−3.738***	−1.354***
	(.395)	(.410)	(.000)	(.374)
Percentage predicted	77.8	77.9	82.0	77.0
Nagelkerke R^2	.251	.212	.248	.225
χ^2	365.082	296.801	331.230	328.119

Note: Entries report unstandardized beta coefficients with standard errors in parentheses.
* $p \leq .05$. ** $p \leq .01$. *** $p \leq .001$.

petitions and of participating in online-initiated offline events. That interest in politics affects online participation was an easily predictable finding, but it also happens to be a normative mixed blessing, as attitudes toward politics in Italy are marred by widespread disinterest and distrust, as we saw in the introductory paragraph of this chapter. In line with the common practice of Italian voter surveys, respondents were asked to grade their level of interest in politics on the same 1–10 scale that is used in school, with 6 corresponding to the "pass" grade. This allowed respondents to anchor their self-evaluations to a scale they are familiar with, while at the same time not biasing their responses toward high grades: in our sample, four in ten graded themselves below 6 and the average grade was 5.81, with only one in ten respondents grading themselves between 9 and 10. Although political interest is slightly more common among internet users (average score of 6.16) and even more common among those who log on at least daily (average score of 6.34, with only 28 percent scoring themselves lower than 6), the generally low level of interest in politics among Italians clearly constitutes a ceiling that limits online participation more than technological diffusion and internet literacy.

As for respondents' ideological self-placement, we included two variables that measured, respectively, left-right alignments, originally assessed on a seven-point scale ranging from extreme left to extreme right, recoded as a 0–1 normalized variable for ease of comparison, and the degree of extremism, measured as respondents' propensity to locate themselves toward the extremes or the center of the political spectrum, again recoded as a 0–1 normalized variable for ease of comparison. Thus, the left-right variable allows us to appreciate the effect of an individual's ideological choice in the bipolar competition, whereas the variable measuring extremism allows us to test whether online participation is more popular among politically extremist, and often institutionally marginalized, groups than among citizens espousing mainstream positions.

With respect to ideological self-placement, results of the final step of the regression models confirmed what we found in the second, as left-wing location significantly correlated with (in order of magnitude) signing online petitions, attending offline events after receiving online invitations, and visiting candidate and party websites, whereas the coefficient for expressing political viewpoints online, though positive, was not statistically significant. It should be noted that the gap between left-wing and right-wing respondents in online participation is not, by any means, due to any comparable imbalance in internet use. As Figure 7.1 shows, although our data indicate that citizens who align themselves with the right and center-right of the political spectrum are less likely to claim to have internet access than the rest of the population, among internet users the ideological distribution of those who report accessing the internet at least daily is remarkably symmetrical. Moreover, ideological self-placement still has a sizable and statistically significant effect on three out of four types of online participation even after controlling for political interest. This indicates

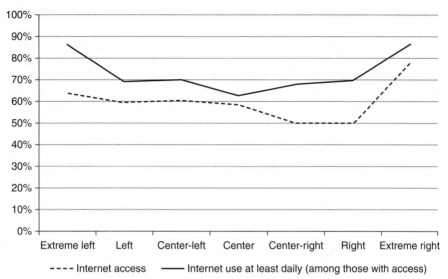

FIGURE 7.1. Relationship between ideological self-placement and internet access ($N =$ 3,516) and use ($N =$ 1,966).

that ideological gaps in internet-based engagement occur not entirely because progressives tend to be more interested in politics than conservatives. Rather, it appears that left-oriented citizens turn to online participation because they perceive the web as a more promising competitive field than the mainstream media, where Berlusconi and the center-right tend to dominate coverage (see Grandi and Vaccari 2009).

In contrast, although in the second step respondents' propensity to declare ideological extremity was found to correlate significantly with visiting political websites and signing online petitions, no statistically significant correlation was found between our measure of political extremism and all our dependent variables, once frequency of internet use and offline information and participation habits were included. This implies that online participation is enhanced by political interest and activism more than by extremism.

As could be expected, one's frequency of internet use significantly affects all types of online political action. Habitual use of the internet enhances internet-based political engagement because frequent users are more likely to encounter opportunities to participate and to have some time to devote to them while online. Offline participation was also found to promote online engagement, as political discussion and particularly attendance at political rallies significantly correlated with three of the four types of online engagement, a finding consistent with the results of our factor analysis. These patterns suggest that internet-based participation supplements and enriches traditional offline political action rather than replacing it: Italians' repertoires of participation are thus augmented rather than impoverished by the new media, as the Beppe Grillo and anti-Berlusconi rallies described earlier illustrate. Results are more ambivalent, however, for offline media use: although reading political articles on newspapers positively affects three out of the four types of online engagement, following politics on television is positively and significantly related only to visiting candidates' and parties' websites, and it has negative effects on the three other types of web-based participation, with a statistically significant coefficient for signing online petitions.

Thus, there seem to be two contradictory tendencies in the relationship between offline information and online participation: reinforcement and complementarity with newspapers, but (at least partial) substitution with television news. Although reading newspapers and participating online enhance each other, watching political programs on television is at best unrelated to most of the online engagement behaviors investigated in this study. This weaker relationship might partially be a result of the fact that watching television is the most common activity among the independent variables that we considered (see Table 7.1), which makes it more difficult to distinguish among our respondents on the basis of this variable. However, the fact that this negative or null effect was found for television also suggests that, again, the Italian political communication context might be playing a role. That is, the particular partisan contours of the Italian mass media system might affect online political action differently, according to citizens' ideological predispositions, which in turn affect their media habits. This hypothesis is corroborated by the fact that ideological self-placement maintains a strong influence on three of the four types of online engagement, even after controlling for offline participation and media use: although the coefficients for all other variables in the first two steps of the hierarchical models decline when the variables of the third step are entered, the strength of association between ideology and internet-based political action remains unaltered for online petition signing and participation in online-organized offline events, and it declines only slightly but maintains statistical significance for visiting websites.

The comparison among the three steps of our hierarchical regression models also allows us to appreciate how different types of engagement are affected by the variables that we considered. For the first dependent variable – visiting a political website – the greatest increase in explained variance (measured by Nagelkerke R^2) was observed when we entered variables measuring offline political habits. The second dependent variable – signing online petitions – was predicted almost equally well by sociodemographic variables, political attitudes, and offline behaviors, with similar increases in explained variance at all steps. With respect to the third dependent variable – attending offline events after receiving an online invitation – offline political habits were more predictive than political attitudes, but both sets of variables explained less variance than sociodemographic ones. Finally, an even greater portion of variance in the fourth variable – expressing political viewpoints online – was accounted for by sociodemographic variables, whereas political attitudes and offline activities, though still relevant, were comparatively less predictive of this behavior. Different types of online political action thus seem to be arranged on a continuum between politically skewed activities (e.g., visiting political websites) that are mostly spawned by interest in politics, ideology, and offline political behaviors, and socially skewed activities (e.g., expressing political viewpoints online) that are more affected by citizens' social location than by their orientations toward politics. Signing online petitions and attending offline events after receiving an online invitation fall closer to the center of the continuum, the former being more politically skewed and the latter more socially skewed.

7.6. Conclusion

This chapter has sought to fill a gap in our knowledge of Italians' online political participation, as no previous study had employed a sample representative of the whole population or measured various types of internet-based engagement. Furthermore, we have considered these behaviors not in isolation but in the context of the Italian political culture and media environment, which allows us to draw more insightful conclusions from our data analysis than would have been the case otherwise.

One of the goals of this study was to improve our understanding of the complexity of online political participation. First, different types of engagement have been found to correlate with different sociodemographic, attitudinal, and behavioral (sets of) variables, and to be distributed differently among the population. Thus, although we still believe that the concept of online participation as a general category is useful, we suggest that future research take steps to delve more deeply into the different facets of this complex phenomenon. Second, online participation turned out to constitute a continuum in which some activities are more tied to citizens' political attitudes and offline behaviors, and others are more related to individuals' social characteristics. Therefore, a one-size-fits-all approach in explaining different types of political action on digital media risks oversimplifying the complex web of influences that we have begun to uncover.

Our findings also allowed us to shed light on the relationship between online and offline political action. On the one hand, the divide between these two realms was confirmed by our factor analysis, which showed that most Italians, if they engage in politics at all, are either active online or offline. On the other hand, we also found overlapping areas between some types of offline involvement that are relatively more demanding and closer to institutional politics and some forms of online participation. These findings lead us to believe that citizens who engage in more demanding offline political activities, such as attending rallies or discussing public affairs, are also more likely to participate online; conversely, those who limit their offline engagement to getting political news through the mass media can sometimes supplement their news diet by visiting parties' or candidates' websites. Therefore, future research should distinguish not only between online and offline activities but also between more and less demanding and institutional endeavors in each realm. Our findings also confirmed that online and offline activities are mutually reinforcing. However, once again, the offline activities that mostly stimulated online behavior were the relatively more demanding ones. Moreover, we also found little and mostly negative correlation between watching politics on television and participating online, which suggests that, at least among parts of the public, digital media might begin to substitute for, rather than complement, Italians' main channel of political news.

To fully appreciate the causes and implications of this phenomenon, we need to place these findings within the Italian political context and combine the findings on the negative relationship between watching political programs and some instances of online participation with the evidence of a strong, positive correlation (controlling for interest in politics, internet use, mass media use, and offline participation) between being ideologically leftist and engaging in digital politics. Our data confirm that the internet has become a political battleground for Italian progressives who have acknowledged that it constitutes a more hospitable communication environment than Berlusconi-dominated television. Although left-wing parties have so far failed to fully take advantage of this potential, social movements loosely affiliated with the left, and directed first and foremost against Berlusconi, have already shown that online participation has remarkable potential to translate into offline action.

Partisan and ideological forces thus seem to be shaping the contours of the online political environment in Italy. This is consistent with the history of mass media development in the country, as Italian newspapers, radio, and television have been characterized by political parallelism from the outset and continuously through different political eras (Hallin and Mancini 2004). The only, but far from irrelevant, difference is that political parallelism in the mass media was of an elite-driven type, as it originated from economic forces, party organization, and governmental decisions. In contrast, the parallelism that we have observed in digital media seems to be of a citizen-driven, or at least citizen-centered type, as it emerges from Italians' autonomous strategies to organize their engagement in coping with a politically asymmetric communication environment (and from outsider groups' efforts to tap into this involvement potential among sympathetic constituencies), rather than from conscious and resourceful direction by political and economic elites. Whether citizen-driven politicization of the new media will achieve a stability and rooting similar to those observed for elite-driven politicization of the mass media is a question that we leave for future inquiries. If citizen-driven parallelism on the internet were to have effects similar to those of elite-driven parallelism on the mass media, then we would expect that digital media will contribute to strengthening the bonds between citizens and parties, as Van Kempen (2007) argues.

Finally, we suggest some implications of this study for comparative research. Although the figure of Berlusconi is peculiar in that he combines media and political power in a way that is unparalleled in Western democracies, his career both as a media tycoon and as a political leader has simply magnified a tendency of entanglement between media and politics that, though extraordinarily well rooted in Italy, is not unique to it. This entanglement can also be found in those media systems that Hallin and Mancini (2004) classified as Mediterranean or polarized pluralist, whose main trait is the politicization of the media. Thus, a first set of countries in which our findings can be expected to at least partially apply includes France, Spain, Portugal, and Greece (which are also classified as polarized pluralist media systems), as well as any other countries in which there are strong ties between politics and at least part of the media system. Although this is true for many developing countries, the politicization of various media sectors or outlets is not uncommon in other types of democratic media systems, for instance, the press of Northern European or democratic corporatist media systems of Germany and Scandinavian countries (Hallin and Mancini 2004); some key players in North Atlantic or liberal media systems, such as the British press (Hallin and Mancini 2004); and the new media, such as cable news channels, blogs, and talk radio, in the United States (Davis and Owen 1998; Baum and Groeling 2008). Thus, a second set of countries in which our findings may be worth testing empirically includes all those Western democracies in which at least part of the media system is politicized. Moreover, even in countries in which the media system is not stably polarized politically, our conclusion that the competitive makeup of the political communication environment creates different types of incentives for different voters may apply to any country in which, either for structural or for contingent reasons, one party or coalition has achieved a more or less stable advantage in a significant part of the mass media realm. The pattern we found for Italy would lead us to expect that, in such a country, citizens from the political side that is losing the mass media battle may be more eager to turn to the new media to counter the other side's communication hegemony.

In summary, in comparative perspective, Italy may be considered a partially deviant case, as it displays properties that most media systems share but with an intensity and diffusion seldom found elsewhere. It is the combination of these similarities and commonalities that make Italy a case worth studying, as it offers theoretically relevant and normatively problematic interactions between social and political context, technological development, and citizen behavior.

7.7. Appendix

Age. Years of age as claimed by respondents.[5]

Expressing political viewpoints online. "During the last year, how often did you use a forum, a blog, or a social networking website such as Facebook and MySpace to express your political viewpoints: often, sometimes, almost never

---

[5] Variables used in the chapter analysis: coding, construction of variables, and survey question wording (alphabetically ordered).

or never?" In the logistic regressions, "often" and "sometimes" were coded as 1; "almost never" and "never" were coded as 0.

Following political programs on TV. "During the last year, how often did you follow political programs on television: often, sometimes, almost never or never?" In the logistic regressions, "often" and "sometimes" were coded as 1; "almost never" and "never" were coded as 0.

Frequency of internet use. "How often do you connect to the internet: more than once a day, once a day, almost twice or thrice a week, once a week, or less than once a week?" (asked only of those respondents who in a previous answer reported having internet access). In the logistic regressions, "more than once a day" and "once a day" were coded as 1; other answers were coded as 0.

Gender. In the logistic regressions, "male" was coded as 1; female as 0.

Ideological self-placement. "Apart from your vote in elections, would you personally define yourself as extreme left, left, center-left, center, center-right, right, or extreme right?" In the logistic regressions, the variable was normalized, ranging from 0 = extreme right to 1 = extreme left.

Interest in politics. "If you were to express your interest in politics with a grade from 1 (low interest) to 10 (high interest), how would you grade yourself?" In the logistic regressions, the variable was normalized, ranging from 0 = low interest to 1 = high interest.

Participating in an offline event after receiving an online invitation. "During the last year, how often did you participate to a political event to which you had been invited online: often, sometimes, almost never or never?" In the logistic regressions, "often" and "sometimes" were coded as 1; "almost never" and "never" were coded as 0.

Participating in rallies and other political activities. "During the last year, how often did you participate to rallies and other political activities organized by parties and political groups: often, sometimes, almost never or never?" In the logistic regressions, "often" and "sometimes" were coded as 1; "almost never" and "never" were coded as 0.

Political extremism. In the logistic regressions, the ideological self-placement variable was recoded on the basis of how far from the center respondents located themselves and was normalized, ranging from 0 = center to 1 = extreme right and extreme left.

Professional status. The original variable featured seventeen categories, which were aggregated into five categories: autonomous workers (entrepreneurs, professionals, retailers, artisans, farmers, other autonomous workers), public and private employees (teachers and professors, managers, private employees, public employees, factory workers, other employees), students, and nonworkers (retired, housewives, unemployed, and other not employed). In the logistic regressions nonworkers were coded as 0 and served as the reference category.

Reading about politics on in newspapers. "During the last year, how often did you read about politics on newspapers: often, sometimes, almost never or never?" In the logistic regressions, these categories were collapsed such that "often" and "sometimes" were coded as 1; "almost never" and "never" were coded as 0.

Signing an online petition. During the last year, how often did you sign a petition online: often, sometimes, almost never or never?" In the logistic regressions, "often" and "sometimes" were coded as 1; "almost never" and "never" were coded as 0.

Talking about politics with friends and acquaintances. "During the last year, how often did you talk about politics with friends and acquaintances: often, sometimes, almost never or never?" In the logistic regressions, "often" and "sometimes" were coded as 1; "almost never" and "never" were coded as 0.

Visiting the website of a candidate or party. "During the last year, how often did you visit the website of a candidate or a party: often, sometimes, almost never or never?" In the logistic regressions, "often" and "sometimes" were coded as 1; "almost never" and "never" were coded as 0.

Years of education. Recoded from respondents' answer to the question, "Which is the latest degree that you have completed: university degree, high-school diploma, high school short diploma, intermediary school, elementary school, or none?" The variable was recoded as the number of years required to complete each diploma: 18 (university degree), 13 (high- school diploma), 11 (high school short diploma), 8 (intermediary school), 5 (elementary school), and 0 (none).

8

On the Causal Nature of the Relationship between Internet Access and Political Engagement

Evidence from German Panel Data

Martin Kroh and Hannes Neiss

8.1. Introduction

Digital media are expected by many scholars to revolutionize democracy (for an overview, see Barber 1999; Ward and Vedel 2006). Although a pessimistic school of thought argues that the internet provides governments opportunities for subtle surveillance and control (Barber 1999; Krueger 2006), more optimistic analysts counter that the internet may strengthen civil societies, grassroots politics, and direct democracy (Coliagnese 2003; Hara and Estrada 2005). This second school of thought expects the internet, among other things, to increase the political involvement of citizens and their propensity to take political action (for a review, see the Introduction and Chapter 1).

The past fifteen years have seen dramatic changes in how citizens and policy makers communicate. Worldwide, the internet and online forums are playing an ever more central role in candidates and parties' efforts to mobilize campaign participation (Norris 2003; Howard 2005), and in many countries, the internet is also replacing newspapers and television as a primary source of political information for an increasing number of groups in society, especially younger people (Norris 2002; Johnson and Kaye 2003; Tolbert and McNeal 2003; De Zúñiga, Puig-i-Abril, and Rojas 2009). Although the internet has changed the forms of political communication, many scholars doubt that it has also changed the prevalence of political engagement in the population at large. These skeptics argue that the internet is "preaching to the converted" (Norris 2003, 21); that is, politically mobilized citizens select themselves into using the internet, but access to the internet does not causally increase political engagement.

A growing body of empirical research analyzes the relationship between internet use and political engagement. In a recent survey of this research, Boulianne (2009) compares the results of thirty-eight empirical studies based on U.S. data. Although some studies report no effect of the internet, a majority of studies do find a positive correlation between internet access and political

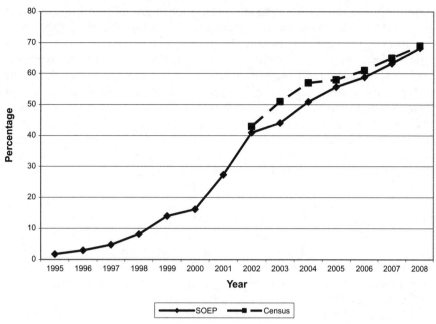

FIGURE 8.1. Internet access in Germany. *Note:* The figure displays the relative frequency of home internet access in Germany based on data from the Socio-Economic Panel analyzed in this chapter and available official census data.

engagement. It is an open question, however, whether results established for the United States can be generalized to other political systems. The U.S. context may be particularly prone to displaying positive effects of the internet on political engagement: online forms of electoral campaigning have been adopted at a much earlier point in time than in other countries (Albrecht, Lübcke, and Hartig-Perschke 2007). In fact, many innovations in e-campaigning and styles have been developed in U.S. primaries (Chadwick 2006). Also, the political blogging scene is much more active in the United States than in other countries. Online communication in the United States is often perceived as transporting unique political information and providing distinctive opportunities to contribute to the political process (Lipton 2009).

The present chapter tests the extent to which a positive internet effect on political engagement can also be identified in Germany, a context that provides a more critical test of the internet-effects hypothesis. Although internet access of private households in Germany has increased sharply since the beginning of the century (see Figure 8.1) and reached similar levels to those in the United States (see also Table I.3), the content and style of online political communication are highly similar to offline political communication. For instance, online campaigning of the major parties is parallel to offline campaigning in traditional mass media (Albrecht et al. 2007; Schweitzer 2008).[1] Also, German citizens seem to use the political opportunities of the internet less actively than, for instance, U.S. citizens. In this sense, the creation of users' own content is rather uncommon, and political communication via the internet is mostly receptive (Vowe, Emmer, and Seifert 2007).[2] This may in part be explained by the high trust of Germans in the traditional mass media: survey data show that Germans – both internet users and nonusers – rate the credibility of traditional media formats considerably higher than that of online political information (Schweiger 2000; see also Nawratil 2006). The internet represents in Germany to a lesser extent – as compared to many other countries – an alternative communication channel for information that is perceived as being suppressed by mainstream media (Schulz, Zeh, and Quiring 2005).

Apart from the question of the generalizability of the U.S. findings, Boulianne (2009) concludes that the causal direction of the correlation between internet access and political engagement has not been fully established. With the exception of the study by Jennings and Zeitner (2003), all of the empirical studies have been based on cross-sectional data, which do not allow a before-after investigation of an internet effect, and some studies even select on the explanatory variable and use internet-based surveys.[3]

The present chapter uses annual panel data on internet access and political engagement that cover the entire period of increasing private internet use since the mid-1990s. The analysis of panel data allows us to compare the level of political engagement in respondents before and after they obtain access to the internet and thus to better estimate the magnitude of a causal internet effect on political engagement than is possible in cross-sectional studies. The chapter compares cross-sectional with panel estimates and focuses largely on indicators of political engagement that neither are formulated online nor are offline specific, namely political interest and general work in political action groups. The results show that the positive correlation between internet access and political

---

[1] Right-wing parties represent the exception to the rule. They provide certain information only online to bypass legal regulations of political contents and recruitment (Chadwick 2006; Copsey 2003).

[2] The recently introduced e-petitions to the national parliament present an exception in this respect. There has been a peak in signatures to e-petitions in 2009 with two petitions receiving more than one hundred thousand signatures. The most successful petitions deal with the internet itself, new media, and educational policies.

[3] The panel study by Jennings and Zeitner (2003) suffers from three problems (Boulianne 2009): first, the analysis is restricted to a single cohort born (around) 1947. Second, the preinternet survey was conducted in 1982 and the postinternet survey in 1997. This large time gap is likely to underestimate self-selection processes. Ideally, one would like to have information on political engagement one year before individuals obtain access to the internet, in the same year, and one year thereafter. Finally, the analysis estimates an internet effect on indicators of political action while controlling for political interest. As Boulianne (2009) points out, political interest is not independent of political action but rather is a condition thereof; it is hard to imagine that individuals become politically active without becoming politically interested at the same time.

engagement is largely due to processes of self-selection: politically active people obtain internet access earlier and at a higher rate than demobilized individuals. However, a small, positive effect of the internet on political engagement survives rigorous empirical testing. This small causal effect is dependent on individual characteristics: particularly the politically mobilized benefit from internet access.

8.2. The Consequences of Internet Use, Self-Selection, and Group Differences

Previous empirical research from the United States suggests that the online community is politically more active than the offline community in many indicators of political engagement: Tolbert and McNeal (2003), for instance, report that internet access increased the probability of voting in the 1996 and 2000 U.S. elections, and Larson (2004) finds similar results for the probability of a donation in the 2004 campaign. De Zúñiga and colleagues (2009), Weber, Loumakis, and Bergman (2003), and Krueger (2002) report positive effects of internet usage in the United States on other forms of political participation, such as contacting politicians and signing petitions.

There is also first evidence of a positive correlation between internet access and various indicators of political engagement in European countries (Norris 2005; Polat 2005; Quintelier and Vissers 2008; Vowe et al. 2007). Most of these studies are based on cross-sectional survey data (but see Chapter 3) and are therefore plagued by uncertainties regarding the extent to which the observed correlation between internet access and political engagement can be attributed to a causal effect of the internet and to the endogenous self-selection of politically mobilized citizens into internet usage (for an overview of this critique, see Boulianne 2009). Both hypotheses are well founded in the broader literature on political engagement (Verba, Schlozman, and Brady 1995) and the literature on internet use (Norris 2002).

8.2.1. The Internet-Effect Hypothesis

The rationale for the internet-effect hypothesis that the internet causally increases the propensity for political engagement is threefold. The most frequently cited argument in favor of the internet-effect hypothesis is that new technologies reduce the costs of becoming politically informed (DiMaggio et al. 2001; Norris 2002, 2005; Larson 2004; Di Gennaro and Dutton 2006; Howard 2005; Grönlund 2007). Because citizens obtain extensive information on certain topics with the click of a mouse, the opportunity costs for becoming politically informed are reduced considerably. Moreover, because many people have access to the internet for nonpolitical reasons, in these cases political information is a free by-product. To the extent that political information expands citizens' knowledge (Coliagnese 2003) and politically knowledgeable individuals are also more likely to be politically engaged, access to the internet causally increases political engagement (Norris 2002; Larson 2004).

The second reason the internet may facilitate political engagement lies in technical features of this medium that make it easier to have a direct political influence. Using the internet, it is much easier not only to obtain political information but also to interactively communicate messages to politicians, media, and like-minded citizens, for instance, by way of blogging and microblogging, as well as e-mail (Lusoli, Ward, and Gibson 2002; Johnson and Kaye 2003; Ward, Gibson, and Lusoli 2003; Trechsel 2007). The internet therefore reduces not only the costs of political information but also the costs of political action and thus causally increases the propensity for political engagement.

The internet also provides a platform for individuals to come into contact with others whom they otherwise would never have met in person. For instance, the internet makes it possible to organize the interests of people geographically dispersed across a country and to form communities around even very small single-issue publics (Norris 2002). These networks may act as vehicles with which to politically mobilize their members (Lusoli et al. 2002).

8.2.2. The Self-Selection Hypothesis

The basic point of critique of the internet hypothesis is that the scale of political engagement in modern societies is a matter of monetary costs: political information is readily available at very limited costs through television news and newspapers, and personal views may be disseminated with limited financial resources by writing traditional letters to politicians and editors. The internet may be more convenient in this respect; however, because the differences in costs are negligible, the internet is said to merely replace traditional forms of political communication and action while leaving the level and structure of political engagement in the population unchanged (Best and Krueger 2005; Norris 2002, 2005; Bimber 2001).

A central aspect of political engagement is the individual motivation: people who are motivated to inform themselves politically, to inform others, and to organize interests will do so irrespective of the marginally reduced costs of internet-based political engagement (Prior 2005). In fact, because the internet makes political engagement more convenient, those who are motivated to become politically active will go online. And the more political information is exclusively available online, the more the internet will become attractive to citizens who are motivated to become politically engaged. The observation of, for instance, higher turnout rates in the online community is the consequence of individuals who intend to vote in an election using the internet to inform themselves about the candidates. The study by Füting (2008) supports this view for German survey data from 2005: attitudes toward one's own role in the political system affect the likelihood of online versus offline political involvement.

A variant of the self-selection hypothesis ascribes the positive correlation between internet access and political engagement to omitted variables that may affect both internet usage and political engagement at the same time (Best and Krueger 2005; Di Gennaro and Dutton 2006; Krueger 2002, 2006). This view is fueled by studies of the digital divide that show that particularly those individual characteristics that are associated with having internet access, such as high income, education, and occupation (Norris 2002), are also correlated with political engagement (Verba et al. 1995). That is, internet users and politically active citizens have the same attributes – high income and education, for instance – but apart from that, the two phenomena are unrelated.

8.2.3. Reciprocal Causation and Group Differences

Many scholars in the debate about the effects of the internet on political engagement take a reconciliatory position between the two poles of the internet-effect hypothesis and the self-selection hypothesis and claim that the two processes may actually be operating at once. Moreover, the causal effect of the internet on political engagement is said to differ in importance between different groups of the population and may often be negligible (Best and Krueger 2005; Barber 1999; Norris 2002, 2005; Krueger 2002, 2006).

Politically motivated citizens may decide to go online because the internet is an attractive tool to achieve their political aims, and those who have internet causally increase their level of political engagement in line with the possibilities for online participation. Norris (2002) refers to this argument of reciprocal causation as the virtuous circle. Because both a selection effect and a causal effect are at work, the internet does increase the political engagement in the public at large but at the expense of making it more unequal than it was before. The internet restricts the politically active population to a very small group of motivated citizens and excludes the passive majority.

The hypothesis of group differences in the internet effect implies that, given that individuals obtain internet access for one reason or another, some groups increase their level of political engagement and some do not. Hypotheses of group differences can be derived directly from the presumed marginal benefits of the internet for becoming politically informed, influencing politics, and forming political networks (Bimber 1998; Barber 1999; Gibson, Howard, and Ward 2000; Di Gennaro and Dutton 2006; Krueger 2005). First, if online political information reduces the direct costs of becoming politically informed, those with the lowest disposable incomes should benefit most from internet access in terms of their propensity for political engagement (Bimber 1998).

Second, online forms of political action should reduce the (opportunity) costs of offline political activities vis-à-vis traditional forms of participation more among individuals with a high affinity to the modern technologies than among those who have difficulties overcoming the technical hurdles of internet use (Best and Krueger 2005). The expectation of age differences in the internet effect is often attributed to this affinity to new technologies (Xie and Jaeger 2008).

Third, those who find it difficult to organize their political interests in their local (offline) community may benefit more from internet access than individuals who hold political interests that many in their local environment share

TABLE 8.1. *Bivariate Association between Internet Access and Political Engagement*

	Observations	Mean	Odds Ratios for Internet Access
Internet access (yes)	20,912	0.582	–
Turnout (definitely)	17,026	0.640	1.450
Attachment to party (yes)	18,126	0.457	1.295
Interest in politics (strong or very strong)	18,159	0.374	1.486
Work in action group (yes)	18,130	0.104	1.616

Source: SOEP 2005.

(Norris 2002; Lusoli et al. 2002; Bimber 1998). For instance, small-issue publics dispersed over the country should benefit more from internet access than local interest groups aiming to improve the situation of their neighborhood.

8.3. Analysis

The analysis in this chapter is based on data from the German Socio-Economic Panel Study (SOEP), a representative household survey with annual interviews since 1984. The survey currently conducts more than twenty thousand personal interviews in more than ten thousand households. Sample selection due to the overrepresentation of subgroups (migrants, East Germans, and so forth) and sample selection due to attrition are compensated for by appropriate longitudinal and cross-sectional weighting variables and regular refreshment samples (Kroh 2009).

8.3.1. Cross-Sectional Estimates

Table 8.1 replicates previous results on the bivariate association between internet access and various indicators of political engagement for a cross-section of the population living in Germany (see also Vowe et al. 2007). The analysis draws on data emanating from the SOEP wave in 2005, a year in which the SOEP surveyed several aspects of political engagement in the population: attachment to a party, interest in politics, active political work, and intention to vote in the parliamentary election (see the Appendix for coding details). Each of the analyzed indicators of engagement is treated as a binary variable.

Although turnout is the most frequent form of political engagement (64 percent report that they would definitely participate in the parliamentary election), work in political action groups is least frequently mentioned (10 percent report spending time in political action groups). The last column of Table 8.1 reports the odds ratio of political engagement between citizens with and without access to the internet. Odds ratios give an idea of the differences in political engagement between the offline and the online community, and in contrast to differences in percentage points, they are invariant to the widely different

TABLE 8.2. *The Effect of Internet Access on Political Engagement in Cross-Sectional Logit Models (odds ratios)*

	Turnout (Definitely)	Attachment to Party (Yes)	Interest in Politics (Very or Strong)	Work in Action Group (Yes)
No controls	1.450	1.295	1.486	1.616
+ Demographic controls	1.923	1.773	2.101	1.672
+ Economic controls	1.337	1.262	1.402	1.335
+ Regional controls	1.291	1.216	1.386	1.328
+ Network controls	1.281	1.209	1.377	1.299
Observations	17,026	18,126	18,159	18,130

Note: All effects significant at $p < .001$.
Source: SOEP 2005.

prevalence of single forms of engagement (see second column of Table 8.1).[4] The reported estimates suggest that the odds of voting versus abstention are 45 percent higher in the online than the offline community, and the odds of being active in political action groups versus no such engagement are 62 percent higher.

Previous research suggests that background variables are related to internet access and political engagement at the same time, and their omission may therefore inflate the positive association between internet access and political engagement reported in Table 8.1 (Best and Krueger 2005; Norris 2002; Jennings and Zeitner 2003). Conversely, this literature suggests that once these third variables are controlled for, one obtains an unbiased estimate of the internet effect on political engagement.

Table 8.2 reports the internet effect on indicators of political engagement in the year 2005 using five different model specifications each. The first model specification, which corresponds to the rightmost column of Table 8.1, contains only a single explanatory variable in the logit model of political engagement: internet access. The second specification adds demographic control variables to the model: gender, age, and migration background. On top of that, the third model specification adds economic control variables, such as income, occupation, and education. The fourth model specification also controls for regional variables – urbanization and East-West differences in Germany – and the last specification additionally controls for measures of the individuals' embeddedness in social networks, such as number of friends, frequency of contacts in the neighborhood, membership in professional associations and labor unions, and church attendance. All these control variables are determinants of both internet

---

[4] For instance, a five-percentage-point difference in an infrequent form of participation, such as active party work, has a different meaning than a five-percentage-point difference in a form that is widely used, such as turnout.

access and political engagement, and their omission may therefore inflate the correlation between both concepts.

For each of the four indicators of political engagement – turnout in the elections, attachment to a party, interest in politics, and active work in politics – findings across the model specifications are highly similar. In model specification without any controls, the odds of a respondent with internet access are higher for all four indicators of political involvement than for respondents without internet access. The magnitude of the difference in political engagement between the offline and online community increases further once the age of respondents is controlled for in model specification 2; given that younger persons are more often internet users, but at the same time politically less engaged than older persons, the difference between the offline and online community conditional on demographical background increases. The remaining sets of control variables reduce the estimate of the internet effect, however. In the final specification (5), the cross-sectional estimates suggest that the internet increases the odds ratio of political engagement by 28 percent in the case of voting in elections, 21 percent in the case of party attachments, 38 percent in the case of political interest, and 30 percent in the case of active political work.

Given the cross-sectional estimates of the internet effect thus far, one would conclude that internet access indeed exerts a positive effect on various indicators of political engagement in Germany. Although the strong bivariate association between internet access and political engagement is to a considerable extent attributable to common background variables – particularly on education, occupation, and income – the difference in political engagement between online and offline community still remains statistically significant even conditional on many background variables.

8.3.2. Event History Estimates

The previous cross-sectional estimates suggest that the internet has a notable positive effect on political engagement. Several scholars have objected to similar findings, claiming that they reflect the reverse causal direction of a self-selection effect (Jennings and Zeitner 2003; Boulianne 2009; Norris 2005). The observation of, for instance, higher turnout rates in the online community is the consequence of those intending to vote in an election using the internet to inform themselves about candidates and policies (Prior 2005). In this second analysis, we investigate this self-selection hypothesis by analyzing the extent to which characteristics of respondents in 1995 – a time when private internet access was still uncommon in the general population (see Figure 8.1) – affected the elapsed time until obtaining internet access in the period up to 2008.

Table 8.3 reports the estimates from a discrete time event-history model of internet use obtained between 1995 and 2008 conditional on personal characteristics in 1995, a point in time when the internet started to become a mass phenomenon. Respondents "exit" the analysis in the year in which they report

TABLE 8.3. *The Effect of Political Engagement on the Duration until Obtaining Internet Access in a Discrete Survival Model (odds ratios)*

	Odds Ratios
Interest in politics	1.106**
Attachment to party	1.112**
Active work in politics	1.148**
Female	0.860***
East Germany	0.733***
Migrant	0.737***
Age	
Under 30	Ref.
30–44	0.865***
45–60	0.395***
Over 60	0.092***
Education	
Primary	Ref.
Secondary	1.443***
Tertiary	1.715***
Occupational status	
Not working	Ref.
High service	1.296***
Low service	1.061
Routine nonmanual	1.116
Routine service sales	0.989
Self-employed	1.122
Skilled manual	0.908
Unskilled manual	0.776***
Unemployed	0.708***
Income	
Lower third	Ref.
Middle third	1.263***
Higher third	1.438***
Urbanization	
Under 20,000	Ref.
20,000–100,000	1.225***
100,000–500,000	1.069
Over 500,000	1.102*
Social network	
Helping friends	0.908**
Meeting friends	0.982
Labor union or professional organization	1.076*
Churchgoing	0.934
Year Effects	Not displayed
Respondents	9401
Observations	83,563
Period	1995–2008

*** $p < 0.001$. ** $p < 0.01$. * $p < 0.05$.
Source: SOEP 2008.

having obtained internet access for the first time or in the year of their "right-censoring," which most often means refusal to participate in the SOEP survey or the end of the period of observation in 2008.

The results reported in Table 8.3 are in line with much of the previous research on the digital divide and show that access to the internet is highly stratified by socioeconomic characteristics: the odds of acquiring internet access are 72 percent higher for a university graduate than for someone with primary education, and they are 44 percent higher for the upper third of the income distribution than for the lower third of the income distribution. Prestigious occupations of the high service class in the Erikson, Goldthorpe, and Porto-carero (EGP) class scheme have above-average chances of obtaining internet access, while unskilled workers and registered unemployed persons have below-average chances of obtaining internet access. Also females, migrants, and Eastern Germans are disadvantaged with respect to their odds of obtaining internet access. Findings on urbanization and social networks (see appendix) suggest no linear relationship. Finally, age in 1995 strongly affects the odds of obtaining internet access in the long run: the odds of someone who was below thirty in 1995 to obtain internet access are $.092^{-1} = 11$ times as high as for someone of age sixty and older in 1995.

Most important, however, conditional on all these background variables, indicators of political engagement in 1995 still exert significant effects on the elapsed time until individuals obtain internet access: the odds ratio is 11 percent higher for someone who reports a party attachment in 1995, also 11 percent higher for someone interested in politics, and 15 percent for politically active respondents. This finding suggests that the causal relation between internet access and political engagement works in both directions and that cross-sectional estimates of the internet effect that do not control for prior levels of political engagement are upward biased.

8.3.3. Fixed-Effects Panel Estimates

Finally, we estimate the magnitude of the internet effect from a before-and-afterperspective of fixed-effects panel models between 1995 and 2008. The SOEP contains three indicators of political engagement that are surveyed in very short intervals, either annually or biannually: attachment to a party, interest in politics, and active political work.

As opposed to cross-sectional models, the internet effect is identified in longitudinal fixed-effects models only by individual changes in political engagement as a function of a change in having access to the internet or not (Wooldridge 2002). Third-variable problems in these models occur only with respect to coinciding events: does, for instance, entering the job market increase the likelihood of having access to the internet and of political engagement at the same time? For this reason, the analysis reported Table 8.4 controls not just for the effect of aging but also for critical life events, such as job mobility, regional mobility, change in households and partnerships, and distance to national elections. Year intercepts, not reported in the table, capture global trends in political

TABLE 8.4. *The Effect of Internet Access on Political Engagement in Panel Fixed-Effects Logit Models (odds ratio)*

	Attachment to Party	Interest in in Politics	Active Work in Politics
Internet	0.988	1.123***	1.154***
Age	0.982	0.934***	0.892***
Age	0.999***	0.999***	0.999***
Log income	1.034	0.968	0.990
First job	0.820**	0.837*	1.289
Job change	1.009	0.960	0.945
Change in partnership	1.059**	0.984	1.052
Regional mobility	0.938	0.939	0.854
Change in household composition	1.004	1.196*	0.817
Further education	0.779	1.067	1.680
Further job training	1.006	1.052	1.135
Distance to election	0.785***	0.798***	0.860***
Year effects	not displayed		
Respondents	15,884	12,735	6,083
Observations	140,235	115,111	40,308
Period	1995–2008		

*** $p < 0.001$. ** $p < 0.01$. * $p < 0.05$.
Source: SOEP 2008.

engagement and internet access that may otherwise spuriously generate correlations between both phenomena.

The fixed-effects panel models suggest weaker effects of internet access on levels of political engagement than the cross-sectional models. The odds ratio of being interested in politics increases by 12 percent and the odds ratio of active work in politics by 15 percent if one compares the levels of political engagement in the same individuals before and after obtaining access to the internet.[5] In case of the attachment to parties, the effect of internet access turns insignificant.

8.3.4. Group Differences

To test the hypothesis that the internet effect varies systematically in magnitude with characteristics of individuals, Figure 8.2 reports the internet effect in odds ratios estimated in fixed-effects panel models for different groups of the sample.

[5] Suppose that 40 percent of the sample is strongly interested in politics and 10 percent of the sample is active in politics. Moreover, 50 percent of the respondents have access to the internet. An odds ratio of, say, 1.12, in that case means that the percentages of politically interested respondents are 41.5 and 38.5, respectively, and the percentages of politically active respondents are 10.6 and 9.4, respectively. That is, in the hypothetical example, an odds ratio of 1.12 suggests a three-percentage-point difference between online and offline community in terms of political interest and a one-percentage-point difference in terms of active work in politics.

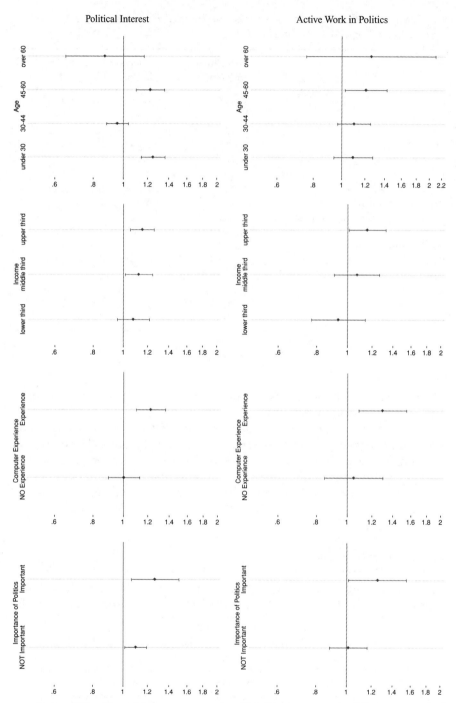

FIGURE 8.2. The effect of internet access on political engagement in different groups of the population (fixed-effects panel estimates, odds ratios).

By way of interactions, these models stratify the internet effect for age groups, income groups, and technical affinity. We use personal computer (PC) use before 1995 as an indicator of this technical affinity, because we suspect that persons using a computer before the internet became a mass phenomenon were better prepared to make use of the new opportunities of online political participation. Those individuals who made their first experiences with the PC at the time when they obtained internet access may have had higher opportunity costs of fully exploiting online opportunities. Moreover, to test the argument that online politics represents a substitute for those who were less involved in non-internet-based politics, we also estimate the internet effect in individuals who report that politics is an important aspect of their lives and in individuals for whom politics is unimportant. The measure of the perceived valence of politics dates to 1995, a time when the internet was hardly used as a political forum.

Because only interest in politics and active work in politics were found to be affected by internet access but not party attachments, we focus solely on the first two indicators of political engagement. The regression models underlying Figure 8.2 include all control variables also reported in Table 8.4. For ease of interpretation, however, we report only the point estimate of the internet effect in different groups of the sample and its respective confidence interval. Confidence intervals that constitute the neutral line indicate that estimated odds ratios do not differ statistically significantly from one, and overlapping confidence intervals between different categories of the same variable indicate statistically insignificant differences between them.

The results in Figure 8.2 suggest that many subgroups considered are affected equally, or at least not significantly differently, by the internet in terms of political engagement. The internet effect on active work in politics is still significantly positive in individuals with technical affinity, the upper third of the income distribution, middle-aged persons (from forty-five to sixty), and those who deemed politics as important before the rise of private internet usage.

The analysis suggests that the increase in political interest as a reaction to internet access is also dependent on personal characteristics: particularly individuals younger than thirty and between forty-five and sixty benefit from an internet connection in terms of political interest. Also, respondents with more income and a certain technical affinity (those with a PC before 1995) increase their level of political interest when having internet access, whereas those with low income and without the technical affinity hardly react to the availability of the internet.

Finally, contrary to expectations, those who were poorly integrated into the political process in 1995 benefit only marginally from internet access. The benefits of internet access are greater for those who deemed politics as important for their lives already before the rise of private internet usage. This holds true for both political action and interest in politics. This finding can be interpreted as the exponential version of the virtuous-circle thesis by Norris (2002): not only do politically attentive citizens select themselves into the (treatment) internet access (see Table 8.3), thus making them more likely to exploit the political benefits of the internet and become more politically active than they used to be (see Table 8.4); if they receive internet access, their marginal benefit is greater than for politically uninvolved citizens.

8.4. Conclusion

As with previous research based on U.S. data, the analysis in this chapter has shown for Germany that most of the cross-sectional correlation between political engagement and internet access is attributable to unspecified background variables and self-selection processes of politically active citizens into internet use.

Cross-sectional regression models show that about 50 percent of the correlation between internet access and political engagement is due to observable third variables on the social position of respondents. An event-history analysis of the acquisition of internet access covering the period between 1995 and 2008 suggests that political involvement in 1995 increases the likelihood of early internet access conditional on various control variables. This analysis is interpreted indicative of the self-selection hypothesis and suggests that political mobilization before the availability of the internet accounts for another 25 percent of the cross-sectional correlation between political engagement and internet access.

The event-history analysis of obtaining internet access does not represent, however, a rigorous test of the causal nature of the self-selection hypothesis, which is beyond the scope of this chapter. The hypothesis states, in essence, that citizens obtain access to the internet at a certain point in time because they intend to become politically active. The reported analysis assumes implicitly that those who report to be politically involved in 1995 also intend to become politically active in the years to come. Even if one can think of more careful tests of the self-selection hypothesis, the analysis does establish that part of the cross-sectional correlation between internet access and political engagement is attributable to previous levels of engagement.

The fixed-effects panel analysis suggests that there is still a small fraction of the correlation attributable to a causal internet effect (about 25 percent). The magnitude of the internet effect on political interest and active work in politics depends on personal characteristics of respondents. Notwithstanding that the causal internet effect is small and dependent on ancillary conditions, it does withstand rigorous empirical testing of the longitudinal analysis in a political context in which one would not expect strong effects of the internet on political engagement. Online campaigning of the major German parties is very similar to offline campaigning in traditional mass media, and German citizens rate the credibility of traditional media formats considerably higher than that of online political information Moreover, German citizens seem to use the political opportunities of the internet less actively than, for instance, U.S. citizens.

Although the internet is found to increase the level of political engagement in the population at large, it does so at the expense of increased inequalities of political interest and action. Not only are politically interested citizens more likely to obtain internet access and therefore more likely to exploit the political benefits thereof, their marginal benefit of internet access is greater than in politically disinterested citizens. Contrary to existing literature on group differences in the magnitude of an internet effect, which conveys a picture of the internet reducing the inequality of traditional political participation, the results of this chapter suggest that the mobilizing effect of the internet is stronger in citizens with high income. The upside is that the internet enhances especially younger people's interest in politics, those who are usually less interested. Nevertheless, the optimistic expectation that the internet provides a platform for those who are poorly integrated into traditional political processes (e.g., the poor, the young, political minorities) seems therefore not to hold true in general. Rather, the internet tends to reproduce existing structures of political inequalities (Barber 1999; Krueger 2002, 2006; Norris 2003; Best and Krueger 2005; Prior 2005).

8.5. Appendix

Political engagement. Each of the four variables measuring political engagement is recoded in binary variables that take the value of 1 when reflecting high levels of political engagement. The question wording is as follows:

- *Active political work* is 1 when people report devoting any amount of time when asked, "How much time do you spend participating in public citizen groups, in political parties, and local politics?"
- *Political interest* is 1 if people say that they are very or quite interested when asked, "Generally speaking, how interested are you in politics?"
- *Party attachment* is 1 if people answer yes to the following question: "Many people in Germany lean toward one party in the long term, even if they occasionally vote for another party. Do you lean toward a particular party?"
- *Voting* is 1 if people report that they would definitely vote when asked: "If the next election to the Bundestag (lower house of parliament) were next Sunday, would you vote?"

Social networks are measured by three variables based on the following question: "Which of the following activities do you take part in during your free time? Please check off how often you do each activity: at least once a week, at least once a month, less often, never" "Meeting with friends, relatives or neighbors," "Helping out friends, relatives or neighbors," and "Attending church, religious events." In addition, membership in a professional organization or a labor union was also added.

Coding of Variables

Variables	Coding
Age	Metric in the cross-sectional and panel fixed-effects models (years of age)
	Categorical in the event-history model (under 30: ref.; 30–44; 45–60; over 60).
Gender (female)	Dummy
Migrant	Dummy
Occupation (based on EGP classification)	
Not working	Reference
Higher service	Dummy
Lower service	Dummy
Routine nonmanual	Dummy
Routine service sales	Dummy
Self-employed	Dummy
Skilled manual	Dummy
Unskilled manual	Dummy
Unemployed	Dummy
Education (based on CASMIN classification)	
Primary	Reference
Secondary	Dummy
Tertiary	Dummy
Household income (OECD weighted)	Metric
Inhabitants	
<20,000	Reference
20,000–100,000	Dummy
100,000–500,000	Dummy
>500,000	Dummy
Residence in East Germany	Dummy
Social networks	
Member of a labor union or professional organization	Dummy
Helping friends and/or neighbors at least once a month	Dummy
Meeting friends at least once a week	Dummy
Visiting church at least once a month	Dummy
Changes within the last year	
First job ever	Dummy
Changed job	Dummy
Changed partner	Dummy
Moved	Dummy
New household member moved in	Dummy
Participated in	
Further education (general or vocational)	Dummy
Further education (political)	Dummy
Days to next national election (log)	Metric

9

The Uses of Digital Media for Contentious Politics in Latin America

Yanina Welp and Jonathan Wheatley

9.1. Introduction

Latin America is a region in constant flux, often in opposing and contradictory directions. After the so-called third wave of democratization that began in the late 1970s and put an end to the authoritarian regimes that held sway in most countries in the region, democracy (understood as a system in which citizens have a real opportunity to change their government through fair, regular, and competitive elections) has gradually become consolidated. However, economic and political crises continue to return to the region and have at times led to institutional breakdown.

A total of fourteen presidents in the region have been unable to complete their presidential mandates since 1980, some as a result of legal proceedings being taken against them over matters such as the violation of human rights (Alberto Fujimori in Peru, in 2000) or over corruption scandals (Fernando Collor de Mello in Brazil, in 1992). Presidents have been impeached by parliament (Abdalá Bucaram in Ecuador, in 1997) or even deposed in a classic military coup (Manuel Zelaya en Honduras, in 2009). There have been presidents who have dismissed their own parliaments (Alberto Fujimori's *autogolpe* in Peru in 1992 and that of Jorge Serrano Elías in 1993 in Guatemala), as well as failed attempts by the opposition to stage a coup (Venezuela, in 2002). These events are not merely machinations by political elites – civil society has been actively involved on many occasions. To cite just a few examples, the Painted Faces (*caras pintadas*) student movement was prominent in Brazil shortly before the resignation of Collor de Mello; a wave of protests known as El Caracazo that began in 1989 and eventually put an end to the government of Andrés Perez in Venezuela (1993); the *cacerolazos* or "pot-banging protests" led to the fall of the presidency of Fernando de la Rúa in Argentina (2001); the Paraguayan March precipitated the downfall of the government of Raúl Cubas Grau in

The authors thank Anita Breuer and the reviewers for their critical comments and suggestions.

1999; in Bolivia President Gonzalo Sánchez de Losada resigned in the midst of protests unleashed by the so-called gas war in 2003, which in 2005 also put an end to the government of his vice-president, Carlos Mesa; and finally, in 2000 President Jamil Mahuad was forced from office in Ecuador by a massive wave of demonstrations orchestrated by the Confederation of Indigenous Nationalities of Ecuador (Confederación de Nacionalidades Indígenas del Ecuador).

The apparent progress made toward consolidating democracy cannot disguise the inherent contradictions in a system that combines a formal commitment to equal rights with high levels of economic inequality and significant dissatisfaction with the institutions of representative democracy.[1] Frequently, tension emerges between governments that tend to ignore the will of the people and the people themselves, who on occasions shed their apathy and mobilize. Governments often elaborate their policies by decree or, when party discipline is strong, promote policies dictated by the leadership of their parties, without any real democratic debate.

An active civil society is key to building democracy, but at the same time if breakthroughs by civil society are not followed by fundamental changes in the socioeconomic structures, then society merely enters a new cycle associated with ever-increasing disenchantment with politics. In a best-case scenario, civil society organizations can force open the political system and reestablish a link between representatives and those who are represented. Behind the social protests that quite often catch the attention of mass media in Latin America, societal organizations with the capacity to engage in – and sustain over time – the politics of protest are becoming increasingly important. In this respect, digital media can provide tools to achieve these objectives (Bennett 2003; Shah et al. 2005).

Social movements are social phenomena based on social networks and resonant frames of collective action, and they have developed the ability to maintain a sustained challenge against powerful opponents. By enhancing the speed, flexibility, and reach of information flows, and by allowing for communication across large distances in real time, digital networks provide the technological infrastructure for the emergence and renovation of social movements (Juris 2005; Garrett 2006). Given their speed, relatively low cost, and extended geographical reach, e-mail and SMS messaging have facilitated the success of spontaneous protests, as ordinary people take to the streets against their governments or their opponents.

Despite the potential uses of digital media for political activism, although in Latin America there is a growing body of literature on social movements and new institutions of participation, studies dealing with digital media are scant and mainly focused on governments and parliaments (see, e.g., Araya

---

[1] Although there are differences between countries, on average, Latin American citizens have more trust in the Catholic Church (67 percent) and television news (52 percent) than in the courts (30 percent), parliament (22 percent), or political parties (15 percent; Barómetro Iberoamericano de Gobernabilidad 2008).

and Barria 2009; Braga 2009; Welp 2008, 2011). By analyzing five political campaigns that have been launched in a bid to influence national policy making, this chapter examines the extent to which the use of digital media is changing the prevalent patterns of civic and political involvement among civil society organizations in Latin America. It also explores the conditions under which social movements take advantage of digital media in their campaigns and the specific characteristics of the political context that condition the way digital media are used.

The selected experiences differ in their objectives and organizational structure, although all have in common that they have been promoted by citizens or civil society organizations to directly influence the definition of policies, for example by trying to repeal an existing law affecting human rights (the Amnesty Law in Uruguay), by fighting against corruption through the promotion of a new law (Campanha Ficha Limpa in Brazil), by repealing a law that has already been approved (the Laws of the Jungle in Peru), or by campaigning against industrial enterprises for environmental reasons (e.g., "No a la cementera en Los Haitises" in the Dominican Republic, "No a la papelera" in Argentina). In the following section a framework for understanding digital media influence in politics is drawn; a third section presents and analyzes the five case studies; finally, in the last section we discuss our conclusions.

9.2. Digital Media and Social Movements

Since the 1980s, media technologies have been undergoing a profound transformation that has revolutionized the way information is transmitted in most societies. These technological changes are reflected in the explosion of cable and satellite television from the late 1980s onward and subsequently in the proliferation of digital media (from the late 1990s), which have allowed for the delivery of online news as well as interactive forms of information transmission such as blogs and podcasts. Still, television remains the most important medium of information.[2] However, the spread of the internet has been continuous, if slower than in Europe or the United States. Data from the International Telecommunication Union (ITU) for 2009 on the five countries that are the focus of this chapter show that 55 percent of Uruguayans, 39.2 percent of Brazilians, 30.4 percent of Argentineans, 27.7 percent of Peruvians, and 26.7 percent of Dominicans use the internet (see also Table I.3 in the Introduction). Figures provided for 2010 by Internet World Stats (IWS) differ, especially in the Argentine case (64.4 percent), but like ITU, IWS locates Argentina, Brazil, and Uruguay among the most intensive users of the internet in the region, whereas the Dominican Republic and Peru rank among the less intensive users (see Table 9.1).

---

[2] According to Latinobarómetro surveys, over four consecutive years, an average of 81 percent of respondents asserted that television was the most important medium for obtaining information on political matters (Latinobarómetro 2008).

TABLE 9.1. *Percentage of Internet Users and Selected Campaigns in Each Country*

Country	Internet Users		Campaign
	ITU[a]	IWS[b]	
Argentina	30.4	64.4	No a la papelera (No to the Paper-Pulp Mill)
Brazil	39.2	37.8	Campanha Ficha Limpa (Clean Sheet Campaign)
Peru	27.7	27.0	Contra la Ley de la Selva (Against the Laws of the Jungle)
Dominican Republic	26.7	30.5	No a la cementera en Los Haitises (No to the Cement Works in Los Haitises)
Uruguay	55.0	52.8	Coordinadora Nacional por la Nulidad de la Ley de Caducidad (National Coordinating Body for the Abrogation of the Amnesty Law)

[a] International Telecommunications Union 2009.
[b] Internet World Statistics 2010.

It is not surprising to find that levels of literacy, wealth, and age are all correlated with internet usage, as literate, wealthier, and younger citizens are most likely to be internet users (see Table 9.2). Among the indigenous population and African Americans the probability of having a computer in 2002 was five times less than it was among the nonindigenous sector of the populations (Comisión Económica para América Latina y el Caribe 2003).[3]

Despite the digital divide, internet usage is expanding. Digital media could have a significant effect on participation given the lower participation costs, the promotion of collective identities, and the creation of communities (Garrett 2006, 204). Another feature of the digital media is its capacity for the geographical dissemination of information on social movements, which is extremely useful for activating national campaigns. This can also help to protect movements by providing protest with international visibility, as has happened in the past with the Ejército Zapatista de Liberación Nacional in Mexico, when the international pressure brought about through digital media contact forced the government to negotiate (Tarrow 2005; see also Chapter 1).

This chapter proposes three distinct hypotheses related to the rate of internet diffusion and adoption, the demographic profile of the campaign members, and the organizational features of the movement. First, regarding the attributes of a social system (opportunity structures) that facilitate or constrain movement activity (Garrett 2006), we propose a diffusion hypothesis. Digital media allow

---

[3] Despite the lack of updated statistics, Latin American countries show a similar pattern in terms of exclusion of poor, older, rural, and nonwhite populations from internet use.

TABLE 9.2. *Internet Use at Least Once in Life, by Age (%)*

Country	18–25	26–40	41–60	61+
Argentina	79	58	33	9
Brazil	76	48	28	8
Dominican Republic	65	38	21	4
Peru	80	45	24	8
Uruguay	69	49	29	10

Source: Latinobarómetro 2008.

for the expansion of social movements through the rapid diffusion of information. In this way they can gain the critical mass needed to have a real political impact. Thus, according to the diffusion hypothesis, campaigns developed in countries with higher levels of internet use among citizens are expected to be more intensive in their use of digital media.

Second, we suggest a demographic hypothesis. The use of digital media by a given social movement depends both on the demographic profile of the movement itself and on the demographic profile of the country. We expect that among certain social groups (the young, urban, nonindigenous, and highly educated citizens) the use of such media is greater. Garrett's (2006) framing process, understood as strategic attempts to craft, disseminate, and contest the narratives used to describe a movement, is relevant here. Among youths, digital media may be used as a way to renovate politics against traditional modes of vertical, hierarchical communication. Another aspect of the demographic hypothesis is functional: digital media are necessary when the participants in a movement are dispersed geographically in such a way that traditional forms of communication (especially face-to-face contact) are difficult. This is most likely if the public space in which the campaign takes place is large in geographical terms, or lacks transport and traditional communications infrastructure, but also has sufficient internet and mobile phone access to make use of digital media possible.

Third, we propose a structural hypothesis. Digital media, based as they are on many-to-many, reciprocal, and nonhierarchical communication, are particularly used in horizontal, nonhierarchical movements. This is because the cultural logic of networking identifies and propagates a set of deeply embedded social and cultural dispositions that orient actors toward building horizontal ties and connections among diverse, autonomous elements through decentralized coordination and directly democratic decision making (Juris 2005; Castells 2007). However, we also suggest that mobilizing structures that encompass not only formal configurations, such as social movement organizations, but also informal configurations, such as networks of activists (Garrett 2006) could promote or inhibit the use of digital media. Horizontal, nonhierarchical movements have an organizational logic that is shared by digital networks, as everyone has an equal opportunity to introduce information and to mobilize other actors. At the same time, movements (especially localized movements) in which face-to-face contacts already serve to organize and mobilize a campaign do not require digital media as a fundamental part of their organizational strategy.

9.3. Methodology

This is an exploratory study, and the selected cases are not intended to represent the entire universe of protest movements in Latin America. The selection of cases was made to test the extent to which the host countries' level of internet use, as well as the profile of the particular groups promoting the selected campaigns (regarding their age composition, rural-urban character, and literacy level) and the structure of the movement (horizontal versus hierarchical), could be related to a more intense use of digital media in the selected campaigns. For this reason we selected cases from countries showing diversity both in terms of the level of internet diffusion (relatively high in Argentina, Brazil, and Uruguay; and relatively low in the Dominican Republic and Peru) and in terms of the age and social status of the groups that spearheaded the campaigns (mainly youths in the Dominican Republic, mainly middle-age, middle-class activists in Argentina and Uruguay; a relatively young activist intelligentsia in Brazil; and relatively poor, indigenous rural communities in Peru).

The five selected experiences also diverge according to the objectives, strategies, and actors involved. Finally, the political contexts of each case and the networks used to mobilize are diverse (see Table 9.3). In one case, traditional organizations such as labor unions and political parties played a dominant role (Uruguay); in another a broad network of organizations worked together to promote a particular issue (Brazil); in the third case the campaign was promoted spontaneously by a network of groups in which young people played a key role (Dominican Republic); the fourth case was motivated by the reaction of civil society in one particular city (Argentina); in the final case the protest was initiated and developed by indigenous movements (Peru).

A first step after the selection of campaigns was the systematic analysis of their digital media use (websites, blogs, and online social networking services such as Twitter, Facebook, MySpace, Sonico, hi5, and Orkut). This allowed us to see how these different devices were used, as well as the extent to which different groups, websites, and blogs were interlinked. A second step in the research process involved in-depth interviews. To select the interviewees we proceeded in different ways: contacting the creators of blogs, identifying people on the relevant websites or in social networks; identifying people through previous personal contact with members of some of the campaigns, approaching political commentators in each country, and eliciting new contacts from those interviewed (snowball sampling).[4] These processes also informed the

---

[4] Six interviews were conducted each for the analysis of the Brazilian, Uruguayan, and Argentine cases and four each for the cases of the Dominican Republic and Peru. These were supplemented by an interview with a specialist in politics and media in each case. The campaigns conducted in

TABLE 9.3. *Key Features of the Five Cases Corresponding to the Three Hypotheses*

Country	Internet Diffusion	Demographic Profile of Users	Structure of the Movement	Intensity of Digital Media Uses
Argentina	Relatively high	Middle age, middle class	Horizontal, assemblies as forum to take decisions, high level of coordination	Middle, oriented toward dissemination
Brazil	Relatively high	Young, professionals, well educated, middle class, urban	Horizontal with a high level of coordination, decentralization of activities	High, oriented toward dissemination, mobilization, pressure, etc.
Dominican Republic	Relatively low	Young, urban, middle class together with more traditional organizations	Horizontal without systematic methods to take decisions nor a unique strategy but complementary actions	High, oriented toward dissemination, to establish national and international networks, and to organize activities
Peru	Relatively low	Indigenous, rural, more marginalized population groups	With elected representatives from affected communities	Low, basic information on the website
Uruguay	Relatively high	Middle age, middle class, led by members of labor unions and political parties	Horizontal	Middle, mainly oriented toward dissemination

research process, as in some cases personal and traditional telephone contact were important whereas in others, e-mail, chat, or internet phone conversations played a more important role.

Interviews were developed around a set of guiding questions that in some cases led to a discussion of other issues (semistructured interviews with some open questions). The core of guiding questions was designed to find out (1) the

Brazil, Uruguay, Argentina, and the Dominican Republic were traced through the digital media during their development (the authors participated as members of Facebook groups and Orkut, receiving information that was circulated on mailing lists). In the case of Brazil, Uruguay, and Argentina the authors had the opportunity to visit the activists and talk to them in situ.

virtual spaces built or used to promote the campaign; (2) the influence of the digital divide on the digital media strategy; (3) the intensity of digital media used to promote activities such as dissemination of information, mobilization, debate, and so forth (intense, occasional, scant, or null); (4) interaction with mass media; (5) the role played by digital media in the campaign (complementary or alternative to more traditional forms of media); (6) the process of decision making inside the movement; and (7) general assessment of how digital media are used for campaign development. Finally, secondary sources (including newspapers and official documents such as laws or official reports) were used to contextualize each movement.

9.4. Case Analysis

9.4.1. *Uruguay: Against the Amnesty Law*

Although today Uruguay is one of the most stable democracies in the world (Moreira 2004), as many Latin American countries, it suffered a harsh dictatorship in the third quarter of the twentieth century (1973–85). As in Spain and Chile, the authoritarian incumbents played an important role in shaping the institutions of the newly reestablished democracy. Law 15848 (Ley de Caducidad de la Pretensión Punitiva del Estado), which provided an amnesty for those involved in human rights violations during the military dictatorship, was a key element in the transition.

Despite the approval of this law by the institutions of representative democracy, the Uruguayan political system possesses two specific features that are unique in the region in terms of challenging the power of these institutions: the obligatory referendum and the popular initiative.[5] In recent years, civil society organizations have entered the political game as actors with veto power, as evidenced by a number of referenda that occurred in the 1990s and stopped certain neoliberal reforms that lacked public support. Further evidence of citizens' involvement in politics is provided by successive Latinobarómetro surveys, which indicate that Uruguayan society embraces democracy with greater enthusiasm than most other societies in the region (Latinobarómetro 2009).

Civil society organizations started collecting signatures to activate a referendum against the Amnesty Law almost as soon as democracy was reestablished. In 1987, just a couple of years after the restoration of democracy, the National Pro-Referendum Commission (Comisión Nacional Pro-Referéndum) presented 634,792 signatures to the electoral court to activate a consultation. After several institutional struggles, a referendum was called in April 1989; however, a majority (57.5 percent of valid votes cast) voted against the abolition of the Amnesty Law. In 2006 the National Coordinating Body for the

---

[5] Even if certain aspects of direct democracy in Latin America are more widespread than previously, Uruguay is unique in that although the president is not allowed to call a referendum, mandatory referenda, abrogative referenda, and citizens' initiatives are frequently used (Welp and Serdült 2009).

Abrogation of the Amnesty Law (Coordinadora Nacional por la Nulidad de la ley Ley de Caducidad) was established to spearhead a new campaign to abrogate the Amnesty Law. The main arguments used in favor of repealing the law were that it was in violation of international human rights agreements signed by Uruguay and that it appeared to be based on an invalid legal principle that "recognizes military pressure as a source of law" (Interview with Gabriel Seré). In September 2007 a new campaign was launched to collect the required 258,000 signatures that would allow for the convocation of an abrogative referendum. In April 2009 the signatures (340,043) were presented to the national parliament. The electoral court organized the referendum to be held in October 2009, to coincide with the presidential election and another referendum called by the parliament to decide on the voting rights of Uruguayans living abroad. However, the proposal was defeated in the referendum by a narrow margin (with 52 percent of valid votes opposing the measure).

Although the initiative was endorsed in a personal capacity by certain members of center-right parties, only parties of the left and center-left (some of them in the governing coalition) gave institutional support. These were Nuevo Espacio, the Socialist Party, the Communist Party, and the Party for the People's Victory. The labor union Plenario Intersindical de Trabajadores y Convención Nacional de Trabajadores (PIT-CNT) and a number of associations, including the Association of Former Political Prisoners of Uruguay (Asociación de Ex-Presos Políticos del Uruguay) and the Federation of University Students of Uruguay (Federación de Estudiantes Universitarios de Uruguay, FEUU), also joined the initiative. The key role in the movement was therefore played by traditional organizations, most notably by political parties and labor unions.

The use of digital media by the Coordinadora was rather moderate. The website presented a simple format, with information on the law it aimed to repeal, the means for financial cooperation, and the members of the platform. There were some links to news releases and television programs and an online survey. In addition to this website, online presentations for the campaign featuring children and other relatives of activists murdered or disappeared during the dictatorship appeared on Facebook and YouTube.[6] The Coordinadora met regularly in assemblies to make decisions on how to run the campaign. Most of the activities were based on face-to-face contact, in meetings, conferences, and lectures. One political analyst argued that this was a traditional campaign that fit well in the Uruguayan tradition of referenda.[7] Digital media were therefore of secondary importance to the campaign.

---

[6] One example is that of MarysYic, daughter of the murdered politician NubleYic, who was interviewed in the course of this research (various exchanges during May 2010). For videos with testimony from family members of those arrested, disappeared, and murdered; fragments of parliamentary debates with statements in favor of the abrogation of the law; shocking historical accounts and other testimonials, see, e.g., http://www.youtube.com/watch?v=E7tPghf9wgk; http://www.youtube.com/watch?v=lem-fRI324k; http://www.youtube.com/watch?v=MUM0Eu8pEsg; and http://www.youtube.com/watch?v=2dLn_4b4RWA.

[7] Interview with Daniel Chasquetti, Uruguayan political analyst (April 5, 2010).

These findings contradict our diffusion hypothesis, as Uruguay is the country with the highest rate of internet diffusion among the countries analyzed in this chapter. Turning to the second hypothesis on the demographic profile of the campaign, at the periphery of the campaign a significant number of young people made use of digital media to collect signatures and promote the vote, especially during the mobilization period. However, the organizers of the campaign were mostly middle age and were not familiar with digital media. The fact that digital media were not central to the campaign may therefore reflect the age profile of the participants, which tends to confirm the demographic hypothesis. Finally, regarding the structural hypothesis, despite the horizontal, nonhierarchical organizational structure of the campaign, the presence of traditional organizations such as parties and labor unions appears to have inhibited a greater use of digital media in favor of a repertoire of more tried and tested campaigning strategies.

9.4.2. *Brazil: Campanha Ficha Limpa*

Brazil has, in recent years, been associated with renewed economic growth persistently accompanied by political corruption. There were scandals involving the parliament in 2005 and 2006, and the Federal Supreme Court has intervened on a number of occasions to sit in judgment on these alleged violations, which are widely considered to be serious (Ayllón 2007; Amorim Neto and Coelho 2008). A particularly egregious form of corruption was an illegal fundraising scheme through which the government attempted to maintain support in Congress by bribing members of smaller opposition parties.

The origins of the Movement against Electoral Corruption (Movimento de Combate à Corrupção Eleitoral, MCCE) go back to 1986, when the Brazilian Commission for Justice and Peace (Comissão Brasileira Justiça e Paz), which is linked to the National Conference of Bishops of Brazil (Conferência Nacional dos Bispos do Brasil, CNBB), began a campaign to prevent vote buying. This initiative led to the adoption of Law 9840/1999 on the corruption of elected officials and fraud in elections. The aim was to amend the electoral law by using a popular initiative procedure that requires the written support of 1 percent of the electorate. The MCCE organized various activities, including a national survey and public hearings, to try to measure the impact of the vote buying and to place this issue on the public agenda. Both the electoral authorities and some media outlets lent their support to the campaign, which helped to strengthen the movement, but many difficulties remained. Resistance came from many of those who lived in poverty and therefore relied on patronage networks.

Since then, an extensive network of organizations, including religious organizations, trade unions, youth organizations, organizations of judges and lawyers, and other nongovernmental organizations (NGOs), has become involved in this struggle across the length and breadth of the country.[8] In April 2008 the network launched the Clean Sheet Campaign (Campanha Ficha Limpa) to

---

[8] The list of institutions in the network is long. The most active are listed at http://mcce.org.br/node/9.

improve the profile of candidates to elective positions in the country and in particular to prevent criminals from entering parliament. As a result of the campaign, a new law that was eventually approved by the parliament and entered into force on June 4, 2010, sought to prevent politicians who have been convicted of serious crimes, such as racism, rape, drug trafficking, misuse of public funds, corruption, and murder, from running in elections and attaining, if elected, immunity from prosecution.[9]

The organizers of the campaign relied on the growing numbers of internet users and the active use of online social networking sites in Brazil.[10] Many forms of digital media were used and combined with already existing websites (such as that of the MCCE[11]) to establish new forms of contact between citizens and activists. A large number of campaign videos and interviews were placed on YouTube,[12] some of which found their way onto mainstream television. One of the more active members of the campaign indicated that, because the MCCE website did not allow the use of properly interactive tools, applications such as Facebook, Twitter, and Orkut were particularly important.[13] The backing of a global organization dedicated to online mobilization, such as Avaaz,[14] allowed thousands of e-mails to be sent to parliamentarians and ordinary citizens to complete the process of collection of signatures: "We collected signatures for months in streets and market places. When we had nearly a million and we saw that time was running out, a youth group was organized to get on the internet and in less than a month four hundred thousand more signatures were obtained."[15] In addition, support committees, regional committees, and even individual members set up blogs in support of the campaign.[16]

---

[9] For the text of the law, see http://www.planalto.gov.br/ccivil_03/Leis/LCP/Lcp135.htm.

[10] Brazilian consumers spend an average of 19.3 hours online for personal use versus 9.8 hours watching television, according to a study released by Deloitte. See http://venturebeat.com/2009/06/22/brazil-social-advertisings-next-frontier/ (accessed September 2010). Another study by the social media company Sysomos shows that Brazil is the fifth-largest nation of Twitter users. See http://latamthought.org/2009/07/13/twitter-in-brazil/ (accessed September 2010).

[11] http://mcce.org.br.

[12] See "Vídeo campanha ficha limpa: Baixe, assista e divulgue!" YouTube, http://www.youtube.com/watch?v=Irs8X_h6REg, http://www.youtube.com/watch?v=lQUIIaTHpNo&feature=related, and http://www.youtube.com/watch?v=geHyotKoJjk&feature=related.

[13] In Facebook, "Campanha Ficha Limpa do Movimento de Combate à Corrupção Eleitoral"; in Twitter, "twitter.com/fichalimpa"; in Orkut, http://www.orkut.com.br/Main#Community.aspx?cmm=5065228.

[14] Avaaz.org (http://www.avaaz.org) is a community of more than 4 million global citizens who take action on the major issues facing the world today. The organization's aim "is to ensure that the views and values of the world's people – and not just political elites and unaccountable corporations – shape global decisions." http://www.avaaz.org/po/brasil_ficha_limpa/?mcce.

[15] Interview with Marlon Reis (March 5, 2010), judge and member of the MCCE, responsible for the Facebook campaign and blog author (http://marlonreis.blogspot.com).

[16] For example: Blog do Comitê de Ponta Grossa (http://www.mccepg.blogspot.com); Campanha em São Paulo (http://campanhafichalimpasp.blogspot.com); Campanha no Espírito Santo (http://fichalimpa-es.blogspot.com/2009/08/o-que-e-campanha-ficha-limpa.html); MCCE Mato Grosso (http://mcce-mt.org); Comitê 9840 de Campinas (http://mccecampinas.blogspot.com).

Regarding the internal organization of the movement, MCCE is primarily a horizontal network coordinated by a national committee and composed of representatives of organizations such as the Lawyers' College and the Bishops' Conference. Given the need to make quick decisions, a committee was elected with a specific informal mandate to take urgent measures regarding the processing of the draft law based on the popular initiative.

Those interviewed agreed that the strategy that developed online occurred naturally as an extension of the normal practices of those involved in social networks. In spite of this, they recognize that, although the internet has taken center stage in the campaign, it is the middle classes that have taken advantage of the internet, whereas the less wealthy sectors of society are involved in more traditional types of activity in the campaign.[17] According to a member of the MCCE, "With the internet, we are able to reach out mostly to the middle and upper classes of Brazil – a lot has been said of how it is something of an 'elite' movement, since most internet users in Brazil are young, educated and urban. Our next challenge is to take this political activism from the virtual world to the streets and from the 'thinking' middle classes to the whole country" (interview with Isabela Nogueira da Gama, May 5, 2010). With respect to the online campaign, all interviewees agreed that it was fundamental in gathering popular support to pass the law and in collecting signatures (digital signatures do not have legal validity): "Through the online campaign, we urged all members from our social network groups to write and call their representatives, to sign the online petition, and it provided a place for them to meet and organize public demonstrations. It helped us obtain support from celebrities who are on Facebook and Twitter, who have a lot more 'followers' than we do, so it was easier to spread the word about the campaign." Digital media were also used to disseminate links to news articles that discussed the campaign or listed politicians who were against the campaign and who tried to keep it from being voted on (da Gama May 5, 2010).

The use of digital media was high, intense, and decentralized in this campaign. The degree of internet diffusion, the profile of most of the leaders of the movement (young, well educated, and middle class, with access to mobile telephones and computer devices), and the network-based, nonhierarchical organization of the campaign created strong incentives to use digital media, so this case seems to fit well with our three hypotheses.

An interesting finding is the extent to which digital media were useful in connecting organizations and people across the territory of a large and decentralized country. This contrasts with the Uruguayan experience, as in Uruguay face-to-face meetings are more easily organized because of the small size of the country. Moreover, the fact that the national political agenda is mainly defined in the capital, Montevideo (where nearly 40 percent of the country's

---

[17] Interview with Luciano Santos, member of the MCCE (http://www.mcce.org) and Articulação Brasileira Contra a Corrupção e a Impunidade (ABRACCI, the Brazilian Network against Corruption and Impunity) (http://abracci.ning.com) (April 30, 2010).

population lives), meant that the campaign was mostly restricted to the relatively narrow geographical boundaries of the capital city. Another relevant finding of the Brazilian case is the way online and offline strategies reinforced each other. An example of this synergy was the launch of a campaign in which mass e-mails were sent to members of parliament as they were about to discuss the new law to prevent criminals from entering parliament. This demonstrated the extent of social pressure and made sure that traditional media outlets paid attention to the protests; as a result, the law was approved without delay.

9.4.3. Dominican Republic: "No a la cementera en Los Haitises"
In May 2009 a government concession granted the Dominican Mining Consortium the right to extract limestone from sedimentary rocks in order to manufacture cement along the border of the national park Los Haitises. Los Haitises is located in the municipality of Gonzalo, one of the poorest municipalities in the country, and is a repository of vast water reservoirs that benefit more than 1 million people. The factory would displace five hundred peasant families.[18] A movement was immediately organized to denounce the potential damage to the environment, as well as the lack of transparency with which the government arrived at its decision, which, opponents claimed, was based on a desire to hide corrupt practices.[19]

During the past decade the Dominican Republic has experienced the emergence and empowerment of protest movements, as well as greater coordination among them (Espinal 2001; Mitchell 2008). Evidence of this trend can be found in the mobilization of various ecological and youth groups, such as the Movimiento Campesino Comunidades Unidas, Espeleogrupo, La Revuelta, Felabel, Juventud Caribe, Projuventud, La Multitud, and Revolución 65. Following the granting of the government concession to the Dominican Mining Consortium, these groups, as well as the main opposition party, the Dominican Revolutionary Party, were united in requesting that the government reverse its decision. Geologists and environmentalists pointed out that the plan for cement production violated more than twenty environmental laws. A report

[18] According to Santos (2009), "Since 1980, thousands of Haitian and Dominican peasants have been forcefully removed from Los Haitises by the military. Though the Dominican government promised to pay compensation for their lands and crops, compensation never arrived in most cases. Prior to carrying out any evictions, the government criminalizes peasants with the aid of the mainstream media by accusing them of cutting down trees and destroying the biodiversity of the park."

[19] There were allegations of conflicts of interest. A source told *Dominican Today* that one of the stakeholders in the project is a private-sector leader whom the government recruited to help manage some of the national parks. The government concession was issued by Jaime David Fernández Mirabal, the environment minister. He is under criticism for going against the advice of his own technicians in the Environment and Natural Resources Department, which issued a report warning of the environmental destruction the construction of a cement factory in Los Haitises could unleash.

issued jointly by the Academy of Science and the Environmental Commission of the State University (UASD) called for the immediate revocation of the government concession and the relocation of peasant communities that had been displaced. As a result of the pressure, in late June 2009 the government agreed to commission a report from the United Nations Development Program (UNDP) on the environmental impact of the project. The mobilization of the protest movement through social networks as well as protest actions in the National national park itself continued until the end of the year, when the UNDP report was published. The report was highly critical of the Dominican government, and its final resolution came out against the installation of the cement factory.[20]

The digital media used most of all by the protest movement was the Facebook group, "Todos unidos contra la cementera en Los Haitises," with more than 5,300 followers, as well as blogs and websites of all the organizations involved. Particularly relevant was the website No Cementera,[21] which contained much information about the national park, as well as maps of the zone. Similarly, political groups, such as Toy Jarto and La Revuelta, disseminated information about a protest camp in the park and organized visits there through their blogs.[22]

According to one of the leaders, despite the digital divide, social networks played a key role in the protests, especially through the use of cell phones. The campaign was coordinated in a simple and open manner: "One of our objectives was to create a space in the social network Facebook in which the network was used as a meeting point, a 'great virtual classroom,' where, through dialogue and participation of supporters, it was possible to reach conclusions about the actions to be implemented not only to fight and defend our opinions but also to do our bit for social awareness on these issues."[23] In the words of Andrés Merejo: "Social networks in cyberspace contribute to a new form of struggle against the dominant discourse and to the decline of traditional forms of media and their social control. 'Digital natives,' in other words young people born in a digital and global age, are pioneers of a new global understanding of social, economic, and environmental problems" (interview April 30, 2010).

What this campaign shows is that even in a context of low internet diffusion, certain groups of people can still successfully use digital media as a campaigning tool. The crucial factor in the Dominican case is that many of the activists involved were young and well familiarized with digital media. As the Brazilian case showed as well, the campaign in the Dominican Republic supports the hypothesis proposed in the Introduction of this book that the most

---

[20] For details, see http://www.hoy.com.do/el-pais/2009/11/26/303612/PNUD-rechaza-instala cion-de-cementera-en-Los-Haitises.

[21] http://nocementera.com.

[22] http://toyjarto.com and http://larevueltard.blogspot.com/2009/05/campamento-de-solidari dad-con-los_13.html.

[23] Interview with Anyelo Rodríguez Morla, student at the Caribbean University and activist (March 5, 2010).

direct consequence of the extension of digital media use for political involvement is the expansion of the repertoire of modes and channels of political
participation, communication, and information. At the same time, it is equally
evident that the context conditions the results. Given that the government and
the institutions were somehow less open and transparent than in cases such
as Brazil or Uruguay, the movement had more incentives to go abroad looking for support to the United Nations, and to look for alternative spaces to
search for information and learn about the decisions, like those provided by
digital media as argued by Jorba and Bimber in Chapter 1. At the same time,
the ecological demands that define this campaign are central to the agenda
of the international environmental movement (more than national issues such
as the derogation or creation of a particular law that is specific to a particular
country), thus reinforcing the salience of digital media in the search for external
support and alliances.

To summarize, the relatively extensive use of digital media in this campaign
seems to reflect the demographic profile of the activists of the campaign. The
campaign was driven to a considerable degree by young people, who used
Facebook and other forms of digital media to expand the campaign to a wider
global audience. This appears to confirm our second hypothesis that the use of
digital media in a campaign is, in part at least, a function of the demographic
profile of its activists. The horizontal, nonhierarchical structure of the movement may also have created positive incentives for the use of digital media as a
campaign tool, supporting our third, structural hypothesis.

9.4.4. *Argentina: Gualeguaychú de Pie*

Mobilization at the local level, the articulation of an issue through networks
that extend beyond this level, the use of an assembly as a forum for decision
making, and the cutting of transport routes as a form of symbolic protest are
characteristics that define many environmental movements in Argentina today,
especially those that oppose the activities of polluting enterprises. The picket, or
closure of transport routes, began to grow as a form of protest in the 1990s, as
it was the only form of protest open for the unemployed, who had no recourse
to the classical method of the workers' struggle, the strike.[24] But this new form
of protest was rapidly adopted as a strategy by other organizations.

The assembly of Gualeguaychú (a city of 76,000 inhabitants) was created
as part of a strategy to oppose the activities of Botnia-UPM's paper-pulp mill,
located nearby across the border in Uruguay on the banks of the estuary of
the Uruguay River, on the grounds that it was polluting the water of the river,
which runs close to the city of Gualeguaychú. Protests began as soon it was

---

[24] The picket is a form of struggle of the industrial age: the aim was to prevent strikebreakers
from entering the factory. The territory of the picket was the factory and its surroundings, and
the objective was to support the strike and prevent production. In the 1990s cutting transport
routes was a new form of protest used by the unemployed, who were excluded from the system
of production and had neither power nor representation (Escobar and Welp 2004).

known that the Uruguayan government was negotiating with industries that produced the pulp that would feed the mill.[25]

Every year since 2005 a march has been organized on April 25, bringing together tens of thousands of inhabitants on the Libertador General San Martín Bridge that crosses the river and links Uruguay to Argentina. A camp was set up in 2006 to prevent traffic from crossing the bridge in a place called Arroyo Verde, which has became a symbol of the struggle. At first the camp was organized on special dates such as weekends or when a meeting between involved politicians took place; but in November 2006 activists decided to install a permanent camp, and this had a very significant (and ever-growing) impact on the economy of the area. For the movement, the campaign has been highly costly in terms of organization and human participation. In particular, the assembly has created committees to carry out high-impact activities that need to be kept secret for the desired objective to be achieved.[26] The assembly and the transport blockade have remained the two basic pillars of the protest right up to the present day.

In September 2009, the Argentinean state, under pressure from the protesters, brought a case before the International Court of Justice at The Hague. In April 2010, the court delivered its verdict, declaring that Uruguay had violated the Uruguay River Statute by failing to communicate its plans to Argentina (as required by the statute), but the court declared itself incompetent to make a judgment on the future of the mill. On April 25, 2010, the annual march to the bridge again brought together tens of thousands of activists, and on May 16 an open assembly resolved to maintain the blockade and continue the struggle. Whatever the final outcome, the achievements of this protest movement are noteworthy. By their actions the protesters have managed to capture the attention of the mass media for a considerable period of time, have influenced the appointment of the highest national authority on environmental matters, and have encouraged Argentina to file an international lawsuit in The Hague. They also managed to ensure that another pulp mill that had been planned for the banks of the Uruguay River had to relocate (Natanson 2010).

---

[25] On May 5, 2006, Argentina's president Néstor Kirchner visited the city and described Gualeguaychú's struggle as a national struggle. However, the attitude of the government toward the Gualeguaychú assembly has been inconsistent. The strict pacifism of the protest, together with the fact that many of those who have joined it belong to the middle classes, as well as an awareness that the use of repression in Argentina led to the fall of the government previous to Kirchner's, explain in part why neither the police nor the military have intervened in the conflict. The local branch of the national Gendarmería, which sympathizes with the protesters, has played a rather supervisory or supporting role, or so declare the members of the assembly themselves.

[26] One emblematic event that gained international visibility was when the local carnival queen entered a summit of presidents of the European Union and Mercosur and, during the photo time, took off her coat and walked around in a bikini with a large placard bearing the slogan "No to the paper-pulp mill" in front of the bewildered gaze of the presidents. See http://www .youtube.com/watch?v=k7ILYrSS5Dc.

In terms of organization, links have been forged between the movement and other environmental actors in the region. One member of the assembly described the process of establishing ties between different assemblies in the following way: "We began alone. Afterwards different assemblies from other places drew together in order to share experience" (interview with Cecilia Alvarez, activist, April 23, 2010). Later the Union of Citizens Assemblies (Unión de Asambleas Ciudadanas, or UAC[27]) was set up, which met every three months in different places and brought together all the citizens' assemblies of the country that were calling for changes in the way natural resources were managed and in the policy of the present government, "which is too tolerant of multinationals and does not listen to the people" (interview with Cecilia Alverez, May 15, 2010). The UAC backed these different movements without attempting to interfere with either the horizontal mode of decision making or the autonomy of local assemblies, but it defended one specific method: "popular consultation and the self-determination of our communities is the only way to arrive at a model for sustainable development at regional level, one that respects the ecosystem, local economies, as well as local cultures and identities . . . There is no steering committee, or management, nor spokespersons" (UAC member).[28]

In terms of the use of digital media, one of the more curious findings of our research on this movement is that the Gualeguaychú campaign combined a horizontal mode of organization and local autonomy in decision making while relying mainly on traditional forms of media rather than the internet. Face-to-face contact and simple telephone conversations have proved the most effective means of communication to organize actions. Although demonstrations have been announced on Facebook, many of the most highly involved activists have neither computers nor internet connections and see no need to acquire them. The internet has functioned merely as a means of disseminating the press releases of the assembly, as well as photos of its different activities and monitoring reports and songs against the pulp mill. There have also been comments (for and against the pulp mill) posted on the blogs of those living on either side of the river (i.e, the international border) in an individual capacity.[29] However, some activists, especially the youngest, have demonstrated a more proactive attitude with regard to digital media, as can be seen in the YouTube videos of concerts in the Arroyo Verde camp, photographs and maps of the area with songs or discourses against the pulp mill, Argentinian and Uruguayan flags

---

[27] http://asambleasciudadanas.org.ar.

[28] UAC members refuse to offer names.

[29] For instance: see http://www.ipodagua.com.ar, http://www.fundavida.com.ar, http://www.elaguamanda.blogspot.com, http://www.guardaelguachazo.blogspot.com, http://www.militantesporlavida.blogspot.com, and http://www.elojodelarazon.blogspot.com. There are also activities on Facebook and Twitter, and YouTube videos of the actions realized. Also people who defend the enterprise have used blogs to do so: http://www.lafraybentina.com.uy and http://www.verdevilla.blogspot.com.

flying together, and especially the emblematic demonstrations with thousands walking along the bridge every April 25.

This case shows some similarities with the Uruguayan case; despite similarly (relatively high) levels of internet use among the population and the similar profile of the activists (middle or upper middle class with access to internet and digital media), the use of digital media during the campaign was moderate and mainly oriented toward dissemination of information. As in Uruguay, most activists were middle-aged, and although some young people used digital media to disseminate information, debate or organization of activities was conducted along more traditional lines. Thus, in both cases tried and tested campaigning techniques tended to predominate over new ways of communication or organization. Appeals to the mass media were used to articulate the demands of the campaign in the national political agenda; traditional face-to-face activities and meetings were predominant at the local level, whereas digital media were used more to disseminate information and to establish links with other organizations.

9.4.5. Peru: Against the Laws of the Jungle

If in the 1970s and 1980s environmental protest seemed more like a luxury enjoyed by "citizens of the first world," since the 1990s this phenomenon has, for various reasons, extended across the length and breadth of Latin America. This we have already seen in our discussion of how plans to build a cement factory along the edge of Los Haitises National Park in the Dominican Republic or the pulp mill in Gualeguaychú (Argentina) were rejected by the local population. The struggle against open-cast mining is also a salient example of a movement that has gained strength in many countries.[30] The origins of this struggle are a consequence of global power relations that have caused developed countries to reject more exploitative forms of production, which have been shifted to the more peripheral regions of the globe.

Peru was the first country in Latin America to export gold to China. The associated extraction and other mining projects have triggered numerous protests across the country. However, the government has not been particularly affected by these protests because the conflicts have tended to be isolated with their own specific actors and dynamics, and have failed to generate a united movement (Tanaka and Vera 2008). The mobilization that we have chosen as our last case study was not directed against any particular enterprise or against the mining industry in general; instead, it focused on the way Peruvian law on the protection of the Amazon rain forest was watered down to conform to the free-trade agreement with the United States. The initiators of the protests

---

[30] Open-cast mining uses particularly aggressive methods to obtain minerals that are not accessible in the form of seams but are instead thinly distributed in rocks; to extract these minerals requires techniques such as the use of large quantities of water and cyanide. Such means of production have a profound impact in the locality: they do not give rise to growth in the local economy (there is no spillover effect), but they have a major impact on the environment of the region, affecting agriculture, fishing, and tourism. For a more detailed analysis, see Svampa and Antonelli (2009).

were indigenous organizations. Already in 2007, the following controversial declaration by President Alan García sparked the indignation of the indigenous community: "There are many resources that are going to waste, that do not receive investment and do not generate work. And all this because of the taboo of an outdated ideology, because of laziness, indolence or the law of the dog in the manger, which states: 'If I do not do it, nobody does it'" (El Comercio, October 28, 2007). In June 2008, the president approved ten legislative decrees (that had been delegated to him by the Congress) that would permit Peruvian law to be adapted to conform to the free-trade agreement. This package, known as "the laws of the jungle," would affect the property rights of indigenous peoples living in a territory of million hectares. The decrees were illegal because they violated both the Indigenous and Tribal Peoples Convention (1989) of the International Labour Organization (also known as ILO Convention 169) and the Peruvian Constitution, which guarantees the inviolability of land ownership of native communities and sustainable development of the Amazon region. Protests broke out almost immediately.

The Interethnic Association for the Development of the Peruvian Rainforest (Asociación Interétnica de Desarrollo de la Selva Peruana, or AIDESEP)[31] and the Confederation of Amazonian Nationalities of Peru (Confederación de Nacionalidades Amazónicas del Peru[32]) initiated the protests. Some 5,000 persons from more than sixty tribes blocked roads and waterways and in August 2008 seized control of two energy installations – a natural gas field and a petroleum pipeline – causing a number of cities to suffer food shortages and power shutdowns. As a response, the government ordered the dismantling of the blockades and sent in the police and the army. There were numerous clashes in the jungle city of Bagua, which led to dozens of deaths.

Toward the end of August, Peru's Congress agreed to vote on the law's possible repeal – on the condition that protesters unblock roads and suspend demonstrations.[33] A few days later, the Peruvian Congress voted to repeal Decree Law (DL) 1015 (effectively abolishing the special regime under which land and forests were managed the native communities) that was particularly vigorously opposed by indigenous communities.[34] However, the Congress retained DL 1013 (centralizing environmental policy by creating a new Ministry of the Environment), which was also strongly opposed by indigenous groups, and the struggle reactivated in 2009.

Despite the fact that the indigenous communities involved in the protests were less likely to have access to digital media than their urban and better-educated counterparts, digital media still played an (albeit minor) role in these

[31] http://www.aidesep.org.pe.
[32] http://www.conap.org.pe.
[33] For more information, see "Peru to Vote on Divisive Land Law," AlJazeera, August 21, 2008, http://english.aljazeera.net/news/americas/2008/08/200882152856900527.html.
[34] For more information, see "Peru Throws out Amazon Land Laws," BBC, August 23, 2008, http://news.bbc.co.uk/2/hi/americas/7578040.stm.

protests. As an example, the website of AIDESEP opened a web forum entitled "Who is the real dog in the manger?" ("¿Quién es el verdadero perro del hortelano?"). Although the internet was used primarily for the purpose of disseminating information, it also allowed its users to open blogs and send e-mails. Even so, political specialists in Peru have observed that the deep digital divide has had an impact on how the movement has – or more often has not – used the digital media, with these forms of media used predominantly by NGOs that are linked to the movement (interview with Fernando TuestaSoldevilla (May 17, 2010). However, according to what Peruvian sociologist Jorge González states on his blog, there is one way in which the digital media played a crucial role and that was in providing an alternative source of information to the mass media and one that many observers believe to have been more reliable.[35] A more recent trend that has been observed in the aftermath of the protests is the proliferation of blogs in support of indigenous demands.[36] Overall, however, the use of digital media by the Peruvian campaign should be characterized as low.

The indigenous organizations that initiated the Peruvian campaign had a clear organizational structure with clearly defined posts and procedures. Decisions are made according to well-defined procedures, and delegates are elected to represent territorial communities. These movements therefore lack the flexibility enjoyed by horizontal organizations such as those that led the protests in the Dominican Republic and Argentina.

In summary, the low level of internet diffusion, the demographic profile of the participants, and the internal and organizational features of the indigenous movement mitigated against the use of digital media during the protests. Only supporters not directly involved in the struggle used digital media to spread their opinions in the country and abroad.

9.5. Conclusion

This exploratory study on the uses of digital media in five campaigns organized by citizens in different Latin American countries has revealed a number of very different scenarios characterized by various degrees of digital media use. Although in some cases new websites were created exclusively for the campaign (e.g., Argentina, Uruguay), in others preexisting websites of the organizations involved were used (e.g., Peru, Brazil, Dominican Republic). The Clean Sheet Campaign in Brazil was clearly the most active in its use of digital media for the purpose of collecting signatures and engaging in the campaign. Moreover, the internet allowed the Clean Sheet movement to gain an additional four hundred thousand signatures in a month to reach the legal threshold needed to submit a petition. The Brazilian case is also characterized by the dissemination of

---

[35] http://blog.pucp.edu.pe/item/65623.
[36] See http://barranquitaperu.blogspot.com, by a bishop, and http://laleydelaselva.blogspot.com, by a journalist.

information and messages through social networks, which played a major role in the campaign.

The second movement to have made extensive use of digital media is the movement opposing the construction of a cement plant in the Los Haitises Park in the Dominican Republic. Although the groups involved in the campaign are diverse (including both peasants and trade unionists), young people have played a particularly prominent role, most notably in the organization of a large protest camp in the park. An intense agenda of activities, including calls to protest, has been organized through the internet. This horizontal mode of organization, in which the internet was used as a forum for recruitment and exchange of ideas, has allowed the movement to grow to such an extent that it was able to virtually force the government to ask the United Nations for an environmental impact report, which in the end came out against the construction.

The assembly of Gualeguaychú is a special case in terms of its horizontal mode of decision making together with its use of shock tactics to grab the attention of traditional mass media. However, although young people have – as in other cases – sent out calls to protest through Facebook and other digital media applications, digital media have not played a central role. This is perhaps surprising given the horizontal mode of organization, which is held to be highly compatible with the use of this form of technology, according to our structural hypothesis. The use of the assembly, the blocking of transport routes, and the establishment of alliances with other national assemblies have been the hallmarks of this protest, although these have mostly been organized through traditional means of communication.

Digital media have opened up a new space for creativity. This was seen in the Uruguayan case, in which the organization of an abrogative referendum corresponded much more closely to a traditional campaign (organized by left-leaning political parties and trade unions). Here, too, there were those who actively supported the campaign by posting images, testimonies, poems, and songs on Facebook, in e-mails, and through YouTube, despite not formally being a part of the coordination process. Overall, however, face-to-face campaigning remained the dominant strategy.

The struggle against the "Laws of the Jungle" in Peru has remained the most disconnected from the digital media. This is due to structural factors such as the social exclusion that many of the communities involved suffer, which is manifested in low levels of both internet access and in low levels of coordination among different sectors and networks. The struggle here has adopted a more traditional form, with the movement taking to the streets and the government turning to repression. Nevertheless, NGOs, religious associations, journalists, and scholars associated with or supporting the network have used the internet to inform a domestic and, above all, international audience of the events as they unfolded.

Our study shows that neither the diffusion hypothesis nor the structural hypothesis can be considered sufficient conditions to fully explain the extent to which digital media are used in protest campaigns. The campaigns in Uruguay and Argentina, where levels of internet diffusion are relatively high, used digital media much less than the campaign in the Dominican Republic, where connectivity is rather low. However, the relatively high levels of internet diffusion in Brazil may have helped the online campaign obtain the critical mass of signatures that allowed the law proposed by the Clean Sheet movement to reach Congress. In terms of the structural hypothesis, the Argentine campaign and, to a lesser extent, the Peruvian campaign were based on a horizontal, nonhierarchical principle of organization, but this was not reflected in greater online activity or the greater use of digital media.

The demographic hypothesis, in contrast, is at least partly borne out. In the Dominican campaign and, to a certain extent, in the Brazilian case, young people were very actively involved, and it was they who helped organize the campaigns through the innovative use of digital media. The Brazilian campaign also shows that digital media can play a key role when the movement is dispersed across a wide territory in which the possibilities for face-to-face contact are limited. The campaign against the cement factory in Los Haitises National Park in the Dominican Republic is also illustrative in terms of this hypothesis: youth involvement meant that the campaign made extensive use of the internet despite the fact that the overall level of internet use in the country as a whole was rather low. In the other campaigns, too, it was predominantly the young members of the movements who pursued the campaign through their personal networks by uploading videos and using blogs as media for dissemination and debate. In the Uruguayan and Argentine campaigns, where activists were predominantly middle aged, however, these methods played only a secondary role, even though internet use in the two countries is actually rather high. In addition to the fact that these activists may be less familiar with digital media than their younger counterparts, middle-aged, middle-class activists in two of Latin America's most developed countries have at their disposal a tried and tested repertoire of traditional campaigning techniques that they can rely on, which younger and poorer activists in less developed countries may lack. However, the flip side of this is what we observed in Peru: poor, rural, and disenfranchised communities simply lack sufficient access to new technologies to be able to use them for political campaigning.

The political context and the perceived efficacy of strategies also play an important role. A well-known repertoire of actions that campaigners have at their disposal can reinforce a preference for traditional strategies. Such a repertoire is more likely to be available to experienced activists in settings in which democratic political institutions function relatively well (e.g., Uruguay) and are able to aggregate and articulate public demands. In relatively mature democracies, digital media serve to reinforce existing political institutions rather than substitute for them, whereas in unstable democracies and systems in which official institutions are weak or dysfunctional, they may constitute an alternative mechanism of political participation and may therefore appear more attractive.

In terms of the demographic profile of campaigners, we have seen that young activists in Latin America, like their counterparts in Western Europe, have a relative monopoly on the use of digital media in political campaigning over their older counterparts. This is primarily because of the way young people use the internet on a daily basis. Although older campaigners use the internet to obtain and even disseminate information, many young people in Latin America, as in other parts of the world, use the internet as a means of social communication.

Overall, the degree of internet diffusion, certain demographic factors, and the degree of political institutionalization interact in a rather complex way to produce divergent outcomes in terms of how digital media are used. In relatively developed countries where high and relatively well-educated, middle-aged, middle-class activists have a tried and tested repertoire of campaign techniques that they can rely on, and where digital media serve to reinforce – rather than substitute for – relatively well-developed political institutions, traditional techniques tend to be fundamental to the campaign, even if they are reinforced by new technologies to facilitate the dissemination of information. This will be the case particularly in relatively small countries, such as Uruguay, where political activity is concentrated in the capital city and face-to-face contact is therefore easier.

In cases in which campaigners are younger, and less well-versed in traditional campaigning techniques but are highly computer literate, where traditional political institutions are sometimes inadequate to aggregate and articulate citizens' demands, but where there is sufficient political openness for activists to operate freely, and where internet diffusion is sufficiently high to allow internet-based social networking to flourish, digital media are widely used as a substitute for more traditional campaigning activities. This tendency may be even more pronounced in settings such as Brazil, where high geographical dispersion of campaigners means that digital media are often necessary for communication across large distances.

In countries with the lowest levels of development and/or the lowest levels of democratic consolidation (e.g., Peru), digital media are unlikely to play a key role in any campaign. Internet diffusion is insufficiently high to allow for the use of such techniques, and the authorities undermine the effectiveness of grassroots campaigns (traditional or otherwise) in terms of policy outcomes. Protests in such settings are likely to involve more radical techniques such as civil disobedience and sabotage to force the government to heed protesters' demands.

10

Opening Closed Regimes

*Civil Society, Information Infrastructure,
and Political Islam*

Muzammil M. Hussain and Philip N. Howard

10.1. Introduction

As Converse (1987, S14) once said of public opinion research, "a sample design which extracts unrelated individuals from the whole and assigns the opinion of each an equal weight is a travesty on any 'realistic' understanding of what the concept of public opinion means." Today, any realistic understanding of public opinion formation in Muslim media systems must come from a critical awareness of the limits to survey data but also from an appreciation that digital information technologies are providing new opportunity structures for inclusion in the process of public opinion formation and measurement.

Ruling elites often try to co-opt civil society groups, and in times of political or military crises they can attempt to control the national information infrastructure. But a defining feature of civil society is independence from the authority of the state, even in countries such as Saudi Arabia and Egypt. And in important ways, digital communication networks are also independent of any particular state authority. What has been the impact of digital media on political communication in Muslim media systems? How have tools such as mobile phones and the internet affected the process of forming political identity, particularly for the young? When do such tools change the opportunity for civic action, and when do they simply empower ruling elites to be more effective censors? In this chapter, we analyze the best available micro-level data on technology use and changing patterns of political identity and macro-level data on networks of civil society actors.

The research in this chapter presents historical case studies. Therefore the events of the Arab Spring do not directly affect our findings. These events indicate that our expectations were if anything quite modest. However, as the ensuing events are not yet over, it is too early to reflect in depth.

Saudi Arabia and Egypt are two strong authoritarian regimes, the first an Islamist monarchy, the latter staunchly secular. Indonesia is an emerging democracy. Pakistan, with a mixed authoritarian and democratic history, is a fragile state. Despite important differences in political culture, technology diffusion is causing new patterns of political communication in all four regimes, with consequences for political participation and collective action. These four cases may be the best instances of governance archetypes in political Islam: Egypt is the largest secular authoritarian regime, Saudi Arabia is the largest Islamist constitutional monarchy, Indonesia is the largest Muslim democracy, and Pakistan is the largest fragile Muslim state. Yet all four are also interesting candidates for comparison: they have among the highest diffusion rates of digital media in the developing world; they are all countries in which digital media have been a means of building a transnational, Muslim political identity; and they are all countries in which the protection of religious and cultural norms has been used to justify levels of censorship and surveillance not tolerated in other parts of the world. We identify the ways in which authoritarian regimes do make effective use of information infrastructure as a means of social control. But we also demonstrate the ways in which civil society groups effectively use information infrastructure to strengthen their own organizational capacity and preserve independence from the state.

In this chapter we analyze changes in the patterns of political communication in four important countries. Even though these regimes are very different, we offer four propositions about what has changed since the introduction of new digital communication technologies. First, we argue that citizens in all four countries have been able to greatly increase the level of international news content in their news diets. Second, a growing portion of the public uses social networking applications in their communications, independent of direct state control. Third, civil society actors have flourished online, even when the state has cracked down domestically. Finally, women have been drawn into political discourse online in ways not available to them in offline spaces.

These four regimes are also among the largest media systems in the Muslim world. Yet the ownership structure of newspapers and radio and television stations has not diversified in recent years, with a few political parties and privately held firms producing most of the broadcast media. Comparatively, Pakistan has the greatest diversity in media and information infrastructure ownership, with minimal state ownership of media assets. In Egypt and Indonesia the state also owns a few media outlets that compete with those owned by political parties and firms, and in Saudi Arabia, state agencies own a controlling interest in most of the media system. Except for Saudi Arabia, the ownership of the digital information infrastructure is generally more diverse than that of broadcast media infrastructure: in Egypt, Indonesia, and Pakistan, policy reforms have resulted in significant competition among internet and mobile phone service providers (Howard, 2010). In these three countries, it is rare to find state agencies with a controlling interest in such service providers. This may be an important reason

citizens report greater levels of trust in the influence of news and media organizations in Pakistan than do citizens in Egypt and Indonesia.[1]

Given the limits of comparable survey data from the region, our argument
is based on two methodological strategies: first, we make use of the few pieces
of reasonably comparable data points from the higher quality studies that are
available; second, we develop short individual case studies about the impact of
new information technologies in each country and offer some comparative perspective on political communication trends that we find are consistent across all
four countries. This approach makes use of the best empirical evidence – qualitative and quantitative – about the impact of digital media on political culture
while also preserving some of the diversity in particular country experiences.
The case studies highlight the most compelling evidence of how digital communication tools have had distinct impacts in individual countries: in Saudi Arabia
such tools have provided an open media space for political discourse with no
offline equivalent but have also allowed social elites to closely manage the production and consumption of political content; in Egypt the regime has used digital media for monitoring, though not restricting, dissent, and online civil society
and journalism have flourished; in Pakistan networks of internet and mobile
phone users have been used to activate and inform partisan publics; in Indonesia these networks have served to entrench democratic practices of election and
issue campaigning. These case studies highlight important differences in the
political consequences of technology diffusion. Subsequently, our comparative
analysis highlights some of the observably consistent consequences across all
four regimes. Digital media diffusion in heterogeneous contexts is likely to
have different political consequences, and as we demonstrate, systems of political communication have in some ways adapted to the new technologies and in
other ways have adapted the technologies to serve existing institutions. In other
words, communication landscapes have been permanently altered through the
adoption of new communication technologies, and states and civil society
actors have also begun to adapt their communication strategies in response.

10.2. Information Technologies and Political Communication: Trends in Four Countries

Cross-case comparison can serve to develop a typology for the kinds of changes
in political communication that occur when digital technologies diffuse.

---

[1] In a 2007 survey, 31 percent of Egyptians, 35 percent of Indonesians, and 36 percent of Pakistanis
reported that the influence of the news organizations and media was very good. Interestingly,
of the subpopulation of internet users, 28 percent of Egyptians, 32 percent of Indonesians, and
fully 47 percent of Pakistanis reported that the influence of the news organizations and media
was very good. This suggests that although Egyptians, even with internet access, are cynical
about news organizations, Pakistanis, especially those with internet access, are more likely to
say positive things about news organizations. Overall, the survey revealed that internet users
are slightly more critical about the influence of political, corporate, and religious institutions
(authors' calculations based on data from Pew Global Attitudes Project 2007).

Public opinion data from the countries we examine here are notoriously inadequate (Pollack 2008), but after evaluating the growing number of sources about political communication in these countries, we can still offer some credible points of comparison. There are some basic statistics that reveal much about the impact of technology diffusion on political communication in the four countries. Television is still the primary source of political news and information for most citizens of these countries, but the internet and mobile phones are a key supplementary source for news that is more personal and relevant to social networks and for information in times of political crisis.

Table 10.1 presents some basic comparative evidence about technology diffusion trends and political communication. The portion of the population that uses the internet is relatively small; however, this portion is also one of the most politically engaged and active. Moreover, it is clear from the data shown that the most important form of digital media in the region is actually the mobile phone, which is far and away the most widely available information technology. Moreover, we have computed several additional measures that add to our interpretation of technology diffusion trends. Technology resources are rarely well distributed among the population of a country, and a common way of measuring how evenly a resource is distributed is through Gini coefficients (Milanovic 2005). Economists often use Gini coefficients to represent the distribution of income in a country, and Gini coefficients are particularly suited as a measure of the distribution of technology by levels of education and income. We have adapted the Gini coefficient to create an index of the distribution of internet access in Egypt, Indonesia, Pakistan, and Saudi Arabia using comparable data from surveys administered in 2006 (Atkinson 1970; Berrebi and Silber 1985).[2] When internet access is concentrated among social elites, the supply of news and information about political life is obviously constrained. In these countries, the two most likely categories of inequality in technology access are socioeconomic status and education. Comparatively, internet access is most concentrated among wealthy and educated elites in Pakistan, moderately concentrated among elites in Egypt and Indonesia, and least concentrated in Saudi Arabia.

In recent years, the OpenNet Initiative has also tracked the kinds of censorship and filtering that different states engage in. Egypt, though an authoritarian regime in many respects, has not been observed filtering political, social, or

---

[2] For example, in a perfectly equal society, 23 percent of the population would be using 23 percent of the internet bandwidth or have access to 23 percent of the internet-enabled computers, and 90 percent of the population would be using 90 percent of the internet bandwidth or have access to 90 percent of the internet-enabled computers. A more equal society has a low Gini coefficient close to 0.00, and a society in which resources are highly concentrated has a high Gini coefficient close to 1.00. In these countries, Gini coefficients could range from equal information technology distribution across categories of education or socioeconomic status to a condition of complete inequality in which all information technology resources are held by the most educated or highest status groups. Table 10.1 presents measures of the distribution of internet access across categories of socioeconomic status and education.

TABLE 10.1. *Digital Media and Political Communication in Four Countries*

Comparative Context	Egypt	Indonesia	Pakistan	Saudi Arabia
Religion[a]	Muslim (mostly Sunni) 90%, Coptic 9%, other Christian 1%	Muslim 86%, Protestant 6%, Roman Catholic 3%, Hindu 2%, other or unspecified 3%	Muslim 95% (Sunni 75%, Shi'a 20%), other (includes Christian and Hindu) 5%	Muslim (mostly Sunni) 100%
Demographics				
Population[b]	80.3 million	234.7 million	164.7 million	27.6 million
Percentage Muslim[b]	94	88	97	99
Literacy, percentage of population older than 15 who can read and write[a]	71	90	50	78
Gross domestic product per capita, purchasing power parity, U.S. dollars, 2009[a]	$6,000	$4,000	$2,600	$20,400
Political communication				
Internet users, percentage of total population 2000[c]	1	1	1	1
Internet users, percentage of total population 2010[c]	15	13	11	27
Mobile phone users, percentage of total population 2010	51	60	56	130
Digital media distribution by socioeconomic status, Gini coefficient, 2006[d]	0.28	0.48	0.64	0.13
Digital media distribution by education, Gini coefficient, 2006[d]	0.61	0.49	0.80	0.39

Comparative Context	Egypt	Indonesia	Pakistan	Saudi Arabia
Do you occasionally use the internet? (percentage of total population, 2007)[c]	20	7	7	n.a.
Percentage of internet users who use the internet as a primary or secondary source of political news and information, 2008[c]	29	7	8	n.a.
Censorship and surveillance[e]				
Political filtering	None	n.a.	Selective	Substantial
Social filtering	None	n.a.	Substantial	Pervasive
Cultural and/or security filtering	None	n.a.	Pervasive	Selective
Internet tool filtering	None	n.a.	Selective	Pervasive

Note: In Saudi Arabia, there are multiple mobile phones per person. See footnote two for explanation of operationalization of Gini coefficients.
[a] From *CIA World Factbook*.
[b] From World Bank, World Development Indicators.
[c] From International Telecommunications Union.
[d] From Howard, Busch, and Cohen (2009).
[e] From OpenNet Initiative.

cultural content, and it has done little to control the kinds of internet tools Egyptians have had access to. Pakistan and Saudi Arabia, in contrast, have demonstrated a willingness to filter content (Indonesia has not been studied by the OpenNet team). Although the two regimes are concerned about different kinds of content, Saudi Arabia is more aggressive in pervasively banning access to information-seeking tools. In 2009, it was regarded as the most aggressive online censorship regime in the Arab Middle East and among North African countries. As in Iran, the Saudi regime routes most, if not all, internet traffic through the King Abdulaziz City for Science and Technology, where content-filtering servers block undesirable content.

10.2.1. Egypt and Authoritarian Secularism
Egypt is one of the largest secular regimes in the Muslim world, and certainly the largest of the Arab nations. Despite frequent government crackdowns and

political censorship by ruling elites, political parties and social movements have turned to digital media as a logistical tool for coordinating social protest, collaborating across organizations, and communicating with members. Political groups like the Muslim Brotherhood have competed with the secular authoritarian regime for political power not only through offline protests and organizing but also through vibrant discussions on various media channels, particularly online. Young Egyptians in particular have taken to the internet, and because Cairo is also a major media and cultural hub, with a reasonably good information infrastructure, the city's politically disaffected youths have built a vibrant public sphere online (Abdulla 2005). Egypt is a country that simultaneously has inspiring examples of how civil society can use the internet for developing policy alternatives and providing services and the worst examples of government oppression of digital activists who appear politically threatening.

Of the four cases, Egypt has the worst record for arresting citizens for political use of digital media. Blogger arrests have gained the most widespread coverage in recent years in Egypt. The earliest known case was of Abdolkarim Nabil Seliman, who in 2005 was arrested and detained for four years after posting comments about political figures and criticizing then President Hosni Mubarak and the state's religious institutions. Despite the crackdowns, political bloggers in Egypt are notoriously resilient in using online spaces to complement their offline activities. Cairo has been the site of many highly publicized human rights abuse and election corruption cases protested by activists using blogs, mobile technology, and alternative media (Human Rights Watch 2005). In 2007, a number of bloggers were arrested for organizing and covering social protests when the Egyptian parliament approved controversial constitutional amendments. Many activist bloggers who have been arrested and harassed have also had to face serious threats to their physical well-being as they were beaten and tortured by Egyptian security personnel (Shapiro 2009).

A regional hub for major news, film, and music industries, Egypt enjoys a historically important position as a major media player in the Middle East, with hundreds of media organizations that serve the wider region (Pintak and Ginges 2008). In Egypt, a number of dailies, weeklies, and magazines are available for consumption in print for the literate. Some of these publications also maintain a heavy online presence, such as *Al-Ahram Weekly*, one of the most popular publications covering culture and politics at the regional and international levels. As many organizations are moving online, some publications have built online discussion spaces for readers to engage more actively and creatively. These online discussion places have become important for citizens to collectively navigate complex identity and gender issues in a society where doing so offline may be more difficult. Arabic news discussion boards, for example, are particularly active spaces for people to discuss Koranic interpretation and debate the value of violent response strategies to the U.S. involvement in Iraq; the publications of cartoons about the prophet Mohammed; and the complexities of religion used to justify the terrorist attacks in New York, London, and Madrid (Abdulla 2007).

On the whole, Egypt's online activists and bloggers, digital news organizations and discussion forums, and political party websites form a virtual ecology of civil society groups debating contentious issues. Furthermore, many of the standard boundaries among these organizations are blurred, for important reasons. For example, banned political parties such as the Muslim Brotherhood rely on their online blogger-activists to speak to power by calling for protest and mobilizing support. Abdel Rahman Fares, a twenty-five-year-old blogger who runs the blog My Tongue Is My Pen, was arrested for inciting citizens to strike. Because many activist blogs, like his, are maintained on off-site servers, governments such as Egypt's are forced to directly censor individuals instead of censoring Google's Blogger service.[3] Politically active youths rely heavily on blogs to express their dissatisfaction with cultural and political issues (Mehanna 2008). Looking across all four countries, Egypt has the largest proportion of citizens who use the internet as either a primary or a secondary source of political news and information. This may be the result of having not just a persecuted opposition that is excluded from mainstream media but also a well-organized opposition that has put significant resources into developing digital news sources to supplement what Egyptians get from official state agencies.

Egypt has a number of active political parties, many of which maintain websites and online newsletters to communicate with their supporters and constituents and with one another. Almost all major parties publish online newspapers, such as the New Wafd Party's *Al-Wafd Daily* the National Progressive Unionist Party's Al-Ahali newspaper, the Arab Democratic Nasserist Party's *Al-Arabi* weekly, and Tomorrow Party's *Al-Ghad* weekly. In addition to the discussion spaces fostered by newspapers, party publications such as these allow for active opportunities for cross-party communication and political negotiation. Moreover, the internet is even more strategically important for parties that have been banned by the government, such as the Muslim Brotherhood. Though banned from participating in Egyptian politics by the government, the Muslim Brotherhood's Ikhwan Online (in Arabic) and Ikhwan Web (in English) allow the organization to maintain an equal, if not more prominent, presence in online Egyptian politics than many legally sanctioned parties.

10.2.2. Indonesia and Democratic Entrenchment
One of the most populated countries in the world, Indonesia by default is also the largest Muslim democracy in the world. Though predominantly Muslim, with its many provinces and hundreds of ethnic groups, Indonesia is also a very diverse society. Religious diversity in particular is a key defining feature of Indonesia's demographic landscape. Christianity, Hinduism, Buddhism, and Confucianism are also represented by significant numbers of followers, and some of the impact of digital media in the social and political arenas translates into conflict and struggle for power between majority and other minorities.

---

[3] Fares's URL is http://abdofares.blogspot.com.

Since the end of the Suharto regime, Indonesia's mainstream media have also become freer. Although costs of internet access are somewhat high and internet diffusion is highly unequal, formal politics, as well as broad issues of gender and identity, have been hotly debated over the growing digital media infrastructures in Indonesia. Mobile phones became a defining feature of new media at this time (Barendregt 2008), with 36 percent having access to cell phones but only 2 percent having computer access and a mere 7 percent using the internet in 2007 (World Bank 2009). The latest figures for technology diffusion in Indonesia are even more revealing: 69 percent of respondents report mobile or cell phone access in their households, of whom 53 percent use it to get news; 21 percent used the internet daily as of 2010.[4]

Strong state censorship has not been experienced in Indonesia since the Suharto era. In recent years, the proliferation of internet infrastructures has coincided with the removal of formal mechanisms for media control used by the government (BBC 1998). A few cases have gained significant focus both in and outside of Indonesia. One such example is that of Prita Mulyasari, a housewife and mother of two who was jailed for complaining about the quality of health care she received (Rumuat 2009). She was charged with violating the Information and Electronic Transaction Law, a law against distributing information that is deemed defamatory, which can lead to a maximum of six years in prison or a fine of one billion rupiah. She exposed private e-mail correspondences between herself and the hospital, and her plight has gained an active online network of supporters via Facebook groups and bloggers. The government prosecutors may have been especially sensitive and nervous about embarrassing expositions such as this given the then-upcoming elections in the emerging democracy. In April 2008 the government also temporarily blocked YouTube and MySpace for showing the anti-Islamic film *Fitna*. Last, the government requires internet cafés to collect and provide identities of internet users to a government agency on a monthly basis (World Association of Newspapers 2009).

Media are big business in Indonesia, with its enormous news-consuming population supporting 1.75 billion sales of paid-for dailies annually. From 2001 to 2004, Indonesia's numerous newspapers also started to increase their online presence and dissemination channels: in 2001, 24 percent of dailies and 26 percent of nondailies were online; but only three years later in 2004, 32 percent of dailies, 33 percent of nondailies, and 72 percent of Sunday newspapers had online editions. Furthermore, the government and politics category of newspaper advertising is the second-largest expenditure, which indicates that politics is popular in news media and that political actors actively invest in Indonesia's vibrant news media as a popular communications medium to reach constituents. Despite market support for journalism in Indonesia, practicing journalism is not entirely a safe endeavor. Violence against journalists

---

[4] Figures computed from InterMedia Survey Research Institute's national survey of Indonesia in April 2010.

is common and well recorded in Indonesia, with sixty-five cases in 2007, and sixty cases of physical violence, threats, reportage prohibition, and lawsuits against journalists in 2008. State officials, police, judges, and even election candidates contributed heavily to these incidents of violence (World Association of Newspapers 2009).

Although internet diffusion is not as widespread and equitable in Indonesia as in the other cases in this comparative analysis, there is reason to believe that it was an essential ingredient in the democratization process of Indonesia in the late 1990s: "There is little doubt that the internet, in the hands of a small university-educated minority in the cities, played some role in the erosion of the political censorship of the Suharto government, and as such contributed to the fall of the three decade old authoritarian regime. From the mid-1990s opposition groups, largely students and professionals, filled newsgroups, chat-rooms and websites with criticism of the Suharto government. In a characteristically Indonesian play on words, one observer in 1997 suggested that INTERNET might stand for '*Indonesian TERkenal NEgatif Terus*' – the acronym is lost in the translation 'Internet = Indonesia is always infamous.'" (Hill and Sen 2002, 171). Although underground e-mail lists and news discussion forums were essential for the democratization movement, after democratization, more than 180 political parties registered but only a few maintained websites. This suggests that though the internet was an essential communication vehicle for elite political activists during a time of political regime change (Hill 2003), forthcoming political parties were more invested in election outcomes and did not invest in digital media given its lack of diffusion in society. In other words, "The Internet had no direct impact on the ballot."

Post-Suharto, the internet continues to serve as an important venue for citizen activists to discuss public affairs issues, (re)negotiate their political identities, and mobilize around shared concerns. In Indonesia's Moluccan Islands, Christian and Muslim cyber-communities engage in online news sharing and aggregation projects (Brauchler 2003). These practices in turn help construct participants' political identities along religious demarcations that have important implications for the future of Indonesia's national identity. Similarly, pro–East Timor activists from around the world rely on the internet to collaborate and collectively organize and smuggle incriminating information regarding the Indonesian government's policies and activities in the region (Hill 2002). Doing so allows them to shape global public opinion and organize sympathy for their struggle. Civil society activists, particularly from the East Timor struggle, have also made heavy use of "hactivism" and cyber-attacks through defacing Indonesian government websites, as in 1997 when they posted proindependence messages on them after hacking forty-five Indonesian domains (the largest known organized hactivism campaign). In summary, the internet's role in Indonesia's struggle as an emerging democracy has been both essential and complicated for the development of a healthy civil society. Without the internet, the student organizers' efforts for democratization would have been severely hampered, but it is not finished yet. Marginalized publics such as from East Timor and the Moluccan Islands continue to use similar tactics to have their needs and concerns addressed by elites as Indonesia cautiously trudges onward to its path for democratic and socioeconomic progress.[5]

10.2.3. Pakistan and Fragile Democracy

Even though there has certainly been an active debate among scholars, policy makers, and pundits about what it means to be a fragile state, Pakistan is often referenced as a fragile democracy. In practical terms, this means that the government is barely able to guarantee the safety of its citizens in most parts of most cities and has nominal authority in some neighborhoods and some parts of the countryside.

Over the past decade of multiple political and military crises in Pakistan, new information technologies have become a fundamental infrastructure for political communication. Although internet use is actively monitored in Pakistan, there have been few high-profile cases of state persecution of bloggers and citizen journalists.[6] Both the Pakistani intelligence services and the country's small but aggressive community of hackers have an international reputation as a disruptive political communication tool. One of the first cyber-conflicts occurred in 1998, when Pakistani intelligence personnel hacked an Indian army website about the status of Kashmir. This escalated into more than two years of denial of service attacks and website defacements. In Pakistan, the Hakerz Club, Gforce Pakistan, and Mos have defaced hundreds of websites worldwide with pro-Kashmiri, anti-Indian content (Wolcott and Goodman 2000). In Pakistan, online journalism is crucial for supplying its literate, far-flung diasporas with news about home and for providing news and information during the frequent security crises in the country. But at home, the internet has allowed for some professionalization of journalists themselves. For example, BBC investments in online ethics and research training, access to electronic resources at public libraries, and an international audience have all had an impact on the quality of journalism in Pakistan (Saeed et al. 2000).

Pakistan has a very vibrant online civil society, and political parties in Pakistan have benefited immensely from the new digital networks. Indeed, internet access is especially important in times of political and security crisis, and it has been since the late 1990s. Internet use spiked during the nuclear tests in the spring of 1998 and the political coup in October 1999 (Wolcott and Goodman 2000). Mainstream parties are better able to read and respond to public opinion, and the digital political communication strategies of mainstream parties help activate large networks of voters. Strategically, the internet and mobile phones have allowed both major and minor parties to activate their members

---

[5] Indonesia's geography plays into this, in that the country's population is distributed over a multitude of islands. However, most survey research in Indonesia samples – as a logistical constraint – is from Java and Sulawesi.

[6] A known exception is Urooj Zia, who posted critical comments about public policy online and was detained for several hours in 2008.

at key moments of political crisis, and they have allowed those parties to tap into wealthy donors both at home and overseas. Political party websites, such as those run by Egypt's Muslim Brotherhood and Pakistan's People's Party, have been able to issue news releases detailing electoral mishaps. Given the country's instability, it is not surprising that many of Pakistan's major political parties have chosen to host their digital infrastructure with services registered outside the country. This provides some stability in times of uncertainty, when media infrastructure can potentially be targeted by government interference.

10.2.4. *Saudi Arabia and Authoritarian Islam*
Internet access was slow to come to Saudi Arabia, and when digital information networks were built, they were deliberately designed to help ruling elites manage the development of political culture. In many Islamic constitutional monarchies, the political opposition had an online presence before those in power. In part, this was because many leaders of political opposition reside in London, New York, Toronto, and Los Angeles, where it was easier to maintain discussion boards and set up websites on .net, .com, or .org domain names. Using their home country's top-level domain name often meant negotiating with political elites at home for permissions. For example, Saudi opposition groups such as the Committee for the Defense of Legitimate Rights and the Movement for Islamic Reform in Arabia managed websites from their offices in London several years before the kingdom itself even began considering offering internet access to its citizens. When the government began planning such a service, it was primarily because of the growing demand for dial-up services in Bahrain that Saudi students and business leaders were using.

In the late 1990s several Islamic states embraced the internet, treating it as another way to promote particular approaches to the Islamic faith, identity, and iconography. Radical Islamic organizations, whether state-entrenched or opposition social movements, competed for the ownership of spiritual iconography online. For example, the Saudi Arabia Ministry of Islamic Affairs, Endowments, Da'wa, and Guidance reserved for its own use the domain name islam.org.sa. This URL was used as the exclusive source for streaming prayers from Medina and Mecca online. This Saudi ministry and others have actively used the internet to promote Wahhabi Islam. One observer noted that "Saudi Arabia invests in the propaganda of the Saudi Arabian-style Islam, the Wahhabi-style Islam, much more than the whole Soviet Union for the whole Soviet history spent on the propaganda of the Communist ideology" (Schwirtz 2007).

Internet censorship certainly constrains the development of civil society in Saudi Arabia. The regime has built into its digital infrastructure the ability to regulate content about politics, social issues, and international security, and the ability to prevent the use of internet tools such as search engines and software download sites (OpenNet, 2010). Access to the entire Israeli domain (.il) is blocked. In addition, internet access can be restricted by means of infrastructural and technical standards. Contracted internet service providers are often assigned limits on the number of modems and ports they can operate;

the filtering software itself can slow down connection speeds. Internet access can be restricted through economic policies: mandated pricing strategies create an information infrastructure that is barely accessible even to the upper middle class. In countries where many people have internet access, the fastest connections, in private homes, belong to social elites.

In Saudi Arabia, there have been some high-visibility arrests of bloggers. But the most notable feature of this country is the way in which ruling elites have actively drafted Saudi internet users to self-police their internet activities. Unlike most countries, the Saudi government encourages its citizens to submit the URL addresses of sites worth banning. Most Saudis are quite aware of the regime's censorship practices, and the justification of cultural protection is an accepted norm in the kingdom.[7] Internet censors in Saudi Arabia publish reports on their activities; when in-country users try to view a blocked URL, they find a page admitting that the content has been blocked. In Saudi Arabia users are invited to suggest new sites for blocking and to request that sites be unblocked, which is effectively crowd-sourcing internet censorship.

Even though political parties and civil society groups are constrained in Saudi Arabia, regime critics can be found online. The Committee for the Defense of Legitimate Rights and Movement for Islamic Reform in Arabia uses its websites to document corruption; criticize the royal family; debate the utility of Shari'a law; and link to content on international websites such as CNN, the *New York Times*, and Amnesty International (Warf and Vincent 2007). But on balance, in Saudi Arabia, digital media have been most useful for the control of political communication, the surveillance of social networks, and the management of cultural production.

10.3. Comparative Perspectives

Broadly speaking, the internet has provided a means and a media for political resistance in all four countries. But more specifically, there are four ways in which the new information infrastructure has had an impact on political communication and public opinion formation. These countries, with very different histories and diverse political cultures, have experienced similar changes in their systems of political communication since the emergence of digital technologies. Even though the regimes are very different, we offer four propositions about how these regimes have opened up in recent years, largely as a result of the proliferation of digital and networked information technologies. In most countries where online news use has been surveyed, researchers have found that the number of people who use the internet for political news and information peaks in times of crisis or during elections, but that most of the time only a fraction

---

[7] For example, in 2007, Fouad al-Farhan was arrested for criticizing government corruption and calling for political reform; he was jailed for four months. In 2008 he was again arrested for "specific violations of nonsecurity laws," and Roshdi Algadir, was detained and beaten for posting a poem.

of the active internet users regularly consume news. The opposite seems to be true within each of the four trends here, but there is obviously some variation in the magnitude of effects.

10.3.1. The Production and Consumption of News
Across all four countries, a growing cohort of citizens is consuming more international news than ever before. There is some evidence to suggest that the news sources, for all four countries, are primarily the BBC, CNN, and Al Jazeera, and that much of the content the average news consumer follows is related to politics and security in other Muslim countries. Nonetheless, this is an important development, because regimes that used to be able to play distinct domestic and international political games can no longer do so. Diplomatic machinations at the international level make it into domestic news, and crises in domestic life are more likely than ever before to be heard by a country's neighbors and its overseas diaspora.

Even the mainstream broadcast and print news sources rely on the internet for content and as a research tool. And of course, for the wealthy in each country the internet affords access to specialized domestic and international news sources. Online news sources still exhibit cultural biases: news sources from the United States and the so-called coalition of the willing produced positive content, human interest stories, and media self-coverage during the Iraq War; news sources in Egypt and Pakistan framed the war in terms of responsibility (Dimitrova et al. 2005). Overall, about two-thirds of Egyptian and Saudi internet users report being frequent consumers of internet news.[8]

Comparatively speaking, new media journalism is valuable in Egypt and Saudi Arabia because it is the primary forum for independent and critical journalism, generated both by professional and citizen journalists. In these countries, online news is produced by loose organizations of journalists, who sometimes write from outside the country, producing content that has no hard-copy or broadcast equivalent and that may not even be hosted on servers located in country. New media journalism is important in Indonesia in that many news outlets have found the freedom to build a domestic multimedia news infrastructure: content may appear in digital and analog formats, hosted on a domestic information infrastructure by a formally incorporated news organization with a dedicated full-time staff. This country has a rapidly growing, politically active, internet user base. So the impact of digital media on news consumption is important but varied: in Egypt and Saudi Arabia it means greater access to

---

[8] News consumption reports often suffer from social desirability effects. Still, the numbers are noteworthy even in comparison to similar figures reported in the Europe and the United States. A majority of Egyptian and Saudi Arabian internet users also report being frequent consumers of internet news (61 percent and 66 percent, respectively). For all those who accessed internet news the previous day, the most popular online news portals in order of preference in Middle Eastern countries are Google News, 23 percent; AlJazeera.net, 13 percent; Yahoo! News, 12 percent; AlArabiya.net, 9 percent; BBC Arabic, 6 percent; and BBC.co.uk, 6 percent (Feld 2009).

international news content from Al Jazeera, CNN, and the BBC; in Pakistan and Indonesia it means greater access to locally produced content.

10.3.2. Social Networking

For the most part, public opinion in countries with large Muslim communities has been a construction of ruling elites and state agencies. By so constraining the media diets of citizens, the ability of journalists to investigate popular sentiment, and the ability of researchers to survey the public, the boundaries of what constituted the public were fundamentally constrained and knowledge of opinion deliberately kept vague. Today, political parties are using the internet to construct political opinion in a different way. By deeply integrating digital tools such as mobile phones and the internet into their systems of political communication, parties are able to reach and activate much greater numbers of people. In this way, the internet is actively used to challenge the basic relations of power, because political parties use it to amass publics that were not previously reachable. Moreover, established political interests – whether traditional political parties in Indonesia and Pakistan or state elites in Egypt and Saudi Arabia – had an easier time controlling broadcast media. Social networking applications have provided a new structure for the flow of political news and information, a structure that does not easily provide political elites with informational choke points. Without mandatory points of passage for political content and with digital hosting services beyond the territorial control of these governments, social networking applications have had implications for who counts as the political public.

In countries where a handful of state agencies own the major media outlets, it is possible to define the public through the selection of topics covered in the news, through the framing of stories, and through the gender and ethnic representation of people who appear as journalists and as characters in news stories. It is rare, for example, to have immigrant Bengalis canvassed for opinion in the nightly newscasts in Saudi Arabia or Indonesia. Increasingly, the internet has become an alternative information source, one that holds content related to those minority voices. But public opinion is shaped by the internet not in the sense that many citizens find interesting new public policy options online, but in the sense that these major media outlets have added the internet to their tool kit for measuring – and manipulating – public opinion. Media systems in these four countries were constructed by the elites to make for easy manipulation by autocratic leaders or the Saudi royal family. Autocrats, by definition, work to constrain the size and diversity of their publics through media systems that distribute limited amounts of information to carefully defined groups. And it is the political parties, legal or not, that make the best use of the internet for extending the definition of who the public is by expanding their membership and increasing the rate of active contact. The social networking applications that facilitate the passage of political content over networks of family and friends provide not simply a competing media system but also an alternative structure for distributing information.

10.3.3. Civil Society Online

Civil society actors have flourished online, largely because much of the internet infrastructure is independent of state control. Civil society is often defined as the self-generating and self-supporting community of people who share a normative order and who volunteer to organize political, economic, or cultural activities that are independent of the state (Diamond 1994). Civil society groups are a crucial part of all democracies, concerned with public affairs, yet autonomous from the state bureaucracies so that government policy itself – and government corruption – is within their purview. Civil society is constituted by a plurality of groups representing diverse perspectives and promoting those perspectives through communications media and cultural institutions. Moreover, a key tenet of the shared normative order is that no one group can claim to represent the whole of society and that society is best served by a multitude of groups that contribute in different ways to the dissemination and exchange of information about public policy options and national development goals (Diamond 1994).

Particularly in Indonesia, Egypt, and Pakistan, civil society leaders have used the internet to reach out to both foreign and domestic publics, to build linkages with like-minded groups, to raise funds from group membership, to activate support in times of crisis, and to provide social services. They also use the internet as a tool for critiquing the government and offering policy alternatives. Such policy alternatives are not always considered by ruling elites, but in Indonesia – and sometimes in Egypt and Pakistan – some are.

The importance of the internet for contemporary civil society actors can be attributed to two factors. Many groups were pushed online because other forms of political communication were inaccessible. Television commercials for advertising to the public were prohibitively expensive and regulated by the state. Radio commercials and newspaper ads were still beyond the budgets of small civic groups and still regulated by the state. The well-monitored broadcast media, even in countries like Pakistan and Indonesia where democracy had strong roots, were a means by which the state and mainstream political parties regulated discourse. The internet allowed for content to be hosted on servers beyond the control of state censors, and it afforded anonymity to those who advanced political critique. During times of crisis when physical spaces for public conversation and debate closed down, the internet provided virtual spaces for political communication.

Over the past decade, civil society organizations were pulled online because of the expanding user base and changing demographics of the internet-using population. In part this was a function of the falling costs: in the year 2000 average residents of Cairo or Jakarta would have spent a quarter of their daily income on an hour of internet access at a cyber café, and average residents of Karachi would have spent three-quarters of their daily income to go online. By 2010, across all three countries, around 5 percent of the average daily income would buy an hour of access at an internet access point (Howard 2007).[9]

---

[9] No information on Saudi Arabia available.

Even though a relatively small portion of the general population in these countries has regular internet access, the portion that is online is politically significant. Internet users are often a country's wealthy and educated elites (as Table 10.1 reveals, this is particularly true for Egypt and Pakistan but less so for Indonesia and Saudi Arabia). They tend to be younger and live in capital cities and urban areas, and they tend to be among the most politically active. So the clients for civil society organizations, whether those organizations are faith based, service oriented, or policy focused, are also potential members and supporters of civic agendas. The proliferation of consumer electronics has made it possible for civic leaders to reach new audiences, but this trend has also empowered local civil society "start-ups" to launch both small, permanent civic organizations and local, issue-specific campaigns. Civil society online has become particularly vibrant in Indonesia and Pakistan. It is vibrant but constrained in Egypt, and it is growing and co-opted in Saudi Arabia.

10.3.4. *Gender Politics and the Politics of Inclusion*
Digital information technologies mediate gender politics in unexpected ways. In the political economy of media, women are playing more dynamic roles in television and film both in front of and behind the camera. But women have, in the opinion of some observers, aggressively invaded the new public space created by digital media (Mernissi 2004). Marcotte (2009), for example, has observed religious discourse regarding gender and sexuality, where forums have been essential spaces to challenge, contest, and even transgress traditional norms. Some have even observed in very conservative societies and families that Muslim women have begun to participate economically by running their own private businesses (NPR 2002). First and foremost, digital media are allowing citizens to learn about the status of women and gender relations in other countries. Second, they allow both men and women to debate specific gender issues relevant in their own cultures (Stowasser 2001). Third, the arrival of digital media in many Muslim communities and households has become an occasion for renegotiating and restructuring gender relationships. Finally, the internet supports women-only online communities, which have become sites for political conversation away from both patriarchal leaders and the public gaze of journalists. Political elites in some countries restrict internet access to prevent such cultural learning, debate, and renegotiations.

The introduction of new digital media does not simply provide the opportunity to redress gender disparities in developing communities; it is providing a platform for learning about gender politics. Three factors impede learning about gender politics in Muslim countries. First, new internet users rarely have the ability to conduct sophisticated searches and critically assess the content they find. This comes with practice, along with coaching from friends and family. Second, political elites in some countries actively work to discourage state programs from providing women with media training and access, or actively block discussion boards, blogs, and chat rooms where young Muslims can have some discourse on gender issues. Third, government regulators establish content filters that block websites they judge to be antithetical to the established edicts of gender relations in their country or to their interpretation of Islam.

Table 10.2 includes data on internet use and attitudes toward gender roles in political, religious, and personal life in Egypt, Pakistan, and Indonesia. Comparatively, Indonesians appear most likely to feel that gender has little to do with being a good political leader and that women have the right to choose their husband. Pakistanis feel that women should choose whether to wear a veil. But in almost all respects, internet users express more moderate opinions about the role of women in society. Most of the internet users surveyed about their gender politics would be young, educated, urban dwellers. Still, there is a growing literature about how exposure to digital media has an impact on users' levels of tolerance and empathy (Robinson, Neustadtl, and Kestnbaum 2004; Brundidge and Rice 2009). For many young Muslims, the online social networking applications and other content are the media by which they learn of life in other countries where faith and freedom can coexist. Networked information technologies are, at the very least, partly responsible for exposing citizens to liberal cultural values, including the notion that two genders have equal worth. Certainly, some internet users in these countries can be radicalized through their internet use, but many will be sensitized by it. And in the case of Saudi Arabia, it may be the broadcast media on state-authorized channels that do more to reinforce conservative and Wahhabi interpretations of Islam. In Egypt and Pakistan, the broadcast media are certainly used to advance secularist perspectives of the role of faith in statecraft. One of the next steps in researching the impact of digital media in countries with large Muslim communities will be to investigate the overall impact of internet use on tolerance.

10.4. Conclusion

It would be unwise to be relentlessly upbeat about the impact of information technologies on political life in the countries examined here. Even as live inspiring popular movements for democracy unfold throughout North Africa and the Arab Middle East, the consequences of digital media for social change are mixed and uneven. Egypt until very recently was one of the toughest authoritarian dictatorships in the world, and Saudi Arabia has a similar status; whereas democratic practices in Indonesia have stabilized over the past decade, such practices in Pakistan appear fleeting. Internet censorship has a chilling effect on many citizens across Egypt, Saudi Arabia, Indonesia, and Pakistan, though for different reasons. All work hard to censor politically – and sometimes culturally – distasteful material from their citizens, but most of what is censored actually originates in these countries (Faris and Villeneuve 2007). After government censors used cultural propriety as the reason to acquire new digital censorship systems, there has been noticeable mission creep as such censors expand to cover more obviously political content. For example, Pakistan began by filtering only websites that contained imagery offensive to Islam, but it now targets political content, such as websites related to the

TABLE 10.2. *Attitudes on Gender and Roles, by Internet Use, 2007*

Percentage of Respondents	Egypt All	Egypt Internet Users	Indonesia All	Indonesia Internet Users	Pakistan All	Pakistan Internet Users	Saudi Arabia All	Saudi Arabia Internet Users
Gender in political leadership								
Men make better leaders	40	37	44	33	58	52	—	—
Women make better leaders	16	11	3	1	8	6	—	—
Both are equal	45	52	53	66	34	43	—	—
Woman's right to choose husband								
Woman should choose	21	14	64	58	6	12	—	—
Family should choose	26	22	9	8	56	39	—	—
Both should have a say	53	64	28	34	38	50	—	—
Woman's right to decide to wear a veil								
Completely agree	29	33	41	41	50	54	—	—
Completely disagree	8	8	1	9	23	21	—	—
Weighted N	1000	198	1008	66	2008	144	—	—
Woman's right to work outside home								
Always	20	32	—	—	—	—	15	32
Only if necessary to help family	60	51	—	—	—	—	52	47
Never	18	16	—	—	—	—	33	20
Not sure	2	1	—	—	—	—	0	0
Weighted N	840	261	—	—	—	—	750	433

Source: Pew Global Attitudes Project (2007).

Baluchistan independence movement. As security situations become unstable, access to digital mapping services or video file-sharing services is the first to be cut.

Knowing that their government may be watching creates an information environment in which Saudis, Egyptians, and Pakistanis restrict their online activities or confine their internet activities according to where they suspect that the state has less oversight, strategically choosing computers that may provide some anonymity – either in very public settings such as cyber-cafés or libraries where personal tasks on public terminals may be difficult to track or in privacy at home, where computer screens cannot be observed by outsiders.

Yet in interesting ways, the diffusion of new technologies has helped nurture a setting that can lead to constitutional moments of change for these regimes. Sometimes, this moment is not so much characterized by radical transformations in political culture, revolutions in political leadership, or radical expansions in electoral franchise. As in the cases of Indonesia and Saudi Arabia, digital media have allowed citizens to slowly enter public discourse who were not allowed to before. They have also allowed citizens to experiment with and nurture civic activities that suit their societies' political cultures and norms. This type of slow and gradated change is characterized by a rapid expansion of the number of people who occupy the public sphere and constitute public opinion. The pace of expansion can primarily be explained by the diffusion of digital media over the past decade, and these can have important consequences for the structure of opportunities for collective action and the exercise of political authority by ruling elites. These large and constitutional changes, though not immediately revolutionary, are certainly apparent with a comparative perspective.

Over the past several years, digital media and global internet infrastructure have allowed marginalized publics to enter public discourse. With this access, they can learn about their regimes, compare what is taking place outside their borders, receive international news in place of state-run media, and eventually hold their leaders accountable. These long-term shifts can eventually lead to rapid and revolutionary change. Between December 2010 and June 2011, there have been serious domestic cascades of uprisings across the twenty-three Arab states in North Africa and the Middle East, popularly dubbed the "Arab Spring." Massive and sustained demonstrations for democratic change sprang up from Tunis to Cairo, and many other major metropolitan hubs, often taking only a day or two to spread. Indeed, most regimes have made major concessions, the ones that did not have had mostly peaceful revolutions, and we are witnessing a novel period in which democracies may be born in a digital age.

However, the sheer speed of how quickly the news has spread, movements have organized, and change is taking place should not understate the significance of the long-term online civil society that made this possible. Despite strict regime censorship and facing real dangers, online citizens and digital activists have made use of the internet to nurture civic spaces over many years. Where the internet and mobile networks have enjoyed significant diffusion, the public has had more opportunities to learn about the rest of the world and compare with their political experiences. Where digital diffusion has been introduced more recently, significant segments of the educated, metropolitan, and economic elite have been the first to gain access. During the Arab Spring, we can witness how these citizens and activists have forged local and international networks with important consequences to their regimes.

Digital Media and Political Attitudes in China

Min Tang, Laia Jorba, and Michael J. Jensen

11.1. Introduction

In the summer of 2009, a judicial case related to the death of a government official in Hubei Province came to national prominence through internet forums.
A female pedicure worker, Deng Yujiao, refused the request for sexual service
from Deng Guida, the director of a local township office. She stabbed him
several times while trying to fend him off, which resulted in his death. Deng
turned herself in to the police and was initially charged with murder. This case
was quickly picked up on the internet and accumulated more than 4 million
posts across different websites (Wines 2009). Internet users were angered by
her treatment in this case. For Chinese netizens, this case exemplifies their
impotence in the face of corrupt and immoral officials, social injustice, and the
lack of respect in the society. Deng Yujiaowas hailed as a national hero who
resisted the abuse of power that is widely perceived in China. National outcry
on the internet even caused several street demonstrations. After a failed attempt
to play down the incident online, Chinese authorities were pressured to drop
the murder charges, grant her bail, and charge her with intentional assault. She
was found guilty but was eventually released without sentencing as a result of
her "mental state."

The Deng Yujiao incident is one of many examples in which internet news
and online discussions influence government policies and decisions and politicians' behavior in China (see Chase and Mulvenon 2002; Yang 2003; Zheng
and Wu 2005; Tai 2006). These kinds of cases are becoming more and more
frequent, and they point to two related trends: attention to the increasing
dynamism in Chinese civil society and increasing demands for individual
and collective rights. In fact, demands that have received positive responses
from the Chinese government span corruption cases, disputes regarding class

This research is supported by Leading Academic Discipline Program, 211 Project for Shanghai
University of Finance and Economics (Project Number 2009330194).

stratification, and some moral issues and concerns related to abuses of power. As those critiques are not a direct threat to the regime itself, they can often produce a favorable response. Yang (2003) notes that the emerging rights consciousness is accompanied by a tendency toward the loosening of political control in certain areas, which leaves more room for political activity among individuals and organizations. Some members of the current regime have challenged the government's censorship powers on the basis of a reading of the constitution that regards its speech protections as an individual right.[1]

These developments are also partially the result of technological change, as the adoption and diffusion of digital media are spreading to larger segments of the population: "The relative 'young' age of Chinese civil society may thus mean that it is more responsive to technological change, especially those technologies that may meet its needs" (Yang 2003, 407). Because of the nascent state of independent civil society in China, digital communication networks can play a particularly important role by serving as communication channels through which nonofficial political discourses can emerge (Tai 2006).

The expansion of nonofficial political communication channels can lead to a more open public sphere, thereby creating increased pressures for democratization and liberalization (Tsagarousianou, Tambini, and Bryan 1998; Hill and Sen 2000; Chase and Mulvenon 2002). This path is not deterministic, as informational authoritarian is an alternative trajectory of development (Jiang 2010). That is, if we assume that technological structures do not determine the resulting structure of politics, it is quite possible that even if some netizens successfully challenge particular government authorities, the regime will still tightly regulate and control online activity. There is evidence that this control is becoming more efficient and widespread (Lagerkvist 2008, 2010). Real change is said to come from economic and technological internal pressures within the government apparatus.

Whichever trajectory emerges, the consensus is that if a Chinese democratic transition occurs, the process of liberalization can be expected to proceed quite slowly (Kalathil and Boas 2003). As Zheng and Wu (2005) argue, the extant evidence points to a discernible direction of the future of the current regime. Although it might be premature to talk about democratization in China, online communications seem to be changing Chinese civil society through the construction of new and augmented spheres for interaction (Jiang 2010), and they might challenge the government itself over the medium to long term.

This argument is framed in an intense and more general way regarding the impact of these technologies in authoritarian regimes, as their diffusion has become more widespread (Dahlgren 2000; Ferdinand 2000a, 2000b; Norris 2003; Kalathil and Boas 2003; Kluver and Banerjee 2005). Predominantly, this research explores state and civil society relations, as well as the possibilities for political participation and collective action. However, scholars have paid

---

[1] "Ex-Chinese Officials Join in Call for Press Freedom," *New York Times*, October 13, 2010 (available at http://www.nytimes.com/2010/10/14/world/asia/14china.html).

comparably little attention to the relationship between political attitudes and digital media,[2] which might form the foundation of an emerging civic culture.

This chapter investigates this relationship specifically in relation to the influence of internet use on political attitudes in China.[3] Compared to traditional media such as television, radio, and newspapers, online news is more likely to frame issues and present information in a way that is unfavorable to the party-state. Therefore, those who consume online news can be expected to hold more negative attitudes toward the regime and its authorities, as the result either of a media effect or of selective exposure, whereby those with more critical attitudes seek out online news. Second, the chapter investigates whether online news consumption has an effect on internal efficacy, given that users are able to access nonofficial news reports. To address these questions, we use the 2008 Asian Barometer Survey.[4]

The chapter first reviews the state of mass media and internet use in China. It then introduces the data and operationalization of the key variables used in the empirical analyses. It finally presents the empirical analyses regarding the effects of internet use on political attitudes and discusses the findings and their implications.

11.2. The State of Traditional Mass Media in China

Since the implementation of the policy of reform and opening of the late 1970s, the Chinese government has relaxed its grip on economic and social activities in China. Unlike the previous totalitarian regime, under which the state directly controlled every aspect of the society, the current Chinese government is somewhat more selective and chooses to control certain key aspects deemed crucial for regime survival. Mass media have traditionally been considered one such critical element. Until recently, most of the major mass media outlets were owned and operated by the state, although the government has continued a monopoly on the supply of most media information, especially information related to political or major policy issues. State agencies like the Chinese

---

[2] Although there are many studies on attitudes in relation to the regime, we found hardly any linking those variables with digital media. An exception can be found in Chen and Shi (2001), who worked on a survey conducted between September 1993 and June 1994 to explore the impact of propaganda of the communist government on people's attitudes toward specific political institutions and toward the government in general. See also Nathan (2003), Li (2004), and Wang (2005, 2006). This is probably because of the lack of reliable and available data, but with new and better surveys on the way, we might see more research on this topic in the near future.

[3] In this article we use frequency of internet use as a proxy for online news consumption, as Chinese use the internet mainly to encounter news and alternative sources on political issues.

[4] Data analyzed in this article were collected by the Asian Barometer Project (2005–2008), which was codirected by Professors Fu Hu and Yun-han Chu and received funding support from Taiwan's Ministry of Education, Academia Sinica, and National Taiwan University. The Asian Barometer Project Office (http://www.asianbarometer.org) is solely responsible for the data distribution. The authors appreciate the assistance and data from the institutes and aforementioned individuals. The analyses and views expressed herein are the authors' own.

Communist Party's (CCP) Central Publicity Department and its propaganda units at each level of government control the content of political news, guide the direction of news reporting, and monitor the operations of news organizations. For almost every important and sensitive political issue, only one voice or a limited range of voices can be heard from the media in China.

Given the tight government control of media in China, most studies of the effects of media equate information in the Chinese mass media to political propaganda, treating it as a means of political control and manipulation (Chen and Shi 2001). It is generally believed that the Chinese media contribute to securing popular support for the government, legitimizing policies, and diminishing demands for political reforms. Most studies assume, and many have found, that media have tremendous success in socializing people to accept official norms and maintaining the legitimacy of the CCP's leadership (Shramm 1976; Hassid 2008a, 2008b; Zhao 1998).

However, in recent years, mass media outlets have experienced fast and fundamental changes in China as well as rapid market reforms. They have expanded in scope, changed in structure, and become more diversified and sophisticated (Polumbaum 1990; Yu 1990; Chan 1993; Lee 1994; Wang 2008). Scholars of Chinese media and politics tend to agree that market reforms have weakened the party's control over the media and liberalized China's media system as an unintentional result of market competition (Chan 1994; Chu 1994; Lynch 1999; Hassid 2008a, 2008b). Driven by the competition for financial resources, many media organizations have increased entertainment content and advertising income. Media content is thus no longer purely dominated by a government propaganda agenda but is filled with a variety of information of political, social, economic, entertainment, and cultural interest (Wang 2009).

News coverage is also changing in this environment. Commercial newspapers compete to attract audiences by pushing the boundaries of control and by covering social and political issues, sometimes even providing controversial opinions (Lynch 1999; Chan 2002; Qiang 2003; Shirk 2007). Negative news stories regarding corruption, poverty, and brutality are regularly seen on Chinese television and in newspapers. A variety of views are occasionally expressed and discussed, albeit within certain limits. For instance, in spring 2010, the delegates to the Eleventh National People's Congress were invited to China Central Television, the official station of the party-state, to discuss and give air to various opinions on widely disputed policy issues such as income inequality, high housing prices, and widespread corruption among politicians. Given this situation, some scholars believe that the media's coverage of controversial issues made it a platform for journalists to influence policy making (Mertha 2008).

With such changes in place, the monopoly power of the state over media has been significantly challenged. That is to say, even though mass media are a key tool for Chinese government propaganda, the content broadcast is not entirely dependent on internal decisions of the CCP. Instead, to manage legitimacy problems, government institutions have found that they also need to

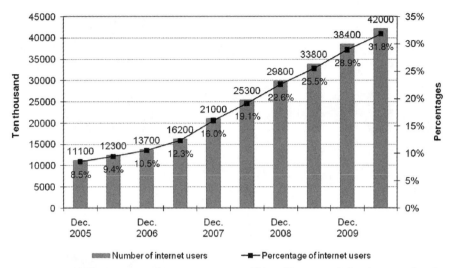

FIGURE 11.1. The increase of internet users in China. Users are defined as people who use the internet at least one hour per week. China Internet Network Information Center was founded in 1997; although it takes orders from the Ministry of Information Industry in conducting its daily business, it is administratively operated by the Chinese Academy of Sciences (http://www.cnnic.net.cn). *Source:* China Internet Network Information Center 2010b.

provide some space for at least a limited plurality of voices and controversial information (Tekwani 2003; see also Chapter 1). This has resulted in a complicated set of dynamics between journalists and government censors. Lagerkvist (2008) observes that the relationship is neither oppositional nor exclusively collaborative. Journalists themselves point to the fact that political authorities and media figures are working with different goals and under different operational norms, although these are not entirely contradictory. In short, there is a movement toward the democratization of the media on three dimensions: demonopolization, professionalization, and certain legal guarantees (Lagerkvist 2010).

The pressure for greater freedom of the press is in part driven by the availability of alternative sources of information online and the need for the mass media to either counterbalance public dissent or to introduce new topics to the political agenda by popular assent (Li, Xuan, and Kluver 2003). In this sense, the internet may have some impact on traditional mass media reporting.

11.3. The State of Digital Media in China

No other change in the media system has been more significant than the expansion of the internet in China. Since the establishment of private internet access in 1994, the growth of internet usage has been virtually exponential year after year. The number of internet users (i.e., people who use the internet at least an hour a week) increased from 10,000 in 1994 to 420 million in 2010

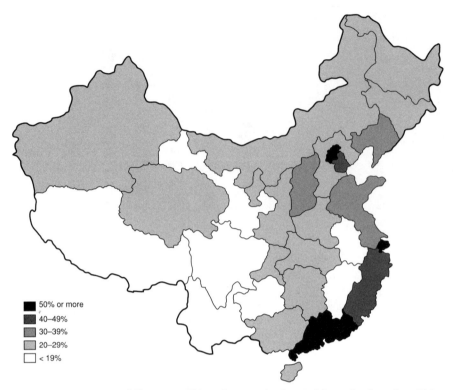

FIGURE 11.2. Internet diffusion in China. *Source:* Authors' elaboration based on China Internet Network Information Center (2010a).

(China Internet Network Information Center 2010b), although the number of internet users as a percentage of the total population is still small compared to advanced democracies (see the Introduction). The semiannual data for the years 2005–2010 are displayed in Figure 11.1. In 2010, about 34 percent of Chinese citizens had used the internet, in contrast with the 69 percent of internet users in developed countries (ITU Statistics 2010). This rapid increase is expected to continue in coming years, particularly in urban areas, although many rural areas remain relatively disconnected (see Figure 11.2). In this sense, even though the digital divide between China and the rest of the world seems to be closing (Tai 2006), the divide remains severe among different Chinese regions. The digital divide within China is due to both a lack of technological diffusion and a lack of skills and resources that allow for the use of technology.[5]

The biggest contrast between China and other countries is online behavior. As Zheng and Wu (2005) note, the online behavior of Chinese citizens differs

---

[5] Big cities in mainland China are widely covered by broadband, but there is no incentive for companies to enter rural markets. The main reasons are lack of market competition, geographic difficulties (as central and western areas are mainly mountainous), poor economic development, high cost of internet, and high rates of illiteracy (Giese 2003).

TABLE 11.1. *Internet Uses*

Types of Use	June 2010 Utilization Rate (% of internet users)
Online music	83
Online news	79
Search engine	76
Instant messaging	72
Online games	71
Online video	63
E-mail	57
Blog	55
Online literature	45
Social network website	50
Online shopping	34
Forum or BBS	32
Online payment	31
E-banking	29
Online stock trading	15
Online travel booking	9

Source: Adapted from China Internet Network Information Center 2010b.

widely from that of their counterparts in advanced democracies in that online news and political information rank among the top uses of the internet (see Table 11.1). This contrasts significantly with netizens in advanced democracies, where leisure and consumer uses predominate (see Chapters 1 and 6).

The data in Table 11.1 confirm that searching for online news is one of the most common internet activities (79 percent), just after listening to music online; commercial uses of the internet (e.g., online shopping, banking) are among the least common activities. However, according to the China Internet Network Information Center (2010b), although online news might be considered an information source alternative to traditional media, a high percentage of internet users report being skeptical about the veracity of online news information: 71 percent of respondents reported partly trusting and partly distrusting internet content. In addition, online news consumption substantially trades off with other forms of media; that is, there is a substitution effect whereby the time an individual spends consuming online news trades off with other forms of media consumption.

Qiang (2003) argues that the internet is the first form of media that provides a forum for Chinese public discussion and debate. Yang (2009) summarizes three major contributions of the internet: it has fostered public debate and the articulation of problems and has demonstrated the potential to play a supervisory role in Chinese politics; it has facilitated the activities of existing organizations while creating a new associational form, the virtual community; and it has introduced new forms of political expression and organizational dynamics into popular protest. Even lacking revolutionary consequences, the internet likely will be "a key pillar of China's slower, evolutionary path toward increased pluralization and possibly even nascent democratization" (Chase and Mulvenon 2002, 90). This has two implications: First, if acquiring political information online motivates attitude change in general (Eveland and Scheufele 2000; Scheufele and Nisbet 2002), then this would appear to be especially true in the Chinese case, given the uniquely pluralizing function of the internet in China's information ecology. Second, the internet has provided additional communication channels, thus enabling greater dissemination of political views and information.

However, it is clear that the internet does not escape from censorship and government control, especially because it was originally established and largely promoted by the government, parallel to the promotion of the internet as the main modernization factor for China (Lagerkvist 2010).[6] The government's system of controlling the internet is one of the most extensive and sophisticated in the world (MacKinnon 2006).[7] Multiple authorities and numerous rules and laws are in place to monitor the flow of information on the web. State control of the internet takes various forms. First and foremost, government authorities try to limit the information users can obtain from the internet. Sophisticated programs like the Golden Shield Project (also known as the Great Firewall) block access to "harmful" or "subversive" websites and monitor activities of internet users. Websites dedicated to the events of Tiananmen Square and other politically sensitive issues are not accessible in China. Other instruments of control have included requirements for computer manufacturers to include special filtering software in their products, although this practice is not widespread.[8]

The state also tries to restrain the anonymity of internet users. Many colleges began to require students to provide a student ID and report their real name when registering online for a campus bulletin board system (BBS). Administrative authorities have been considering a "real name" policy for bloggers, which would require that internet users register their online identification with their real names and proof of identification.[9] Whether this policy will come into place remains unclear, but such a policy consideration reflects the stepped-up

---

[6] In referring to mainland China we exclude Hong Kong and Macau because these districts are under special independent laws and judicial power, and no censorship laws apply.

[7] The government authorities administrating the internet include the Department of Propaganda and the Surveillance Center for National Information Security. More than sixty laws have been enacted since 1996.

[8] For instance, the controversy around Green Dam Youth Escort, a filter meant to stop "pornographic" content, caused such a negative reaction that the information technology minister, Li Yizhong, had to change the initial project and instead propose that the filtering software be used voluntarily rather than compulsorily and targeted mainly at computers used in schools and other public spaces (see "China Pulls Back from Edict on Web-Filtering Software," *Wall Street Journal*, August 14, 2009 (available at http://online.wsj.com/article/SB125013563611828325.html).

[9] "China Targets Online Commentator Anonymity." *BBC News*. May 11, 2010 (available at http://news.bbc.co.uk/2/hi/8671856.stm).

efforts of the Chinese government to limit and control the diversity of views accessible online. The government takes direct action against controversial opinions either by closing and banning blogs and certain web pages containing social or political commentaries or by harassing digital activists. These actions contribute to a climate of threat and fear of being arrested, which is conducive to effective self-censorship.

In addition to centralized control efforts, government agencies hire cooperative internet users to monitor the activities of other users and post comments favorable to government policies. These users are called the 50-Cent Party (Wumao Dang), named after the equivalent of what they are paid for each post.[10] The compliance and collaboration of main international internet providers are also a major problem, although those companies, including Yahoo!, Microsoft, Skype, and until recently Google, argue that restricted internet access better serves the interest of political openness than no internet at all (MacKinnon 2006).

However, despite all these measures and efforts, backing down on internet diffusion and access is not on the government agenda, as such steps would represent a step backward in commercial and economic terms. Rather, the regime is attempting to minimize what it perceives as the negative impacts of internet use (i.e. access to content which the deem inappropriate for public consumption; Tai 2006). At the same time, the internet has proved much more difficult to control. On the one hand, the connection to outside content and net servers, and the flexibility to open new internet sites when others are shut down, increases exponentially difficulties for government control; no firewall is completely effective and increasingly services are offered to citizens to evade those filters (MacKinnon 2006; Yang 2009). Even when online content is removed, there is always a lag providing time for contraband material to be seen and read by many citizens.

On the other hand, commercial interests and private entrepreneurs have played a large role in the development of China's internet, and sometimes their interests collide with the policy aims of certain Chinese agencies and departments. Some companies offer software to bypass censorship or to mask blocked addresses and services that enable access to blocked pages. Moreover, since 2005, some companies began to sign corporate responsibility codes promoted by international organizations like the United Nations.

The relative freedom of online journalism in relation to traditional state media stems from the differentiated societal functions that motivated the expansion of internet access and the development of mass media in China. Mass media outlets have traditionally served a propaganda function while the internet has played a critical role in the development of the knowledge economy. Therefore, rooted in its inception, the internet had to be a freer environment where ideas could be developed. Today internet journalists and bloggers can

---

[10] For a detailed and exhaustive review of the tools the Chinese government uses to control digital content and structure, see Chase and Mulvenon (2002).

more easily evade the strict guidelines about what, how, and when to report certain news that broadcast journalists are subject to following. That is, while the Chinese government tries to update internet legislation, regulation quickly becomes outdated (Tai 2006), and there are not enough people to control internet activity.

As a result, in China, innovations in cloaking software and use practices are changing too quickly for the government to keep up. This creates certain gaps in the dissemination of information on the internet, which allows for the internet to become a place where people can access alternative information and perspectives, express different views about social and political issues, and even engage in some antiregime activities. This also explains the previous popularity of campus BBSs among college students, who often made extensive use of these networks to communicate with fellow students.[11] Students used the BBS to make friends, look for dates, and seek entertainment. Most important, they bravely reported events on the basis of firsthand observation, spread censored information, and exchanged different opinions about social and political issues.

To counterbalance this online information, both state media and commercial internet sites have begun online news reporting. The official newspaper *People's Daily* opened the online forum Strong Nation Forum, which became a popularly visited site where nationalist sentiment and criticism of certain policies or officials are frequently seen. Commercial internet portals like Sina.com and Sohu.com are browsed by tens of millions of viewers every day.[12] Most news websites have also opened discussion forums and message boards, which give users a chance to comment on news stories. These online platforms become readers' outlet for expressing dissatisfaction, criticism, and even cynicism. Most major commercial news websites also provide free blogging services. Professionals, writers, and celebrities post their views or commentaries (not necessarily favorable to the party-state) on their personal blogs. For the most part, blog readers can comment on blog posts as they like. Although the party has attempted to moderate blog content, dissenting views are widely encountered as a result of the inherent difficulties in controlling the internet. In a country where no freelance reporting can be published in the official press, blogging has become the most convenient way for dissidents to express opinions. Beyond official news reporting and commercial internet portals, numerous unofficial online forums (e.g., Tianya.cn, Popyard.com) have developed into sites where one can find the harshest criticism of the government and its policies. This

---

[11] Most major universities have one or more BBS. The most famous ones include Beijing University's BeidaWeiming, Tsinghua University's ShuimuQinghua, Nanking University's Xiao Baihe, and Nankai University's Wo Ai Nankai. However, their popularity has declined in recent years.

[12] These sites are owned and run by private entrepreneurs. Although they are supposed to operate under the general guidance of the government, they are not considered state media and enjoy greater freedom in reporting news.

sphere of freer speech is becoming more important as the internet has become extensively integrated into the lives of young people and is beginning to influence the lives of older generations as well.

Online news reporting and cyber-discussion have began to affect government decisions and politicians' behavior, with regard not only to the protection of rights but also to policies and the, albeit limited, degree of allowed information pluralism (Tai 2006; Yang 2009). The Deng Yujiao incident is just one of many such stories. President Hu Jintao and Premier Wen Jiabao have openly expressed that they pay special attention to online news and discussion. Wen publicly claimed that he browses the internet every day for up to an hour to know what people are talking about on the web. The two have even joined lively discussion with online viewers in web chat rooms. Online information is particularly crucial for party officials: the internet is one of the few places where political leaders can encounter negative reporting, which can be useful feedback for officials, as it enables them to anticipate and formulate responses to issues.

This feedback is particularly important because officials fear or are often uncertain about the possible effects from negative online news, and widespread online news stories tend to receive considerable attention from other politicians. Local officials typically act swiftly to resolve the exposed problems largely because they do not want top-level leaders to notice and penalize them. Internet reporting makes the voices of ordinary citizens powerful enough to make politicians change their behavior on some issues. During a meeting of the National People's Congress in March 2011, journalists and meeting attendees exposed the inappropriate remarks of the delegates during panel discussions on housing prices, income disparity, and other controversial issues. These remarks received harsh criticism from netizens and created sufficient public pressure that officials had to respond and in some cases publicly apologize for their remarks or behavior.

The previous paragraphs tell us about the complex dynamics between civil society and Chinese government, and a critical dimension of those dynamics is the potential for change in the political attitudes of those who engage online – particularly as internet use becomes more common across a broader segment of society. Chen and Shi (2001) conducted one of the few empirical studies on public opinion to explore the impact of government propaganda on Chinese attitudes. They found that state news media in China in general have negative effects on political attitudes toward political institutions and in particular lead to greater distrust of the government. The authors conclude that mass media–based propaganda fails to mobilize support for the regime. Given the countervailing forces between the politically pluralizing tendencies of Chinese internet users and the efforts by the Chinese government to control those forces, this chapter explores whether online news consumption in China influences internet users' political attitudes, specifically trust in institutions, attitudes toward democracy, and sense of political efficacy.

TABLE 11.2. *News Sources*

	% of Users(n)[a]	% Regarding this as the Most Important Source (n)
Television	87 (4456)	82 (4180)
Newspaper	22 (1117)	3 (135)
Radio	12 (597)	1 (65)
Internet	7 (372)	2 (125)
Instant messaging	8 (404)	0 (22)
Personal contacts	18 (931)	2 (121)
Other	1 (26)	0.3 (15)

Note: Percentages based on weighted data. Figures for *n* are rounded to the nearest whole number.
[a] Figures do not add up to 100 percent because of multiple responses.
Source: Asian Barometer Survey 2008.

11.4. Data, Variables, and Measurement

To analyze the relationship between digital media use and political attitudes, this study uses the data from the 2008 Asian Barometer Survey (ABS). The ABS is a Taiwan-based public opinion survey across seventeen Asian countries and territories.[13] The 2008 wave was collected between December 2007 and December 2008. The China survey was conducted by the Research Center for Contemporary China, based at Peking University. The survey used a national probability sampling method representative of the adult population older than eighteen years.[14] Nevertheless, the calculations are based on the sample weights to more accurately reflect known population parameters. The survey contains 5,098 respondents and had a 73 percent response rate in urban areas and a 87 percent response rate in rural areas. The ABS asks a wide range of questions covering media consumption, religion, ideology, party identification, and other political attitudes and behaviors.[15]

According to the data presented in Table 11.2, less than 20 percent of the Chinese public uses the internet; however, that still ranks China among those countries with the greatest number of internet users. There is a bimodal

[13] The territories included are Japan, Mongolia, South Korea, Taiwan, Hong Kong, mainland China, the Philippines, Thailand, Vietnam, Cambodia, Singapore, Indonesia, India, Pakistan, Bangladesh, Sri Lanka, and Nepal.
[14] The survey excludes those living in the Tibetan Autonomous Region, mainly because of difficulties in carrying out fieldwork. Based on the statistics of China's annual population (from the State Council Population Census Office), a stratified multistage-area sampling procedure with probabilities proportional to size measures (PPS) was employed to select the sample and guarantee coverage of rural areas and minority populations. For more details on the sampling and information on the data, see the website of the Asian Barometer project, at http://www.asianbarometer.org.
[15] See the Appendix for specific variable wordings and coding details.

TABLE 11.3. *Internet Access and Exposure to Online News, by Sociodemographic Characteristics*

Population Segment	Percentage of Population that Uses the Internet (*n*)
Total Population	17
Age	
18 to 30 years old	34 (251)
31 to 40 years old	11 (127)
41 to 50 years old	7 (75)
51 to 60 years old	2 (22)
61 and older	3 (23)
Gender	
Male	10 (259)
Female	9 (179)
Education	
No formal education	0.3 (4)
Primary education	3 (47)
Secondary education	16 (325)
Tertiary education	70 (124)
Location	
Megacity	50 (207)
Major city	50 (354)
Small town	20 (633)
Village	10 (3786)

Note: All figures are based on weighted data. Figures for *n* are rounded to the nearest whole number. An internet user is anyone who reports having used the internet at least several times a year.
Source: Asian Barometer 2008.

distribution in the frequency of internet use in China: 6 percent rarely use the internet, 4 percent use the internet daily or almost daily, 4 percent use the internet weekly, and the remaining one percent use it less often than weekly. Hence, internet use is either a relatively rare or regular event in Chinese life without many occasional users.

Table 11.3 presents the proportion of internet users by age, education, gender, and residence. It shows that internet use is much higher among young, highly educated urban citizens, but there are not significant differences by gender, which is consistent with the China Internet Network Information Center (2010b) data. These figures show that there is a highly stratified digital divide, with internet access concentrated in the young, urban, and educated segment of the population.

We move now to the dependent variables. Institutional trust is operational-ized as an additive scale consisting of eight different government institutions at national and local levels, resulting in an index ranging from 0 to 24. Cron-bach's α for the scale is 0.88 (standardized. $\alpha = 0.88$), and the elimination of no item improves the scale fit. The scale mean is 18.28 (s.d. = 4.21), well above the scale midpoint (12), which shows that respondents express a great deal of confidence in political institutions.

Support for democracy is operationalized in terms of the extent to which respondents "would like China to be democratic now" on a scale ranging from 1 to 10. This question captures respondents' preference for democracy. As section 11.5 shows, popular conceptions of democracy in China diverge in subtle but important ways from its general understanding in the West. Given the normative distance from the status quo implied by this question, it may shed some light on the trajectory of political evolution in China. The average value of this variable is 8.58 (s.d. = 1.31), which indicates strong and widespread support for democracy in China.

Last, internal efficacy is computed from an additive index of two variables (with a Kendall's tau b of 0.28, $p < .001$) measuring the extent to which respondents believe that they have the ability to participate in politics and the extent to which they regard politics as too complicated for them. The scale for this item ranges from 0 to 6. The mean value of the index is of 2.27 (s.d. = 0.52), which indicates that respondents tend to feel that they lack political efficacy, although this average is slightly more than one standard deviation from the scale midpoint.

11.5. Analysis of Political Attitudes

Chinese political attitudes have been a curiosity to researchers in the West. Empirical research generally shows that the Chinese have high levels of trust in government and a positive evaluation of government performance (Li 2004; Wang 2005, 2006; Wang 2009). These figures are notably higher than the lev-els of political support reported in most industrial democracies (Klingemann 1999). The evidence indicates that fear or intimidation (Wang 2006) and pro-paganda (Chen and Shi 2001) fail to explain this phenomenon.[16] Wang (2006) offers an alternative explanation that is related to the economic performance of the government and individual well-being, as well as the limited political

---

[16] Wang (2006) points to the weak correlation between political fear and expressed confidence in the government. Chen and Shi (2001) found that only between 4 percent and 14 percent of expressed confidence was attributable to fear. Li (2004) also reported a decreasing concern about negative consequences of criticizing the government between 1999 and 2001. The correlation between trust in institutions and strong agreement that people are free to speak what they think without fear is not high but is still positive and significant, at $p = 0.01$. Thus, it may be that in our case, part of the explanation has to do with fear. Obviously, a better measurement and detailed exploration of those two variables could provide a better understanding of this relationship, but that is beyond the scope of this chapter.

reforms that the government has implemented.[17] This effect is so strong that it even surpasses and counterbalances the negative effect of limits on personal self-expression and trust of government. Li (2004) advances another explanation based on citizens' differentiation between the government's intention to meet the needs of citizens and government capacity to carry out those intentions. As a result, positive evaluations regarding the government's intentions and its capacity to carry them out can result in higher levels of institutional trust predicated on government outputs, even in the absence of political efficacy.

Wang (2009) noted that the emerging middle class – which is also the segment of the population in which we see the largest levels of internet use – was opposed to government and democratic reforms, as they would entail a somewhat chaotic transformation and impede economic progress. They were content with the current pace of liberalization: "Although they were not against democracy, they were much less enthusiastic about supporting democratic movement" (Wang 2009, 54).

The definition of democracy that is popularly internalized in China has generated some debate. Wang (2007) argues on the basis of the 2004 ABS data that support for democracy indicates genuine democratic attitudes as understood in the West. Self-identification with democracy indicates people's general feeling toward the substantive meaning denoted by democracy, a system previously considered unacceptable or inappropriate. The 2008 ABS contains an open-ended question on the meaning of democracy, and the most frequent responses on the definition of democracy include "people as their own masters" (14.2 percent), "freedom of speech, press and expression" (13.9 percent), and "election, popular vote or electoral choice" (8.1 percent).

However, attaching significance to these statements on the meaning of democracy for Chinese citizens is problematic given their polysemic nature. Concepts such as those listed here are perfectly "compatible not only with the doctrine of socialist democracy but also with classic Confucian ideals of benevolent dictatorship" (Shi 2008, 215). For instance, a modal characterization of democracy was "election, popular vote or electoral choice," but options such as "the rotation of government," "a competitive party system," "participation and citizen empowerment," and the "ability to select or change government" were not as frequent. This suggests that the context in which concepts such as democracy are used has a significant role in governing their meaning. As a result, popular conceptions of democracy in China are largely uncritical of the current regime structure.

Perhaps because of this, previous studies have reported that a high percentage of the population desires democracy while also believing that China is

---

[17] The ABS data also show that a respondent's perception that his or her current economic family situation is better than a few years ago is significantly correlated with trust in government. As economic growth has been significant in China, this can also explain part of the high mean observed in the level of trust.

already a democracy (Shi 2008). According to the 2008 ABS, about 20 percent of Chinese believe that China is a "fully functioning democracy," and 37 percent support the view that China is a democracy but one with minor problems. Only 16 percent consider China a democracy with major problems, and less than 2 percent of those surveyed think that China is not a democracy at all. Similarly, when respondents were asked to rate the level of democracy on a 10-point scale where 1 meant "complete dictatorship" and 10 meant "complete democracy," the mean value was 7.4 (s.d. = 1.5).

Furthermore, when asked about how democracy functioned in their country, 68 percent reported that they were "fairly" or "very satisfied with the way democracy works" in China. These data show that, in general, the Chinese regard their country as fairly democratic, or at least they are unwilling to state publicly otherwise. For these questions about democracy in China, however, an average of one in five respondents declined to answer for one reason or another.[18]

We now move to the analysis of the association between internet use and political attitudes, controlling for sociodemographic variables (education, age, gender), attitudes toward government control of speech, and political interest.[19] Using proportional-odds logistic regression models, we predict levels of support for institutional trust and democracy, as well as levels of internal political efficacy. Internet users can be expected to be more critical of officials and the functioning of the current system, because online information is more critical of the regime. However, they are not expected to significantly differ from other Chinese in their support of democracy, given the middle class's investment in the current regime structure. Finally, because the internet opens additional opportunities for voice, we expect internet users to have greater levels of internal efficacy. The results are presented in Table 11.4.

The regressions show that internet users are notably less trusting of political institutions, which suggests that they evince lower levels of political support than their offline counterparts. In addition, those who reject government control of political speech are significantly more critical of the current regime. By contrast, those who live in small towns or the countryside are considerably more trusting of government institutions than those who live in the largest cities. This may be explained in part by lower internet access rates. However, in larger cities, even those who do not have internet access are more likely to be in contact with social networks, conversational partners, and informal opinion leaders who are online. Age is positively associated with institutional trust, which is consistent with evidence that the youngest generation does not have the same ties to the political regime as generations that came before. Those who are most critical of political institutions in China are young internet users

---

[18] Shi (2008, 214) has shown that this high nonresponse is not related to political fear but to lower levels of education and political interest.
[19] Household income was omitted because of the high nonresponse rate (90%) for the item.

TABLE 11.4. *Internet Use and Political Attitudes*

	Institutional Trust β (s.e.)	Support for Democracy β (s.e.)	Internal Efficacy β (s.e.)
Education	−0.06 (0.07)	0.04 (0.08)	0.90 (0.14)***
Gender (female)	0.06 (0.03)	0.08 (0.04)*	−0.22 (0.07)***
Age	0.01 (0.00)***	0.01 (0.00)***	0.00 (0.00)
Political interest	0.10 (0.06)	0.24 (0.07)***	1.40 (0.13)***
Urban-rural: Major city	0.08 (0.10)	0.25 (0.11)*	0.33 (0.20)
Urban-rural: Small city	0.33 (0.09)***	0.13 (0.09)	0.47 (0.18)**
Urban-rural: Countryside	0.63 (0.09)***	0.35 (0.09)***	0.62 (0.16)***
Free speech	−0.19 (0.03)***	−0.18 (0.04)***	−0.41 (0.07)***
Internet use	−0.29 (0.07)***	−0.08 (0.07)	0.41 (0.14)**
Deviance	19,524.41	9646.80	7943.90
AIC	19,588.41	9682.80	7973.90
N	3792	3163	3474

Note: All figures are based on weighted data. AIC = Akaike information criterion.
Source: Asian Barometer 2008.

who live in China's largest cities and tend to reject the government's control of speech.

Given the nature of common understandings of democracy in China, we should not expect that support for democracy has the same estimators as those for a critical view of government institutions. These results show that internet use has no relationship with support for democracy or becoming more democratic. However, although the Chinese tend to associate free speech with democracy, they have reconciled this conception with the right of the government to regulate speech to pursue certain goals (Lagerkvist 2008). These data indicate that those who reject the government's right to limit public discussion of certain topics are also more critical of democracy as they understand it. As with institutional trust, those in rural areas and with more political interest tend to be more supportive of democracy. However, the youngest generation also is more skeptical of democracy in China, which suggests that they may have different conceptualizations of democracy or profess different political values in relation to older cohorts.

The final model, regarding political efficacy, may shed some additional insight on China's political future. As in most Western democracies, education is a positive predictor of internal efficacy, as is political interest. Also, internet use is a positive estimator of political efficacy, as it is in Western Europe and the United States. Women have notably lower levels of political efficacy, which may reflect dominant cultural beliefs regarding the public role of women. Women in more rural areas tend to have greater levels of political efficacy than their counterparts who live in the largest cities. As internet use expands, changes in the economy continue the movement from rural areas to cities, and as generational replacement produces widespread value change, we may see changes in the path of China's political future. Although at the moment, those who are most critical of the current regime tend to feel less politically efficacious, that may change over time as the younger generation replaces their parents and grandparents.

11.6. Conclusion

This chapter presented an analysis of internet use in relation to political attitudes in China. The general finding of the chapter is that internet users tend to be more critical of the current regime and believe that they are more politically efficacious. Irrespective of whether this relationship is endogenous or tied to other factors, such as postmaterialism, internet use is concentrated among a segment of the population that is already more critical of the current regime. Although this segment of young, educated urbanites otherwise express lower levels of political efficacy, internet use is linked with higher levels of political efficacy overall. And the more this segment uses the internet, the more efficacious and critical their attitudinal dispositions.

Even when the question of support for democracy was framed so as to create normative distance from the status quo, respondents still seem to identify democratization as a process in the framework of the current regime. This suggests that the direction of democratic political development (as it exists in China) diverges from liberal democracy – at least as things stand today. However, this is a vision of democracy that is distinctly tied to the older generations. What that future will look like is somewhat unclear, given that we lack a complete picture of the prevailing political vision underlying the current generation's discontent.

Younger and more highly educated cohorts have decidedly more negative views of the current institutions. Even if those who oppose the government's right to control political speech tend to have greater doubts about their political efficacy, the educated and those online do not. The internet's reach is still relatively low, at roughly 15 percent, but if the digital divide shrinks and dissident online politics becomes more normalized, and if political opportunities for change begin to open, digital spaces may become a place where critical counternarratives and alternative visions of the political system can flourish. Given that broadcast media do not operate as an entirely separate system and are not functionally differentiated from the aims of the regime, the internet could play an important role in the formation of political networks pushing for change. During the Tiananmen Square protests in 1989, ChinaNet, a nascent computer network linking students and other academics, played a key role in demonstrators being able to communicate with one another (Calhoun 1989). If political change occurs in China's future, digitally networked communications could prove crucial, and China's netizens could once again be in the vanguard.

11.7. Appendix[20]

Age. Years of age.

Education. Ordinal variable with four categories: none, primary, secondary, tertiary.

Institutional trust. The index of institutional trust is computed from respondent assessments of trust in nine government institutions (the president and executive branch, the judicial system, the national government in Beijing, political parties, parliament, the civil service, the military, the police, and local government). Respondents were asked to indicate whether they had "a great deal of trust," "quite a lot of trust," "not very much trust," or "none at all" These items were summed together resulting in scale values ranging from 0 to 27.

Interest in politics. Interest in politics is measured on a four-point scale based on the question "How much would you say you are interested in politics?" with responses ranging from 1 (not at all interested) to 4 (very interested).

Internal political efficacy. This index is computed from two items based on respondents' agreement with the statements "I think I have the ability to participate in politics" and "sometimes politics and government seems so complicated that a person like me can't really understand what is going on." The answers range from 0 (strongly agree) to 3 (strongly disagree) for each item, which results in a scale from 0 to 6.

Internet, television, newspapers, radio news consumption. These four dummy variables identify whether respondents use each form of media for political information (question wording is "What is your main source of information about politics and government?" – multiple responses possible).

Support for democracy. Support for democracy is operationalized in terms of respondents' answer to the question, "To want extent would you want our country to be democratic now?" on a scale ranging from 1 (complete dictatorship) to 10 (complete democracy).

---

[20] Variable used in the chapter analysis: coding, construction of variables, and survey question wording (alphabetically ordered)

Conclusion

Laia Jorba, Michael J. Jensen, and Eva Anduiza

This book has dealt with two research questions: how does digital media use influence political engagement, and which contextual variables may condition this relationship? The evidence analyzed across the fifteen cases considered in this book suggests that engagement with digital environments is having an effect on users and that contextual features play a significant role in shaping digital politics.

The cases presented in this volume have isolated evidence for both cross-national generalizations and system-level effects, indicating that the role of a particular variable depends on its interaction with institutional elements, media systems, and the digital divide in a political system. In addition, the cases provide evidence that digital media create political opportunity structures in political systems, which in turn depend on contextual factors. We first consider the evidence linking digital media use to higher levels of political engagement, and we then move to the question of the role of contextual features of political systems and their immediate environments in shaping the development of digital politics in a polity.

Political Engagement around the World

The most sustained empirical observation throughout the analyses carried out in this volume is that, despite all the nuances, there is evidence of a positive and significant effect of digital media on political engagement, regardless of the political context under consideration. In particular, the research assembled here shows that internet use is positively associated with a variety of forms of

The conclusions here indeed result from many exchanges with the contributors of this volume, to whom we are very grateful. We are also grateful for the detailed comments of two volume reviewers. Any errors remain, of course, the sole responsibility of the editors, who acknowledge the financial support of the Spanish Ministry of Science and Innovation (research grants SEJ 2007–80062, CSO2009–05975-E, CSO2010-09901).

political engagement – both behavioral and attitudinal. Jorba and Bimber's as well as Chadwick's review of the literature show that this is consistent with the preponderance of previous research regarding digital media. This has been confirmed throughout the book, ranging from electoral turnout in the 2008 U.S. elections to critical evaluations of the current regime in China. That this finding holds up independent of the methodology used and the context involved demonstrates its robustness.

The detection of a positive effect of internet use on political engagement – behavioral and attitudinal – is found to varying degrees across Western Europe, using both survey and qualitative evidence, as the chapters by Colombo, Galais, and Gallego; Cantijoch; Vaccari; and Kroh and Neiss show. Moreover, the American and German panel studies in Chapters 3 (Hamilton and Tolbert) and 8 (Kroh and Neiss) demonstrate that this effect holds even when controlling for the fact that politically involved citizens have been more likely to use the internet. This relationship may strengthen over time as internet use becomes more widespread and integrated into everyday life and political practices.

These analyses cannot be directly extended to other cases that are advanced democracies, both because of significant differences in legally sanctioned participatory repertoires and because of limitations on data availability. However, even when institutions are closed to citizen politics, individuals are finding other spaces in which to participate politically, and this often occurs in digital domains. In these political systems, digitally networked devices open channels of political information and communication that otherwise would not exist. The results presented in this volume show that even in such nondemocratic systems, there are rich repertoires of digital politics and online participation, and information consumption may have significant effects on political attitudes.

Explaining this general effect of digital media use on political engagement is complicated. Pinning down, let alone generalizing, the paths and mechanisms through which this posited causal relationship works requires further empirical development. However, we find broad similarities across the majority of cases. It appears evident that there are multiple processes at work at the same time. In line with the expectations outlined in the Introduction, we can differentiate direct and indirect paths from digital media use to political engagement. On the one hand, the diffusion of digital media has brought into the political arena additional means and modes for political engagement. This effect is likely more significant where media systems are relatively closed, as in Italy, or where political institutions greatly constrain political rights, as in China and to varying degrees in the Islamic world. In these cases online engagement has a particular relevance. As our systematic comparison of the Spanish and U.S. cases shows, online engagement seems to largely follow a similar explanatory model across countries where resources such as internet skills and motivations such as political interest play an important role, and others such as education or political efficacy are secondary. Thus, beyond country differences, which we consider later, there are some fundamental common patterns that must be highlighted.

On the other hand, the relationship between the use of digital media and political participation is not always direct; there are also indirect effects that operate through the generation of resources and attitudes (both self-referential beliefs – political efficacy and political interest – and beliefs about the nature of the political system) that result from digital media use and that in turn affect engagement. Regarding resources, Jensen and Anduiza as well as Cantijoch find that internet use and online resources are significant predictors of offline political participation in the Spanish case. Hamilton and Tolbert find that with increasing internet use over time, individuals show higher levels of political interest. This result, combined with even stronger concomitant effects for television news and newspaper consumption, is evidence against the media-malaise thesis (Norris 2000; Coleman and Blumler 2009). Kroh and Neiss found similar effects in Germany, also from panel data. In their study of European countries, Colombo, Galais, and Gallego likewise found a link between internet use and political interest and efficacy. Although the magnitudes of the effects are not uniform across countries – suggesting contextual features condition this relationship – the authors find broad-based support for a connection between internet use and political efficacy.

The book also shows that digital media use influences political attitudes beyond these advanced democracies. In these contexts, attitudes and interests are not limited to psychological involvement with the political system. We have found that in some cases internet users hold different normative beliefs regarding the constitution of the political system and who should have standing in public life. Particularly in societies where the political system is relatively closed, internet users are more likely to challenge the boundaries of political inclusion.

One consistent finding across cases in the nondemocratic world is a relationship between internet use and support for greater democracy, however that is understood. Despite institutionalized censorship, information flows challenging official accounts persist online, which leads to low levels of trust in institutions. Likewise, Hussain and Howard find that internet-using populations are more likely to support some democratization in the cultural and political spheres, and thereby support of certain political and civic rights, especially in Indonesia and Pakistan, as well as equal rights for women in the public sphere. These cases provide evidence that internet users are more likely to favor individualism than dominant modes of political exclusion in these societies. This finding is consistent with previous work regarding early adopters in the United States and Europe that showed that internet users are significantly more individualistic and support government transparency (Norris 2001).

Of course, the strength of an internet effect is not constant across countries or situations. A number of important nuances and qualifications are in order. First, it is clear that contextual factors are fundamental aspects that condition these relationships, even in relatively similar cases such as Western European countries, as Colombo, Galais, and Gallego demonstrate. The comparison between Spain and the United States also illustrates several interesting differences. Jensen and Anduiza's chapter shows that the role of internet resources is somewhat more important in Spain than in the United States. In addition, Hamilton and Tolbert's and Cantijoch's studies show that, although exposure to online political information is important in both countries, only in the United States does it seem to affect voting and campaign-related participation. These differences may be because the U.S. survey data were gathered in the midst or wake of a national election campaign in which online mobilization efforts by parties and candidates was commonplace. Meanwhile, the Spanish data were collected during a period of electoral peace before the 2008 Spanish electoral campaign when political parties were less intensively communicating with the electorate. This suggests that comparative analyses of digital politics should consider not only ongoing elements of the political opportunity structure but also the mobilization processes that, despite their short temporal durations, are part of the context.

Second, the analyses sustained throughout the book provide support for the conclusion that the effect of digital media depends on the modes of political engagement considered. Thus, although we have used the terms *political engagement* and *political involvement* to encompass different political attitudes and behaviors, the empirical analyses in this volume have found differences in classes of attitudes and modes of behavior.

Kroh and Neiss find relatively stronger effects of internet access for work in political action groups than for voting intentions and party attachment in Germany. These differences are even more acute in Cantijoch's and Hamilton and Tolbert's studies. Cantijoch's chapter differentiates participatory modes and shows that although there is an effect of internet use, and particularly of the degree of consumption of political information on extrarepresentational forms of participation, the same does not happen for representational modes of participation. Hamilton and Tolbert identify significant effects of changes in online information exposure on offline participation in the campaign and on electoral turnout in the presidential election, but not on the primaries.

The multidimensionality and expanded repertoire of political engagement increase when we consider online political involvement, which appears even more diverse than traditional offline involvement. Jensen and Anduiza distinguish between web 1.0 modes of political participation and web 2.0's participatory architecture. Vaccari considers three different modes of online engagement in Italy, each of them attracting citizens with different sociopolitical profiles. In the chapter by Howard and Hussain on Islamic countries, different modes of engagement and value orientations are considered, such as online information exposure, use of online social networks, the development of online civil society, and attitudes regarding the role of women in society.

In addition, beyond traditional categories of political participation, it is clear that the boundaries among information seeking, communication, political discussion, and political participation have become more difficult to distinguish online. Digital media position information consumers to easily modify and retransmit information they receive, and in many nondemocratic regimes, even information seeking can be a transgressive political act.

A third consideration has emerged from the chapters: in the same way as different dimensions of political engagement must be distinguished for meaningful empirical analysis and generalizations, differences in uses and in digital media platforms available must also be taken into account. Although digital networks may have a global expanse, use of these networks is not global and general but specific and partial, in the sense that the purposes, requirements, and logics of concrete networks differ greatly from one another. Chadwick's contribution develops several concepts that help give definition to online politics. His research suggests that undifferentiated measures of digital media use may be unsatisfactory given the variety of digital architectures and the uses to which they are put.

Hence, the mobilization-versus-reinforcement debate, which has significantly shaped the development of digital politics, is no longer by itself an adequate conceptual vocabulary for describing and explaining online participation. Whether mobilization or reinforcement is occurring is not reducible to the demographic traits of users, as who participates online depends in part on the type of participation. Rather, the work presented here suggests the need for discriminating the different ways in which people are connecting to the political system and for classifying the impacts of different connections on both the political system and the individuals using the technology.

As the digital divide recedes and both individuals and political organizations become increasingly sophisticated consumers and producers of online political information, there is a great deal of differentiation in their practical politics and political experiences online. This is even more important online than it is offline. Chadwick's and Jorba and Bimber's chapters show the potential for a greater diversity of online political forms, including self-organized and dispersed political activities. Although in many places the first to engage online were the most interested in politics and had more socioeconomic resources, as internet diffusion and adoption reach their saturation points, we find more diversity among those who engage online. This means that the online population is changing not only in numbers but also in political and demographic characteristics.

In this respect, we can identify two trends: first, the greater the extension and domestication of digital media use, the greater is the plurality of people who are engaged online and the greater and more diverse political practices are developed. Early adopters are known to have particular characteristics that often mirror extant participatory inequalities (Norris 2001). However, as diffusion reaches a saturation point, the internet becomes domesticated. Jensen and Anduiza show that in the United States, at least during a campaign period, socioeconomic stratification was less pronounced, and Hamilton and Tolbert find an internet effect for people who were otherwise less participatory.

Second, although it is true that younger cohorts are most engaged online, age stratification may disappear through a process of generational replacement.

The link between age and internet use may have several sources. Technology uptake has a large literature in the study of informatics. One general finding is the relative reluctance of individuals to alter ingrained practices (Danziger et al. 1982; Dutton 1999; Kling 2007), which may lead to younger cohorts being relatively more open to using technology. Younger cohorts may also feel more comfortable in digital networks that provide opportunities for involvement outside traditional political organizations for a variety of political causes, networking on their own terms, and pursing political issues that sometimes fall outside mainstream agendas (De Certeau 1997; Collin 2008; Marsh, O'Toole, and Jones 2007). This contrasts with the empirical findings regarding offline activity in political and civil society organizations (Rosenstone and Hansen 1993; Putnam 2000).

Whether and how people become politically involved online are deeply embedded contextual elements of the political system and its environment. Welp and Wheatley find that movements' online strategies were affected in part by the extent of the digital divide, the level of political development of the country, the demographic characteristics of the activists, and their past experiences in mobilization strategies. Participation strategies in countries as diverse as Italy, some Islamic countries, and Spain use digital media to transmit alternatives to dominant narratives contained in traditional broadcast media. Vaccari shows that in Italy people engaged online are ideologically distinct, as the political right monopolizes traditional media. In some Islamic countries, Hussain and Howard note, one can encounter use of the internet to propagate both secular and radical Islamic narratives. In Spain, online arenas are used more by individuals and groups countering government information and policies.

Thus, digital media use may promote a diversity of attitudes and practices of political engagement. A thorough analysis of this relationship must take into account different dimensions of digital media use, different dimensions of political engagement, and the specific role of contextual variables. Although we have already outlined some elements for which contextual variables are expected to play a relevant role, we move into a more thorough analysis of this matter.

The Role of Context in Digital Politics

Online practices do not exist in a vacuum but are related and linked to institutional contexts, levels of technological development, and extant political practices and orientations. Political systems differ in their configurations of incentives for the emergence of digital politics. Comparative analysis plays an important role in the development of the study of digital politics, as it allows for exploration of relationships between these contextual elements and digital politics. We can therefore move from descriptive statements to more explanatory analyses of digital politics.

From the chapters included in this volume, three broad contextual dimensions appear as useful elements for understanding the question of how digital media influence political engagement and who engages online: the digital divide, the media system, and the institutional environment. The research presented here shows that digital media alter the contour of political systems in many cases by providing communication opportunities that would not otherwise exist. These contextual dimensions are not unrelated, as the chapters here have documented: political institutions may supervene on the operation of media systems and the digital divide, and likewise, media systems and the digital divide may influence each other and the behavior of political institutions.

The digital divide operates at a macro and micro level. At a macro level, different stages of digital media diffusion can be distinguished in the countries considered in this volume: from countries with low levels of diffusion to countries approaching a ceiling level or saturation stage, in which most people are online (e.g., Germany, the United Kingdom, or the United States; see Table I.3). The digital divide plays an important role in the development of digital politics because it serves as a material limiting constraint on the possibilities for digital politics in a political system. In general, the lowest levels of internet diffusion are found in the countries with more closed structures of political opportunity (as shown in Table I.3), and this is not without consequences. However, our analyses show that even in countries that rank among the lowest in internet use, there is nevertheless significant political activity that makes use of a range of digitally networked devices. In these cases, political interactions are often limited to a small, highly educated, and middle- or upper-class segment of the population or aid in connecting individuals with individuals and international organizations, as in the Dominican Republic in Chapter 9.

The chapters here illustrate a wide range of government dispositions toward digital politics. In countries that are politically open and with widespread internet access and use, digital politics has reached a relatively high degree of normalization, becoming integrated into government-citizen interactions and electoral politics. In countries where access is highly limited, the views expressed and political organization that results are limited – a reflection of the interests of the narrow segment in a society with internet access. We found that in areas with low levels of diffusion, internet access is concentrated among higher educated and upper-middle-class to upper-class populations. Even in Saudi Arabia, where internet access is least stratified in the Islamic world, the highest connection speeds are found mostly in the private homes of social elites. However, it is precisely in contexts of low internet diffusion that online involvement may be more important in terms of its consequences, even if restricted to a small fraction of the population.

At a micro level, the digital divide affects the digital political practices of individuals. We found in general that countries with higher levels of internet access have higher levels of online participation. This suggests that the digital divide limits the opportunities available at an individual level. As Jensen and Anduiza found, for people with the same level of education, income, and age, American internet users were somewhat more likely than their Spanish counterparts to participate online. In addition, the digital divide in internet skills and the domestication of technology plays a key role. A consistent finding in the chapters by Cantijoch as well as Jensen and Anduiza showed that the diversity of nonpolitical uses of the internet was one of the strongest predictors of digital participation. The material divide and the skills-domestication divide therefore operate at both macro and micro levels, thereby creating and delimiting the range of opportunities for digital political engagement.

However, the existence or absence of the digital divide does not explain, per se, the political use of those media. In countries with similar diffusion levels, there are still significant differences in the amount of online political engagement. Thus, to understand the use of digital media and its effectiveness, we turn to the political opportunity structures and incentives created by media systems and institutional environments.

A second contextual element influencing digital politics is the media system. The cases presented in this volume highlight the importance of several aspects of the media system: the institutional regimes regulating the operation of media systems; the level of partisanship permitted; a commercial versus a public charter; and the level of professionalism, which may affect the degree to which the public trusts the media's reporting.

Beginning with media independence, Hussain and Howard's work reveals that in places like Egypt and Pakistan with strong government control, low levels of trust in broadcast media have given rise to amateur journalism among dissidents with internet access. In some countries dissidents use online forums and blogs to voice political and cultural criticism. Correspondingly, the authors find that individuals who have access in each of these countries – apart from Pakistan, which has the lowest levels of internet access among this group of countries – have notably lower levels of trust in traditional broadcast media news. Tang, Jorba, and Jensen's research on China also shows that frequency of internet use is related to lower levels of institutional trust and greater internal efficacy.

In cases where governments do not actively censor online information and where there is no threat of prosecution, the level of media professionalism and trust in broadcast media can influence reliance on internet sources. Welp and Wheatley find that, despite Peru's significantly lower levels of internet access, nongovernmental organizations made extensive use of online diffusion mechanisms to spread information considered more reliable, given the lack of independence between Peruvian broadcast media outlets and the government. By contrast, countries with high levels of trust in traditional media (e.g., United States, Germany) may have less divergence between digitally networked and broadcast news sources. The degree to which media systems are commercialized and revenue driven rather than public service driven can also influence online information seeking. In countries like Spain, which has a mixed public and private media system, the public broadcaster is the primary outlet for news consumption, and other channels are constrained by a public charter. Hence, as Cantijoch argues here, online sources are important channels of information on political causes that challenge dominant, narrower conceptions of political space.[1] Vaccari's chapter on Italian politics shows a highly concentrated media environment in which even mainstream opposition politics may depend greatly on digital media. In addition to the state-owned media outlets, the leader of the center-right coalition and his family own a significant portion of the print and broadcast media outlets. Hence, those who identify with the political left are more inclined to rely on political information from the internet and to participate online.

Thus, statutory regulations, market forces, and perceived trust in media systems can have an effect on digital politics. In contrast to broadcast media, digital media have a decentralized communication structure that, we have seen, makes it harder for governments and broadcasters to regulate and control. This fact structurally empowers individuals to provide alternative accounts and political narratives, and to connect across fields of operations (Couldry 2008). As a result, the use of digital media has expanded the political opportunity structures available even in societies with the highest levels of political freedom.

Finally, the third contextual element considered regards the characteristics of the political context, both in terms of a system's institutional structures and in terms of more spatially and temporally contingent structural dimensions that are institutionally defined, such as political campaigning and electoral cycles. The political opportunity structure is not entirely exogenous to digital politics, as these promote or limit the use of new technologies for political purposes and are in turn affected by iterated communication and actions by individuals, organizations, and governments (Crozier 2007; Hanseth and Lyytinen 2010, 4; Chapter 2). The chapters in this volume pointed to three political dimensions that significantly influenced the development of digital politics: the level of institutional responsiveness, the level of political mobilization, and the legal regulation of political speech and political organizations.

Perceptions of institutional responsiveness function both as a motivation for digital modes of participation and as a consequence of digital information consumption. Where political institutions are considered less responsive and levels of institutional trust are low, digital media are often used to circumvent these institutions or to involve other actors, which can bring effective pressure to bear. Welp and Wheatley noted that in the face of an unresponsive government in the Dominican Republic, demonstrators made use of online groups to raise awareness about the dangers of a cement production facility that was finally halted under pressure from the United Nations.

Jensen and Anduiza found some evidence for this even in a consolidated democracy like Spain: where levels of institutional trust and confidence in parties are particularly low, there are correspondingly significantly lower levels

---

[1] As we saw in May 2011 in Spain, new issues and discussions for an alternative way of doing politics have arisen in online spaces, in parallel with – and as part of the process of – offline mobilizations. Through online channels, this movement and their claims have achieved sufficient recognition to receive mostly sympathetic attention of mainstream broadcast media.

of direct contact with political officials and higher levels of horizontal connections with the political community via blogging. In a similar vein, Cantijoch found a link in Spain between internet use and extrarepresentational forms of participation, but not representational modes of political participation, though the two modes are not unrelated.

Elections or other political events can also produce temporary openings for digital participation. The data for the United States used in Hamilton and Tolbert's and Jensen and Anduiza's chapters were collected during a highly mobilized moment in the U.S. electoral cycle: the 2008 elections. During this period, parties and candidates were actively soliciting political involvement online, and there was an abundance of information transmitted both to those actively seeking political information and via accidental exposure. Although there is not a baseline in these cases for comparison, the data presented in both chapters show that there was considerable attention paid to the election, that online participation was widespread, and that internet use was linked to offline participation. To the extent that modern campaigns are characterized by what Chadwick (Chapter 2) calls informational exuberance, or the vast quantities of information often produced by citizens, campaigns continue to have success collecting donations online, raising public awareness, and transforming passive supporters into active organizers online, and campaigns create additional opportunities for persons to become involved online.

Moreover, political mobilization matters in nondemocratic contexts. Digital media are sometimes used intensely in times of crisis and around crucial political events, like revolutionary moments, the rise of intense political controversies, and other times when the political system is under intense stress. Where the temporal dynamics of a situation give advantage to rapid political organization and response, digital communication structures offer organizational flexibility and scalability, which can be decisive in the outcome of a situation – particularly for those out of formal positions of authority. The Indonesian case is paradigmatic in this respect: online engagement contributed largely to the fall of Suharto's dictatorship and the country's subsequent democratization, but after the transition, engagement via digital media dropped dramatically. It seems clear in this case that the rise of online participation is mainly explained by the mobilization of opposition political parties and organizations, which used these technologies in the absence of other institutionalized channels for voice and organization, a motive that faded with regime change.

Digitally networked communications would likely prove even more crucial for the emergence of oppositional narratives and movements in the absence of civil society. We have seen some evidence of this in the Arab Spring uprisings. The wave of revolutions that spread from Tunisia to Egypt and neighboring countries in part built on the momentum of narratives transmitted via television and social media channels that conveyed the personal narratives of those encountering similar circumstances throughout the region. These narratives quickly spread beyond the limits of internet access, as most people in Egypt, for example, either had internet access or knew people who had access (Zhuo,

Wellman, and Yu 2011). The consequences of these changes have yet to play out.

Political actors such as parties and social movements play a crucial role in these mobilization processes, as they differ in the degree to which they make use of digital media. In this sense, the success of certain groups and movements in online communities is explained by those political actors' adaptation to this new creative digital culture rather than by a more or less traditional use of digital technologies as a one-way information channel. This adaptation may explain successful outcomes, for example Obama's online campaign or the civic campaigns in Brazil and the Dominican Republic analyzed in Welp and Wheatly's chapter.

Certainly, online politics to some extent runs parallel to traditional institutions, and the degree to which these will try to adapt their practices to this new language, or to control the emergence of this autonomous world, will presumably influence the success or failure of traditional politics and the connection with emerging forms of political engagement. The battle to control the content and the creation of digital spaces is found across all the countries analyzed here, although the creation of new structures is a more crucial debate in developing countries. Digital infrastructures are evolving, and traditional political institutions are still reacting to these changes, looking for ways to take advantage of new political opportunities. Although governments and political institutions are working to open vertical online communication paths that are easier to control, civil society is creating its own horizontal spaces and paths of communication, which often are subject to less political control. Attention to the degrees of horizontality and verticality will likely become more important as the structural differentiation of these channels promotes greater variance in online organizational forms.

In addition, legal regulations and limitations on political participation and freedom of speech can create incentives to engage in digital politics. Restrictions on the formation of political parties and other movements can drive political organization online, where formal mechanisms of political association are otherwise prohibited. Tang, Jorba, and Jensen's chapter on China showed that lacking formal government opposition or institutional recourse, Chinese citizens often resort to blogging and posting in online forums to raise issues and communicate demands. Even though internet access is relatively limited, this can be an effective means of holding officials to account – at least to a limited range of demands that do not seriously challenge the regime. Likewise, Hussain and Howard's chapter provides evidence of Egyptian bloggers organizing a strike – an action that, without the relative anonymity afforded by digital environments, would otherwise be impossible. In cases in both of these chapters, legal limitations on freedom of speech and social taboos often drive subversive political discourse, online where it is relatively harder to track and regulate. Jorba and Bimber as well as Hussain and Howard observed that even under regimes with a strong concentration of political power and in which individual political and civil rights are limited, there are still some spaces for politically disruptive uses of digital media. Given the decentralized structure of digital networks, the internet is much harder to control, which effectively enables online dissent to continue but at some risk to its participants.

There are two final observations that, though not directly addressed in the chapters, emerge when analyzing the evidence gathered in this volume. First, we are seeing the emergence of horizontal political practices in all the countries analyzed here. The Anglo-American experience with the diffusion and adoption of digital media finds the rise of an increasingly horizontal and social dimension in political and economic life, and it would be a surprise if this dimension did not follow a similar pattern elsewhere, as it partially results from the architecture of technology. Even in authoritarian regimes and in the face of the absence of a dynamic civil society, technology allows for the construction of horizontal networks linking individuals and information sources. The horizontal structure of social digital communications facilitates the constitution of political society in a self-organizing fashion, parallel to and outside of traditional institutions. The emergent sociality of politics that some of the chapters here hint at may play a key role in both transformations in political organization and the level of participatory inclusion.

Second, digital media support the expansion of political repertoires and favor the proliferation of available sources of information. In a very short time we have witnessed the transition in politics from a period of information abundance (Bimber 2003) to information exuberance, where the strategic production and transmission of information have become the modern political currency (Chapter 2; Crozier 2007). Government agencies are regularly bombarded with e-mail campaigns organized by interest groups (Shulman 2009). For government officials, the inundation of political information and participation in advanced democracies may leave them overloaded without sufficient capacity to process the deluge of inputs. It is therefore becoming more important for governments and political authorities to devise ways to navigate the sheer volume of these communications and incorporate them into processes of interest aggregation, collective decision making, and policy implementation.

Both of these developments point to the general expansion of opportunity structures, as the structural affordances of digital media permit the creation of new connections between citizens and governments. Digitally networked technologies can open new political spaces and allow for forms of involvement not previously available, with the possibility of engaging previously uninvolved segments of the population. This is particularly clear and important in less developed democracies, where there are often fewer communication channels for influencing government or for self-organization in civil society.

Jorba and Bimber as well as Chadwick noted, however, that the expansion of participatory opportunities and repertoires raised questions regarding two fundamental issues: pluralism and equality. The trajectory toward greater pluralism generally carries throughout the cases, although digital channels matter most when there is little opportunity for political communication elsewhere.

The second question is about the effects of digital politics on political equality. The extent to which online participation predominantly represents privileged segments of the population and the consequences of that bias for public policies are of concern to advanced and developing democracies. Given these changes, we anticipate that before long research will indicate changing structures of political influence and self-organization.

We assume here that the expansion of repertoires and the sociality and horizontality of online engagement practices encourage voice and loyalty by opening up new channels to promote changes in public policies and the political system. But this also brings some challenges regarding plurality and polarization, as well as equality and influence. In nonadvanced industrial democracies and in developed countries, the relevance and implications of these two issues may differ, but they still are the center of our concerns.

References

Abbott, Jason P. 2001. Democracy@internet.asia? The challenges to the emancipatory potential of the net: Lessons from China and Malaysia. *Third World Quarterly* 22(1): 99–114.

Abdulla, Rasha A. 2005. Taking the e-train: The development of the internet in Egypt. *Global Media and Communication* 1(2): 149–165.

Abdulla, Rasha A. 2007. Islam, jihad, and terrorism in post-9/11 Arabic discussion boards. *Journal of Computer-Mediated Communication* 12(3): article 15. http://jcmc .indiana.edu/vol12/issue3/abdulla.html.

Adams, Paul C. 2009. *Geographies of media and communication: A critical introduction.* Oxford, U.K.: Wiley-Blackwell.

Albrecht, Steffen, Maren Lübcke, and Rasco Hartig-Perschke. 2007. Weblog campaigning in the German Bundestag election 2005. *Social Science Computer Review* 25(4): 504–520.

Almond, Gabriel, and Sidney Verba. 1963. *The civic culture: Political attitudes and democracy in five nations.* Princeton, NJ: Princeton University Press.

Althaus, Scott L., and David Tewksbury. 2000. Patterns of internet and traditional news media use in a networked community. *Political Communication* 17(1): 21–45.

Amorim Neto, Octavio, and Carlos Frederico Coelho. 2008. Brasil en el 2007: El desencuentro entre la economía y la política. *Revista de Ciencia Política* 28(1): 81–102.

Anderson, Jon W. 1997. Cybernauts of the Arab diaspora: Electronic mediation in transnational cultural identities. Paper presented at the Couch-Stone Symposium "Postmodern culture, global capitalism and democratic action," April 10–12, University of Maryland. http://www.naba.org.uk/content/articles/diaspora/cybernauts_ of_the_arab_diaspora.htm (accessed January 2010).

Anderson, Mary. 2005. Beyond membership: A sense of community and political action. Ph.D. diss., Political Science Department, Florida State University.

Anduiza, Eva, Marta Cantijoch, Aina Gallego, and Jorge Salcedo. 2010. *Internet y participación política en España.* Madrid: Centro de Investigaciones Sociológicas.

Anduiza, Eva, Aina Gallego, and Marta Cantijoch. 2010. Online participation in Spain: The impact of traditional and internet resources. *Journal of Information Technology and Politics* 7(4): 356–368.

Anstead, Nick, and Andrew Chadwick. 2009. Parties, elections, campaigning, and the Internet: Toward a comparative institutional approach. In *Routledge handbook of internet politics*, ed. Andrew Chadwick and Phillip Howard, 56–71. London: Routledge.

Anttiroiko, Ari-Veikko. 2010. Innovation in democratic e-governance: Benefiting from web 2.0 applications in the public sector. In *Citizens and e-government: Evaluating policy and management*, ed. Christopher G. Reddick, 110–130. Hershey, PA: IGI Global.

Araya, Eduardo, and Diego Barria. 2009. E-Participación en el senado chileno: ¿Aplicaciones deliberativas? *Convergencia* 16(51): 239–268.

Atkinson, Anthony. 1970. On the measurement of inequality. *Journal of Economic Theory* 2(3): 244–293.

Ayllón, Bruno. 2007. El segundo mandato de Lula: Obstáculos políticos y planes de crecimiento económico para un Brasil sub-emergente. *ARI* 96(2007). http://www.realinstitutoelcano.org/analisis/ARI2007/ARI96-2007_Ayllon_Lula_Brasil.pdf (accessed September 2010).

Bakker, Tom P., and Claes H. de Vreese. 2011. Good news for the future? Young people, internet use, and political participation. *Communication Research* 38(4): 451–470.

Banda, Fackson, Wisdom J. Tettey, and Okoth Fred Mudhai. 2009. Introduction: New media and democracy in Africa – a critical interjection. In *African media and the digital public sphere*, ed. Okoth Fred Mudhai, Wisdom J. Tettey, and Fackson Banda, 1–20. Hampshire, U.K.: Palgrave.

Bang, Henrik. 2005. Among everyday makers and expert citizens. In *Remarking governance: Peoples, politics, and the public sphere*, ed. Janet Newman, 159–178. Bristol, U.K.: Policy Press.

Bang, Henrik, and Anders Esmark. 2009. Good governance in network society: Reconfiguring the political from politics to policy. *Administrative Theory and Praxis* 31(1): 7–37.

Barber, Benjamin. 1984. *Strong democracy: Participatory politics for a new age.* Berkeley: University of California Press.

Barber, Benjamin. 1997. The new telecommunications technology: Endless frontier or the end of democracy. *Constellations* 4(2): 208–228.

Barber, Benjamin R. 1999. Three scenarios for the future of technology and strong democracy. *Political Science Quarterly* 113(4): 573–589.

Bardi, Luciano. 2002. Italian parties: Change and functionality. In *Political parties in advanced industrial democracies*, ed. Paul Webb, David M. Farrell, and Ian Holliday, 46–75. New York: Oxford University Press.

Bardi, Luciano, Piero Ignazi, and Oreste Massari. 2007. *I partiti italiani: Iscritti, dirigenti, eletti.* Milan: Egea, Università Bocconi Editore.

Bardi, Luciano, and Gianfranco Pasquino. 1995. Politicizzati e alienati. In *Sulla soglia del cambiamento*, ed. Arturo M. L. Parisi, and Hans Schadee, 17–42. Bologna: Il Mulino.

Barendregt, Bart. 2008. Sex, cannibals, and the language of cool: Indonesian tales of the phone and modernity. *Information Society* 24(3): 160–170.

Barnes, Samuel H., Max Kaase, Klaus Rallerback, Barbara Farah, Felix Heunks, Ronald Inglehart, M. Kent Jennings, Hans D. Klingemann, Allan Marsh, and Leopold Rosenmayr. 1979. *Political action: Mass participation in five Western democracies.* Beverly Hills, CA: Sage Publications.

Baum, Matthew, and Tim Groeling. 2008. New media and the polarization of American political discourse. *Political Communication* 25: 345–365.

BBC. 1998. Despatches Indonesia lifts media controls. *BBC News*, June 15. http://news.bbc.co.uk/2/hi/despatches/10737 (accessed March 21, 2010).

Beck, Ulrich. 1997. *The reinvention of politics: Rethinking modernity in the global social order*. Malden, MA: Polity Press.

Benkler, Yochai. 2006. *The wealth of networks: How social production transforms markets and freedom*. New Haven, CT: Yale University Press.

Bennett, W. Lance. 2003. Communicating global activism. *Information, Communication, and Society* 6(2): 143–168.

Bennett, W. Lance. 2008. Changing citizenship in the digital age. In *Civic life online: Learning how digital media can engage youth*, ed. W. Lance Bennett, 1–24. Cambridge, MA: MIT Press.

Bennett, W. Lance, and Shanto Iyengar. 2008. A new era of minimal effects? The changing foundations of political communication. *Journal of Communication* 58(4): 707–731.

Bentivegna, Sara. 2006. *Campagne elettorali in rete*. Rome: Laterza.

Berrebi, Z. M., and Jacques Silber. 1985. Income inequality indices and deprivation: A generalization. *Quarterly Journal of Economics* 100(3): 807–810.

Best, Samuel J., and Brian S. Krueger. 2005. Analyzing the representativeness of internet political participation. *Political Behavior* 27(2): 183–216.

Bimber, Bruce. 1998. The internet and political mobilization: Research note on the 1996 election season. *Social Science Computer Review* 16(4): 391–401.

Bimber, Bruce. 1999. The internet and citizen communication with government: Does the medium matter? *Political Communication* 16(4): 409–428.

Bimber, Bruce. 2000. The study of information technology and civic engagement. *Political Communication* 17(4): 329–333.

Bimber, Bruce. 2001. Information and political engagement in America: The search for effects of information technology at the individual level. *Political Research Quarterly* 54(1): 53–67.

Bimber, Bruce. 2003. *Information and American democracy: Technology in the evolution of political power*. Cambridge: Cambridge University Press.

Bimber, Bruce, and Richard Davis. 2003. *Campaigning online: The internet in U.S. elections*. New York: Oxford University Press.

Bimber, Bruce, Cynthia Stohl, and Andrew J. Flanagin. 2009. Technological change and the shifting nature of political organization. In *Routledge handbook of internet politics*, ed. Andrew Chadwick and Phillip Howard, 72–85. New York: Routledge.

Blais, André. 2000. *To vote or not to vote? The merits and limits of rational choice theory*. Pittsburgh, PA: University of Pittsburgh Press.

Blumler, Jay G., and Michael Gurevitch 1995. *The crisis of public communication*. New York: Routledge.

Bode, Leticia. 2010. Accidentally informed 2.0: Incidental learning on Facebook. Paper presented at the annual meeting of the Midwest Political Science Association, April 23, Chicago.

Bollen, Kenneth. 1989. *Structural equations with latent variables*. New York: Wiley.

Bonchek, Mark S. 1997. From broadcast to netcast: The internet and the flow of political information. Ph.D. dissertation, Harvard University.

Bonet, Eduard, Irene Martín, and José Ramón Montero. 2006. Actitudes políticas de los españoles. In *Ciudadanos, asociaciones y participación política en España*, by

Joan Font, José Ramón Montero, and Mariano Torcal, 105–132. Madrid: Centro de Investigaciones Sociológicas.

Bonfadelli, Heinz. 2002. The internet and knowledge gaps: A theoretical and empirical investigation. *European Journal of Communication* 17(1): 65–84.

Borge, Rosa and Ana Cardenal. 2011. "Surfing the net: A pathway to participation for the politically uninterested?" *Policy & Internet*, 3(1), 1–29.

Bosco, Anna, and Leonardo Morlino, eds. 2007. *Party change in Southern Europe*. London: Routledge.

Boulianne, Shelley. 2009. Does internet use affect engagement? A meta-analysis of research. *Political Communication* 26(2): 193–211.

Braga, Sergio. 2009. Internet and representative institutions in Brazil: Information technology in Brazilian Houses of Representatives (2007–2011). Paper presented at the Joint Sessions of Workshops, European Consortium for Political Research (ECPR), April 14–19, Lisbon.

Brauchler, Birgit. 2003. Cyberidentities in war: Religion, identity, and the internet in the Moluccan conflict. *Indonesia* 75: 123–151.

Bray, John. 2000. Tibet, democracy and the internet bazaar. *Democratization* 7(1): 157–173.

Breindl, Yana, and Pascal Francq. 2008. Can web 2.0 applications save e-democracy? A study of how new internet applications may enhance citizen participation in the political process online. *International Journal of Electronic Democracy* 1(1): 14–31.

Brundidge, Jennifer, and Ronald E. Rice. 2009. Political engagement online: Do the information rich get richer and the like-minded more similar? In *Routledge handbook of internet politics*, ed. Andrew Chadwick and Philip N. Howard, 144–156. London: Routledge.

Calenda, Davide, and Albert Meijer. 2008. Young people, the internet and political participation: Findings of a web survey in Italy, Spain, and the Netherlands. *Information, Communication, and Society* 12(6): 879–898.

Calenda, Davide, and Lorenzo Mosca. 2007. The political use of the internet: Some insights from two surveys of Italian students. *Information, Communication, and Society* 10(1): 29–47.

Calhoun, Craig. 1989. Tiananmen, television and the public sphere: Internationalization of culture and the Beijing spring of 1989. *Public Culture* 2(1): 54–71.

Cantijoch, Marta, and Rachel Gibson. 2011. Contextualising and measuring e-participation. Paper presented at the Internet, Voting, and Democracy Conference (II), Center for the Study of Democracy, May 14, University of California, Irvine.

Cantijoch, Marta, Laia Jorba, and Josep San Martín. 2009. Exposure to political information in new and old media: Which impact on political participation? Paper presented at the 104th American Political Science Association Annual Meeting, August 28–31, Boston.

Carlson, Tom, and Görab Djupsun. 2001. Old wine in new bottles? The 1999 Finnish election campaign on the internet. *Harvard International Journal of Press/Politics* 1(6): 68–87.

Castells, Manuel. 1989. *The informational city: Information technology, economic restructuring, and the urban regional process*. Cambridge, MA: Blackwell.

Castells, Manuel. 2006. The network society: From knowledge to policy. In *The network society: From knowledge to policy*, ed. Manuel Castells and Gustavo Cardoso, 3–21. Washington, DC: Center for Transatlantic Relations.

Castells, Manuel. 2007. Communication, power and counter-power in the network society. *International Journal of Communication* 1: 238–266.

Castells, Manuel. 2009. *Communication power.* New York: Oxford University Press.

Castles, Stephen. 2002. Migration and community formation under conditions of globalization. *International Migration Review* 36(4): 1143–1168.

Censis. 2008. *42° rapporto sulla situazione sociale del paese/2008.* Milan: Franco Angeli.

Central Intelligence Agency. 2011. *The World Factbook.* https://www.cia.gov/library/publications/the-world-factbook/.

Comisión Económica Para América Latina y el Caribe. 2003. *Los caminos hacia una sociedad de la información en América Latina y el Caribe.* Santiago de Chile: United Nations. http://www.cepal.cl/publicaciones/xml/9/12899/lcg2195e2.pdf.

Chadwick, Andrew. 2003. Bringing e-democracy back in: Why it matters for future research on e-governance. *Social Science Computer Review* 21(4): 443–455.

Chadwick, Andrew. 2006. *Internet politics: States, citizens, and new communication technologies.* New York: Oxford University Press.

Chadwick, Andrew. 2007. Digital network repertoires and organizational hybridity. *Political Communication* 24(3): 283–301.

Chadwick, Andrew. 2009a. The internet and politics in flux. *Journal of Information Technology and Politics* 63(4): 195–196.

Chadwick, Andrew. 2009b. Web 2.0: New challenges for the study of e-democracy in an era of informational exuberance. *I/S: A Journal of Law and Policy for the Information Society* 5(1): 9–41.

Chadwick, Andrew. 2011a. Explaining the failure of an online citizen engagement initiative: The role of internal institutional variables. *Journal of Information Technology and Politics* 8(1): 21–40.

Chadwick, Andrew. 2011b. The political information cycle in a hybrid news system: The British prime minister and the "Bullygate" affair. *International Journal of Press/Politics* 16(1): 3–29.

Chadwick, Andrew, and Philip N. Howard. 2009a. Introduction: New directions in internet politics research. In *Routledge handbook of internet politics*, ed. Andrew Chadwick and Philip N. Howard, 1–9. London: Routledge.

Chadwick, Andrew, and Philip N. Howard, eds. 2009b. *Routledge handbook of internet politics.* London: Routledge.

Chadwick, Andrew, and Christopher May. 2003. Interaction between states and citizens in the age of the internet: "E-government" in the United States, Britain and the European Union. *Governance: An International Journal of Policy, Administration, and Institutions* 16(2): 271–300.

Chan, Alex. 2002. From propaganda to hegemony: Jiaodian Fangtan and China's media policy. *Journal of Contemporary China* 30(11): 35–51.

Chan, Joseph. 1993. Commercialization without independence: Media development in China. *China Review* 25(1): 1–25.

Chan, Joseph. 1994. Media internationalization in China: Processes and tensions. *Journal of Communication* 44(3): 70–88.

Chase, Michael S., and James C. Mulvenon. 2002. *You've got dissent! Chinese dissident use of the internet and Beijing's counterstrategies.* Santa Monica, CA: RAND.

Chen, Hsinchun, Lawrence Brandt, Valerie Gregg, Roland Traunmüller, Sharon Dawes, Eduard Hovy, Ann Macintosh, and Catherine A. Larson, eds. 2008. *Digital government: E-government research, case studies, and implementation.* New York: Springer.

Chen, Xueyi, and Tianjian Shi. 2001. Media effects on political confidence and trust in the People's Republic of China in the post-Tiananmen period. *East Asia* 19(3): 84–118.

Chu, Leonard L. 1994. Continuity and change in China's media reform. *Journal of Communication* 44(3): 4–21.

Chun, Li. 2009. New media: The rising road for public involvement in China. Paper presented at the International Workshop on New Media and Politics, May 28–31, Barcelona, Spain.

Cleaver, Harry M., Jr. 1998. The Zapatista effect: The internet and the rise of an alternative political fabric. *Journal of International Affairs* 51(2): 621–640.

Clément, Marc. 2002. Internet, l'avenir radieux! In *L'Internet en politique: Des États-Unis à l'Europe*, ed. Viviane Serfaty, 267–273. Strasbourg, France: Presses Universitaires de Strasbourg.

China Internet Network Information Center. 2010a. 25th Statistical survey report on internet development in China, January. http://www.cnnic.net.cn.

China Internet Network Information Center. 2010b. 26th Statistical survey report on internet development in China, July. http://www.cnnic.net.cn.

Coleman, Stephen, and Jay Blumler. 2009. *The internet and democratic citizenship*. New York: Cambridge University Press.

Coleman, Stephen, ed. 2001. *Elections in the age of the internet*. London: Hansard Society.

Coleman, Stephen. 2005. *E-democracy from the ground up down: An evaluation of community focused approaches to e-democracy Bristol City Council*. London: Bristol City Council for the Local E-democracy National Project.

Coliagnese, Cary. 2003. The internet and public participation in rulemaking. Working paper, Harvard University.

Collin, Philippa. 2008. The internet, youth participation policies, and the development of young people's political identities in Australia. *Journal of Youth Studies* 11(5): 527–542.

Consorcio Iberamericano de MercadosAsesoramientos, Barómetro Iberoamericano de Gobernabilidad, 2008. http://www.cimaiberoamerica.com (accessed May 2010).

comScore. 2010. Social networking explodes worldwide as sites increase their focus on cultural relevance. http://www.comscore.com/Press_Events/Press_Releases/2008/08/Social_Networking_World_Wide/(language)/eng-US (accessed March 17, 2010).

Converse, Philip E. 1987. Changing conceptions of public opinion in the political process. *Public Opinion Quarterly* 51(4): S12–S24.

Copsey, Nigel. 2003. Extremism on the net: The extreme right and the value of the internet. In *Political parties and the internet: Net gain?* ed. Rachel Gibson, Paul Nixon, and Stephen Ward, 218–233. London: Routledge.

Cornfield, Michael. 2003. Adding in the net: Making citizenship count in the digital age. In *The civic web: Online politics and democratic values*, ed. David M. Anderson and Michael Cornfield, 97–112. Lanham, MD: Rowman and Littlefield.

Couldry, Nick. 2008. Mediatization or mediation? Alternative understandings of the emergent space of digital storytelling. *New Media and Society* 10(3): 373–391.

Crozier, Michael. 2007. Recursive governance: Contemporary political communication and public policy. *Political Communication* 24(1): 1–18.

Crozier, Michael. 2008. Listening, learning, steering: New governance, communication and interactive policy formation. *Policy and Politics* 36(1): 3–19.

Crozier, Michael P. 2010. Rethinking systems. *Administration and Society* 42(5): 504–525.

Currant, James, Shanto Iyengar, Anker Brink Lund, and Inka Salovaara-Moring. 2009. Media system, public knowledge and democracy. *European Journal of Communication* 24(1): 5–26.

Curtice, John, and Pippa Norris. 2004. E-politics? The impact of the internet in political trust and participation. In *British social attitudes: The 21st report*, ed. Alison Park, John Curtice, Katarina Thomson, Catherine Bromley, and Miranda Phillips, 99–118. London: Sage.

Dahlgren, Peter. 2000. The internet and the democratization of civic culture. *Political Communication* 17(4): 335–340.

Dalton, Russell J. 2000. Value change and democracy. In *Disaffected democracies*, ed. Susan J. Pharr, and Robert D. Putnam, 252–269. Princeton, NJ: Princeton University Press.

Dalton, Russell J. 2004. *Democratic challenges, democratic choices: The erosion of political support in advanced industrial democracies*. New York: Oxford University Press.

Dalton, Russell J. 2008. *Citizen politics: Public opinion and political parties in advanced industrial democracies*, 5th ed. Washington, DC: Congressional Quarterly Press.

Dalton, Russell J. 2008. *The good citizen: How a younger generation is reshaping American politics*. Washington, D.C.: Congressional Quarterly Press.

Dalton, Russell J., and Martin P. Wattenberg. 2000. *Parties without partisans: Political change in advanced industrial democracies*. Oxford: Oxford University Press.

Danziger, James N., William H. Dutton, Rob Kling, and Kenneth A. Kraemer. 1982. *Computers and politics: High technology in American local governments*. New York: Columbia University Press.

Davis, Richard. 1999. *The web of politics: The internet's impact on the American political system*. New York: Oxford University Press.

Davis, Richard, and Diana Owen. 1998. *New media and American politics*. New York: Oxford University Press.

D'Costa, Anthony P. 2003. Catching up and falling behind: Inequality, IT, and the Asian diaspora. In *Asia.com: Asia encounters the internet*, ed. K. C. Ho, Randolph Kluver, and Kenneth C. C. Yang, 44–66. London: Routledge.

De Certeau, Michel. 1997. *The capture of speech and other political writings*. Minneapolis: University of Minnesota Press.

Delli Carpini, Michael X. 2000. Gen.com: Youth, civic engagement, and the new information environment. *Political Communication* 17(4): 341–349.

Delli Carpini, Michael X., Fay Lomax Cook, and Lawrence R. Jacobs. 2004. Public deliberation, discursive participation, and citizen engagement: A review of the empirical literature. *Annual Review of Political Science* 7: 315–344.

Delli Carpini, Michael X., and Scott Keeter. 1997. *What Americans know about politics and why it matters*. New Haven, CT: Yale University Press.

Delli Carpini, Michael X., and Scott Keeter. 2002. The internet and an informed citizenry. In *The civic web*, ed. David Anderson, and Michael Cornfield, 129–153. Lanham: Rowman & Littlefield.

Deibert, Ronald, John Palfrey, Rafal Rohozinski, and Jonathan Zittrain. 2008. *Access denied: The practice and policy of global internet filtering*. Cambridge, MA: MIT Press.

De Zúñiga, Homero Gil, Eulàlia Puig-i-Abril, and Hernando Rojas. 2009. Weblogs, traditional sources online and political participation: An assessment of how the internet is changing the political environment. *New Media Society* 11(4): 553–574.

Diamond, Lawrence. 1994. Rethinking civil society: Toward democratic consolidation. *Journal of Democracy* 5(3): 4–17.

Di Gennaro, Corina, and William Dutton. 2006. The internet and the public: Online and offline political participation in the United Kingdom. *Parliamentary Affairs* 59(2): 299–313.

Dillman, Don. 1978. *Mail and telephone surveys: The total design method.* New York: John Wiley and Sons.

DiMaggio, Paul, Eszter Hargitta, W. Russell Neuman, and John P. Robinson. 2001. Social implications of the internet. *Annual Review of Sociology* 27: 307–336.

Dimitrova, Daniela V., Lynda Lee Kaid, Andrew Paul Williams, and Kaye D. Trammell. 2005. War on the web: The immediate news framing of Gulf War II. *Harvard International Journal of Press/Politics* 10(1): 22–44.

Donovan, Todd, and Shaun Bowler. 2004. *Reforming the republic: Democratic institutions for the new America.* Upper Saddle River, NJ: Pearson Prentice Hall.

Downs, Anthony. 1957. *An economic theory of democracy.* New York: Harper and Row.

Drew, Dan, and David Weaver. 2006. Voter learning in the 2004 presidential elections: Did the media matter? *Journalism and Mass Communication Quarterly* 83(1): 25–42.

Dutton, William H. 1999. *Society on the line: Information politics in the digital age.* New York: Oxford University Press.

Easton, David. 1990. *An analysis of political structure.* New York: Routledge.

Egorov, Georgy, Sergei Guriev, and Konstantin Sonin. 2009. Why resource-poor dictators allow freer media: A theory and evidence from panel data. *American Political Science Review* 103(4): 645–668.

Eickelman, Dale F., and Jon W. Anderson, eds. 1999. *New media in the Muslim world: The emerging public sphere.* Bloomington: Indiana University Press.

Escobar, Patricio, and Yanina Welp. 2004. La Argentina piquetera. *Guaraguao: Revista de Cultura Latinoamericana* 8(19): 67–75.

Espinal, Rosario. 2001. La sociedad civil movilizada y las reformas democráticas en la República Dominicana. *Espiral, Estudios sobre Estado y Sociedad* 7(21): 101–132.

Eurobarometer. 2009. Standard Eurobarometer 71. http://ec.europa.eu/public_opinion/archives/eb/eb71/eb71_en.htm (accessed January 22, 2010).

European Commission. 2009. *Europe's digital competitiveness report.* Vol. 1, *i2010 – Annual Information Society Report 2009.* Commission Staff Working Document, SEC(2009) 1103. Brussels: Commission of the European Communities.

European Social Survey. 2009. Revised datasets. http://www.europeansocialsurvey.org.

Eurostat. 2010. Information Society statistics. http://epp.eurostat.ec.europa.eu/portal/page/portal/information_society/data/main_tables (accessed January 22, 2010).

Eveland, William, P., and Sharon Dunwoody. 2000. Examining information processing on the world wide web using think aloud protocols. *Media Psychology* 2(3): 219–244.

Eveland, William P., and Dietram A. Scheufele. 2000. Connection news media use with gaps in knowledge and participation. *Political Communication* 17(3): 2215–2237.

Facebook Downing Street e-petitions. 2008. http://www.facebook.com/s.php?q=downing±street±petition&n=-1&k=200000010&init=r (accessed August 2010).

Facebook. 2009a. Facebook applications: Politics. http://www.facebook.com/apps/directory.php (accessed August 2010).

Facebook. 2009b. Facebook causes application. http://www.facebook.com/causes (accessed August 2010).

Faris, Robert, and Nart Villeneuve. 2007. Access denied. In *Access denied: The practice and policy of global internet filtering*, ed. Ronald J. Deibert, John G. Palfrey, Rafal Rohozinski, and Jonathan Zittrain, 5–28. Cambridge, MA: MIT Press.

Farmer, Rick, and Rich Fender. 2005. E-parties: Democratic and republican state parties in 2000. *Party Politics* 111(1): 47–58.

Farthing, Rys. 2010. The politics of youthful antipolitics: Representing the "issue" of youth participation in politics. *Journal of Youth Studies* 13(2): 181–195.

Ferdinand, Peter. 2000a. Conclusion. *Democratization* 71(1): 174–182.

Ferdinand, Peter. 2000b. The internet, democracy and democratization. *Democratization* 71(1): 1–17.

Ferrer, Mariona. 2005. Participación política. In *España: Sociedad y política en perspectiva comparada*, ed. Mariano Torcal, Laura Morales, and Santiago Pérez-Nievas, 221–236. Valencia: Tirant lo Blanch.

Flanagin, Andrew J., and Miriam J. Metzger. 2001. Internet use in the contemporary media environment. *Human Communication Research* 27(1): 153–181.

Fowler, Floyd J. 2002. *Survey research methods*, 3rd ed. Thousand Oaks, CA: Sage.

Foot, Kirsten M., and Steven M. Schneider. 2006. *Web campaigning*. Cambridge, MA: MIT Press.

Franda, Marcus. 2001. *Launching into cyberspace: Internet development and politics in five world regions*. Boulder, CO: Lynne Rienner Publishers.

Freedman, Paul, Michael Franz, and Kenneth Goldstein. 2004. Campaign advertising and democratic citizenship. *American Journal of Political Science* 48(4): 723–741.

Friedman, Jay. 2005. The reality of virtual reality: The internet and gender equality advocacy in Latin America. *Latin American Politics and Society* 47(3): 1–34.

Froehling, Oliver. 1997. The cyberspace "war of ink and internet" in Chiapas, Mexico. *Geographical Review* 87(2): 291–307.

Fung, Archon. 2007. Democratic theory and political science: A pragmatic method of constructive engagement. *American Political Science Review* 101(3): 443–458.

Furutani, Kaichiro, Tetsuro Kobayashi, and Mitsuhiro Ura. 2007. Effects of internet use on self-efficacy: Perceived network-changing possibility as a mediator. *AI and Society* 23(2): 251–263.

Füting, Angelika. 2008. Wer ist die "Politische online elite" in Deutschland? In *Düsseldorfer Forum politische Kommunikation: Schriftenreihe: Band 3*, ed. Esra Aydin, Matthias Begenat, Christian Michalek, Jasmin Schemann, and Ingo Stefes, 55–76. Berlin: Lit Verlag.

Garrett, Kelly. 2005. Exposure to controversy in an information society. Ph.D. diss., University of Michigan.

Garrett, Kelly. 2006. Protest in an information society: A review of literature on social movements and new ICTs. *Information, Communication, and Society* 9(2): 202–224.

Garrett, Kelly. 2009. Echo chambers online? Politically motivated reinforcement seeking. *Journal of Computer-Mediated Communication* 14(2): 265–285.

Gentzkow, Matthew, and Jesse M. Shapiro. 2010. Ideological segregation online and offline. Chicago Booth Research Paper 10–19, University of Chicago.

Gibson, Rachel K., Philip N. Howard, and Steven Ward. 2000. Social capital, internet connectedness and political participation: A four-country study. Paper prepared for the International Political Science Association, Quebec, Canada, August 1–5.

Gibson, Rachel K., Wainer Lusoli, and Stephen J. Ward. 2005. Online participation in the UK: Testing a "contextualised" model of internet effects. *British Journal of Politics and International Relations* 7(4): 561–583.

Gibson, Rachel K., Paul Nixon, and Stephen J. Ward, eds. 2003. *Political parties and the internet: Net gain?* London: Routledge.

Gibson, Rachel K., and Andrea Römmele. 2001. A party-centered theory of profession-alized campaigning. *International Journal of Press/Politics* 6(4): 31–43.

Gibson, Rachel K., and Stephen J. Ward. 2000. *Reinvigorating democracy: British politics and the internet*. Aldershot, U.K.: Ashgate.

Giese, Karsten. 2003. Internet growth and the digital divide: Implications for spatial development. *In China and the internet: Politics of digital leap forward (Politics in Asia)*, ed. Christopher R. Hughes and Gudrun Wacker, 30–57. London: Routledge-Gurzon.

Gil de Zúñiga, Homero, Lauren Copeland, and Bruce Bimber. 2011. Political con-sumerism and political communication: The social networking connection. Paper prepared for presentation at the annual meeting of the Midwest Association for Pub-lic Opinion Research.

Gimpel, James G., Karen M. Kaufmann, and Shanna Perason-Merkowitz. 2007. The battleground vs. the blackout states: The behavioral implications of modern presi-dential campaigns. *Journal of Politics* 69(3): 786–779.

Giner, José Miguel, María Carmen Tolosa, and Antonio Fuster. 2004. The new economy in Spain: A regional analysis. Paper presented at the European Conference for the European Regional Science Association, August 25–29, Porto, Portugal.

Graber, Doris A. 1988. *Processing the news: How people tame the information tide*, 2nd ed. New York: Longman.

Graber, Doris A. 1996. The "new" media and politics: What does the future hold? *PS: Political Science and Politics* 29(1): 157–168.

Graham, Mark, and Shahram Khosravi. 2002. Reordering public and private in Iranian cyberspace: Identity, politics, and mobilization. *Identities* 9(2): 219–246.

Grandi, Roberto, and Cristian Vaccari. 2009. Election campaigning and the new media. In *Resisting the tide: Cultures of opposition under Berlusconi (2001–06)*, ed. Daniele Albertazzi, Clodagh Brook, Charlotte Ross, and Nina Rothenberg, 46–56. New York: Continuum.

Granovetter, Mark S. 1973. The strength of weak ties. *American Journal of Sociology* 78(6): 1360–1380.

Gray, Mark, and Miki Caul. 2000. Declining voter turnout in advanced industrial democracies, 1950 to 1997: The effects of declining group mobilization. *Comparative Political Studies* 33(9): 1091–1122.

Greenberg, Edward S. 1986. *Workplace democracy: The political effects of participa-tion*. Ithaca, NY: Cornell University Press.

Greenberg, Edward S., Leon Grunberg, and Kelley Daniel. 1996. Industrial work and political participation: Beyond "simple spillover." *Political Research Quarterly* 49(2): 305–330.

Grönlund, Kimmo. 2007. Knowing and not knowing: The internet and political infor-mation. *Scandinavian Political Studies* 30(3): 397–418.

Gunther, Richard, José Ramón Montero, and Joan Botella, eds. 2004. *Democracy in modern Spain*. New Haven, CT: Yale University Press.

Gunther, Richard, José Ramón Montero, and Hans-Jürgen Puhle, eds. 2007. *Democ-racy, intermediation, and voting on four continents*. New York: Oxford University Press.

Gunther, Richard, and Anthony Mughan, eds. 2000. *Democracy and the media: A comparative perspective*. Cambridge: Cambridge University Press.

Guillén, Mauro F., and Sandra L. Suárez. 2005. Explaining the global digital divide: Economic, political and sociological drivers of cross-national internet use. *Social Forces* 84(2): 681–708.

Gurin, Patricia, and Edgar Epps. 1975. *Black consciousness, identity and achievement: A study of students in historically black colleges*. New York: Wiley.

Gurin, Patricia, Shirley Hatchett, and James Sidney Jackson. 1989. Methodological issues in telephone surveys of black Americans: The 1984 national black election study. In *Hope and independence: Blacks' response to electoral and party politics*, ed. Patricia Gurin, Shirley Hatchett, and James Sidney Jackson, 265–278. New York: Russell Sage Foundation.

Habermas, Jürgen. 1996. *Between facts and norms*. Oxford, U.K.: Polity Press.

Hallin, Daniel C., and Paolo Mancini. 2004. *Comparing media systems: Three models of media and politics*. Cambridge: Cambridge University Press.

Hansard Society. 2007. *Digital dialogues second phase report, August 2006–August 2007*. London: Hansard Society.

Hanseth, Ole, and Kalle Lyytinen. 2010. Design theory for dynamic complexity in information infrastructures: The case of building internet. *Journal of Information Technology* 25(1): 1–19.

Hara, Noriko, and Zilia Estrada. 2005. Analyzing the mobilization of grassroots activities via the internet: A case study. *Journal of Information Science* 31(6): 503–514.

Harkness, Janet, Beth-Ellen Pennell, and Alisú Schoua-Glusberg. 2004. Survey questionnaire translation and assessment. In *Questionnaire development evaluation and testing methods*, ed. Stanley Presser, Jennifer M. Rothgeb, Mick P. Couper, Judith L. Lessler, Elizabeth Martin, Jean Martin, and Eleanor Singer, 453–473. New York: Wiley.

Harwit, Eric, and Duncan Clark. 2001. Shaping the internet in China: Evolution of political control over network infrastructure and content. *Asian Survey* 41(3): 377–408.

Hassid, Jonathan. 2008a. China's contentious journalists: Reconceptualizing the media. *Problems of Post-Communism* 55(4): 52–61.

Hassid, Jonathan. 2008b. Controlling the Chinese media: An uncertain business. *Asian Survey* 48(3): 414–430.

Hay, Colin. 2007. *Why we hate politics*. Cambridge, U.K.: Polity Press.

Helle-Valle, Jo, and Dag Slettemeas. 2008. ICTs, domestication and language-games: A Wittgensteinian approach to media uses. *New Media and Society* 10(1): 45–66.

Heng, Michael S. H., and Aldo De Moor. 2003. From Habermas's communicative theory to practice on the internet. *Info Systems* 13(4): 331–352.

Hill, David. 2002. East Timor and the internet: Global political leverage in/on Indonesia. *Indonesia: Modern Indonesia Project* 73: 25–51.

Hill, David. 2003. Communication for a new democracy: Indonesia's first online elections. *Pacific Review* 16(4): 525–547.

Hill, David T., and Krishna Sen. 2000. *The internet in Indonesia's new democracy*. New York: Routledge.

Hill, David T., and Krishna Sen. 2002. Netizens in combat: Conflict on the internet in Indonesia. *Asian Studies Review* 26(2): 165–187.

Hill, Kevin A., and John E. Hughes. 1998. *Cyberpolitics: Citizen activism in the age of the internet*. New York: Rowman & Littlefield.

Hillygus, Sunshine, and Todd G. Shields. 2008. *The persuadable voter: Wedge issues in presidential campaigns.* Princeton, NJ: Princeton University Press.

Hindman, Matthew. 2009. *The myth of digital democracy.* Princeton, NJ: Princeton University Press.

Hirschman, Albert O. 1970. *Exit, voice, and loyalty: Responses to decline in firms, organizations, and states.* Cambridge, MA: Harvard University Press.

Ho, K. C., Randolph Kluver, and Kenneth C. C. Yang, eds. 2003. *Asia.com: Asia encounters the internet.* New York: Routledge.

Hoff, Jens. 2006. *Internet, governance and democracy: Democratic transitions from Asian and European perspectives.* Copenhagen: Nordic Institute of Asian Studies.

Hoff, Jens, Ivan Horrocks, and Pieter Tops. 2000. *Democratic governance and new technology: Technologically mediated innovations in political practice in Western Europe.* London: Routledge.

Holbert, R. Lance, R. Kelly Garrett, and Laurel S. Gleason. 2010. A new era of minimal effects? A response to Bennett and Iyengar. *Journal of Communication* 60(1): 15–34.

Howard, Philip N. 2005. Deep democracy, thin citizenship: The impact of digital media in political campaign strategy. *Annals of the American Academy of Political and Social Science* 597(1): 153–170.

Howard, Philip N. 2006. *New media campaigns and the managed citizen.* New York: Cambridge University Press.

Howard, Philip N. 2007. WIA Report 2007 – Wired States. Seattle: University of Washington. http://www.wiareport.org.

Howard, Philip N. 2008. *World information access project: World information access report – 2008.* Seattle: University of Washington. http://www.wiareport.org/index.php/176/2008-briefing-booklet (accessed February 2010).

Howard, Philip N. 2010. Inside the cyberwar for Iran's future, January 21. http://www.miller-mccune.com/politics/inside-the-cyberwar-for-iran-s-future-6535/.

Howard, Philip. 2011. *The digital origins of dictatorship and democracy: Information technology and political Islam.* New York: Oxford University Press.

Howard, Philip N., Laura Busch, and Spencer Cohen. 2009. *ICT diffusion and distribution dataset, 1990–2007.* Ann Arbor, MI: Inter-University Consortium for Political and Social Research. http://arc.irss.unc.edu/dvn/dv/ICPSR/faces/study/StudyPage.xhtml?studyId=50578&studyListingIndex=0_2cccc2fecde461efbfef40ea9e83.

Howard, Philip N., and Steve Jones. 2004. *Society online: The internet in context.* Thousand Oaks: Sage Publications.

Hughes, Christopher R. 2000. Nationalism in Chinese cyberspace. *Cambridge Review of International Affairs* 13(2): 195–209.

Hughes, Christopher R., and Gudrun Wacker, eds. 2003. *China and the internet: Politics of the digital leap forward.* London: Routledge.

Human Rights Watch. 2005. False freedom: Online censorship in the Middle East and North Africa. *Human Rights Watch Report* 17(10): 17–41. http://www.hrw.org/en/node/11563/section/5 (accessed March 20, 2010).

Hwang, Hyunseo, Michael Schmierbach, Hye-Jin Paek, Homero Gil de Zúñiga, and Dhavan Shah. 2006. Media dissociation, internet use, and antiwar political participation: A case study of political dissent and action against the war in Iraq. *Mass Communication and Society* 9(4): 461–483.

Inglehart, Ronald. 1990. *Culture shift in advanced industrial society.* Princeton, NJ: Princeton University Press.

Inglehart, Ronald. 1997. *Modernization and postmodernization: Cultural, economic, and political change in 43 societies.* Princeton, NJ: Princeton University Press.

Inglehart, Ronald. 1999. Postmodernization erodes respect for authority but increases support for democracy. In *Critical citizens: Global support for democratic governance,* ed. Pippa Norris, 236–255. New York: Oxford University Press.

Inglehart, Ronald, and Gabriela Catterberg. 2003. Trends in political action: The developmental trend and the post-honeymoon decline. *International Journal of Comparative Sociology* 43(3–5): 300–316.

Inglehart, Ronald, and Christian Welzel. 2005. *Modernization, cultural change, and democracy.* London: Cambridge University Press.

International Telecommunications Union. 2007. Information and Communication Technology Statistics. http://www.itu.int/ITU-D/ict.

International Telecommunications Union. 2010. Information and Communication Technology Statistics. http://www.itu.int/ITU-D/ict.

International Telecommunications Union. 2011. Information and Communication Technology Statistics. http://www.itu.int/ITU-D/ict.

Internet World Stats. 2009. Usage and Population Statistics. http://www.internet worldstats.com.

Internet World Stats. 2011. Usage and Population Statistics. http://www.internet worldstats.com.

Iyengar, Shanto, and Kyu S. Hahn. 2009. Red media, blue media: Evidence of ideological selectivity in media use. *Journal of Communication* 59(1): 19–39.

Jackman, Simon, and Lynn Vavreck. 2009. *The 2008 cooperative campaign analysis project.* Palo Alto, CA: YouGov/Polimetrix.

Jackman, Simon, and Lynn Vavreck. 2010. Primary politics: Race, gender, and age in the 2008 democratic primary. *Journal of Elections, Public Opinion and Parties* 20(2): 153–186.

Jackson, Nigel A., and Darren G. Lilleker. 2009. Building an architecture of participation? Political parties and web 2.0 in Britain. *Journal of Information Technology and Politics* 63(4): 232–250.

Jenkins, Henry, and David Thorburn. 2003. *Democracy and the media.* Cambridge, MA: MIT Press.

Jennings, M. Kent, and Vicki Zeitner. 2003. Internet use and civic engagement: A longitudinal analysis. *Public Opinion Quarterly* 67(3): 311–334.

Jensen, Jakob Linaa. 2006. Minnesota e-democracy: Mobilizing the mobilized? In *The internet and politics: Citizens, voters, and activists,* ed. Sarah Oates, Diana Marie Owen, and Rachel K. Gibson, 39–58. New York: Routledge.

Jensen, Michael J., James N. Danziger, and Alladi Venkatesh. 2007. Civil society and cyber society: The role of the internet in community associations and democratic politics. *Information Society* 23(1): 39–50.

Jian, Guowei, and Leo Jeffres. 2008. Spanning the boundaries of work: Workplace participation, political efficacy, and political involvement. *Communication Studies* 59(1): 35–50.

Jiang, Min. 2010. Authoritarian informationalism: China's approach to internet sovereignty. *SAIS Review* 30(2): 71–89.

Johnson, Thomas J., and Barbara K. Kaye. 2000. Using is believing: The influence of reliance on the credibility of online political information among politically interested internet users. *Journalism and Mass Communication Quarterly* 77(4): 865–879.

Johnson, Thomas J., and Barbara K. Kaye. 2003. A boost or bust for democracy? How the web influenced political attitudes and behaviors in the 1996 and 2000 presidential elections. *International Journal of Press/Politics* 8(3): 9–34.

Jöreskog, Karl G., and Dag Sörbom. 1996. *LISREL 8: User's reference guide*. Lincolnwood, IL: Scientific Software International.

Juris, Jeffrey. 2005. The new digital media and activist networking within anti-corporate globalization movements. *Annals of the American Academy of Political and Social Science* 597(1): 189–208.

Kagami, Mitsuhiro, Masatsugu Tsuji, and Emmanuele Giovannetti. 2004. *Information technology policy and the digital divide: Lessons for developing countries*. Northampton, U.K.: Edward Elgar Publishing.

Kahn, Kim Fridkin, and Patrick J. Kenney. 1999. *The spectacle of U.S. senate campaigns*. Princeton, NJ: Princeton University Press.

Kalathil, Shanthi, and Taylor C. Boas. 2003. *Open networks, closed regimes: The impact of the internet on authoritarian rule*. Washington, DC: Carnegie Endowment for International Peace and Brookings Institution.

Kallinikos, Jannis. 2002. Reopening the black box of technology artifacts and human agency. In *International Conference on Information Systems (ICIS)*, 287–294, December 15–18, Barcelona, Spain.

Kallinikos, Jannis. 2004. Farewell to constructivism: Technology and context-embedded action. In *The social study of information and communication technology: Innovation, actors, and contexts*, ed. Chrisanthi Avgerou, Claudio Ciborra, and Frank Land, 140–161. New York: Oxford University Press.

Kallinikos, Jannis, Aleksi Aaltonen, and Attila Marton. 2010. A theory of digital objects. *First Monday* 15(6–7). http://firstmonday.org/htbin/cgiwrap/bin/ojs/index.php/fm/article/viewArticle/3033/2564.

Kalnes, Øyvind. 2009. Norwegian parties and web 2.0. *Journal of Information Technology and Politics* 6(3–4): 251–266.

Karakaya, Rabia. 2005. The internet and political participation. Exploring the explanatory links. *European Journal of Communication* 20(4): 435–559.

Karan, Kavita, Jacques D. M. Gimeno, and Edson Tandoc. 2009. The internet and mobile technologies in elections campaigns: The Gabriela women's party during the 2007 Philippine elections. *Journal of Information Technology and Politics* 63(4): 326–338.

Karpf, David. 2009. Don't think of an online elephant: Explaining the dearth of conservative political infrastructure online in America. Paper presented at the Annual Meeting of American Political Science Association, September 2–6, Toronto.

Katz, James E., and Ronald E. Rice. 2002. *Social consequences of internet use: Access, involvement and interaction*. Cambridge, MA: MIT Press.

Kavanaugh, Andrea, Joon B. Kim, Manuel A. Perez-Quinones, Joseph Schmitz, and Philip Isenhour. 2008. Net gains in political participation: Secondary effects of internet on community. *Information, Communication and Society* 11(7): 933–963.

Kavanaugh, Andrea, and Scott Patterson, S. J. 2001. The impact of community computer networks on social capital and community involvement. *American Behavioural Scientist* 45(3): 496–509.

Kaye, Barbara K., and Thomas J. Johnson. 2002. Online and in the know: Uses and gratifications of the web for political information. *Journal of Broadcasting and Electronic Media* 46(1): 54–71.

Kearney, Michael. 1995. The local and the global: The anthropology of globalization and transnationalism. *Annual Review of Anthropology* 24: 547–565.

Keele, Luke. 2005. The authorities really do matter: Party control and trust in government. *Journal of Politics* 67(3): 873–886.

Keen, Andrew. 2007. *The cult of the amateur: How today's internet is killing our culture and assaulting our economy.* London: Nicholas Brealey.

Kenski, Kate, and Natalie Jomini Stroud. 2006. Connections between internet use and political efficacy, knowledge, and participation. *Journal of Broadcasting and Electronic Media* 50(2): 173–192.

Kitschelt, Herbert P. 1986. Political opportunity structures and political protest: Antinuclear movements in four democracies. *British Journal of Political Science* 16: 57–85.

Kling, Rob. 2007. What is social informatics and why does it matter? *Information Society* 23(4): 205–220.

Klingemann, Hans-Dieter. 1999. Mapping political support in the 1990s: A global analysis. In *Critical citizens: Global support for democratic government*, ed. Pippa Norris, 31–56. New York: Cambridge University Press.

Klotz, Robert J. 2004. *The politics of internet communication.* Oxford, U.K.: Rowman & Littlefield.

Kluver, Randolph, and Indrajit Banerjee. 2005. The Internet in nine Asian nations. *Information Communication Society* 8(1): 30–46.

Kluver, Randolph, Nicholas W. Jankowski, Kirsten A. Foot, and Steven M. Schneider, eds. 2007. *The internet and national elections: A comparative study of web campaigning.* New York: Routledge.

Kobayashi, Tetsuro, Ken'ichi Ikeda, and Kakuko Miyata. 2006. Social capital online: Collective use of the internet and reciprocity as lubricants of democracy. *Information, Communication and Society* 9(5): 582–611.

Kok Wah, Francis Loh, and Khoo Boo Teik. 2002. *Democracy in Malaysia: Discourses and practices.* Richmond, VA: Curzon Press.

Kraut, Robert, Sara Kiesler, Bonka Boneva, Jonathan Cummings, Vicki Helgeson, and Anne Crawford. 2002. Internet paradox revisited. *Journal of Social Issues* 58(1): 49–74.

Kriesi, Hanspeter. 2008. Political mobilisation, political participation and the power of the vote. *West European Politics* 31(1): 147–168.

Kroh, Martin. 2009. Documentation of sample sizes and panel attrition in the German Socio Economic Panel (SOEP), 1984–2008. *Data Documentation* 47. Berlin: Deutsches Institut für Wirtschaftsforschung.

Krueger, Brian S. 2002. Assessing the potential of internet political participation in the United States: A resource approach. *American Politics Research* 30(5): 476–498.

Krueger, Brian S. 2005. Government surveillance and political participation on the internet. *Social Science Computer Review* 23(4): 439–452.

Krueger, Brian S. 2006. A comparison of conventional and internet political mobilization. *American Politics Research* 34(6): 759–776.

Kunreuther, Laura. 2006. Technologies of the voice: FM radio, telephone, and the Nepali diaspora in Kathmandu. *Cultural Anthropology* 21(3): 323–353.

Lagerkvist, Johan. 2008. China's online news industry: Control giving way to Confucian virtue. In *China's science and technology sector and the forces of globalisation*, ed. Elspeth Thomson and Jon Sigurdson, 191–206. Singapore: World Scientific Publishing.

Lagerkvist, Johan. 2010. *After the internet, before democracy: Competing norms in Chinese media and society*. Bern: Peter Lang, International Academic Publishers.

Larson, Karen Geneva. 2004. The internet and political participation: The effect of internet use on voter turnout. Ph.D. diss., Graduate School of Arts and Sciences, Georgetown University.

Latinobarómetro. 2008. *Latinobarómetro report 2008*. Santiago de Chile: Corporación Latinobarómetro. http://www.latinobarometro.org.

Latinobarómetro. 2009. *Latinobarómetro report 2009*. Santiago de Chile: Corporación Latinobarómetro. http://www.latinobarometro.org.

Lazarsfeld, Paul, Bernard Berelson, and Hazel Gaudet. 1944. *The people's choice*. New York: Free Press.

Lee, Kwan Min. 2006. Effects of internet use on college students' political efficacy. *Cyber Psychology and Behavior* 9(4): 415–422.

Lee, Paul Siu-Nam. 1994. Mass communication and national development in China: Media roles reconsidered. *Journal of Communication* 44(2): 22–37.

Lee, Yeon-Ok. 2009. Internet election 2.0? Culture, institutions, and technology in the Korean presidential elections of 2002 and 2007. *Journal of Information Technology and Politics* 63(4): 312–325.

Lei, Ya-Wen. 2011. The political consequences of the rise of the internet: Political beliefs and practices of Chinese netizens. *Political Communication* 28(3): 291–322.

Leighley, Jan E. 1990. Social interaction and contextual influences on political participation. *American Politics Research* 18(4): 459–475.

Lessig, Lawrence. 2006. *Code: Version 2.0*. New York: Perseus Books.

Levi, Margaret, and Laura Stoker. 2000. Political trust and trustworthiness. *Annual Review of Political Science* 3: 475–507.

Li, Lianjiang. 2004. Political trust in rural China. *Modern China* 30(2): 228–258.

Li, Xiguang, Qin Xuan, and Randolph Kluver. 2003. Who is setting the Chinese agenda? The impact of online chatrooms on party presses in China. In *Asia.com: Asia encounters the internet*, ed. K. C. Ho, Randolph Kluver, and Kenneth C. C. Yang, 143–158. London: Routledge.

Lim, Merlyna. 2003. From real to virtual and back again: Civil society, public sphere, and the internet in Indonesia. In *Asia.com: Asia encounters the internet*, ed. K. C. Ho, Randolph Kluver, and Kenneth C. C. Yang, 113–128. London: Routledge.

Lipton, Jacqueline D. 2009. From domain names to video games: The rise of the internet in presidential politics. *Denver University Law Review* 86: 693–708.

Little, Adrian. 2008. *Democratic piety: Complexity, conflict and violence*. Edinburgh, U.K.: Edinburgh University Press.

Liu, Xiaobo. 2009. The internet is God's present to China. *London Times*, April 28. http://www.timesonline.co.uk/tol/comment/columnists/guest_contributors/article6181699.ece (accessed October 22, 2010).

Löfgren, Karl. 2000. Danish political parties and new technology: Interactive parties or new shop windows. In *Democratic governance and new technology: Technologically mediated innovations in political practice in Western Europe*, ed. Jens Hoff, Ivan Horrocks, and Pieter Tops, 57–71. London: Routledge.

Löfgren, Karl. 2003. Intraparty use of new ITCs: Bringing party membership back in? Paper presented at the European Consortium for Political Research Joint Sessions, March 28–April 2, Edinburgh, United Kingdom.

Luo, Michael. 2008. Obama recasts the fund-raising landscape. *New York Times*, October 19. http://www.nytimes.com/2008/10/20/us/politics/20donate.html?ref=politics (accessed March 5, 2010).

Lupia, Arthur, and Tasha S. Philpot. 2005. Views from inside the net: How websites affect young adults' political interest. *Journal of Politics* 67(4): 1122–1142.

Luskin, Robert. 1990. Explaining political sophistication. *Political Behaviour* 12(4): 331–361.

Lusoli, Wainer. 2005. A second-order medium? The internet as a source of electoral information in 25 European countries. *Information Polity* 10(3–4): 247–265.

Lusoli, Wainer, and Janelle Ward. 2005. "Politics makes strange bedfellows": The internet and the 2004 European Parliament Election in Britain. *Harvard International Journal of Press/Politics* 10(4): 71–97.

Lusoli, Wainer, Steven Ward, and Rachel Gibson. 2002. Political organisations and online mobilisation: Different media – same outcomes? *New Review of Information Networking* 8(1): 89–107.

Lynch, Daniel C. 1999. *After the propaganda state: Media, politics, and thought work in reformed China*. Stanford, CA: Stanford University Press.

Lyon, David. 2003. Cyberspace, surveillance, and social control: The hidden face of the internet in Asia. In *Asia.com: Asia encounters the internet*, ed. K. C. Ho, Randolph Kluver, and Kenneth C. C. Yang, 67–82. London: Routledge.

Macintosh, Ann. 2003. Using information and communication technologies to enhance citizen engagement in the policy process. In *Promises and problems of e-democracy: Challenges of online citizen engagement*, ed. Organisation for Economic Co-operation and Development, 20–141. Paris: Organisation for Economic Co-operation and Development.

Macintosh, Ann, Stephen Coleman, and Mansur Lalljee. 2005. *E-methods for public engagement: Helping local authorities communicate with citizens*. Bristol, U.K.: Bristol City Council.

MacKinnon, Rebecca. 2006. *Race to the bottom: Corporate complicity in Chinese internet censorship*. New York: Human Rights Watch. http://www.hrw.org/en/reports/2006/08/09/race-bottom (accessed July 14, 2011).

Maeda, John. 2008. *The laws of simplicity*. Cambridge, MA: MIT Press.

Maraffi, Marco. 2002. Per che cosa si è votato il 13 maggio? Le mappe cognitive degli elettori italiani. In *Le ragioni dell'elettore*, ed. Mario Caciagli and Piergiorgio Corbetta, 301–338. Bologna, Italy: Il Mulino.

Marcotte, Roxanne D. 2009. Gender and sexuality online in Australian Muslim forums. *Contemporary Islam* 4(1): 117–138.

Margolis, Michael, and Davis Resnick. 2000. *Politics as usual: The cyberspace "revolution."* Thousand Oaks, CA: Sage Publications.

Marien, Sofie, Marc Hooghe, and Ellen Quintelier. 2010. Inequalities in non-institutionalised forms of political participation: A multi-level analysis of 25 countries. *Political Studies* 58(1): 187–213.

Marsh, Alan. 1977. *Protest and political consciousness*. Beverly Hills, CA: Sage.

Marsh, Alan, and Max Kaase. 1979. Measuring political action. In *Political Action: Mass participation in five western democracies*, ed. Samuel H. Barnes, and Max Kaase, Klaus R. Allerback, Barbara Farah, Felix Heunks, 57–96. Beverly Hills: Sage.

Marsh, David, Therese O'Toole, and Su Jones. 2007. *Young people and politics in the UK: Apathy or alienation?* New York: Palgrave Macmillan.

Martín, Irene. 2005. Interés por la política y desapego político. In *España: Sociedad y política en perspectiva comparada – un análisis de la primera ola de la Encuesta Social Europea*, ed. Mariano Torcal, Santiago Perez Nievas, and Laura Morales, 63–82. Valencia, Spain: Tirant lo Blanch.

Martín, Irene, and Jan W. van Deth. 2007. Political involvement. In *Citizenship, involvement and democracy: A comparative analysis*, ed. Jan W. van Deth, José Ramon Montero, and Anders Westholm, 303–333. London: Routledge.

Mason, Ronald. 1982. *Participatory and workplace democracy: A theoretical development in critique of liberalism*. Carbondale: Southern Illinois University Press.

Mayo, Ed, and Tom Steinberg. 2007. The power of information review. Available at http://www.opsi.gov.uk/advice/poi/power-of-information-review.pdf.

Mazzoleni, Gianpietro. 1999. La revolución simbólica de internet. Paper presented at the International Seminar Technological Innovation and Political Communication, December 2–4, Perugia, Italy.

McDonald, Michael P., and Samuel L. Popkin. 2001. The myth of the vanishing voter. *American Political Science Review* 95(4): 963–974.

McGlinchey, Eric. 2009. Transitions 2.0: The internet, political culture and autocracy in Central Asia. Paper presented at the annual meeting of the American Political Science Association, September 3–6, Toronto.

Mehanna, Omnia. 2008. Internet and the Egyptian public sphere. *CODESRIA*: 1–18.

Mercer, Claire. 2005. Telecentres and transformations: Modernizing Tanzania through the internet. *African Affairs* 105(419): 243–264.

Mernissi, Fatema. 2004. The satellite, the prince, and Scheherazade: The rise of women and communicators in digital Islam. *Transnational Broadcasting Studies* 12: 101–115.

Mertha, Andrew. 2008. *China's water warriors: Citizen action and policy change*. Ithaca, NY: Cornell University Press.

Merton, Robert K. 1957. *Social theory and social structure*. New York: Free Press.

Micheletti, Michele. 2003. *Political virtue and shopping: Individuals, consumerism, and collective action*. New York: Palgrave Macmillan.

Milanovic, Branko. 2005. *Worlds apart: Measuring international and global inequality*. Princeton, NJ: Princeton University Press.

Milbrath, Lester, and Madan Lal Goel. 1977. *Political participation: How and why do people get involved in politics?* Lanham, MD: University Press of America.

Miller, John H., and Scott E. Page. 2004. The standing ovation problem. *Complexity* 9(5): 8–16.

Min, Seong-Jae. 2010. From the digital divide to the democratic divide: Internet skills, political interest, and the second-level digital divide in political internet use. *Journal of Information Technology and Politics* 7(1): 22–35.

Mitchell, Christopher. 2008. La República Dominicana 2007: Buscando la institucionalidad. *Revista de Ciencia Política* 28(1): 171–187.

Mitscherlich, Alexander, and John J. Francis. 1970. Panel on "Protest and revolution." *International Journal of Psycho-Analysis* 51: 211–218.

Montero, José Ramón, Richard Gunther, and Mariano Torcal. 1997. Democracy in Spain: Legitimacy, discontent and disaffection. *Studies in Comparative International Development* 32(3): 124–160.

Morales, Laura. 2003. Ever less engaged citizens? Political participation and associational membership in Spain. Working Paper No. 220, Institut de Ciències Polítiques i Socials, Barcelona.

Morales, Laura. 2005 ¿Existe una crisis participativa? La evolución de la participación política y asociacionalismo en España. *Revista Española de Ciencia Política* 13: 51–87.

Morales, Laura, and Laia Jorba. 2009. Transnational links and the political incorporation of migrant associations in European cities. Paper presented at the European Consortium for Sociological Research, December 11–12, Paris.

Morales, Laura, and Laia Jorba. 2010. The transnational links and practices of migrants' organisations in Spain. In *Diaspora and transnationalism*, ed. Rainer Baubock, Thomas Faist, and Eduardo Romanos. Amsterdam: International Migration Integration and Social Cohesion Series, Amsterdam University Press.

Moreira, Constanza. 2004. Resistencia política y ciudadanía: Plebiscitos y referéndums en el Uruguay de los 90. *América Latina Hoy* 36: 17–45.

Morozov, Evgeny. 2011. *The net delusion: The dark side of internet freedom*. New York: Public Affairs.

Mosca, Lorenzo. 2010. From the streets to the net? The political use of the internet by social movements. *International Journal of E-Politics* 1(1): 1–21.

Mossberger, Karen, and Caroline J. Tolbert. 2010. Digital democracy. In *Oxford encyclopedia of American elections and political behavior*, ed. Jan Leighley. New York: Oxford University Press.

Mossberger, Karen, Caroline J. Tolbert, and D. Bowen. 2007. Who is mobilized by the internet? Online and offline political participation. Paper presented at the Third Karlstad Seminar on Studying Political Action, October 18–20, Karlstad University, Karlstad, Sweden.

Mossberger, Karen, Caroline J. Tolbert, and Ramona S. McNeal. 2008. *Digital citizenship: The internet, society, and participation*. Cambridge, MA: MIT Press.

Mossberger, Karen, Caroline Tolbert, Ramona NcNeal, and Jason McDonald. 2008. The benefits of society online: Civic engagement. In *Digital citizenship: The internet, society, and participation*, ed. Karen Mossberger, Caroline Tolbert, and Ramona NcNeal, 47–66. Cambridge, MA: MIT Press.

Mossberger, Karen, Caroline J. Tolbert, and Mary Stansbury. 2003. *Virtual inequality: Beyond the digital divide*. Washington, DC: Georgetown University Press.

Muhlberger, Peter. 2003. Political values, political attitudes, and attitude polarization in internet political discussion: Political transformation or politics as usual? *Communications* 28(2): 107–133.

Muhlberger, Peter. 2004. Access, skill and motivation in online political discussion: Testing cyberrealism. In *Democracy online: The prospects for political renewal through the internet*, ed. Peter Shane, 225–237. New York: Routledge.

Mulder, Bert. 1999. Parliamentary futures: Re-presenting the issue – information, technology and the dynamics of democracy. *Parliamentary Affairs* 52: 553–566.

Mutz, Diana C. 2008. Is deliberative democracy a falsifiable theory? *Annual Review of Political Science* 11: 521–538.

Mutz, Diana, and Paul Martin. 2001. Facilitating communication across lines of political difference: The role of mass media. *American Political Science Review* 95(1): 97–114.

Natanson, José. 2010. Usos y abusos de la sociedad civil. *Página 12*, April 25. http://www.pagina12.com.ar/diario/elpais/1-144543-2010-04-25.html (accessed September 2010).

Nathan, Andrew J. 2003. Authoritarian resilience. *Journal of Democracy* 14(1): 6–17.

National Public Radio. 2002. Islam on the internet: Three-part series exploring intersections of faith and technology. http://www.npr.org/programs/watc/cyberislam/ (accessed August 20, 2010).

National Telecommunications and Information Administration. 2010. *Digital nation: 21st century America's progress toward universal broadband internet access*. Washington, DC: U.S. Department of Commerce. http://www.ntia.doc.gov.

Nawratil, Ute. 2006. *Glaubwürdigkeit in der sozialen kommunikation*. Munich: Westdeutscher Verlag.

Negroponte, Nicholas. 1995. *Being digital*. New York: Random House.

Neustadtl, Alan, and John P. Robinson. 2002. Social contact differences between internet users and nonusers in the general social survey. *IT and Society* 1(1): 73–102.

Newell, James L. 2001. Italian political parties on the web. *Harvard International Journal of Press/Politics* 4(6): 60–87.

Nie, Norman H., and Lutz Erbring. 2002. Internet and society. A preliminary report. *IT and Society* 1(1): 275–283.

Nielsen, Jakob. 1999. *Designing web usability: The practice of simplicity*. Indianapolis, IN: New Riders.

Niemi, Richard G., and Jane Junn. 1998. *Civic education: What makes students learn*. New Haven, CT: Yale University Press.

Norris, Pippa. 1999a. *Critical citizens: Global support for democratic government*. New York: Oxford University Press.

Norris, Pippa. 1999b. Who surfs? New technology, old voters and virtual democracy in US elections 1992–2000. In *Democracy.com: Governance in a networked world*, ed. Elaine Ciulla Kamarck and Joseph S. Nye, 71–94. Hollis, NH: Hollis Publishing.

Norris, Pippa. 2000. *A virtuous circle: Political communications in postindustrial societies*. New York: Cambridge University Press.

Norris, Pippa. 2001. *Digital divide: Civic engagement, information poverty, and the internet worldwide*. New York: Cambridge University Press.

Norris, Pippa. 2002. *Democratic phoenix: Reinventing political activism*. Cambridge: Cambridge University Press.

Norris, Pippa. 2003. Preaching to the converted: Pluralism, participation and party websites. *Party Politics* 9(1): 21–45.

Norris, Pippa. 2005. The impact of the internet on political activism: Evidence from Europe. *International Journal of Electronic Government Research* 1(1): 20–39.

Norris, Pippa. 2011. *Democratic deficits: Rising aspirations, negative news, or failing performance*. New York: Cambridge University Press.

Norris, Pippa, and John Curtice. 2007. Getting the message out: A two-step model of the role of the internet in campaign communication flows during the 2005 British general election. *Journal of Information Technology and Politics* 4(4): 3–13.

Norris, Pippa, and Ronald Inglehart. 2009. *Cosmopolitan communications: Cultural diversity in a globalized world*. New York: Cambridge University Press.

Noveck, Beth Simone. 2000. Paradoxical partners: Electronic communication and electronic democracy. In *The internet, democracy, and democratization*, ed. Peter Ferdinand, 18–34. London: Frank Cass.

Nye, Joseph S., Jr., Phillip D. Zelikow, and David C. King, eds. 1997. *Why people don't trust government*. Cambridge, MA: Harvard University Press.

Oldenburg, Ray. 1997. *The great good place: Coffee shops, bookstores, bars, hair salons, and other hangouts at the heart of a community*, 2nd ed. New York: Marlowe.

O'Loughlin, Ben. 2001. The political implications of digital innovations: The internet and trade-offs of democracy and liberty in the developed world. *Information, Communication and Society* 4(4): 595–614.

Olson, Mancur. 1965. *The logic of collective action: Public goods and the theory of groups.* Cambridge, MA: Harvard University Press.

OpenNet Initiative. http://opennet.net/about-oni (accessed March 2010).

O'Reilly, Tim. 2007. What is web 2.0? Design patterns and business models for the next generation of software. *International Journal of Digital Economics* 65(1): 17–37.

Organization for Economic Cooperation and Development. 2009 The future of news and the internet. Report for the Organization for Economic Cooperation and Development. http://www.oecd.org/dataoecd/30/24/45559596.pdf.

Ouyang, Zhonghui. 2005. The epitome of middle city's e-government in China: Quanzhou. *ACM International Conference Proceeding Series* 113: 505–513 http://portal.acm.org/toc.cfm?id=1089551&type=proceeding&coll=GUIDE&dl=GUIDE&CFID=74937358&CFTOKEN=25158849 – _blank.

Owen, Diana. 2006. The internet and youth civic engagement in the United States. In *The internet and politics: Citizens, voters, and activists*, ed. Sarah Oats, Diana M. Owen, and Rachel Gibson, 20–38. New York: Routledge.

Papacharissi, Zizi. 2009. The virtual sphere 2.0: The internet, the public sphere and beyond. In *Routledge handbook of internet politics*, ed. Andrew Chadwick and Philip N. Howard, 230–245. New York: Routledge.

Parry, Geraint, George Moyser, and Neil Day. 1992. *Political participation and democracy in Britain.* Cambridge: Cambridge University Press.

Pasek, Josh, Eian More, and Daniel Romer. 2009. Realizing the social internet? Online social networking meets offline social capital. *Journal of Information Technology and Politics* 6(3–4): 197–215.

Pasquino, Gianfranco. 2002. Una cultura poco cívica. In *Le ragioni dell'elettore*, ed. Mario Caciagli and Piergiorgio Corbetta, 53–78. Bologna, Italy: Il Mulino.

Pasquino, Gianfranco. 2007. Tricks and treats: The 2005 Italian electoral law and its consequences. *South European Society and Politics* 12(1): 79–93.

Pateman, Carole. 1970. *Participation and democratic theory.* New York: Cambridge University Press.

Patterson, Thomas E. 2002. *The vanishing voter: Public involvement in an age of uncertainty.* New York: Knopf.

Pedersen, Karina, and Jo Saglie. 2005. New technology in ageing parties: Internet use in Danish and Norwegian parties. *Party Politics* 3(11): 359–377.

Penfold, Carolyn. 2003. Global technology meets local environment: State attempts to control internet content. In *Asia.com: Asia encounters the Internet*, ed. K. C. Ho, Randolph Kluver, and Kenneth C. C. Yang, 83–96. London: Routledge.

Peterson, Steven A. 1992. Workplace politicization and its political spillovers: A research note. *Economic and Industrial Democracy* 13(4): 511–524.

Pew Global Attitudes Project. 2007. *Rising environmental concern in 47-nation survey.* Washington, D.C.: Pew Research Center.

Pew Internet and American Life Project. 2008. Trend data: Online activities. http://www.pewinternet.org/Static-Pages/Trend-Data/Online-Activities20002009.aspx.

Pew Internet and American Life Project. 2010. Trend data: Demographics of internet users. http://www.pewinternet.org/Static-Pages/Trend-Data/Whos-Online.aspx.

Pharr, Susan J., and Robert D. Putnam. 2000. *Disaffected democracies: What's troubling the trilateral countries?* Princeton, NJ: Princeton University Press.

Pintak, Lawrence, and Jeremy Ginges. 2008. The mission of Arab journalism: Creating change in a time of turmoil. *International Journal of Press/Politics* 13(3): 193–227.

Plutzer, Eric. 2002. Becoming a habitual voter: Inertia, resources, and growth in young adulthood. *American Political Science Review* 96(1): 41–56.

Polat, Rabia Karakaya. 2005. The internet and political participation: Exploring the explanatory links. *European Journal of Communication* 20(4): 435–459.

Pollack, David. 2008. Slippery polls: Uses and abuses of opinion surveys from Arab states. Washington, DC: Washington Institute for Near East Affairs. http://www.washingtoninstitute.org/templateC04.php?CID=290 (accessed March 18, 2010).

Polumbaum, Judy. 1990. The tribulations of China's journalists after a decade of reform. In *Voices of China: The interplay of politics and journalism*, ed. Chin-Chuan Lee, 38–68. New York: Guilford Press.

Pool, Sola. 1990. *Technologies without boundaries*. Cambridge, MA: Harvard University Press.

Portes, Alejandro, Luis E. Guarnizo, and Patricia Landolt. 1999. The study of transnationalism: Pitfalls and promise of an emergent research field. *Ethnic and Racial Studies* 22(2): 217–237.

Poster, Mark. 2001. *What's the matter with the Internet?* Minneapolis: University of Minnesota Press.

Prior, Markus. 2005. News vs. entertainment: How increasing media choice widens gaps in political knowledge and turnout. *American Journal of Political Science* 49(3): 577–592.

Prior, Markus. 2007. *Post-broadcast democracy: How media choice increases inequality in political involvement and polarizes elections*. New York: Cambridge University Press.

Putnam, Robert D. 2000. *Bowling alone: The collapse and revival of American community*. New York: Simon and Schuster.

Putnam, Robert D., ed. 2002. *Democracies in flux*. New York: Oxford University Press.

Qiang, Xiao. 2003. Cyber speech: Catalyzing free expression and civil society. *Harvard International Review* 25(2): 70–76.

Quintelier, Ellen, and Sara Vissers. 2008. The effect of internet use on political participation: An analysis of survey results for 16-year olds in Belgium. *Social Science Computer Review* 26(4): 411–442.

R Development Core Team. 2010. *R: A language and environment for statistical computing*. Vienna: R Foundation for Statistical Computing.

Rao, Sandhya, and Bruce C. Klopfenstein, eds. 2002. *Cyberpath to development in Asia: Issues and challenges*. Westport, CT: Praeger Publishers.

Resnick, David. 1998. The normalisation of cyberspace. In *The politics of cyberspace*, ed. Chris Toulouse, and Timothy W. Luke, 48–68. London: Routledge.

Rheingold, Howard. 1993. *The virtual community: Homesteading on the electronic frontier*. Reading, MA: Addison-Wesley.

Richards, Russell. 2006. Users, interactivity and generation. *New Media and Society* 8(4): 531–550.

Rinnawi, Khalil. 2009. The internet and the Arab world as a virtual public sphere. http://cmsprod.bgu.ac.il/NR/rdonlyres/E1D4CA76–9BEF-49A3–8B70-ADF2B3AF68FB/12231/Rinnawi.pdf (accessed February 2010).

Rizopoulos, Dimtris. 2006. Ltm: An R package for latent variable modeling and item response theory analyses. *Journal of Statistical Software* 17: 1–25.

Robinson, John P., Alan Neustadtl, and Meyer Kestnbaum. 2004. Technology and tolerance: Public opinion differences among internet users and non-users. In *Society online: The internet in context*, ed. Philip N. Howard and Steve Jones, 237–253. Thousand Oaks, CA: Sage.

Rodan, Garry. 1998. The internet and political control in Singapore. *Political Science Quarterly* 113(1): 63–89.

Römmele, Andrea. 2003. Political parties, party communication and new information and communication technologies. *Party Politics* 9(1): 7–20.

Rosenstone, Steven J., and John Mark Hansen. 1993. *Mobilization, participation, and democracy in America*. New York: Macmillan.

Rospars, Joe. 2009. Obama 2008. Paper presented at Campaigning for the Net Generation Conference Progress/Blue State Digital Labour 2.0. February 2, Canary Wharf, London.

Rucht, Dieter. 2007. The spread of protest politics. In *The Oxford handbook of political behavior*, ed. Russell J. Dalton, and Hans-Dieter Klingemann, 708–723. New York: Oxford University Press.

Rumuat, Carolina. 2009. Indonesia: Jailed for complaining. *Global Voices Online*, May 31. http://globalvoicesonline.org/2009/05/31/indonesia-jailed-for-complaining/.

Saeed, Hamid, Muhammad Asghar, Muhammad Anwar, and Muhammad Ramzan. 2000. Internet use in university libraries of Pakistan. *Online Information Review* 24(2): 154–160.

Santos, Emanuel. 2009. Dominicans defend biodiversity. *Socialist Worker*, May 28. http://socialistworker.org/ (accessed November 2010).

Sartori, Giovanni. 1976. *Parties and party systems: A framework for analysis*. Cambridge: Cambridge University Press.

Scarrow, Susan. 2007. Political activism and party members. In *The Oxford handbook of political behavior*, ed. Russell J. Dalton, and Hans-Dieter Klingemann, 636–654. New York: Oxford University Press.

Scheufele, Dietram A., and Matthew C. Nisbet. 2002. Being a citizen online: New opportunities and dead ends. *Harvard International Journal of Press/Politics* 7(3): 55–75.

Schlozman, Kay Lehman, Sidney Verba, and Henry E. Brady. 2010. Weapon of the strong? Participatory inequality and the internet. *Perspectives on Politics* 8(2): 487–509.

Schulz, Winfried, Reimar Zeh, and Oliver Quiring. 2005. Voters in a changing media environment: A data-based retrospective on consequences of media change in Germany. *European Journal of Communication* 20(1): 55–88.

Schweiger, Wolfgang. 2000. Media credibility: Experience or image? A survey on the credibility of the world wide web in Germany in comparison to other media. *European Journal of Communication* 15(1): 37–59.

Schweitzer, Eva Johanna. 2005. Election campaigning online: German party websites in the 2002 national elections. *European Journal of Communication* 20(3): 327–351.

Schweitzer, Eva Johanna. 2008. Innovation or normalization in e-campaigning? A longitudinal content and structural analysis of German party websites in the 2002 and 2005 national elections. *European Journal of Communication* 23(4): 449–470.

Schwirtz, Michael. 2007. An overflowing of Islamic fervor in Russia. *International Herald Tribune*, December 17.

Semetko, Holli A., and Natalya Krasnoboka. 2003. The political role of the internet in societies in transition: Russia and Ukraine compared. *Party Politics* 19(1): 77–104.

Shah, Dhavan V., Jaeho Cho, William P. Eveland Jr., and Nojin Kwak. 2005. Information and expression in a digital age: Modeling internet effects on civic participation. *Communication Research* 32(5): 531–565.

Shah, Dhavan V., Jaeho Cho, Seungahn Nah, Melissa R. Gotlieb, Hyunseo Hwang, Nam-Jin Lee, Rosanne M. Scholl, and Douglas M. McLeod. 2007. Campaign ads, online messaging, and participation: Extending the communication mediation model. *Journal of Communication* 57(4): 676–703.

Shah, Dhavan V., Nojin Kwak, and R. Lance Holbert. 2001. "Connecting" and "disconnecting" with civic life: Patterns of internet use and the production of social capital. *Political Communication* 18(2): 141–162.

Shah, Dhavan V., Jack M. McLeod, and So-Hyang Yoon. 2001. Communication, context, and community: An exploration of print, broadcast, and internet influences. *Communication Research* 28(4): 464–506.

Shapiro, Samantha M. 2009. Revolution, Facebook style. *New York Times*, January 25.

Shi, Tianjian. 2008. China: Democratic values supporting an authoritarian system. In *How East Asians view democracy*, ed. Yun-han Chu, Larry Diamond, Andrew J. Nathan, and Doh Chul Shin, 209–237. New York: Columbia University Press.

Shirk, Susan. 2007. *China – fragile superpower: How China's internal politics could derail its peaceful rise?* Oxford: Oxford University Press.

Shirky, Clay. 2010. *Cognitive surplus: Creativity and generosity in a connected age.* New York: Penguin Press.

Shramm, Wilbur. 1976. China's experience and development communication: How transferable is it? In *Communication and development*, ed. Chu Godwin, 85–105. Honolulu, HI: East-West Center.

Shulman, Stuart W. 2006. Whither deliberation? Mass e-mail campaigns and U.S. regulatory rulemaking. *Journal of E-Government* 3(3): 41–64.

Shulman, Stuart. W. 2009. The case against mass e-mails: Perverse incentives and low quality public participation in U.S. federal rulemaking. *Policy and Internet* 1(1): 23–53.

Shynkaruk, Anton. 2005. Re@l and virtual power: Political technologies in parties' development in Ukraine and Russia. Working paper, Centro Argentino de Estudios Internacionales, Buenos Aires.

Smith, Aaron. 2009. *The internet's role in campaign 2008.* Washington, DC: Pew Internet and American Life Project. http://www.pewinternet.org (accessed March 3, 2010).

Smith, Aaron, and Lee Rainie. 2008. *The internet and the 2008 election.* Washington, DC: Pew Internet and American Life Project.

Smith, Daniel A., and Caroline J. Tolbert. 2004. *Educated by initiative: The effects of direct democracy on citizens and political organizations in the American states.* Ann Arbor: University of Michigan Press.

Smith, Glenn R. 2010. Politicians and the news media: How elite attacks influence perceptions of media bias. *International Journal of Press/Politics* 15(3): 319–343.

Sobel, Richard. 1993. From occupational involvement to political participation: An exploratory analysis. *Political Behavior* 15(4): 339–353.

Soon, Carol, and Randolph Kluver. 2007. The internet and online political communities in Singapore. *Asian Journal of Communication* 17(3): 246–265.

Stanley, J. Woody, and Christopher Weare. 2004. The effects of internet use on political participation: Evidence from an agency online discussion forum. *Administration and Society* 36(5): 503–527.

Stoker, Gerry. 2006. *Why politics matters: Making democracy work*. New York: Palgrave Macmillan.

Stolle, Dietlind, and Marc Hooghe. 2004a. Consumers as political participants? Shifts in political action repertoires in Western societies. In *Politics, products, and markets: Exploring political consumerism past and present*, ed. Michele Micheletti, Andreas Føllesdal, and Dietlind Stolle, 265–288. New Brunswick, NJ: Transaction Publishers.

Stolle, Dietlind, and Marc Hooghe. 2004b. Emerging repertoires of political action? A review of the debate on participation trends in Western societies. Paper presented at the European Consortium for Political Research Joint Sessions, April 13–18, Uppsala, Sweden.

Stolle, Dietlind, Marc Hooghe, and Michele Micheletti. 2005. Politics in the supermarket: Political consumerism as a form of political participation. *International Political Science Review* 26(3): 245–269.

Stolle, Dietlind, and Michele Micheletti. 2005. The expansion of political action repertoires: Theoretical reflections on results from the Nike email exchange internet campaign. Paper presented at the 101st Annual Meeting of the American Political Science Association, August 28–31, Washington DC.

Stowasser, Barbara. 2001. Old shayks, young women, and the internet: The rewriting of women's political rights in Islam. *Muslim World* 91(1): 99–120.

Stromer-Galley, Jennifer. 2003. Diversity of political conversation on the internet: Users' perspectives. *Journal of Computer-Mediated Communication* 8(3). http://jcmc .indiana.edu/vol8/issue3/stromergalley.html.

Sun, Wanning. 2002. *Leaving China: Media, migration, and transnational imagination*. Lanham, MD: Rowman & Littlefield.

Sunstein, Cass R. 2001. *Republic.com*. Princeton, NJ: Princeton University Press.

Sunstein, Cass R. 2006. *Infotopia: How many minds produce knowledge*. New York: Oxford University Press.

Sunstein, Cass R. 2007. *Republic.com 2.0*. Princeton, NJ: Princeton University Press.

Svampa, Marisvella, and Mirta Antonelli, eds. 2009. *Minería transnacional, narrativas del desarrollo y resistencias sociales*. Buenos Aires: Biblos.

Tabellini, Guido. 2005. Culture and institutions: Economic development in the regions of Europe. Center for Economic Studies Working Paper No. 1492.

Tai, Zixue. 2006. *The internet in China: Cyberspace and civil society*. New York: Routledge.

Tanaka, Martín, and Sofía Vera. 2008. El neodualismo de la política peruana. *Revista de Ciencia Política* 28(1): 347–365.

Tarrow, Sidney. 2000. Mad cows and social activists: Contentious politics in the trilateral democracies. In *Disaffected democracies: What's troubling the trilateral countries?*, ed. Susan J. Pharr, and Robert D. Putnam, 270–290. Princeton, NJ: Princeton University Press.

Tarrow, Sydney. 2005. *The new transnational activism*. New York: Cambridge University Press.

Tate, Katherine. 1994. *From protest to politics: The new black voters in American elections*. Cambridge, MA: Harvard University Press.

Taubman, Geoffrey. 1998. A not-so world wide web: The internet, China, and the challenges to nondemocratic rule. *Political Communication* 15(2): 255–272.

Tedesco, John C. 2007. Examining internet interactivity effects on young adult political information efficacy. *American Behavioral Scientist* 50(9): 1183–1194.

Tekwani, Shyam. 2003. The Tamil diaspora. Tamil militancy, and the internet. In *Asia.Com: Asia encounters the internet*, ed. K. C. Ho, Rudolph Kluver, and Kenneth C. C. Yang, 175–192. New York: Routledge.

Teorell, Jan, Mariano Torcal, and José Ramón Montero. 2007. Political participation: Mapping the terrain. In *Citizenship and involvement in European democracies: A comparative analysis*, ed. Jan W. van Deth, José Ramón Montero, and Anders Westholm, 334–357. London: Routledge.

Terranova, Tiziana. 2004. *Network culture: Politics for the information age*. London: Pluto Press.

Tewksbury, David. 2003. What do Americans really want to know? Tracking the behavior of news readers on the internet. *Journal of Communication* 53(4): 694–710.

Tewksbury, David, and Jason Rittenberg. 2009. Online news creation and consumption: Implications for modern democracies. In *Routledge handbook of internet politics*, ed. Andrew Chadwick, and Philip N. Howard, 186–200. London: Routledge.

Tewksbury, David, Andrew Weaver, and Brett D. Maddex. 2001. Accidentally informed: Incidental news exposure on the world wide web. *Journalism and Mass Communication Quarterly* 78(3): 533–554.

Thompson, Dennis F. 2008. Deliberative democratic theory and empirical political science. *Annual Review of Political Science* 11: 497–520.

Tolbert, Caroline J, Amanda Keller, and Todd Donovan. 2010. A modified national primary: State losers and support for changing the Presidential nominating process. *Political Science Quarterly* 125(3): 393–424.

Tolbert, Caroline J., and Ramona S. McNeal. 2003. Unraveling the effects of the internet on political participation. *Political Research Quarterly* 56(2): 175–185.

Topf, Richard. 1995. Beyond electoral participation. In *Citizens and the state*, ed. Hans-Dieter Klingemann and Dieter Fuchs, 52–93. New York: Oxford University Press.

Torcal, Mariano, and José Ramón Montero. 2006. Political disaffection in comparative perspective. In *Political disaffection in contemporary democracies: Social capital, institutions, and politics*, ed. Mariano Torcal, and José Ramón Montero, 3–19. New York: Routledge.

Torcal, Mariano, José Ramón Montero, and Jan Teorell. 2006. La participación política en España: Modos y niveles en perspectiva comparada. In *Ciudadanos, asociaciones y participación en España*, ed. José Ramón Montero, Joan Font, and Mariano Torcal, 22–45. Madrid: Centro de Investigaciones Sociológicas.

Torney-Purta, Judith. 2004. Adolescents' political socialization in changing contexts: An international study in the spirit of Nevitt Sanford. *Political Psychology* 25(3): 465–478.

Trechsel, Alexander H. 2007. E-voting and electoral participation. In *Dynamics of referendum campaigns: An international perspective*, ed. Claes de Vreese, 159–182. London: Palgrave.

Tsagarousianou, Rosa, Damian Tambini, and Cathy Bryan, eds. 1998. *Cyberdemocracy: Technology, cities and civic networks*. London: Routledge.

U.K. Foreign Office. 2008. FCO bloggers: Global conversations. http://blogs.fco.gov.uk.

U.K. National Health Service. 2008. Our NHS, our future: Have your say. http://www.ournhs.nhs.uk.

U.K. Office of Communications. 2010. *The communications market 2010*. London: HMSO.

U.K. Prime Minister's Office. 2008. E-petitions website. http://petitions.pm.gov.uk.

United Nations. 2010. The Millenium Development Goals report. http://www.un.org/millenniumgoals/reports.shtml.

U.S. White House. 2009. Open for questions. http://www.whitehouse.gov/OpenForQuestions/.

Uslaner, Eric M. 2004. Trust, civic engagement and the internet. *Political Communication* 21(2): 223–242.

Vaccari, Cristian. 2006. La campagna 2006 su internet: Pubblico, siti e agenda. *Comunicazione Politica* 7(2): 329–341.

Vaccari, Cristian. 2008a. Più informazione che partecipazione: I siti Internet dei partiti nella campagna elettorale 2008. *Comunicazione Politica* 9(2): 183–198.

Vaccari, Cristian. 2008b. Research note: Italian parties' web sites in the 2006 elections. *European Journal of Communication* 23(1): 69–77.

Vaccari, Cristian. 2009. Web challenges to Berlusconi: An analysis of oppositional sites. In *Resisting the tide: Cultures of opposition under Berlusconi (2001–06)*, ed. Daniele Albertazzi, Clodagh Brook, Charlotte Ross, and Nina Rothenberg, 135–147. New York: Continuum.

van Deursen, Alexander J. A. M., and Jan A. G. M. van Dijk. 2010. Internet skills and the digital divide. *New Media and Society* 13(6): 893–911.

Van Dijk, Jan. 2005. *The deepening divide: Inequality in the information society*. Thousand Oaks, CA: Sage Publications.

Van Dijk, Jan. 2006. *The network society, social aspects of the new media*. Thousand Oaks, CA: Sage Publications.

Van Kempen, Hetty. 2007. Media-party parallelism and its effects: A cross-national comparative study. *Political Communication* 24: 303–320.

Vavreck, Lynn, and Douglas Rivers. 2008. The 2006 cooperative Congressional election study. *Journal of Elections, Public Opinion, and Parties* 18: 355–366.

Venkatesh, Alladi. 2008. Digital home technologies and transformation of households. *Information Systems Frontiers* 10(4): 391–395.

Verba, Sidney, and Norman H. Nie. 1972. *Participation in America: Political democracy and social equality*. Chicago: University of Chicago Press.

Verba, Sidney, Norman H. Nie, and Jae-o Kim. 1978. *Participation and political equality: A seven-nation comparison*. Cambridge: Cambridge University Press.

Verba, Sidney, Kay L. Schlozman, and Henry E. Brady. 1995. *Voice and equality: Civic voluntarism in American politics*. Cambridge, MA: Harvard University Press.

Vissers, Sara, Marc Hooghe, Dietlind Stolle, and Valérie-Anne Mahéo. 2009. The impact of online and offline mobilization on participation modes. Paper presented at the International Workshop on New Media and Politics, May 28–31, Barcelona, Spain.

Vowe, Gerhard, Martin Emmer, and Markus Seifert. 2007. Abkehr oder mobilisierung? Zum einfluss des internets auf die individuelle politische kommunikation empirischer befunde zu alten fragen im kontext neuer medien. In *Fortschritte der politischen kommunikationsforschung*, ed. Birgit Krause, Benjamin Fretwurst, and Jens Vogelsang, 109–130. Wiesbaden: VS Verlag.

Wang, Jing. 2008. *Brand new China: Advertising, media, and commercial culture*. Cambridge, MA: Harvard University Press.

Wang, Xin. 2009. Seeking channels for engagement: Media use and political communication by China's rising middle class. *China: An International Journal* 7(1): 31–56.

Wang, Zhengxu. 2005. Before the emergence of critical citizens: Economic development and political trust in China. *International Review of Sociology* 15(1): 155–171.

Wang, Zhengxu. 2006. Explaining regime strength in China. *China: An International Journal* 4(2): 217–237.

Wang, Zhengxu. 2007. Public support for democracy in China. *Journal of Contemporary China* 16(53): 561–579.

Ward, Stephen, and Thierry Vedel. 2006. Introduction: The potential of the internet revisited. *Parliamentary Affairs* 59(2): 210–225.

Ward, Steven, Rachel K. Gibson, and Wainer Lusoli. 2003. Online participation and mobilisation in Britain: Hype, hope and reality. *Parliamentary Affairs* 56(4): 652–668.

Ward, Stephen, and Wainer Lusoli. 2003. Dinosaurs in cyberspace? British trade unions and the internet. *European Journal of Communication* 18(2): 147–179.

Warf, Barney, and Peter Vincent. 2007. Multiple geographies of the Arab internet. *Area* 39(1): 83–96.

Warschauer, Mark. 2003. *Technology and social inclusion: Rethinking the digital divide*. Cambridge, MA: MIT Press.

Wattenberg, Martin. 1996. *The decline of American political parties*. Cambridge, MA: Harvard University Press.

Wattenberg, Martin P. 2007. *Is voting for young people?* New York: Pearson Longman.

Weber, Lori M., Alysha Loumakis, and James Bergman. 2003. Who participates and why? An analysis of citizens on the internet and the mass public. *Social Science Computer Review* 21(1): 26–42.

Wellman, Barry. 1997. An electronic group is virtually a social network. In *Culture of the internet*, ed. Sara Kiesler. 179–205. Mahwah, NJ: Lawrence Erlbaum.

Wellman, Barry, Anabel Quan-Haase, James Witte, and Keith Hampton. 2001. Does the internet increase, decrease, or supplement social capital? *American Behavioral Scientist* 45(3): 436–455.

Welp, Yanina, and Uwe Serdült, eds. 2009. *Armas de doble filo: La participación ciudadana en la encrucijada*. Buenos Aires: Prometeo.

Welp, Yanina. 2008. América Latina en la era del gobierno electrónico: Análisis de la introducción de nuevas tecnologías para la mejora de la democracia y el gobierno. *Revista del CLAD Reforma y Democracia* 41. http://www.clad.org/portal/publicaciones-del-clad/revista-clad-reforma-democracia/articulos/041-junio-2008.

Welp, Yanina. 2011. Bridging the political gap? The adoption of ICTs for the improvement of Latin American parliamentary democracy. In *E-parliament and ICT-based legislation: Concept, experience and lessons*, ed. Mehmet Zahid Sobaci, 217–236. Hershey, PA; IGI Global.

Whiteley, Paul, and Patrick Seyd. 1998. The dynamics of party activism in Britain: A spiral of demobilization? *British Journal of Political Science* 28: 113–137.

Williams, Bruce, and Michael X. Delli Carpini. 2004. Monica and Bill all the time and everywhere: The collapse of gatekeeping and agenda setting in the new media environment. *American Behavioral Scientist* 47(9): 1208–1230.

Wines, Michael. 2009. Civic-minded Chinese find a voice online. *New York Times*, June 16. http://www.nytimes.com/2009/06/17/world/asia/17china.html?hp (accessed September 2010).

Witte, Barbara, Kirsten Rautenberg, and Claudia Auer. 2010. No profound change: Web 2.0 and the German election campaign. Bremen University, Unpublished manuscript.

Wojcieszak, Magdalena E., and Diana C. Mutz. 2009. Online groups and political discourse: Do online discussion spaces facilitate exposure to political disagreement? *Journal of Communication* 59(1): 40–56.

Wolcott, Peter, and Seymour Goodman. 2000. The internet in Turkey and Pakistan: A comparative analysis. Palo Alto: Center for International Security and Cooperation, Stanford University.

Wolfinger, Raymond E., and Steven J. Rosenstone. 1980. *Who votes?* New Haven, CT: Yale University Press.

Wooldridge, Jeffrey M. 2002. *Econometric analysis for cross-section and panel data.* Cambridge, MA: MIT Press.

World Association of Newspapers. 2009. Indonesia: Media market description. *World Press Trends* 2009: 497–501.

World Bank. 2009. Indonesia: ICT at a glance. *Information and communication for development* 2009: 220.

Wright, Scott. 2006. Government-run online discussion fora: Moderation, censorship and the shadow of control. *British Journal of Politics and International Relations* 8(4): 550–568.

Xenos, Michael A., and Patricia Moy. 2007. Direct and differential effects of the internet on political participation and civic engagement. *Journal of Communication* 57(4): 704–718.

Xie, Bo, and Paul T. Jaeger. 2008. Older adults and political participation on the internet: A cross-cultural comparison of the USA and China. *Journal of Cross-Cultural Gerontology* 23(1): 1–15.

Xing, Chunxiao, Jijiang Yang, Wei He, Yong Zhang, and Chen Chen. 2008. Research and development of key technologies for e-government: Case studies in China. In *Digital government: E-government research, case studies, and implementation,* ed. Hsinchun Chen, Lawrence Brandt, Valerie Gregg, Roland Traunmüller, Sharon Dawes, Eduard Hovy, Ann Macintosh, and Catherine A. Larson, 615–645. New York: Springer.

Yang, Guobin. 2003. The co-evolution of the internet and civil society in China. *Asian Survey* 43(3): 405–422.

Yang, Guobin. 2009. *The power of the internet in China: Citizen activism online.* New York: Columbia University Press.

Yildiz, Helene. 2002. Internet, un nouvel outil de communication multidimensionnel. In *L'internet en politique: Des États-Unis à l'Europe,* ed. Viviane Serfaty, 275–290. Strasbourg, France: Presses Universitaires de Strasbourg.

Young, Iris M. 2000. *Inclusion and democracy.* New York: Oxford University Press.

Yu, Jinglu. 1990. The structure and function of Chinese television 1979–1989. In *Voices of China the interplay of politics and journalism,* ed. Chin-Chuan Lee, 69–87. New York: Guilford Press.

Zhang, Pengzhu, Xiaoning Mao, Tang Xieping, and Daniel Zeng. 2008. A hybrid e-government model: Case studies in Shanghai. In *Digital government: E-government research, case studies, and implementation,* ed. Hsinchun Chen, Lawrence Brandt, Valerie Gregg, Roland Traunmüller, Sharon Dawes, Eduard Hovy, Ann Macintosh, and Catherine A. Larson, 697–718. New York: Springer.

Zhao, Yuezhi. 1998. *Media, market and democracy in China between the party line and the bottom line.* Urbana: University of Illinois Press.

Zheng, Yongnian, and Guoguang Wu. 2005. Information technology, public space, and collective action in China. *Comparative Political Studies* 38(5): 507–536.

Zhuo, Xiaolin, Barry Wellman, and Justine Yu. 2011. Egypt: The first internet revolt? *Peace Magazine* 27(3). http://www.peacemagazine.org/archive/?id=2176 (accessed July 2011).

Zittel, Thomas. 2009. Lost in technology? Political parties and the online campaigns of constituency candidates in Germany's mixed member electoral system. *Journal of Information Technology and Politics* 63(4): 298–311.

Zmerli, Sonjua, Ken Newton, and José Ramón Montero. 2007. Trust in people, confidence in political institutions, and satisfaction with democracy. In *Citizenship and involvement in European democracies: A comparative analysis*, ed. Jan van Deth, José Ramón Montero, and Anders Westholm, 35–65. London: Routledge.

Zukin, Cliff, Scott Keeter, Molly Andolina, Krista Jenkins, and Michael X. Delli Carpini. 2006. *A new engagement? Political participation, civic life, and the changing American citizen.* New York: Oxford University Press.

Index

Other Books in the Series (*continued from page iii*)